Mastering PostgreSQL
Third Edition

Advanced techniques to build and administer scalable and reliable PostgreSQL database applications

Hans-Jürgen Schönig

BIRMINGHAM - MUMBAI

Mastering PostgreSQL 12
Third Edition

Copyright © 2019 Packt Publishing

Commissioning Editor: Amey Varangaokar
Acquisition Editor: Devika Battike
Content Development Editor: Athikho Sapuni Rishana
Senior Editor: Sofi Rogers
Technical Editor: Utkarsha S. Kadam and Manikandan Kurup
Copy Editor: Safis Editing
Project Coordinator: Aishwarya Mohan
Proofreader: Safis Editing
Indexer: Rekha Nair
Production Designer: Aparna Bhagat

First published: January 2018
Second edition: October 2018
Third edition: November 2019

Production reference: 1281119

Published by Packt Publishing Ltd.
Livery Place
35 Livery Street
Birmingham
B3 2PB, UK.

ISBN 978-1-83898-882-1

www.packt.com

Packt.com

Subscribe to our online digital library for full access to over 7,000 books and videos, as well as industry leading tools to help you plan your personal development and advance your career. For more information, please visit our website.

Why subscribe?

- Spend less time learning and more time coding with practical eBooks and Videos from over 4,000 industry professionals

- Improve your learning with Skill Plans built especially for you

- Get a free eBook or video every month

- Fully searchable for easy access to vital information

- Copy and paste, print, and bookmark content

Did you know that Packt offers eBook versions of every book published, with PDF and ePub files available? You can upgrade to the eBook version at www.packt.com and as a print book customer, you are entitled to a discount on the eBook copy. Get in touch with us at customercare@packtpub.com for more details.

At www.packt.com, you can also read a collection of free technical articles, sign up for a range of free newsletters, and receive exclusive discounts and offers on Packt books and eBooks.

Contributors

About the author

Hans-Jürgen Schönig has 18 years' experience with PostgreSQL. He is the CEO of a PostgreSQL consulting and support company called Cybertec Schönig and Schönig GmbH. It has successfully served countless customers around the globe. Before founding Cybertec Schönig and Schönig GmbH in the year 2000, he worked as a database developer at a private research company that focused on the Austrian labor market, where he primarily worked on data mining and forecast models. Besides, he has written several books on PostgreSQL.

About the reviewers

Daniel Durante is a consultant and strategist for Fortune 100 companies, and has been a full-stack developer since the age of 12. He is also an author and technical reviewer for Packt Publishing. His code exists in infrastructures such as Hubcash, Stripe, and Walmart. He has worked on text-based browser games that have surpassed 1,000,000 active players. Further he has created bin packing software for CNC machines, worked with embedded programming with cortex-m and PIC circuits, produced high-frequency trading applications, and helped contribute to and maintain one of the oldest **object-relational mappers** (**ORMs**) of Node.js (SequelizeJS).

Marcelo Diaz is a software engineer with more than 15 years of experience with a special focus on PostgreSQL. He is passionate about open source and has promoted its application in critical and high-demand environments where
he has worked as a software developer and consultant on private and public companies. He currently works very happily at Cybertec and as a technical reviewer for Packt Publishing.

He enjoys spending his leisure time with his daughter, Malvina, and his wife, Romina. He also likes playing football.

Packt is searching for authors like you

If you're interested in becoming an author for Packt, please visit `authors.packtpub.com` and apply today. We have worked with thousands of developers and tech professionals, just like you, to help them share their insight with the global tech community. You can make a general application, apply for a specific hot topic that we are recruiting an author for, or submit your own idea.

Table of Contents

Preface

This third edition of *Mastering PostgreSQL 11* presents expert techniques for developing, managing, and administering PostgreSQL databases efficiently. In this edition, we'll cover advanced development and administration aspects, such as partitioning, clustering, logical replication, fault tolerance, optimizing performance, and more, allowing you to become a true PostgreSQL expert.

The book begins with an introduction to the newly released features in PostgreSQL 11 to help you build efficient and fault-tolerant PostgreSQL applications. You'll examine all the advanced aspects of PostgreSQL in detail, including logical replication, database clusters, performance tuning, monitoring, and user management. You will also work with the PostgreSQL optimizer, learn how to configure PostgreSQL for high performance, and explore how to move from Oracle to PostgreSQL. As you progress through the chapters, you will cover transactions, locking, indexes, and optimizing queries to improve performance.

Additionally, you'll learn how to manage network security and explore backups and replications while understanding the useful extensions of PostgreSQL so that you can optimize speed and performance when using large databases.

By the end of this book, you will be able to use your database to its utmost capacity by implementing advanced administrative tasks with ease.

Who this book is for

This book is ideal for PostgreSQL developers and administrators, as well as database admins who have some familiarity with PostgreSQL and database management. Prior exposure to PostgreSQL and familiarity with the basics of database administration is expected.

What this book covers

Chapter 1, *PostgreSQL 12 Overview*, provides an overview of PostgreSQL and its features. You will learn about the new functionalities available in PostgreSQL 12.

Chapter 2, *Understanding Transactions and Locking*, covers one of the most important aspects of any database system: proper database work is usually not possible without the existence of transactions. Understanding transactions and locking is vital to performance, as well as professional work.

Chapter 3, *Making Use of Indexes*, covers everything you need to know about indexes. Indexes are key to performance and are therefore an important cornerstone if you want a good user experience and high throughput. All the important aspects of indexing will be covered in this chapter.

Chapter 4, *Handling Advanced SQL*, introduces you to some of the most important concepts of modern SQL. You will learn about windowing functions as well as other important current elements of SQL.

Chapter 5, *Log Files and System Statistics*, guides you through administrative tasks such as log file management and monitoring. You will learn how to inspect your servers and extract runtime information from PostgreSQL.

Chapter 6, *Optimizing Queries for Good Performance*, tells you everything you need to know about good PostgreSQL performance. The chapter covers SQL tuning and information about memory management.

Chapter 7, *Writing Stored Procedures*, teaches you some of the advanced topics related to server-side code. In this chapter, the most important server-side programming languages are covered and important aspects are pointed out.

Chapter 8, *Managing PostgreSQL Security*, is designed to help you improve the security of your server. The chapter features everything from user management to **Row-Level Security (RLS)**. Information about encryption is also included.

Chapter 9, *Handling Backup and Recovery*, is all about backups and data recovery. You will learn how to back up your data, which will enable you to restore things in the event of a disaster.

Chapter 10, *Making Sense of Backups and Replication*, is all about redundancy. You will learn how to asynchronously and synchronously replicate PostgreSQL database systems. All modern features are covered as extensively as possible.

Chapter 11, *Deciding on Useful Extensions*, describes the widely used modules that add more functionality to PostgreSQL. You will also learn about the most common extensions.

Chapter 12, *Troubleshooting PostgreSQL*, offers a systematic approach to fixing problems in PostgreSQL. It will enable you to spot common problems and approach them in an organized way.

Chapter 13, *Migrating to PostgreSQL*, is the final chapter of this book and it shows you how to migrate from commercial databases to PostgreSQL. This chapter covers the most important databases migrated these days.

To get the most out of this book

This book has been written for a broad audience. In order to follow the examples presented in this book, it makes sense to have at least some experience with SQL and, perhaps, even PostgreSQL in general (although, this is not a mandatory requirement). In general, it is a good idea to have some familiarity with the Unix command line as well.

Conventions used

There are a number of text conventions used throughout this book.

CodeInText: Indicates code words in text, database table names, folder names, filenames, file extensions, pathnames, dummy URLs, user input, and Twitter handles. Here is an example: "Mind that the order in the ENUM type does matter."

Any command-line input or output is written as follows:

```
test=# CREATE TYPE currency AS ENUM ('USD', 'EUR', 'GBP');
CREATE TYPE
```

Bold: Indicates a new term, an important word, or words that you see onscreen. For example, words in menus or dialog boxes appear in the text like this. Here is an example: "This configuration allows you to authenticate using **lightweight directory access protocol (LDAP)**."

Warnings or important notes appear like this.

 Tips and tricks appear like this.

Get in touch

Feedback from our readers is always welcome.

General feedback: If you have questions about any aspect of this book, mention the book title in the subject of your message and email us at customercare@packtpub.com.

Errata: Although we have taken every care to ensure the accuracy of our content, mistakes do happen. If you have found a mistake in this book, we would be grateful if you would report this to us. Please visit www.packtpub.com/support/errata, selecting your book, clicking on the Errata Submission Form link, and entering the details.

Piracy: If you come across any illegal copies of our works in any form on the Internet, we would be grateful if you would provide us with the location address or website name. Please contact us at copyright@packt.com with a link to the material.

If you are interested in becoming an author: If there is a topic that you have expertise in and you are interested in either writing or contributing to a book, please visit authors.packtpub.com.

Reviews

Please leave a review. Once you have read and used this book, why not leave a review on the site that you purchased it from? Potential readers can then see and use your unbiased opinion to make purchase decisions, we at Packt can understand what you think about our products, and our authors can see your feedback on their book. Thank you!

For more information about Packt, please visit packt.com.

Section 1: Basic Overview

This introductory section aims to provide an overview of the latest version of PostgreSQL and ensuring that you understand some of the basic concepts around it.

This section contains the following chapters:

- Chapter 1, *PostgreSQL 12 Overview*
- Chapter 2, *Understanding Transactions and Locking*

PostgreSQL 12 Overview 1

After the usual development cycle, PostgreSQL 12 was released to the public in autumn 2019. The new release offers a variety of new features and provides a rich set of functionality to users, which will make application development faster, improve performance, and generally make PostgreSQL even more usable than it previously was. Many of the new features open the door for further development in the future and will enable developers to implement cutting edge technologies in the decades to come. In this chapter, you will be introduced to those new features and will get an overview of what has been improved, added, and even changed.

The following topics will be covered:

- What's new in PostgreSQL 12?
- SQL and developer-related features
- Backup, recovery, and replication
- Performance-related topics
- Storage-related topics

All relevant features will be covered. Of course, there is always more, and thousands of tiny changes have made it into PostgreSQL 12. What you will see in this chapter are the highlights of the new release.

What's new in PostgreSQL 12?

PostgreSQL 12 is a major milestone and a lot of infrastructure has made it into the core this time. This is especially important in the long run. In this chapter, you will be introduced to the most important developments in the PostgreSQL world. Let's get started and see what the developers have come up with.

Digging into SQL and developer-related topics

PostgreSQL 12 provides some new features that are especially important to developers.

Improving psql and database documentation

In PostgreSQL, two major improvements have been made:

- Adding figures to the documentation
- Adding links to `psql`

The PostgreSQL documentation has traditionally been very good. However, in the past, the documentation did not contain any figures or graphical explanations; it was purely text, which made it hard for some people to quickly understand some aspects of the database. PostgreSQL has finally put an end to this and images have been introduced. This might sound like a minor thing, but it required some changes to the way documentation is handled in general. More figures will be added in the future.

The second change that is immediately visible to `psql` users is that `\h` does not point to the documentation directly. The following listing shows an example:

```
test=# \h SHOW
Command:     SHOW
Description: show the value of a run-time parameter
Syntax:
SHOW name
SHOW ALL

URL: https://www.postgresql.org/docs/12/sql-show.html
```

The URL is really useful here. It avoids a lot of unnecessary searching and digging.

Displaying output as CSV

For those of you using psql to work with PostgreSQL, there is more—psql can't display data in CSV format, as shown in the next listing:

```
test=# \pset format csv
Output format is csv.
test=# SELECT id, id FROM generate_series(1, 4) AS id;
id,id
1,1
2,2
3,3
4,4
```

This is especially useful if you are using psql in a shell script and if you are piping data from one program to the next. If you always want to get data in CSV format, you can add the pset command to your .psqlrc file.

Rebuilding indexes concurrently

Once in a while, it can be necessary (in rare circumstances) to recreate an index. For quite some time, PostgreSQL has provided CREATE INDEX CONCURRENTLY, which allows end users to create an index while a table is under a heavy write load. A normal CREATE INDEX statement blocks the table while the index is created and, therefore, it is hardly possible to create large indexes in a 24 x 7 OLTP database.

However, in some cases, it might be necessary to recreate all indexes in a database or a specific schema. PostgreSQL 12 allows you to run REINDEX CONCURRENTLY on an entire database, schema, or table:

```
test=# \h REINDEX
Command:     REINDEX
Description: rebuild indexes
Syntax:
REINDEX [ ( VERBOSE ) ] { INDEX | TABLE | SCHEMA | DATABASE | SYSTEM } [
CONCURRENTLY ] name

URL: https://www.postgresql.org/docs/12/sql-reindex.html
```

REINDEX CONCURRENTLY will dramatically reduce the pain caused by REINDEX and achieve results with minimal locking.

Storing the result of a computation

PostgreSQL 12 has more features that can simplify development. In many cases, the content of a column has to be derived from some other column. Traditionally, this has been implemented using a trigger. However, writing a trigger needs some coding and manual work. PostgreSQL has a better solution to the problem.

Suppose we want to store data in kilometers and nautical miles. One nautical mile translates to 1.852 km.

For those of you who know nothing about nautical miles: A nautical mile is $1/60^{th}$ of a degree on the equator.

To make sure that nautical miles are always generated, the following syntax can be used:

```
test=# CREATE TABLE t_measurement (
    t        timestamp,
    km       numeric,
    nm       numeric GENERATED ALWAYS AS (km * 1.852) STORED
);
CREATE TABLE
```

GENERATED ALWAYS AS is an elegant way to pre-calculate the content of a column. As you can see, the definition does exactly what we expect:

```
test=# INSERT INTO t_measurement (t, km) VALUES (now(), 100) RETURNING *;
            t                | km |   nm
-----------------------------+-----+----------
 2019-09-30 15:02:31.004481 | 100 | 185.200
(1 row)

INSERT 0 1
```

However, there is more than instantly meets the eye—GENERATED ALWAYS AS also ensures that the content of the column cannot be changed to ensure that the value is always correct:

```
test=# INSERT INTO t_measurement (t, km, nm) VALUES (now(), 100, 1000)
RETURNING *;
ERROR: cannot insert into column "nm"
DETAIL: Column "nm" is a generated column.
```

Performance-wise, the new feature is also faster than the traditional method of using a trigger.

Improving ENUM handling

The possibility to create ENUM types (CREATE TYPE ... AS ENUM) has been around for quite some time now. In PostgreSQL 12, some improvements have been made to make sure that the type can be used even more efficiently. Let's create a simple type first and see how this works:

```
test=# CREATE TYPE currency AS ENUM ('USD', 'EUR', 'GBP');
CREATE TYPE
```

For the sake of simplicity, I have created a data type storing a couple of currencies. Mind that the order in the ENUM type does matter. If you order by a currency column, you will notice that the order returned by PostgreSQL is exactly as specified in the ENUM type.

What has been added in PostgreSQL is the ability to modify an ENUM type inside a single transaction. The following example shows how that works:

```
test=# BEGIN;
BEGIN
test=# ALTER TYPE currency ADD VALUE 'CHF' AFTER 'EUR';
ALTER TYPE
test=# SELECT 'USD'::currency;
 currency
----------
 USD
(1 row)
```

However, there is one restriction: as you can see, the old ENUM values can be used inside the transaction directly. However, the new ones are not available within the same transaction:

```
test=# SELECT 'CHF'::currency;
ERROR:  unsafe use of new value "CHF" of enum type currency
LINE 1: SELECT 'CHF'::currency;
                      ^
HINT:  New enum values must be committed before they can be used.
test=# COMMIT;
ROLLBACK
```

The transaction will error out if we want to access the new value inside the transaction.

Making use of JSONPATH

JSONPATH is also one of those features that are highly relevant to developers. Many people have asked for this functionality in the past and PostgreSQL 12 finally provides the desired capability.

Here are some examples:

```
test=# SELECT jsonb_path_exists('{"a": 1}', '$.a');
 jsonb_path_exists
-------------------
 t
(1 row)

test=# SELECT '{"a": 1}'::jsonb @? '$.a';
 ?column?
----------
 t
(1 row)

test=# SELECT jsonb_path_match('{"a": 1}', '$.a == 1');
 jsonb_path_match
-------------------
 t
(1 row)

test=# SELECT '{"a": 1}'::jsonb @@ '$.a == 1';
 ?column?
----------
 t
(1 row)
```

As you can see, a couple of new functions have been added to dissect a JSON document quickly and easily. This will greatly boost PostgreSQL 12's ability to handle NoSQL-style workloads.

Understanding backup and recovery related features

In the new release, we can also see some changes that are backup- and replication-related. Some means to configure replication and backup have changed in the new release.

Note that you might have to adjust your script to make sure that your automation still works. Existing code might fail.

The most important change is that `recovery.conf` is no more. All necessary configuration steps can now be done directly in `postgresql.conf` as well as using empty files to control the desired behavior.

To figure out how this works, we recommend reading `Chapter 10`, *Making Sense of Backups and Replication*. All changes will be explained in great detail.

Making use of performance improvements

PostgreSQL 12 adds a couple of performance improvements. In this section, you will learn about some of the more relevant improvements that can make a difference in real life.

Optimizing common table expressions and planner support functions

Common table expressions (**CTEs**) are often used to make queries more readable. However, in older versions (pre 12), CTEs came with some PostgreSQL specifics. The result of a CTE is always calculated—just like an independent query. The optimizer could not inline the query and turn it into something faster. A CTE was an optimization barrier that greatly limited the freedom of the planner to do smart things. In PostgreSQL, the situation has changed. The optimizer is now a lot smarter and has more options to deal with CTEs in general.

Let's take a look at an example. The following plan was created in PostgreSQL 11:

```
test=# explain WITH x AS (SELECT * FROM generate_series(1, 5) AS id)
       SELECT * FROM x;
                              QUERY PLAN
------------------------------------------------------------------------
 CTE Scan on x  (cost=10.00..30.00 rows=1000 width=4)
   CTE x
     ->  Function Scan on generate_series id  (cost=0.00..10.00 rows=1000
 width=4)
 (3 rows)
```

As you can see, PostgreSQL executes CTE as is and scans the result. But there's more: the planner estimates that the generate_series function returns 1000 rows, which is, of course, not true.

Let's take a look at the plan produced by PostgreSQL 12:

```
test=# explain WITH x AS (SELECT * FROM generate_series(1, 5) AS id)
       SELECT * FROM x;
                            QUERY PLAN
-------------------------------------------------------------------
 Function Scan on generate_series id  (cost=0.00..0.05 rows=5 width=4)
(1 row)
```

There are two things we can see here. First of all, the CTE scan is gone, which means that PostgreSQL simply inlined the CTE and optimized it away. But there's more. Let's take a closer look at the number of rows estimated. In this case, the estimate is correct. The reason for that is support functions. When writing a function, we can provide PostgreSQL with an additional function providing estimates to the optimizer:

```
test=# \h CREATE FUNCTION
Command:     CREATE FUNCTION
Description: define a new function
Syntax:
CREATE [ OR REPLACE ] FUNCTION
    ...
    | SUPPORT support_function
    ...
URL: https://www.postgresql.org/docs/12/sql-createfunction.html
```

This is incredibly useful if you are dealing with set-returning functions returning thousands or even millions of rows at a time. By telling the optimizer what to expect, it can make smarter decisions, which is, of course, beneficial to overall performance.

Speeding up partitions

Every major release of PostgreSQL provides the end user with improved partitioning. The same holds true for PostgreSQL 12. This time, partition pruning has been speeded up dramatically. Why should we care? If you have got more than just a handful of partitions, fast removal of partitions during planning and execution is vital to ensure that the overhead of partitioning does not go through the roof.

Let's do a small test and see what happens. Let's execute the following SQLs in PostgreSQL 11 as well as in PostgreSQL 12:

```
test=# CREATE TABLE part (id int) PARTITION BY RANGE (id);
CREATE TABLE
```

First of all, a normal range partitioned table is created. The second challenge is to create a really large number of partitions to do our test. The easiest way to achieve that is to generate the desired SQL commands using plain SQL, as shown in the next example. Make sure that this SQL statement is executed on PostgreSQL 11 as well as PostgreSQL 12:

```
test=# SELECT 'CREATE TABLE part_' || id || ' PARTITION OF part
           FOR VALUES FROM (' || id || ') TO (' || id + 1 || ')'
       FROM generate_series(1, 1000) AS id;
                              ?column?
------------------------------------------------------------------
 CREATE TABLE part_1 PARTITION OF part FOR VALUES FROM (1) TO (2)
 CREATE TABLE part_2 PARTITION OF part FOR VALUES FROM (2) TO (3)
 CREATE TABLE part_3 PARTITION OF part FOR VALUES FROM (3) TO (4)
 . . .
```

The SQL statement will create 1,000 SQL statements to create partitions. The beauty now is that `psql` has the `builting \gexec` command. `resultset` that was just created will be seen as SQL input. In my judgment, this is the easiest way to create large numbers of tables:

```
test=# \gexec
CREATE TABLE
CREATE TABLE
CREATE TABLE
```

Now that 1,000 partitions should be in both databases, we can try to compare the results. To do that, I am using a simple `explain analyze` statement, which is totally sufficient to prove my point:

```
test=# explain analyze SELECT * FROM part WHERE id = 545;
                              QUERY PLAN
------------------------------------------------------------------
 Append  (cost=0.00..41.94 rows=13 width=4)
         (actual time=0.029..0.029 rows=0 loops=1)
   ->  Seq Scan on part_545  (cost=0.00..41.88 rows=13 width=4)
         (actual time=0.028..0.028 rows=0 loops=1)
         Filter: (id = 545)
 Planning Time: 17.747 ms
 Execution Time: 0.057 ms
(5 rows)
```

In PostgreSQL 11, the planner needs `17.747 ms` to come up with the desired plan. Running the same in PostgreSQL 12 will show somewhat better results:

```
test=# explain analyze SELECT * FROM part WHERE id = 545;
                        QUERY PLAN
----------------------------------------------------------------
 Seq Scan on part_545  (cost=0.00..41.88 rows=13 width=4)
      (actual time=0.005..0.005 rows=0 loops=1)
   Filter: (id = 545)
 Planning Time: 0.146 ms
 Execution Time: 0.029 ms
(4 rows)
```

Wow! The time needed by the planner has increased by more than 100 times. The more partitions we have, the more important this feature is going to be in a real-world environment.

Creating special indexes more efficiently

In PostgreSQL 12, index creation has been improved once again. This time, the GiST, GIN, and SP-GiST indexes were the ones receiving an extra boost. From now on, these index types will produce less WAL during index creation, which, in turn, saves space if you are archiving a transaction log.

Understanding new storage-related features

Let's now turn our attention to one of the biggest achievements (in my judgment) of the past 10 years in the PostgreSQL universe: pluggable storage engines. What is the general problem? For the past, roughly, 30 years, the PostgreSQL community has focused its attention and development efforts on one single storage engine, the `heap`. While a general-purpose storage engine performs well in many cases, some situations demand different approaches to storage. This is especially true if you are running analytics or high volumes of `UPDATE` statements changing millions or even billions of rows, given an OLTP workload.

So, what is the problem with a conventional row store? Suppose you are running analytics on a large table. Your table might consist of dozens of columns and you have got to read them all to retrieve just a handful of columns. Of course, this is inefficient. By storing data in a column-oriented way, you have only got to fetch the data you really needed. But there is more to this: the content of a column contains a lot more redundancy than a row. `id`, `name`, `date` is definitely less redundant than `name`, `name`, `name`.

In short, you can apply a lot more optimizations for certain workloads. However, this is not true for all kinds of applications. A classical row store is king if you are running classical OLTP operations or if you tend to need the entire row anyway.

The bottom line is: PostgreSQL 12 offers great opportunities for future developments and will lead the way for an explosion of storage engines.

Summary

PostgreSQL offers many new features that cover all aspects of PostgreSQL, including security, SQL capabilities, replication, storage, and a lot more. Many of these new features create new infrastructure, which will open the door for future developments and pave the way for even greater releases in the future.

In the next chapter, you will be introduced to transactions and locking, which are important for scalability and storage management, as well as performance.

2
Understanding Transactions and Locking

Now that we've covered the introduction to PostgreSQL 12, we want to focus our attention on the next important topic. Locking is a vital concept for any kind of database. It is not enough to understand just how it works to write proper or better applications—it is also essential from a performance point of view. Without handling locks properly, your applications might not only be slow; they might also behave in very unexpected ways. In my opinion, locking is the key to performance, and having a good overview of this will certainly help. Therefore, understanding locking and transactions is important for administrators and developers alike. In this chapter, you will learn about the following topics:

- Working with PostgreSQL transactions
- Understanding basic locking
- Making use of `FOR SHARE` and `FOR UPDATE`
- Understanding transaction isolation levels
- Observing deadlocks and similar issues
- Utilizing advisory locks
- Optimizing storage and managing cleanups

By the end of this chapter, you will be able to understand and utilize PostgreSQL transactions in the most efficient way possible. You will see that many applications can benefit from improved performance.

Working with PostgreSQL transactions

PostgreSQL provides you with highly advanced transaction machinery that offers countless features to developers and administrators alike. In this section, we will look at the basic concept of transactions.

The first important thing to know is that, in PostgreSQL, everything is a transaction. If you send a simple query to the server, it is already a transaction. Here is an example:

```
test=# SELECT now(), now();
             now             |             now
-----------------------------+-----------------------------
 2019-07-10 14:25:08.406051+02 | 2019-07-10 14:25:08.406051+02
(1 row)
```

In this case, the SELECT statement will be a separate transaction. If the same command is executed again, different timestamps will be returned.

> Keep in mind that the now() function will return the transaction time. The SELECT statement will, therefore, always return two identical timestamps. If you want the **real time**, consider using clock_timestamp() instead of now().

If more than one statement has to be a part of the same transaction, the BEGIN statement must be used, as follows:

```
test=# \h BEGIN
Command: BEGIN
Description: start a transaction block
Syntax:
BEGIN [ WORK | TRANSACTION ] [ transaction_mode [, ...] ]

where transaction_mode is one of:

  ISOLATION LEVEL { SERIALIZABLE | REPEATABLE READ | READ COMMITTED | READ
UNCOMMITTED }
  READ WRITE | READ ONLY
  [ NOT ] DEFERRABLE

URL: https://www.postgresql.org/docs/12/sql-begin.html
```

The BEGIN statement will ensure that more than one command is packed into a transaction. Here is how it works:

```
test=# BEGIN;
BEGIN
test=# SELECT now();
              now
-------------------------------
 2019-07-10 14:26:55.665943+02
(1 row)

test=# SELECT now();
              now
-------------------------------
 2019-07-10 14:26:55.665943+02
(1 row)

test=# COMMIT;
COMMIT
```

The important point here is that both timestamps will be identical. As we mentioned earlier, we are talking about transaction time.

To end the transaction, COMMIT can be used:

```
test=# \h COMMIT
Command: COMMIT
Description: commit the current transaction
Syntax:
COMMIT [ WORK | TRANSACTION ] [ AND [ NO ] CHAIN ]

URL: https://www.postgresql.org/docs/12/sql-commit.html
```

There are a couple of syntax elements here. You can just use COMMIT, COMMIT WORK, or COMMIT TRANSACTION. All three commands have the same meaning. If this is not enough, there's more:

```
test=# \h END
Command:   END
Description: commit the current transaction
Syntax:
END [ WORK | TRANSACTION ]
```

The END clause is the same as the COMMIT clause.

ROLLBACK is the counterpart of COMMIT. Instead of successfully ending a transaction, it will simply stop the transaction without ever making things visible to other transactions, as shown in the following code:

```
test=# \h ROLLBACK
Command: ROLLBACK
Description: abort the current transaction
Syntax:
ROLLBACK [ WORK | TRANSACTION ] [ AND [ NO ] CHAIN ]

URL: https://www.postgresql.org/docs/12/sql-rollback.html
```

Some applications use ABORT instead of ROLLBACK. The meaning is the same. What is new in PostgreSQL is the concept of a chained transaction. What is the point of all this? The following listing shows an example:

```
test=# SHOW transaction_read_only;
 transaction_read_only
-----------------------
 off
(1 row)

test=# BEGIN TRANSACTION READ ONLY;
BEGIN
test=# SELECT 1;
 ?column?
----------
        1
(1 row)

test=# COMMIT AND CHAIN;
COMMIT
test=# SHOW transaction_read_only;
 transaction_read_only
-----------------------
 on
(1 row)

test=# COMMIT AND NO CHAIN;
COMMIT
test=# SHOW transaction_read_only;
 transaction_read_only
-----------------------
 off
(1 row)
```

```
test=# COMMIT;
psql: WARNING: there is no transaction in progress
COMMIT
```

Let's go through this example step by step:

1. Display the content of the transaction_read_only setting. It is off because, by default, we are in read/write mode.
2. Start a read-only transaction using BEGIN. This will automatically adjust the transaction_read_only variable.
3. Commit the transaction using AND CHAIN, then PostgreSQL will automatically start a new transaction featuring the same properties as the previous transaction.

In our example, we will also be in read-only mode, just like the transaction before. There is no need to explicitly open a new transaction and set whatever values again, which can dramatically reduce the number of roundtrips between application and server. If a transaction is committed normally (= NO CHAIN) the read-only attribute of the transaction will be gone.

Handling errors inside a transaction

It is not always the case that transactions are correct from beginning to end. Things might just go wrong for whatever reason. However, in PostgreSQL, only error-free transactions can be committed. The following listing shows a failing transaction, which errors out due to a division-by-zero error:

```
test=# BEGIN;
BEGIN
test=# SELECT 1;
 ?column?
----------
        1
(1 row)
test=# SELECT 1 / 0;
psql: ERROR: division by zero
test=# SELECT 1;
psql: ERROR: current transaction is aborted, commands ignored until end of
transaction block
test=# COMMIT;
ROLLBACK
```

Note that division by zero did not work out.

In any proper database, an instruction similar to this will instantly error out and make the statement fail.

It is important to point out that PostgreSQL will error out, unlike MySQL, which is far less strict. After an error has occurred, no more instructions will be accepted, even if those instructions are semantically and syntactically correct. It is still possible to issue COMMIT. However, PostgreSQL will roll back the transaction because it is the only correct thing to be done at that point.

Making use of SAVEPOINT

In professional applications, it can be pretty hard to write reasonably long transactions without ever encountering a single error. To solve this problem, users can utilize something called SAVEPOINT. As the name indicates, a savepoint is a safe place inside a transaction that the application can return to if things go terribly wrong. Here is an example:

```
test=# BEGIN;
BEGIN
test=# SELECT 1;
 ?column?
----------
        1
(1 row)

test=# SAVEPOINT a;
SAVEPOINT
test=# SELECT 2 / 0;
psql: ERROR:  division by zero
test=# SELECT 2;
psql: ERROR:  current transaction is aborted, commands ignored until end of
transaction block
test=# ROLLBACK TO SAVEPOINT a;
ROLLBACK
test=# SELECT 3;
 ?column?
----------
        3
(1 row)

test=# COMMIT;
COMMIT
```

After the first `SELECT` clause, I decided to create a savepoint to make sure that the application can always return to this point inside the transaction. As you can see, the savepoint has a name, which is referred to later.

After returning to the savepoint called `a`, the transaction can proceed normally. The code has jumped back to before the error, so everything is fine.

The number of savepoints inside a transaction is practically unlimited. We have seen customers with over 250,000 savepoints in a single operation. PostgreSQL can easily handle this.

If you want to remove a savepoint from inside a transaction, there's the `RELEASE SAVEPOINT` command:

```
test=# \h RELEASE
Command: RELEASE SAVEPOINT
Description: destroy a previously defined savepoint
Syntax:
RELEASE [ SAVEPOINT ] savepoint_name

URL: https://www.postgresql.org/docs/12/sql-release-savepoint.html
```

Many people ask what will happen if you try to reach a savepoint after a transaction has ended. The answer is that the life of a savepoint ends as soon as the transaction ends. In other words, there is no way to return to a certain point in time after the transactions have been completed.

Transactional DDLs

PostgreSQL has a very nice feature that is unfortunately not present in many commercial database systems. In PostgreSQL, it is possible to run DDLs (commands that change the data's structure) inside a transaction block. In a typical commercial system, a DDL will implicitly commit the current transaction. This does not occur in PostgreSQL.

Apart from some minor exceptions (`DROP DATABASE`, `CREATE TABLESPACE`, `DROP TABLESPACE`, and so on), all DDLs in PostgreSQL are transactional, which is a huge advantage and a real benefit to end users.

Here is an example:

```
test=# \d
No relations found.
test=# BEGIN;
BEGIN
```

```
test=# CREATE TABLE t_test (id int);
CREATE TABLE
test=# ALTER TABLE t_test ALTER COLUMN id TYPE int8;
ALTER TABLE
test=# \d t_test
     Table "public.t_test"
 Column |  Type  | Modifiers
--------+--------+-----------
 id     | bigint |

test=# ROLLBACK;
ROLLBACK
test=# \d
No relations found.
```

In this example, a table has been created and modified, and the entire transaction has been aborted. As you can see, there is no implicit COMMIT command or any other strange behavior. PostgreSQL simply acts as expected.

Transactional DDLs are especially important if you want to deploy software. Just imagine running a **content management system** (CMS). If a new version is released, you'll want to upgrade. Running the old version would still be OK; running the new version would also be OK, but you really don't want a mixture of old and new. Therefore, deploying an upgrade in a single transaction is highly beneficial as it upgrades an atomic operation.

 To facilitate good software practices, we can include several separately coded modules from our source control system into a single deployment transaction.

Understanding basic locking

In this section, you will learn about basic locking mechanisms. The goal is to understand how locking works in general and how to get simple applications right.

To show you how things work, we will create a simple table. For demonstrative purposes, I will add one row to the table using a simple INSERT command:

```
test=# CREATE TABLE  t_test (id int);
CREATE TABLE
test=# INSERT INTO t_test VALUES (0);
INSERT 0 1
```

The first important thing is that tables can be read concurrently. Many users reading the same data at the same time won't block each other. This allows PostgreSQL to handle thousands of users without any problems.

The question now is what happens if reads and writes occur at the same time? Here is an example. Let's assume that the table contains one row and its `id = 0`:

Transaction 1	Transaction 2
BEGIN;	BEGIN;
UPDATE t_test SET id = id + 1 RETURNING *;	
User will see 1	SELECT * FROM t_test;
	User will see 0
COMMIT;	COMMIT;

Two transactions are opened. The first one will change a row. However, this is not a problem as the second transaction can proceed. It will return the old row as it was before UPDATE. This behavior is called **Multi-Version Concurrency Control (MVCC)**.

A transaction will only see data if it has been committed by the write transaction before the initiation of the read transaction. One transaction cannot inspect the changes that have been made by another active connection. A transaction can see only those changes that have already been committed.

There is also a second important aspect—many commercial or open source databases are still (as of 2018) unable to handle concurrent reads and writes. In PostgreSQL, this is absolutely not a problem—reads and writes can coexist.

Write transactions won't block read transactions.

After the transaction has been committed, the table will contain 1.

What will happen if two people change data at the same time? Here is an example:

Transaction 1	Transaction 2
`BEGIN;`	`BEGIN;`
`UPDATE t_test SET id = id + 1 RETURNING *;`	
It will return 2	`UPDATE t_test SET id = id + 1 RETURNING *;`
	It will wait for transaction 1
`COMMIT;`	It will wait for transaction 1
	It will reread the row, find 2, set the value, and return 3
	`COMMIT;`

Suppose you want to count the number of hits on a website. If you run the preceding code, no hit will be lost because PostgreSQL guarantees that one `UPDATE` statement is performed after the other.

 PostgreSQL will only lock rows affected by `UPDATE`. So, if you have 1,000 rows, you can theoretically run 1,000 concurrent changes on the same table.

It is also worth noting that you can always run concurrent reads. Our two writes will not block reads.

Avoiding typical mistakes and explicit locking

In my life as a professional PostgreSQL consultant (`https://www.cybertec-postgresql. com`), I have seen a couple of mistakes that are repeated frequently. If there are constants in life, these typical mistakes are definitely some of the things that never change.

Here is my favorite:

Transaction 1	Transaction 2
BEGIN;	BEGIN;
SELECT max(id) FROM product;	SELECT max(id) FROM product;
User will see 17	User will see 17
User will decide to use 18	User will decide to use 18
INSERT INTO product ... VALUES (18, ...)	INSERT INTO product ... VALUES (18, ...)
COMMIT;	COMMIT;

In this case, there will be either a duplicate key violation or two identical entries. Neither variation of the problem is all that appealing.

One way to fix this problem is to use explicit table locking. The following code shows us the syntax definition of LOCK:

```
test=# \h LOCK
Command: LOCK
Description: lock a table
Syntax:
LOCK [ TABLE ] [ ONLY ] name [ * ] [, ...] [ IN lockmode MODE ] [ NOWAIT ]

where lockmode is one of:

    ACCESS SHARE | ROW SHARE | ROW EXCLUSIVE | SHARE UPDATE EXCLUSIVE
    | SHARE | SHARE ROW EXCLUSIVE | EXCLUSIVE | ACCESS EXCLUSIVE

URL: https://www.postgresql.org/docs/12/sql-lock.html
```

As you can see, PostgreSQL offers eight types of locks to lock an entire table. In PostgreSQL, a lock can be as light as an ACCESS SHARE lock or as heavy as an ACCESS EXCLUSIVE lock. The following list shows what these locks do:

- ACCESS SHARE: This type of lock is taken by reads and conflicts only with ACCESS EXCLUSIVE, which is set by DROP TABLE and so on. Practically, this means that SELECT cannot start if a table is about to be dropped. This also implies that DROP TABLE has to wait until a reading transaction is complete.
- ROW SHARE: PostgreSQL takes this kind of lock in the case of SELECT FOR UPDATE/SELECT FOR SHARE. It conflicts with EXCLUSIVE and ACCESS EXCLUSIVE.

- ROW EXCLUSIVE: This lock is taken by INSERT, UPDATE, and DELETE. It conflicts with SHARE, SHARE ROW EXCLUSIVE, EXCLUSIVE, and ACCESS EXCLUSIVE.
- SHARE UPDATE EXCLUSIVE: This kind of lock is taken by CREATE INDEX CONCURRENTLY, ANALYZE, ALTER TABLE, VALIDATE, and some other flavors of ALTER TABLE, as well as by VACUUM (not VACUUM FULL). It conflicts with the SHARE UPDATE EXCLUSIVE, SHARE, SHARE ROW EXCLUSIVE, EXCLUSIVE, and ACCESS EXCLUSIVE lock modes.
- SHARE: When an index is created, SHARE locks will be set. It conflicts with ROW EXCLUSIVE, SHARE UPDATE EXCLUSIVE, SHARE ROW EXCLUSIVE, EXCLUSIVE, and ACCESS EXCLUSIVE.
- SHARE ROW EXCLUSIVE: This one is set by CREATE TRIGGER and some forms of ALTER TABLE and conflicts with everything except ACCESS SHARE.
- EXCLUSIVE: This type of lock is by far the most restrictive one. It protects against reads and writes alike. If this lock is taken by a transaction, nobody else can read or write to the table that's been affected.
- ACCESS EXCLUSIVE: This lock prevents concurrent transactions from reading and writing.

Given the PostgreSQL locking infrastructure, one solution to the max problem we outlined previously would be as follows. The example in the following code shows how to lock a table:

```
BEGIN;
LOCK   TABLE   product IN ACCESS EXCLUSIVE MODE;
INSERT INTO  product SELECT max(id) + 1,  ... FROM product;
COMMIT;
```

Keep in mind that this is a pretty nasty way of doing this kind of operation because nobody else can read or write to the table during your operation. Therefore, ACCESS EXCLUSIVE should be avoided at all costs.

Considering alternative solutions

There is an alternative solution to this problem. Consider an example where you are asked to write an application to generate invoice numbers. The tax office might require you to create invoice numbers without gaps and without duplicates. How would you do this? Of course, one solution would be a table lock. However, you can really do better. Here is what you can do to handle the numbering problem we are trying to solve:

```
test=# CREATE TABLE t_invoice (id int PRIMARY KEY);
CREATE TABLE
```

```
test=# CREATE TABLE  t_watermark (id int);
CREATE TABLE
test=# INSERT INTO  t_watermark VALUES (0);
INSERT 0
test=# WITH  x AS (UPDATE t_watermark SET id = id + 1 RETURNING *)
        INSERT INTO  t_invoice
        SELECT * FROM  x RETURNING *;
id
----
  1
(1 row)
```

In this case, we introduced a table called t_watermark. It contains just one row. The WITH command will be executed first. The row will be locked and incremented, and the new value will be returned. Only one person can do this at a time. The value returned by the CTE is then used in the invoice table. It is guaranteed to be unique. The beauty is that there is only a simple row lock on the watermark table, which leads to no reads being blocked in the invoice table. Overall, this way is more scalable.

Making use of FOR SHARE and FOR UPDATE

Sometimes, data is selected from the database, then some processing happens in the application, and finally, some changes are made back on the database side. This is a classic example of SELECT FOR UPDATE.

Here is an example that shows the way SELECT is often executed in the wrong way:

```
BEGIN;
SELECT * FROM  invoice WHERE  processed = false;
** application magic  will  happen here  **
UPDATE invoice SET processed = true  ...
COMMIT;
```

The problem here is that two people might select the same unprocessed data. Changes that are made to these processed rows will then be overwritten. In short, a race condition will occur.

To solve this problem, developers can make use of SELECT FOR UPDATE. Here's how it can be used. The following example will show a typical scenario:

```
BEGIN;
SELECT * FROM invoice WHERE processed = false FOR UPDATE;
** application magic  will  happen here  **
UPDATE invoice SET processed = true ...
COMMIT;
```

SELECT FOR UPDATE will lock rows just like UPDATE would. This means that no changes can happen concurrently. All locks will be released on COMMIT as usual.

If one SELECT FOR UPDATE command is waiting for another SELECT FOR UPDATE command, you will have to wait until the other one completes (COMMIT or ROLLBACK). If the first transaction doesn't want to end, for whatever reason, the second transaction may potentially wait forever. To avoid this, it is possible to use SELECT FOR UPDATE NOWAIT:

Transaction 1	Transaction 2
BEGIN;	BEGIN;
SELECT ... FROM tab WHERE ... FOR UPDATE NOWAIT;	
Some processing	SELECT ... FROM tab WHERE ... FOR UPDATE NOWAIT;
Some processing	ERROR: could not obtain lock on row in relation tab

If NOWAIT is not flexible enough for you, consider using lock_timeout. It will contain the amount of time you want to wait on locks. You can set this on a per-session level:

```
test=# SET lock_timeout TO 5000;
SET
```

In this case, the value is set to 5 seconds.

While SELECT does basically no locking, SELECT FOR UPDATE can be pretty harsh. Just imagine the following business process: we want to fill up an airplane that has 200 seats. Many people want to book seats concurrently. In this case, the following might happen:

Transaction 1	Transaction 2
BEGIN;	BEGIN;
SELECT ... FROM flight LIMIT 1 FOR UPDATE;	

Waiting for user input	`SELECT ... FROM flight LIMIT 1 FOR UPDATE;`
Waiting for user input	It has to wait

The trouble is that only one seat can be booked at a time. There are potentially 200 seats available, but everybody has to wait for the first person. While the first seat is blocked, nobody else can book a seat, even if people don't care which seat they get in the end.

`SELECT FOR UPDATE SKIP LOCKED` will fix the problem. Let's create some sample data first:

```
test=# CREATE TABLE t_flight AS
        SELECT * FROM generate_series(1, 200) AS id;
SELECT 200
```

Now comes the magic:

Transaction 1	Transaction 2
BEGIN;	BEGIN;
SELECT * FROM t_flight LIMIT 2 FOR UPDATE SKIP LOCKED;	SELECT * FROM t_flight LIMIT 2 FOR UPDATE SKIP LOCKED;
It will return 1 and 2	It will return 3 and 4

If everybody wants to fetch two rows, we can serve 100 concurrent transactions at a time without having to worry about blocking transactions.

 Keep in mind that waiting is the slowest form of execution. If only one transaction can be active at a time, it is pointless to buy ever more expensive servers if your real problems are caused by locking and conflicting transactions in general.

However, there's more. In some cases, FOR UPDATE can have unintended consequences. Most people are not aware of the fact that FOR UPDATE will have an impact on foreign keys. Let's assume that we have two tables: one to store currencies and the other to store accounts. The following code shows an example of this:

```
CREATE TABLE t_currency (id int, name text, PRIMARY KEY (id));
INSERT INTO t_currency VALUES (1, 'EUR');
INSERT INTO t_currency VALUES (2, 'USD');

CREATE TABLE t_account (
        id              int,
        currency_id     int             REFERENCES t_currency (id)
                                ON UPDATE CASCADE
```

```
                                       ON DELETE CASCADE,
balance        numeric);
INSERT INTO t_account VALUES (1, 1, 100);
INSERT INTO t_account VALUES (2, 1, 200);
```

Now, we want to run SELECT FOR UPDATE on the account table:

Transaction 1	Transaction 2
BEGIN;	
SELECT * FROM t_account FOR UPDATE;	BEGIN;
Waiting for user to proceed	UPDATE t_currency SET id = id * 10;
Waiting for user to proceed	It will wait on transaction 1

Although there is a SELECT FOR UPDATE command on accounts, the UPDATE command on the currency table will be blocked. This is necessary because, otherwise, there is a chance of breaking the foreign key constraint altogether. In a fairly complex data structure, you can therefore easily end up with contentions in an area where they are least expected (some highly important lookup tables).

As well as FOR UPDATE, there's also FOR SHARE, FOR NO KEY UPDATE, and FOR KEY SHARE. The following list describes what these modes actually mean:

- FOR NO KEY UPDATE: This one is pretty similar to FOR UPDATE. However, the lock is weaker and, therefore, it can coexist with SELECT FOR SHARE.
- FOR SHARE: FOR UPDATE is pretty strong and works on the assumption that you are definitely going to change rows. FOR SHARE is different because more than one transaction can hold a FOR SHARE lock at the same time.
- FOR KEY SHARE: This behaves similarly to FOR SHARE, except that the lock is weaker. It will block FOR UPDATE but will not block FOR NO KEY UPDATE.

The important thing here is to simply try things out and observe what happens. Improving locking behavior is really important as it can dramatically improve the scalability of your application.

Understanding transaction isolation levels

Up until now, you have seen how to handle locking, as well as some basic concurrency. In this section, you will learn about transaction isolation. To me, this is one of the most neglected topics in modern software development. Only a small fraction of software developers are actually aware of this issue, which in turn leads to mind-boggling bugs.

Here is an example of what can happen:

Transaction 1	Transaction 2
`BEGIN;`	
`SELECT sum(balance) FROM t_account;`	
User will see 300	`BEGIN;`
	`INSERT INTO t_account (balance) VALUES (100);`
	`COMMIT;`
`SELECT sum(balance) FROM t_account;`	
User will see 400	
`COMMIT;`	

Most users would actually expect the first transaction to always return 300, regardless of the second transaction. However, this isn't true. By default, PostgreSQL runs in the READ COMMITTED transaction isolation mode. This means that every statement inside a transaction will get a new snapshot of the data, which will be constant throughout the query.

 A SQL statement will operate on the same snapshot and will ignore changes by concurrent transactions while it is running.

If you want to avoid this, you can use TRANSACTION ISOLATION LEVEL REPEATABLE READ. In this transaction isolation level, a transaction will use the same snapshot through the entire transaction. Here's what will happen:

Transaction 1	Transaction 2
`BEGIN TRANSACTION ISOLATION LEVEL` `REPEATABLE READ;`	
`SELECT sum(balance) FROM t_account;`	

User will see 300	BEGIN;
	INSERT INTO t_account (balance) VALUES (100);
	COMMIT;
SELECT sum(balance) FROM t_account;	SELECT sum(balance) FROM t_account;
User will see 300	User will see 400
COMMIT;	

As we've outlined, the first transaction will freeze its snapshot of the data and provide us with constant results throughout the entire transaction. This feature is especially important if you want to run reports. The first and last page of a report should always be consistent and operate on the same data. Therefore, the repeatable read is key to consistent reports.

Note that isolation-related errors won't always pop up instantly. Sometimes, trouble is noticed years after an application has been moved to production.

> Repeatable read is not more expensive than read committed. There is no need to worry about performance penalties. For normal **online transaction processing** (OLTP), read committed has various advantages because changes can be seen much earlier and the odds of unexpected errors are usually lower.

Considering Serializable Snapshot Isolation transactions

On top of read committed and repeatable read, PostgreSQL offers **Serializable Snapshot Isolation** (SSI) transactions. So, overall, PostgreSQL supports three isolation levels. Note that read uncommitted (which still happens to be the default in some commercial databases) is not supported: if you try to start a read uncommitted transaction, PostgreSQL will silently map to read committed. Let's get back to the serializable isolation level.

> If you want to know more about this isolation level, consider checking out https://wiki.postgresql.org/wiki/Serializable.

The idea behind serializable isolation is simple; if a transaction is known to work correctly when there is only a single user, it will also work in the case of concurrency when this isolation level is chosen. However, users have to be prepared; transactions may fail (by design) and error out. In addition to this, a performance penalty has to be paid.

> Consider using serializable isolation only when you have a decent understanding of what is going on inside the database engine.

Observing deadlocks and similar issues

Deadlocks are an important issue and can happen in every database. Basically, a deadlock will happen if two transactions have to wait on each other.

In this section, you will see how this can happen. Let's suppose we have a table containing two rows:

```
CREATE TABLE t_deadlock (id int);
INSERT INTO t_deadlock VALUES (1), (2);
```

The following example shows what can happen:

Transaction 1	Transaction 2
BEGIN;	BEGIN;
UPDATE t_deadlock SET id = id * 10 WHERE id = 1;	UPDATE t_deadlock SET id = id * 10 WHERE id = 2;
UPDATE t_deadlock SET id = id * 10 WHERE id = 2;	
Waiting on transaction 2	UPDATE t_deadlock SET id = id * 10 WHERE id = 1;
Waiting on transaction 2	Waiting on transaction 1
	Deadlock will be resolved after 1 second (deadlock_timeout)
COMMIT;	ROLLBACK;

As soon as the deadlock is detected, the following error message will show up:

```
psql: ERROR: deadlock detected
DETAIL: Process 91521 waits for ShareLock on transaction 903;
    blocked by process 77185.
Process 77185 waits for ShareLock on transaction 905;
blocked by process 91521.
HINT: See server log for query details.
CONTEXT: while updating tuple (0,1) in relation "t_deadlock"
```

PostgreSQL is even kind enough to tell us which row has caused the conflict. In my example, the root of all evil is a tuple, (0, 1). What you can see here is ctid, which is a unique identifier of a row in a table. It tells us about the physical position of a row inside the table. In this example, it is the first row in the first block (0).

It is even possible to query this row if it is still visible to your transaction. Here's how it works:

```
test=# SELECT ctid, * FROM t_deadlock WHERE ctid = '(0,  3)';
ctid   | id
-------+-----
(0,1)  |  10
(1 row)
```

Keep in mind that this query might not return a row if it has already been deleted or modified.

However, this isn't the only case where deadlocks can lead to potentially failing transactions. Transactions can also not be serialized for various reasons. The following example shows what can happen. To make this example work, I assume that you've still got the two rows, id = 1 and id = 2:

Transaction 1	Transaction 2
BEGIN ISOLATION LEVEL REPEATABLE READ;	
SELECT * FROM t_deadlock;	
Two rows will be returned	
	DELETE FROM t_deadlock;
SELECT * FROM t_deadlock;	
Two rows will be returned	
DELETE FROM t_deadlock;	
The transaction will error out	
ROLLBACK; - we cannot COMMIT anymore	

In this example, two concurrent transactions are at work. As long as the first transaction is just selecting data, everything is fine because PostgreSQL can easily preserve the illusion of static data. But what happens if the second transaction commits a DELETE command? As long as there are only reads, there is still no problem. The trouble begins when the first transaction tries to delete or modify data, which is already dead at this point. The only solution for PostgreSQL is to error out due to a conflict caused by our transactions:

```
test=# DELETE FROM t_deadlock;
psql: ERROR: could not serialize access due to concurrent update
```

Practically, this means that end users have to be prepared to handle erroneous transactions. If something goes wrong, properly written applications must be able to try again.

Utilizing advisory locks

PostgreSQL has highly efficient and sophisticated transaction machinery that is capable of handling locks in a really fine-grained and efficient way. A few years ago, people came up with the idea of using this code to synchronize applications with each other. Thus, advisory locks were born.

When using advisory locks, it is important to mention that they won't go away on COMMIT like normal locks do. Therefore, it is really important to make sure that unlocking is done properly and in a totally reliable way.

If you decide to use an advisory lock, what you really lock is a number. So, this isn't about rows or data; it is really just a number. Here's how it works:

Session 1	Session 2
BEGIN;	
SELECT pg_advisory_lock(15);	
	SELECT pg_advisory_lock(15);
	It has to wait
COMMIT;	It still has to wait
SELECT pg_advisory_unlock(15);	It is still waiting
	Lock is taken

The first transaction will lock 15. The second transaction has to wait until this number has been unlocked again. The second session will even wait after the first one has committed. This is highly important as you cannot rely on the fact that the end of the transaction will nicely and miraculously solve things for you.

If you want to unlock all locked numbers, PostgreSQL offers the `pg_advisory_unlock_all()` function to do exactly this:

```
test=# SELECT pg_advisory_unlock_all();
pg_advisory_unlock_all
-----------------------

(1 row)
```

Sometimes, you might want to see whether you can get a lock and error out if this isn't possible. To achieve this, PostgreSQL offers a couple of functions; to see a list of all such available functions, enter `\df *try*advisory*` at the command line.

Optimizing storage and managing cleanup

Transactions are an integral part of the PostgreSQL system. However, transactions come with a small price tag attached. As we've already shown in this chapter, sometimes, concurrent users will be presented with different data. Not everybody will get the same data returned by a query. In addition to this, DELETE and UPDATE are not allowed to actually overwrite data since ROLLBACK would not work. If you happen to be in the middle of a large DELETE operation, you cannot be sure whether you will be able to COMMIT or not. In addition to this, data is still visible while you perform DELETE, and sometimes data is even visible once your modification has long since finished.

Consequently, this means that cleanup has to happen asynchronously. A transaction cannot clean up its own mess and COMMIT/ROLLBACK might be too early to take care of dead rows.

The solution to this problem is VACUUM. The following code block provides you with a syntax overview:

```
test=# \h VACUUM
Command: VACUUM
Description: garbage-collect and optionally analyze a database
Syntax:
VACUUM [ ( option [, ...] ) ] [ table_and_columns [, ...] ]
VACUUM [ FULL ] [ FREEZE ] [ VERBOSE ] [ ANALYZE ] [ table_and_columns [,
...] ]

where option can be one of:

    FULL [ boolean ]
    FREEZE [ boolean ]
    VERBOSE [ boolean ]
    ANALYZE [ boolean ]
```

```
        DISABLE_PAGE_SKIPPING [ boolean ]
        SKIP_LOCKED [ boolean ]
        INDEX_CLEANUP [ boolean ]
        TRUNCATE [ boolean ]

    and table_and_columns is:

        table_name [ ( column_name [, ...] ) ]

    URL: https://www.postgresql.org/docs/12/sql-vacuum.html
```

VACUUM will visit all of the pages that potentially contain modifications and find all the dead space. The free space that's found is then tracked by the **free space map** (**FSM**) of the relation.

Note that VACUUM will, in most cases, not shrink the size of a table. Instead, it will track and find free space inside existing storage files.

> Tables will usually have the same size after VACUUM. If there are no valid rows at the end of a table, file sizes can go down, although this is rare. This is not the rule, but rather the exception.

What this means to end users will be outlined in the *Watching VACUUM at work* section of this chapter.

Configuring VACUUM and autovacuum

Back in the early days of PostgreSQL projects, people had to run VACUUM manually. Fortunately, those days are long gone. Nowadays, administrators can rely on a tool called autovacuum, which is part of the PostgreSQL server infrastructure. It automatically takes care of cleanup and works in the background. It wakes up once per minute (see autovacuum_naptime = 1 in postgresql.conf) and checks whether there is work to do. If there is work, autovacuum will fork up to three worker processes (see autovacuum_max_workers in postgresql.conf).

The main question is, when does autovacuum trigger the creation of a worker process?

> Actually, the autovacuum process doesn't fork processes itself. Instead, it tells the main process to do so. This is done to avoid zombie processes in the case of failure and to improve robustness.

The answer to this question can, again, be found in `postgresql.conf`, as shown in the following code:

```
autovacuum_vacuum_threshold = 50
autovacuum_analyze_threshold = 50
autovacuum_vacuum_scale_factor = 0.2
autovacuum_analyze_scale_factor = 0.1
```

The `autovacuum_vacuum_scale_factor` command tells PostgreSQL that a table is worth vacuuming if 20% of its data has been changed. The trouble is that if a table consists of one row, one change is already 100%. It makes absolutely no sense to fork a complete process to clean up just one row. Therefore, `autovacuum_vacuuum_threshold` says that we need 20%, and this 20% must be at least 50 rows. Otherwise, VACUUM won't kick in. The same mechanism is used when it comes to the creation of optimizer statistics. We need 10% and at least 50 rows to justify new optimizer statistics. Ideally, `autovacuum` creates new statistics during a normal VACUUM to avoid unnecessary trips to the table.

Digging into transaction wraparound-related issues

There are two more settings in `postgresql.conf` that are quite important to understand to really make use of PostgreSQL. As we have stated already, understanding VACUUM is key to performance:

```
autovacuum_freeze_max_age = 200000000
autovacuum_multixact_freeze_max_age = 400000000
```

To understand the overall problem, it is important to understand how PostgreSQL handles concurrency. The PostgreSQL transaction machinery is based on the comparison of transaction IDs and the states transactions are in.

Let's look at an example. If I am transaction ID `4711` and if you happen to be `4712`, I won't see you because you are still running. If I am transaction ID `4711` but you are transaction ID `3900`, I will see you. If your transaction has failed, I can safely ignore all of the rows that are produced by your failing transaction.

The trouble is as follows: transaction IDs are finite, not unlimited. At some point, they will start to wraparound. In reality, this means that transaction number 5 might actually be after transaction number 800 million. How does PostgreSQL know what was first? It does so by storing a watermark. At some point, those watermarks will be adjusted, and this is exactly when VACUUM starts to be relevant. By running VACUUM (or `autovacuum`), you can ensure that the watermark is adjusted in a way that there are always enough future transaction IDs left to work with.

Not every transaction will increase the transaction ID counter. As long as a transaction is still reading, it will only have a virtual transaction ID. This ensures that transaction IDs are not burned too quickly.

The `autovacuum_freeze_max_age` command defines the maximum number of transactions (age) that a table's `pg_class.relfrozenxid` field can attain before a VACUUM operation is forced to prevent transaction ID wraparound within the table. This value is fairly low because it also has an impact on clog cleanup (the clog or commit log is a data structure that stores two bits per transaction, which indicates whether a transaction is running, aborted, committed, or still in a subtransaction).

The `autovacuum_multixact_freeze_max_age` command configures the maximum age that a table's `pg_class.relminmxid` field can attain before a VACUUM operation is forced to prevent the `multixact` ID wraparound within the table. Freezing tuples is an important performance issue, and there will be more on this process in Chapter 6, *Optimizing Queries for Good Performance*, where we will discuss query optimization.

In general, trying to reduce the VACUUM load while maintaining operational security is a good idea. A VACUUM instance on large tables can be expensive, and therefore keeping an eye on these settings makes perfect sense.

A word on VACUUM FULL

Instead of the normal VACUUM, you can also use VACUUM FULL. However, I really want to point out that VACUUM FULL actually locks the table and rewrites the entire relation. In the case of a small table, this might not be an issue. However, if your tables are large, the table lock can really kill you in minutes! VACUUM FULL blocks upcoming writes and, therefore, some people talking to your database might have the feeling that it is actually down. Hence, a lot of caution is advised.

To get rid of VACUUM FULL, I recommend that you check out `pg_squeeze` (`http://www.cybertec.at/introducing-pg_squeeze-a-postgresql-extension-to-auto-rebuild-bloated-tables/`), which can rewrite a table without blocking writes.

Watching VACUUM at work

Now, it is time to see VACUUM in action. I have included this section here because my practical work as a PostgreSQL consultant and supporter (http://www.postgresql-support.com/) indicates that most people only have a very vague understanding of what happens on the storage side.

To stress this point again, in most cases, VACUUM will not shrink your tables; space is usually not returned to the filesystem.

Here is my example, which shows how to create a small table with customized autovacuum settings. The table is filled with 100000 rows:

```
CREATE TABLE t_test (id int) WITH (autovacuum_enabled = off);
INSERT INTO t_test
    SELECT * FROM generate_series(1, 100000);
```

The idea is to create a simple table containing 100000 rows. Note that it is possible to turn autovacuum off for specific tables. Usually, this is not a good idea for most applications. However, there is a corner case, where autovacuum_enabled = off makes sense. Just consider a table whose life cycle is very short. It doesn't make sense to clean out tuples if the developer already knows that the entire table will be dropped within seconds. In data warehousing, this can be the case if you use tables as staging areas. VACUUM is turned off in this example to ensure that nothing happens in the background. Everything you see is triggered by me and not by some process.

First of all, consider checking the size of the table by using the following command:

```
test=# SELECT pg_size_pretty(pg_relation_size('t_test'));
pg_size_pretty
----------------
 3544 kB
(1 row)
```

The pg_relation_size command returns the size of a table in bytes.
The pg_size_pretty command will take this number and turn it into something human-readable.

Then, all of the rows in the table will be updated using a simple UPDATE statement, as shown in the following code:

```
test=# UPDATE t_test SET id = id + 1;
UPDATE 100000
```

What happens is highly important to understand PostgreSQL. The database engine has to copy all the rows. Why? First of all, we don't know whether the transaction will be successful, so the data cannot be overwritten. The second important aspect is that a concurrent transaction might still be seeing the old version of the data.

The UPDATE operation will copy rows.

Logically, the size of the table will be larger after the change has been made:

```
test=# SELECT pg_size_pretty(pg_relation_size('t_test'));
 pg_size_pretty
----------------
 7080 kB
(1 row)
```

After UPDATE, people might try to return space to the filesystem:

```
test=# VACUUM t_test;
VACUUM
```

As we stated previously, VACUUM does not return space to the filesystem in most cases. Instead, it will allow space to be reused. The table, therefore, doesn't shrink at all:

```
test=# SELECT pg_size_pretty(pg_relation_size('t_test'));
 pg_size_pretty
----------------
 7080 kB
(1 row)
```

However, the next UPDATE will not make the table grow because it will eat the free space inside the table. Only a second UPDATE would make the table grow again because all the space is gone and so additional storage is needed:

```
test=# UPDATE t_test SET id = id + 1;
UPDATE 100000
test=# SELECT pg_size_pretty(pg_relation_size('t_test'));
 pg_size_pretty
----------------
 7080 kB
(1 row)
```

```
test=# UPDATE t_test SET id = id + 1;
UPDATE 100000
test=# SELECT pg_size_pretty(pg_relation_size('t_test'));
 pg_size_pretty
----------------
 10 MB
(1 row)
```

If I had to decide on a single thing you should remember after reading this book, this is it. Understanding storage is the key to performance and administration in general.

Let's run some more queries:

```
VACUUM t_test;
UPDATE t_test SET id = id + 1;
VACUUM t_test;
```

Again, the size is unchanged. Let's see what's inside the table:

```
test=# SELECT ctid, * FROM t_test ORDER BY ctid DESC;
  ctid       | id
-------------+--------
...
(1327, 46) | 112
(1327, 45) | 111
(1327, 44) | 110
...
(884, 20)  | 99798
(884, 19)  | 99797
...
```

The `ctid` command is the physical position of a row on a disk. By using `ORDER BY ctid DESC`, you will basically read the table backward in physical order. Why should you care? Because there are some very small values and some very big values at the end of the table. The following code shows how the size of the table changes when data is deleted:

```
test=# DELETE FROM t_test
            WHERE id > 99000
                OR id < 1000;
DELETE 1999
test=# VACUUM t_test;
VACUUM
test=# SELECT pg_size_pretty(pg_relation_size('t_test'));
 pg_size_pretty
----------------
 3504 kB
(1 row)
```

Although only 2% of the data has been deleted, the size of the table has gone down by two-thirds. The reason for this is that if VACUUM only finds dead rows after a certain position in the table, it can return space to the filesystem. This is the only case in which you will actually see the table size go down. Of course, normal users have no control over the physical position of data on the disk. Therefore, storage consumption will most likely stay somewhat the same unless all rows are deleted.

 Why are there so many small and big values at the end of the table anyway? After the table is initially populated with 100,000 rows, the last block is not completely full, so the first UPDATE will fill up the last block with changes. This shuffles the end of the table a bit. In this carefully crafted example, this is the reason for the strange layout at the end of the table.

In real-world applications, the impact of this observation cannot be stressed enough. There is no performance tuning without really understanding storage.

Limiting transactions by making use of snapshot too old

VACUUM does a good job and it will reclaim free space as needed. However, when can VACUUM actually clean out rows and turn them into free space? The rule is this: if a row cannot be seen by anybody anymore, it can be reclaimed. In reality, this means that everything that is no longer seen, even by the oldest active transaction, can be considered to be really dead.

This also implies that really long transactions can postpone cleanup for quite some time. The logical consequence is table bloat. Tables will grow beyond proportion, and performance will tend to go downhill. Fortunately, starting with PostgreSQL 9.6, the database has a nice feature that allows the administrator to intelligently limit the duration of a transaction. Oracle administrators will be familiar with the **snapshot too old error.** Since PostgreSQL 9.6, this error message is also available. However, it is more of a feature than an unintended side effect of bad configuration (which it actually is in Oracle).

To limit the lifetime of snapshots, you can make use of a setting in PostgreSQL's `config` file, `postgresql.conf`, which has all of the configuration parameters that are needed for this:

```
old_snapshot_threshold = -1
        # 1min-60d; -1 disables; 0 is immediate
```

If this variable is set, transactions will fail after a certain amount of time. Note that this setting is on an instance level and that it cannot be set inside a session. By limiting the age of a transaction, the risk of insanely long transactions will decrease drastically.

Making use of more VACUUM features

VACUUM has steadily been improved over the years. In this section, you will learn about some of the more recent improvements.

In many cases, VACUUM can skip pages. This is especially true when the visibility map suggests that a block is visible to everyone. VACUUM may also skip a page that is heavily used by some other transaction. DISABLE_PAGE_SKIPPING disables this kind of behavior and ensures that all pages are cleaned during this run.

One more way to improve on VACUUM is to use SKIP_LOCKED: the idea here is to make sure that VACUUM does not harm concurrency. If SKIP_LOCKED is used, VACUUM will automatically skip over relations, which cannot instantly be locked, thus avoiding conflict resolution. This kind of feature can be very useful in the event of heavy concurrency.

One of the important and sometimes overlooked aspects of VACUUM is the need to clean up indexes. After VACUUM has successfully processed a heap, indexes are taken care of. If you want to prevent this from happening you can make use of INDEX_CLEANUP. By default, INDEX_CLEANUP is `true` but depending on your workload you might decide to skip index cleanup in some rare cases. So, what are those rare cases? Why might anybody not want to clean up indexes? The answer is simple: if your database may potentially soon shut down due to transaction wraparound, it makes sense to run VACUUM as quickly as possible. If you've got a choice between downtime and some kind of postponed cleanup, you should opt for VACUUM quickly to keep your database alive.

Summary

In this chapter, you learned about transactions, locking and its logical implications, and the general architecture the PostgreSQL transaction machinery can have for storage, concurrency, and administration. You saw how rows are locked and some of the features that are available in PostgreSQL.

In Chapter 3, *Making Use of Indexes*, you will learn about one of the most important topics in database work: indexing. You will also learn about the PostgreSQL query optimizer, as well as various types of indexes and their behavior.

Questions

1. What is the purpose of a transaction?
2. How long can a transaction in PostgreSQL be?
3. What is transaction isolation?
4. Should we avoid table locks?
5. What do transactions have to do with VACUUM?

Section 2: Advanced Concepts 2

This section expands upon the key topics of PostgreSQL 12.

This section contains the following chapters:

3
Making Use of Indexes

In `Chapter 2`, *Understanding Transactions and Locking*, you learned about concurrency and locking. In this chapter, it is time to attack indexing head on. The importance of this topic cannot be stressed enough—indexing is (and will most likely remain) one of the most important topics in the life of every database engineer.

After 18 years of professional, full-time PostgreSQL consulting and PostgreSQL 24x7 support (`www.cybertec-postgresql.com`), I can say one thing for sure—bad indexing is the main source of bad performance. Of course, it is important to adjust memory parameters and all that. However, it is all in vain if indexes are not used properly. There is simply no replacement for a missing index. To make my point: there is no way to achieve good performance without proper indexing, so always make it a point to check the indexing if performance is bad.

This is the reason behind dedicating an entire chapter to indexing alone. This will give you as many insights as possible.

In this chapter, we will cover the following topics:

- Understanding simple queries and the cost model
- Improving speed using clustered tables
- Understanding additional B-tree features
- Introducing operator classes
- Understanding PostgreSQL index types
- Achieving better answers with fuzzy searching
- Understanding full-text search

By the end of this chapter, you will understand how indexes can be used beneficially in PostgreSQL.

Understanding simple queries and the cost model

In this section, we will get started with indexes. To understand how things work, some test data is needed. The following code snippet shows how data can be created easily:

```
test=# DROP TABLE IF EXISTS t_test;
DROP TABLE
test=# CREATE TABLE t_test (id serial, name text);
CREATE TABLE
test=# INSERT INTO t_test (name) SELECT 'hans'
    FROM generate_series(1, 2000000);
INSERT 0 2000000
test=# INSERT INTO t_test (name) SELECT 'paul'
    FROM generate_series(1, 2000000);
INSERT 0 2000000
```

In the first line, a simple table is created. Two columns are used; the first is an auto-increment column that just keeps creating numbers, and the second is a column that will be filled with static values.

The generate_series function will generate numbers from 1 to 2 million. So, in this example, 2 million static values for hans and 2 million static values for paul are created.

In all, 4 million rows have been added:

```
test=# SELECT name, count(*) FROM t_test GROUP BY 1;
 name | count
------+---------
 hans | 2000000
 paul | 2000000
(2 rows)
```

These 4 million rows have some nice properties, which we will be using throughout this chapter. IDs are ascending, and there are only two distinct names.

Let's run a simple query:

```
test=# \timing
Timing is on.
test=# SELECT * FROM t_test WHERE id = 432332;
   id   | name
--------+------
 432332 | hans
(1 row)

Time: 176.949 ms
```

In this case, the `timing` command will tell `psql` to show the runtime of a query.

 This is not the real execution time on the server, but the time measured by `psql`. In the event of very short queries, network latency can be a substantial part of the total time, so this has to be taken into account.

Making use of EXPLAIN

In this example, reading 4 million rows has taken more than 100 milliseconds. From a performance point of view, this is a total disaster. To figure out what went wrong, PostgreSQL offers the EXPLAIN command, which is defined as shown in the following code:

```
test=# \h EXPLAIN
Command: EXPLAIN
Description: show the execution plan of a statement
Syntax:
EXPLAIN [ ( option [, ...] ) ] statement
EXPLAIN [ ANALYZE ] [ VERBOSE ] statement

where option can be one of:

    ANALYZE [ boolean ]
    VERBOSE [ boolean ]
    COSTS [ boolean ]
    SETTINGS [ boolean ]
    BUFFERS [ boolean ]
    TIMING [ boolean ]
    SUMMARY [ boolean ]
    FORMAT { TEXT | XML | JSON | YAML }

URL: https://www.postgresql.org/docs/12/sql-explain.html
```

When you have a feeling that a query is not performing well, EXPLAIN will help you to reveal the real performance problem.

Here is how it works:

```
test=# EXPLAIN SELECT * FROM t_test WHERE id = 432332;
                             QUERY PLAN
-------------------------------------------------------------------
 Gather  (cost=1000.00..43463.92 rows=1 width=9)
   Workers Planned: 2
   -> Parallel Seq Scan on t_test
          (cost=0.00..42463.82 rows=1 width=9)
            Filter: (id = 432332)
(4 rows)
```

What you see in this listing is an execution plan. In PostgreSQL, an SQL statement will be executed in four stages. The following components are at work:

- The **parser** will check for syntax errors and obvious problems
- The **rewrite** system takes care of rules (views and other things)
- The **optimizer** will figure out how to execute a query in the most efficient way and work out a plan
- The **plan** provided by the optimizer will be used by the executor to finally create the result

The purpose of EXPLAIN is to see what the planner has come up with to run the query efficiently. In my example, PostgreSQL will use a parallel sequential scan. This means that two workers will cooperate and work on the filter condition together. The partial results are then united through a thing called a **gather** node, which was introduced in PostgreSQL 9.6 (it is part of the parallel query infrastructure). If you look at the plan more closely, you will see how many rows PostgreSQL expects at each stage of the plan (in this example, rows = 1; that is, one row will be returned).

 In PostgreSQL 9.6 through 10.0, the number of parallel workers will be determined by the size of the table. The larger the operation is, the more parallel workers PostgreSQL will fire up. For a very small table, parallelism is not used, as it would create too much overhead.

Parallelism is not a must. It is always possible to reduce the number of parallel workers to mimic pre-PostgreSQL 9.6 behavior by setting the following variable to 0:

```
test=# SET max_parallel_workers_per_gather TO 0;
SET
```

Note that this change has no side effect as it is only in your session. Of course, you can also make this change in the `postgresql.conf` file, but I would advise against doing this as you might lose quite a lot of performance that's provided by the parallel queries.

Digging into the PostgreSQL cost model

If only one CPU is used, the execution plan will look like this:

```
test=# EXPLAIN SELECT * FROM t_test WHERE id = 432332;
                         QUERY PLAN
--------------------------------------------------------------
 Seq Scan on t_test (cost=0.00..71622.00 rows=1 width=9)
   Filter: (id = 432332)
(2 rows)
```

PostgreSQL will sequentially read (sequential scan) the entire table and apply the filter. It expects the operation to cost `71622` penalty points. Now, what does this mean? Penalty points (or costs) are mostly an abstract concept. They are needed to compare different ways to execute a query. If a query can be executed by the executor in many different ways, PostgreSQL will decide on the execution plan by promising the lowest cost possible. The question now is, how did PostgreSQL end up with `71622` points?

Here is how it works:

```
test=# SELECT pg_relation_size('t_test') / 8192.0;
      ?column?
--------------------
 21622.000000
(1 row)
```

The `pg_relation_size` function will return the size of the table in bytes. Given this example, you can see that the relation consists of `21622` blocks (8,000 each). According to the cost model, PostgreSQL will add a cost of one for each block it has to read sequentially.

The configuration parameter to influence that is as follows:

```
test=# SHOW seq_page_cost;
 seq_page_cost
---------------
 1
(1 row)
```

However, reading a couple of blocks from a disk is not everything we have to do. It is also necessary to apply the filter and to send these rows through a CPU. Two parameters shown in the block shown here account for these costs:

```
test=# SHOW cpu_tuple_cost;
 cpu_tuple_cost
----------------
 0.01
(1 row)
test=# SHOW cpu_operator_cost;
 cpu_operator_cost
-------------------
 0.0025
(1 row)
```

This leads to the following calculation:

```
test=# SELECT 21622*1 + 4000000*0.01 + 4000000*0.0025;
   ?column?
-------------
 71622.0000
(1 row)
```

As you can see, this is exactly the number that's shown in the plan. Costs will consist of a CPU part and an I/O part, which will all be turned into a single number. The important thing here is that costs have nothing to do with real execution, so it is impossible to translate costs into milliseconds. The number the planner comes up with is really just an estimate.

Of course, there are some more parameters outlined in this brief example. PostgreSQL also has special parameters for index-related operations, as follows:

- random_page_cost = 4: If PostgreSQL uses an index, there is usually a lot of random I/O involved. On traditional spinning disks, random reads are much more important than sequential reads, so PostgreSQL will account for them accordingly. Note that, on SSDs, the difference between random and sequential reads does not exist anymore, so it can make sense to set random_page_cost = 1 in the postgresql.conf file.
- cpu_index_tuple_cost = 0.005: If indexes are used, PostgreSQL will also consider that there is some CPU cost invoiced.

If you are utilizing parallel queries, there are even more cost parameters:

- `parallel_tuple_cost = 0.1`: This defines the cost of transferring one tuple from a parallel worker process to another process. It basically accounts for the overhead of moving rows around inside the infrastructure.
- `parallel_setup_cost = 1000.0`: This adjusts the costs of firing up a worker process. Of course, starting processes to run queries in parallel is not free, and so this parameter tries to model those costs associated with process management.
- `min_parallel_tables_scan_size = 8 MB`: This defines the minimum size of a table that's considered for parallel queries. The larger a table grows, the more CPUs PostgreSQL will use. The size of the table has to triple to allow for one more worker process.
- `min_parallel_index_scan_size = 512kB`: This defines the size of an index, which is necessary to consider a parallel scan.

Deploying simple indexes

Firing up more worker processes to scan ever larger tables is sometimes not the solution. Reading entire tables to find just a single row is usually not a good idea.

Therefore, it makes sense to create indexes:

```
test=# CREATE INDEX idx_id ON t_test (id);
CREATE INDEX
test=# SELECT * FROM t_test WHERE id = 43242;
  id   | name
-------+------
 43242 | hans
(1 row)
Time: 0.259 ms
```

PostgreSQL uses Lehman-Yao's high concurrency B-tree for standard indexes (https://www.csd.uoc.gr/~hy460/pdf/p650-lehman.pdf). Along with some PostgreSQL-specific optimizations, these trees provide end users with excellent performance. The most important thing is that Lehman-Yao allows you to run many operations (reading and writing) on the very same index at the same time, which helps to improve throughput dramatically.

However, indexes are not free:

```
test=# \di+
                        List of relations
  Schema | Name   | Type  | Owner | Table  | Size  | Description
 --------+--------+-------+-------+--------+-------+-------------
  public | idx_id | index | hs    | t_test | 86 MB |
 (1 row)
```

As you can see, our index containing 4 million rows will eat up 86 MB of disk space. In addition to this, the writes to the table will be slower because the index has to be kept in sync all the time.

In other words, if you insert into a table featuring 20 indexes, you also have to keep in mind that we have to write to all those indexes on INSERT, which seriously slows down the writing.

 With the introduction of version 11, PostgreSQL now supports parallel index creation. It is possible to utilize more than one CPU core to build an index, thereby speeding up the process considerably. For now, this is only possible if you want to build a normal B-tree—there is no support for other index types yet. However, this will most likely change in the future. The parameter to control the level of parallelism is max_parallel_maintenance_workers. It tells PostgreSQL how many processes it can use as an upper limit.

Making use of sorted output

B-tree indexes are not only used to find rows; they are also used to feed sorted data to the next stage in the process:

```
test=# EXPLAIN SELECT *
            FROM  t_test
            ORDER BY id DESC
            LIMIT 10;
                          QUERY PLAN
 ---------------------------------------------------------------
  Limit (cost=0.43..0.74 rows=10 width=9)
    -> Index Scan Backward using idx_id on t_test
          (cost=0.43..125505.43 rows=4000000 width=9)
 (2 rows)
```

In this case, the index already returns data in the right sort order, and therefore there is no need to sort the entire set of data. Reading the last `10` rows of the index will be enough to answer this query. Practically, this means that it is possible to find the top *N* rows of a table in a fraction of a millisecond.

However, ORDER BY is not the only operation that requires sorted output. The `min` and `max` functions are also all about sorted output, so an index can be used to speed up these two operations as well. Here is an example:

```
test=# explain SELECT min(id), max(id) FROM t_test;
                        QUERY PLAN
----------------------------------------------------------------
 Result  (cost=0.93..0.94 rows=1 width=8)
   InitPlan 1 (returns $0)
     -> Limit  (cost=0.43..0.46 rows=1 width=4)
           -> Index Only Scan using idx_id on t_test
                   (cost=0.43..135505.43 rows=4000000 width=4)
                     Index Cond: (id IS NOT NULL)
   InitPlan 2 (returns $1)
     -> Limit  (cost=0.43..0.46 rows=1 width=4)
           -> Index Only Scan Backward using idx_id on t_test t_test_1
                   (cost=0.43..135505.43 rows=4000000 width=4)
                     Index Cond: (id IS NOT NULL)
 (9 rows)
```

In PostgreSQL, an index (a B-tree, to be more precise) can be read in normal order or backward. The thing now is that a B-tree can be seen as a sorted list. So, naturally, the lowest value is at the beginning and the highest value is at the end. Therefore, `min` and `max` are perfect candidates for a speedup. What is also worth noting is that, in this case, the main table doesn't need to be referenced at all.

In SQL, many operations rely on sorted input; therefore, understanding these operations is essential because there are serious implications on the indexing side.

Using more than one index at a time

Up until now, you have seen that one index at a time has been used. However, in many real-world situations, this is nowhere near sufficient. There are cases demanding more logic in the database.

PostgreSQL allows the use of multiple indexes in a single query. Of course, this makes sense if many columns are queried at the same time. However, that's not always the case. It can also happen that a single index is used multiple times to process the very same column.

Here is an example:

```
test=# explain SELECT * FROM t_test WHERE id = 30 OR id = 50;

                         QUERY PLAN
--------------------------------------------------------------
 Bitmap Heap Scan on t_test (cost=8.88..16.85 rows=2 width=9)
   Recheck Cond: ((id = 30) OR (id = 50))
   -> BitmapOr (cost=8.88..8.88 rows=2 width=0)
         -> Bitmap Index Scan on idx_idv
               (cost=0.00..4.44 rows=1 width=0)
               Index Cond: (id = 30)
         -> Bitmap Index Scan on idx_id (cost=0.00..4.44 rows=1 width=0)
               Index Cond: (id = 50)
(7 rows)
```

The point here is that the id column is needed twice. First, the query looks for 30, and then for 50. As you can see, PostgreSQL will go for a bitmap scan.

 A bitmap scan is not the same as a bitmap index, which people who have a good Oracle background might know of. They are two totally distinct things and have nothing in common. Bitmap indexes are an index type in Oracle, while bitmap scans are a scan method.

The idea behind a bitmap scan is that PostgreSQL will scan the first index, collecting a list of blocks (pages of a table) containing the data. Then, the next index will be scanned to—again—compile a list of blocks. This works for as many indexes as desired. In the case of OR, these lists will then be unified, leaving us with a long list of blocks containing the data. Using this list, the table will be scanned to retrieve these blocks.

The trouble now is that PostgreSQL has retrieved a lot more data than needed. In our case, the query will look for two rows; however, a couple of blocks might have been returned by the bitmap scan. Therefore, the executor will do a recheck to filter out these rows, that is, the ones that do not satisfy our conditions.

Bitmap scans will also work for AND conditions or a mixture of AND and OR. However, if PostgreSQL sees an AND condition, it does not necessarily force itself into a bitmap scan. Let's suppose that we have a query looking for everybody living in Austria and a person with a certain ID. It really makes no sense to use two indexes here, because, after searching for the ID, there is really not much data left. Scanning both indexes would be much more expensive because there are 8 million people (including me) living in Austria, and reading so many rows to find just one person is pretty pointless from a performance standpoint. The good news is that the PostgreSQL optimizer will make all these decisions for you by comparing the costs of different options and potential indexes, so there is no need to worry.

Using bitmap scans effectively

The question naturally arising now is, when is a bitmap scan most beneficial and when is it chosen by the optimizer? From my point of view, there are really only two use cases:

- To avoid fetching the same block over and over again
- To combine relatively bad conditions

The first case is quite common. Suppose you are looking for everybody who speaks a certain language. For the sake of this example, we can assume that 10% of all people speak the required language. Scanning the index would mean that a block in the table has to be scanned all over again, since many skilled speakers might be stored in the same block. By applying a bitmap scan, it is ensured that a specific block is only used once, which of course leads to better performance.

The second common use case is to use relatively weak criteria together. Let's suppose we are looking for everybody between 20 and 30 years of age owning a yellow shirt. Now, maybe 15% of all people are between 20 and 30 and maybe 15% of all people actually own a yellow shirt. Scanning a table sequentially is expensive, and so PostgreSQL might decide to choose two indexes because the final result might consist of just 1% of the data. Scanning both indexes might be cheaper than reading all of the data.

In PostgreSQL 10.0, parallel bitmap heap scans are supported. Usually, bitmap scans are used by comparatively expensive queries. Added parallelism in this area is, therefore, a huge step forward and definitely beneficial.

Using indexes in an intelligent way

So far, applying an index feels like the Holy Grail, always improving performance magically. However, this is not the case. Indexes can also be pretty pointless in some cases.

Before digging into things more deeply, here is the data structure we have used for this example. Remember that there are only two distinct names and unique IDs:

```
test=# \d t_test
                Table "public.t_test"
 Column |  Type   | Modifiers
--------+---------+------------------------------------------
 id     | integer | not null default nextval('t_test_id_seq'::regclass)
 name   | text    |
Indexes:
    "idx_id" btree (id)
```

At this point, one index has been defined, which covers the `id` column. In the next step, the `name` column will be queried. Before doing this, an index on the name will be created:

```
test=# CREATE INDEX idx_name ON t_test (name);
CREATE INDEX
```

Now, it is time to see if the index is used correctly; consider the following code block:

```
test=# EXPLAIN SELECT * FROM t_test WHERE name = 'hans2';
                    QUERY PLAN
----------------------------------------------------------
Index Scan using idx_name on t_test
    (cost=0.43..4.45 rows=1 width=9)
    Index Cond: (name = 'hans2'::text)
(2 rows)
```

As expected, PostgreSQL will decide on using the index. Most users would expect this. But note that my query says `hans2`. Remember, `hans2` does not exist in the table and the query plan perfectly reflects this. `rows=1` indicates that the planner only expects a very small subset of data being returned by the query.

There is not a single row in the table, but PostgreSQL will never estimate zero rows because it would make subsequent estimations a lot harder, since useful cost calculations of other nodes in the plan would be close to impossible.

Let's see what happens if we look for more data:

```
test=# EXPLAIN SELECT *
        FROM t_test
        WHERE name = 'hans'
            OR name = 'paul';
                    QUERY PLAN
----------------------------------------------------------
  Seq Scan on t_test (cost=0.00..81622.00 rows=3000011 width=9)
    Filter: ((name = 'hans'::text) OR (name = 'paul'::text))
(2 rows)
```

In this case, PostgreSQL will go for a straight sequential scan. Why is that? Why is the system ignoring all indexes? The reason is simple: `hans` and `paul` make up the entire dataset because there are no other values (PostgreSQL knows that by checking the system statistics). Therefore, PostgreSQL figures that the entire table has to be read anyway. There is no reason to read all of the index and the full table if reading the table is sufficient.

In other words, PostgreSQL will not use an index just because there is one. PostgreSQL will use indexes when they make sense. If the number of rows is smaller, PostgreSQL will again consider bitmap scans and normal index scans:

```
test=# EXPLAIN SELECT *
       FROM t_test
       WHERE name = 'hans2'
            OR name = 'paul2';
                        QUERY PLAN
------------------------------------------------------------------
 Bitmap Heap Scan on t_test (cost=8.88..12.89 rows=1 width=9)
    Recheck Cond: ((name = 'hans2'::text) OR (name = 'paul2'::text))
    -> BitmapOr (cost=8.88..8.88 rows=1 width=0)
          -> Bitmap Index Scan on idx_name
             (cost=0.00..4.44 rows=1 width=0)
                Index Cond: (name = 'hans2'::text)
          -> Bitmap Index Scan on idx_name
             (cost=0.00..4.44 rows=1 width=0)
                Index Cond: (name = 'paul2'::text)
```

The most important point to learn here is that execution plans depend on input values.

They are not static and not independent of the data inside the table. This is a very important observation, which has to be kept in mind at all times. In real-world examples, the fact that plans change can often be the reason for unpredictable runtimes.

Improving speed using clustered tables

In this section, you will learn about the power of correlation and the power of clustered tables. What is this about? Imagine that you want to read a whole area of data. This might be a certain time range, some block, IDs, and so on.

The runtime of these queries will vary, depending on the amount of data and the physical arrangement of data on the disk. So, even if you are running queries that return the same number of rows, two systems might not provide the answer within the same time span, as the physical disk layout might make a difference.

Here is an example:

```
test=# EXPLAIN (analyze true, buffers true, timing true)
    SELECT *
    FROM    t_test
    WHERE   id < 10000;
                    QUERY PLAN
-----------------------------------------------------------------
```

```
Index Scan using idx_id on t_test
   (cost=0.43..370.87 rows=10768 width=9)
   (actual time=0.011..2.897 rows=9999 loops=1)
  Index Cond: (id < 10000)
  Buffers: shared hit=85
 Planning time: 0.078 ms
 Execution time: 4.081 ms
(5 rows)
```

As you can see, the data has been loaded in an organized and sequential way. Data has been added ID after ID, and so it can be expected that the data will be on the disk in a sequential order. This holds true if data is loaded into an empty table using an auto-increment column.

You have already seen EXPLAIN in action. In this example, EXPLAIN (analyze true, buffers true, and timing true) has been utilized. The idea is that analyze will not just show the plan but also execute the query and show us what has happened.

EXPLAIN analysis is perfect for comparing planner estimates with what really happened. It is the best way to figure out whether the planner was correct or way off. The buffers true parameter will tell us how many 8,000 blocks were touched by the query. In this example, a total of 85 blocks were touched. A shared hit means that data was coming from the PostgreSQL I/O cache (shared buffers). Altogether, it took PostgreSQL around 4 milliseconds to retrieve the data.

What happens if the data in your table is somewhat random? Will things change?

To create a table containing the same data but in a random order, you can simply use ORDER BY random(). It will make sure that the data is indeed shuffled on disk:

```
test=# CREATE TABLE t_random AS SELECT * FROM t_test ORDER BY random();
SELECT 4000000
```

To ensure a fair comparison, the same column is indexed:

```
test=# CREATE INDEX idx_random ON t_random (id);
CREATE INDEX
```

To function properly, PostgreSQL will need optimizer statistics. These statistics will tell PostgreSQL how much data there is, how values are distributed, and whether the data is correlated on disk. To speed things up even more, I have added a VACUUM call. Please note that VACUUM will be discussed in more depth later in this book:

```
test=# VACUUM ANALYZE t_random;
VACUUM
```

Now, let's run the same query that we ran previously:

```
test=# EXPLAIN (analyze true, buffers true, timing true)
       SELECT * FROM t_random WHERE id < 10000;
                          QUERY PLAN
----------------------------------------------------------------
 Bitmap Heap Scan on t_random
         (cost=203.27..18431.86 rows=10689 width=9)
         (actual time=5.087..13.822 rows=9999 loops=1)
   Recheck Cond: (id < 10000)
   Heap Blocks: exact=8027
   Buffers: shared hit=8057
   -> Bitmap Index Scan on idx_random
         (cost=0.00..200.60 rows=10689 width=0)
         (actual time=3.558..3.558 rows=9999 loops=1)
       Index Cond: (id < 10000)
       Buffers: shared hit=30
 Planning time: 0.075 ms
 Execution time: 14.411 ms
(9 rows)
```

There are a couple of things to observe here. First of all, a staggering total of 8057 blocks were needed, and the runtime has skyrocketed to over 14 milliseconds. The only thing here that somewhat rescued performance was the fact that data was served from memory and not from disk. Just imagine what it would mean if you had to access the disk 8,057 times just to answer this query. It would be a total disaster because the disk wait would certainly slow things down dramatically.

However, there's more to see. You can even see that the plan has changed. PostgreSQL now uses a bitmap scan instead of a normal index scan. This is done to reduce the number of blocks needed in the query to prevent even worse behavior.

How does the planner know how data is stored on the disk? `pg_stats` is a system view containing all the statistics about the content of the columns. The following query reveals the relevant content:

```
test=# SELECT tablename, attname, correlation
       FROM  pg_stats
       WHERE tablename IN ('t_test', 't_random')
       ORDER BY 1, 2;
 tablename | attname | correlation
-----------+---------+-------------
 t_random  | id      | -0.0114944
 t_random  | name    |   0.493675
 t_test    | id      |           1
 t_test    | name    |           1
(4 rows)
```

You can see that PostgreSQL takes care of every single column. The content of the view is created by ANALYZE, defined as shown here, and is vital to performance:

```
test=# \h ANALYZE
Command: ANALYZE
Description: collect statistics about a database
Syntax:
ANALYZE [ ( option [, ...] ) ] [ table_and_columns [, ...] ]
ANALYZE [ VERBOSE ] [ table_and_columns [, ...] ]

where option can be one of:

    VERBOSE
    SKIP_LOCKED

and table_and_columns is:

    table_name [ ( column_name [, ...] ) ]

URL: https://www.postgresql.org/docs/12/sql-analyze.html
```

Usually, ANALYZE is automatically executed in the background using the autovacuum daemon, which will be covered later in this book.

Back to our query. As you can see, both tables have two columns (id and name). In the case of t_test.id, the correlation is 1, which means that the next value somewhat depends on the previous one. In my example, numbers are simply ascending. The same applies to t_test.name. First, we have entries containing hans, and then we have entries containing paul. All identical names are therefore stored together.

In t_random, the situation is quite different; a negative correlation means that data is shuffled. You can also see that the correlation for the name column is around 0.5. In reality, this means that there is usually no straight sequence of identical names in the table, but that names keep switching all the time when the table is read in the physical order.

Why does this lead to so many blocks being hit by the query? The answer is relatively simple. If the data we need is not packed together tightly but spread out over the table evenly, more blocks are needed to extract the same amount of information, which in turn leads to worse performance.

Clustering tables

In PostgreSQL, there is a command called CLUSTER that allows us to rewrite a table in the desired order. It is possible to point to an index and store data in the same order as the index:

```
test=# \h CLUSTER
Command: CLUSTER
Description: cluster a table according to an index
Syntax:
CLUSTER [VERBOSE] table_name [ USING index_name ]
CLUSTER [VERBOSE]

URL: https://www.postgresql.org/docs/12/sql-cluster.html
```

The CLUSTER command has been around for many years and serves its purpose well. However, there are some things to consider before blindly running it on a production system:

- The CLUSTER command will lock the table while it is running. You cannot insert or modify data while CLUSTER is running. This might not be acceptable on a production system.
- Data can only be organized according to one index. You cannot order a table by zip code, name, ID, birthday, and so on, at the same time. This means that CLUSTER will make sense if there are search criteria that are used most of the time.
- Keep in mind that the example outlined in this book is more of a worst-case scenario. In reality, the performance difference between a clustered and a non-clustered table will depend on the workload, the amount of data retrieved, cache hit rates, and a lot more.
- The clustered state of a table will not be maintained as changes are made to a table during normal operations. Correlation will usually deteriorate as time goes by.

Here is an example of how to run the CLUSTER command:

```
test=# CLUSTER t_random USING idx_random;
CLUSTER
```

Depending on the size of the table, the time needed to cluster will vary.

Making use of index-only scans

So far, you have seen when an index is used and when it is not. In addition to this, bitmap scans have been discussed.

However, there is more to indexing. The following two examples will only differ slightly, although the performance difference might be fairly large. Here is the first query:

```
test=# EXPLAIN SELECT * FROM t_test WHERE id = 34234;
                        QUERY PLAN
-----------------------------------------------------------------
  Index Scan using idx_id on t_test
    (cost=0.43..8.45 rows=1 width=9)
    Index Cond: (id = 34234)
```

There is nothing unusual here. PostgreSQL uses an index to find a single row. What happens if only a single column is selected?

```
test=# EXPLAIN SELECT id FROM t_test WHERE id = 34234;
                        QUERY PLAN
-----------------------------------------------------------------
  Index Only Scan using idx_id on t_test
    (cost=0.43..8.45 rows=1 width=4)
    Index Cond: (id = 34234)
(2 rows)
```

As you can see, the plan has changed from an index scan to an index-only scan. In our example, the id column has been indexed, so its content is naturally in the index. There is no need to go to the table in most cases if all the data can already be taken out of the index. Going to the table is (almost) only required if additional fields are queried, which is not the case here. Therefore, the index-only scan will promise significantly better performance than a normal index scan.

Practically, it can even make sense to include an additional column in an index here and there to enjoy the benefit of this feature. In MS SQL, adding additional columns is known as **covering indexes**. Since PostgreSQL 11, we have the same functionality, which uses the INCLUDE keyword in CREATE INDEX.

Understanding additional B-tree features

In PostgreSQL, indexing is a large field and covers many aspects of database work. As I have outlined in this book already, indexing is the key to performance. There is no good performance without proper indexing. Therefore, it is worth inspecting the indexing-related features that we will cover in the following subtopics in detail.

Combined indexes

In my job, as a professional PostgreSQL support vendor, I am often asked about the difference between combined and individual indexes. In this section, I will try to shed some light on this question.

The general rule is that if a single index can answer your question, it is usually the best choice. However, you cannot index all possible combinations of fields people are filtering on. What you can do instead is use the properties of combined indexes to achieve as much gain as possible.

Let's suppose we have a table containing three columns: `postal_code`, `last_name`, and `first_name`. A telephone book would make use of a combined index like this. You will see that data is ordered by location. Within the same location, data will be sorted by last name and first name.

The following table shows which operations are possible, given the three-column index:

Query	Possible	Remarks

`postal_code = 2700`
   `AND last_name = 'Schönig'`
   `AND first_name = 'Hans'`
	Yes	This is the ideal use case for this index.

`postal_code = 2700` `AND last_name = 'Schönig'`	Yes	No restrictions.
`last_name = 'Schönig` `AND postal_code = 2700`	Yes	PostgreSQL will simply swap conditions.
`postal_code = 2700`	Yes	This is just like an index on `postal_code`; the combined index just needs more space on the disk.
`first_name = 'Hans'`	Yes, but a different use case	PostgreSQL cannot use the sorted property of the index anymore. However, in some rare cases (usually very broad tables, including countless columns), PostgreSQL will scan the entire index if it is as cheap as reading the very broad table.

If columns are indexed separately, you will most likely end up seeing bitmap scans. Of course, a single, hand-tailored index is better.

Adding functional indexes

So far, you have seen how to index the content of a column as it is. However, this might not always be what you really want. Therefore, PostgreSQL allows . / ' as the creation of functional indexes. The basic idea is very simple: instead of indexing a value, the output of a function is stored in the index.

The following example shows how the cosine of the `id` column can be indexed:

```
test=# CREATE INDEX idx_cos ON t_random (cos(id));
CREATE INDEX
test=# ANALYZE;
ANALYZE
```

All you have to do is put the function on the list of columns, and you are done. Of course, this won't work for all kinds of functions. Functions can only be used if their output is immutable, as shown in the following example:

```
test=# SELECT age('2010-01-01 10:00:00'::timestamptz);
          age
------------------------
 6 years 9 mons 14:00:00
(1 row)
```

Functions such as `age` are not really suitable for indexing because their output is not constant. Time goes on and, consequently, the output of `age` will change too. PostgreSQL will explicitly prohibit functions that have the potential to change their result given the same input. The `cos` function is fine in this respect because the cosine of a value will still be the same 1,000 years from now.

To test the index, I have written a simple query to show what will happen:

```
test=# EXPLAIN SELECT * FROM t_random WHERE cos(id) = 10;
                          QUERY PLAN
---------------------------------------------------------------------
 Index Scan using idx_cos on t_random (cost=0.43..8.45 rows=1 width=9)
   Index Cond: (cos((id)::double precision) = '10'::double precision)
(2 rows)
```

As expected, the functional index will be used just like any other index.

Reducing space consumption

Indexing is nice, and its main purpose is to speed up things as much as possible. As with all good stuff, indexing comes with a price tag: space consumption. To work its magic, an index has to store values in an organized fashion. If your table contains 10 million integer values, the index belonging to the table will logically contain these 10 million integer values, plus additional overhead.

A B-tree will contain a pointer to each row in the table, and so it is certainly not free of charge. To figure out how much space an index will need, you can ask `psql` using the `\di+` command:

```
test=# \di+
                        List of relations
  Schema | Name       | Type  | Owner | Table     | Size
 --------+------------+-------+-------+-----------+-------
  public | idx_cos    | index | hs    | t_random  | 86 MB
  public | idx_id     | index | hs    | t_test    | 86 MB
  public | idx_name   | index | hs    | t_test    | 86 MB
  public | idx_random | index | hs    | t_random  | 86 MB
 (4 rows)
```

In my database, a staggering amount of 344 MB has been burned to store these indexes. Now, compare this to the amount of storage that's burned by the underlying tables:

```
test=# \d+
                        List of relations
  Schema | Name          | Type     | Owner | Size
 --------+---------------+----------+-------+------------
  public | t_random      | table    | hs    | 169 MB
  public | t_test        | table    | hs    | 169 MB
  public | t_test_id_seq | sequence | hs    | 8192 bytes
 (3 rows)
```

The size of both tables combined is just 338 MB. In other words, our indexing needs more space than the actual data. In the real world, this is common and actually pretty likely. Recently, I visited a Cybertec customer in Germany and I saw a database in which 64% of the database size was made up of indexes that were never used (not a single time over a period of months). So, over-indexing can be an issue, just like under-indexing. Remember, these indexes don't just consume space. Every INSERT or UPDATE must maintain the values in the indexes as well. In extreme cases, such as our example, this vastly decreases write throughput.

If there are just a handful of different values in the table, partial indexes are a solution:

```
test=# DROP INDEX idx_name;
DROP INDEX
test=# CREATE INDEX idx_name ON t_test (name)
        WHERE name NOT IN ('hans', 'paul');
CREATE INDEX
```

In the following case, the majority has been excluded from the index and a small, efficient index can be enjoyed:

```
test=# \di+ idx_name
                      List of relations
 Schema |   Name    | Type  | Owner | Table  | Size
--------+-----------+-------+-------+--------+-----------
 public | idx_name  | index | hs    | t_test | 8192 bytes
(1 row)
```

Note that it only makes sense to exclude very frequent values that make up a large part of the table (at least 25% or so). Ideal candidates for partial indexes are gender (we assume that most people are male or female), nationality (assuming that most people in your country have the same nationality), and so on. Of course, applying this kind of trickery requires some deep knowledge of your data, but it certainly pays off.

Adding data while indexing

Creating an index is easy. However, keep in mind that you cannot modify a table while an index is being built. The CREATE INDEX command will lock up the table using a SHARE lock to ensure that no changes happen. While this is clearly no problem for small tables, it will cause issues on large ones on production systems. Indexing 1 TB of data or so will take some time, and therefore blocking a table for too long can become an issue.

The solution to this problem is the CREATE INDEX CONCURRENTLY command. Building the index will take a lot longer (usually, at least twice as long), but you can use the table normally during index creation.

Here's how it works:

```
test=# CREATE INDEX CONCURRENTLY idx_name2 ON t_test (name);
CREATE INDEX
```

Note that PostgreSQL doesn't guarantee success if you are using the CREATE INDEX CONCURRENTLY command. An index can end up being marked as invalid if the operations running on your system somehow conflict with the index creation. If you want to figure out if your indexes are invalid, use \d on the relation.

Introducing operator classes

So far, the goal has been to figure out what to index and whether to blindly apply an index on this column or on a group of columns. There is one assumption, however, that we have silently accepted to make this work. Up until now, we have worked on the assumption that the order in which the data has to be sorted is a somewhat fixed constant. In reality, this assumption might not hold true. Sure, numbers will always be in the same order, but other kinds of data will most likely not have a predefined, fixed sort order.

To prove my point, I have compiled a real-world example. Take a look at the following two records:

```
1118 09 08 78
2345 01 05 77
```

My question now is, are these two rows ordered properly? They might be, because one comes before another. However, this is wrong because these two rows do have some hidden semantics. What you see here are two Austrian social security numbers. 09 08 78 actually means August 9, 1978, and 01 05 77 actually means May 1, 1977. The first four numbers consist of a checksum and some sort of auto-incremented three-digit number. So, in reality, 1977 comes before 1978, and we might consider swapping those two lines to achieve the desired sort order.

The problem is that PostgreSQL has no idea what these two rows actually mean. If a column is marked as text, PostgreSQL will apply the standard rules to sort the text. If the column is marked as a number, PostgreSQL will apply the standard rules to sort numbers. Under no circumstances will it ever use something as odd as I've described. If you think that the facts I outlined previously are the only things to consider when processing those numbers, you are wrong. How many months does a year have? 12? Far from true. In the Austrian social security system, these numbers can hold up to 14 months. Why? Remember . . . three digits are simply an auto-increment value. The trouble is that if an immigrant or a refugee has no valid paperwork and if their birthday is not known, they will be assigned an artificial birthday in the 13th month.

During the Balkan wars in 1990, Austria offered asylum to over 115,000 refugees. Naturally, this three-digit number was not enough, and a 14th month was added. Now, which standard data type can handle this kind of COBOL-leftover from the early 1970s (which was when the layout of the social security number was introduced)? The answer is none.

To handle special-purpose fields in a sane way, PostgreSQL offers operator classes:

```
test=# \h CREATE OPERATOR CLASS
Command: CREATE OPERATOR CLASS
Description: define a new operator class
Syntax:
CREATE OPERATOR CLASS name [ DEFAULT ] FOR TYPE data_type
  USING index_method [ FAMILY family_name ] AS
  { OPERATOR strategy_number operator_name [ ( op_type, op_type ) ]
    [ FOR SEARCH | FOR ORDER BY sort_family_name ]
  | FUNCTION support_number [ ( op_type [ , op_type ] ) ]
    function_name ( argument_type [, ...] )
  | STORAGE storage_type
  } [, ... ]

URL: https://www.postgresql.org/docs/12/sql-createopclass.html
```

An operator class will tell an index how to behave. Let's take a look at a standard binary tree. It can perform five operations:

Strategy	Operator	Description
1	<	Less than
2	<=	Less than or equal to
3	=	Equal to
4	>=	Greater than or equal to
5	>	Greater than

The standard operator classes support the standard data types and standard operators we have used throughout this book. If you want to handle social security numbers, it is necessary to come up with your own operators that are capable of providing you with the logic you need. Those custom operators can then be used to form an operator class, which is nothing more than a strategy that's passed to the index to configure how it should behave.

Creating an operator class for a B-tree

To give you a practical example of what an operator class looks like, I have put together some code to handle social security numbers. To keep it simple, I have paid no attention to details such as checksum.

Creating new operators

The first thing we must do is come up with the desired operators. Note that five operators are needed. There is one operator for each strategy. A strategy of an index is really like a plugin that allows you to put in your own code.

Before getting started, I have compiled some test data:

```
CREATE TABLE t_sva (sva text);

INSERT INTO t_sva VALUES ('1118090878');
INSERT INTO t_sva VALUES ('2345010477');
```

Now that the test data is there, it is time to create an operator. For this purpose, PostgreSQL offers the CREATE OPERATOR command:

```
test=# \h CREATE OPERATOR
Command: CREATE OPERATOR
Description: define a new operator
Syntax:
CREATE OPERATOR name (
    PROCEDURE = function_name
    [, LEFTARG = left_type ] [, RIGHTARG = right_type ]
    [, COMMUTATOR = com_op ] [, NEGATOR = neg_op ]
    [, RESTRICT = res_proc ] [, JOIN = join_proc ]
    [, HASHES ] [, MERGES ]
)

URL: https://www.postgresql.org/docs/12/sql-createoperator.html
```

Basically, the concept is as follows: operator calls a function, which gets one or two parameters; one for the left argument and one for the right argument of operator.

As you can see, an operator is nothing more than a function call. So, consequently, it is necessary to implement the logic needed in those functions that are hidden by the operators. In order to fix the sort order, I have written a function called `normalize_si`:

```
CREATE OR REPLACE FUNCTION normalize_si(text) RETURNS text AS $$
    BEGIN
    RETURN substring($1, 9, 2) ||
            substring($1, 7, 2) ||
            substring($1, 5, 2) ||
            substring($1, 1, 4);
    END; $$
LANGUAGE 'plpgsql' IMMUTABLE;
```

Calling this function will return the following result:

```
test=# SELECT normalize_si('1118090878');
 normalize_si
--------------
 7808091118
(1 row)
```

As you can see, all we did is swap some digits. It is now possible to just use the normal string sort order. In the next step, this function can already be used to compare social security numbers directly.

The first function that's needed is the `less than` function, which is needed by the first strategy:

```
CREATE OR REPLACE FUNCTION si_lt(text, text) RETURNS boolean AS $$
    BEGIN
            RETURN normalize_si($1) < normalize_si($2);
        END;
$$ LANGUAGE 'plpgsql' IMMUTABLE;
```

There are two important things to note here:

- The function must not be written in SQL. It only works in a procedural or compiled language. The reason for this is that SQL functions can be inlined under some circumstances, and this would cripple the entire endeavor.
- The second issue is that you should stick to the naming convention used in this chapter—it is widely accepted by the community. `Less than` functions should be called `_lt`, less than or equal to functions should be called `_le`, and so on.

Given this knowledge, the next set of functions that are needed by our future operators can be defined:

```
-- lower equals
CREATE OR REPLACE FUNCTION si_le(text, text)
  RETURNS boolean AS
$$
  BEGIN
    RETURN normalize_si($1) <= normalize_si($2);
  END;
$$
LANGUAGE 'plpgsql' IMMUTABLE;

-- greater equal
CREATE OR REPLACE FUNCTION si_ge(text, text)
  RETURNS boolean AS
$$
BEGIN
  RETURN normalize_si($1) >= normalize_si($2);
END;
$$
LANGUAGE 'plpgsql' IMMUTABLE;

-- greater
CREATE OR REPLACE FUNCTION si_gt(text, text)
  RETURNS boolean AS
$$
BEGIN
  RETURN normalize_si($1) > normalize_si($2);
END;
$$
LANGUAGE 'plpgsql' IMMUTABLE;
```

So far, four functions have been defined. A fifth function for the `equals` operator is not necessary. We can simply take the existing operator because `equals` does not depend on sort order anyway.

Now that all the functions are in place, it is time to define these operators:

```
-- define operators
CREATE OPERATOR <# ( PROCEDURE=si_lt,
                     LEFTARG=text,
                     RIGHTARG=text);
```

The design of the operator is actually very simple. The operator needs a name (in my case, <#), a procedure, which is supposed to be called, and the data type of the left and the right argument. When the operator is called, the left argument will be the first parameter of si_lt, and the right argument will be the second argument.

The remaining three operators follow the same principle:

```
CREATE OPERATOR <=# ( PROCEDURE=si_le,
                  LEFTARG=text,
                  RIGHTARG=text);

CREATE OPERATOR >=# ( PROCEDURE=si_ge,
                  LEFTARG=text,
                  RIGHTARG=text);

CREATE OPERATOR ># ( PROCEDURE=si_gt,
                  LEFTARG=text,
                  RIGHTARG=text);
```

Depending on the type of index you are using, a couple of support functions are needed. In the case of standard B-trees, there is only one support function needed, which is used to speed things up internally:

```
CREATE OR REPLACE FUNCTION si_same(text, text) RETURNS int AS $$
     BEGIN
               IF normalize_si($1) < normalize_si($2)
               THEN
                       RETURN -1;
               ELSIF normalize_si($1) > normalize_si($2)
               THEN
                       RETURN +1;
               ELSE
                       RETURN 0;
               END IF;
     END;
$$ LANGUAGE 'plpgsql' IMMUTABLE;
```

The si_same function will either return -1 if the first parameter is smaller, 0 if both parameters are equal, and 1 if the first parameter is greater. Internally, the _same function is the workhorse, so you should make sure that your code is optimized.

Creating operator classes

Finally, all the components are in place, and it is possible to create the operator class that's needed by the index:

```
CREATE OPERATOR CLASS sva_special_ops
FOR TYPE text USING btree
AS
    OPERATOR 1 <# ,
    OPERATOR 2 <=# ,
    OPERATOR 3 = ,
    OPERATOR 4 >=# ,
    OPERATOR 5 ># ,

    FUNCTION 1 si_same(text, text);
```

The CREATE OPERATOR CLASS command connects strategies and operators to OPERATOR 1. <# means that strategy 1 will use the <# operator. Finally, the the _same function is connected with the operator class.

Note that the operator class has a name, and that it has been explicitly defined to work with B-trees. The operator class can already be used during index creation:

```
CREATE INDEX idx_special ON t_sva (sva sva_special_ops);
```

Creating an index works in a slightly different way than before: sva sva_special_ops means that the sva column is indexed using the sva_special_ops operator class. If sva_special_ops is not explicitly used, then PostgreSQL will not go for our special sort order, and will instead decide on the default operator class.

Testing custom operator classes

In our example, the test data consists of just two rows. Therefore, PostgreSQL will never use an index because the table is just too small to justify the overhead of even opening the index. To be able to still test without having to load too much data, you can advise the optimizer to make sequential scans more expensive.

Making operations more expensive can be done in your session using the following instruction:

```
SET enable_seqscan TO off;
```

The index works as expected:

```
test=# explain SELECT * FROM t_sva WHERE sva = '0000112273';
                           QUERY PLAN
-----------------------------------------------------------------
 Index Only Scan using idx_special on t_sva
   (cost=0.13..8.14 rows=1 width=32)
   Index Cond: (sva = '0000112273'::text)
(2 rows)

test=# SELECT * FROM t_sva;
    sva
------------
 2345010477
 1118090878
(2 rows)
```

Understanding PostgreSQL index types

So far, only binary trees have been discussed. However, in many cases, B-trees are just not enough. Why is that? As we've already discussed in this chapter, B-trees are basically based on sorting. The <, <=, =, >=, and > operators can be handled using B-trees. The trouble is, not every data type can be sorted in a useful way. Just imagine a polygon. How would you sort these objects in a useful way? Sure, you can sort by the area covered, its length, and so on, but doing this won't allow you to actually find them using a geometric search.

The solution to this problem is to provide more than just one index type. Each index will serve a special purpose and do exactly what is needed. The following six index types are available (as of PostgreSQL 10.0):

```
test=# SELECT * FROM pg_am;
 amname  |  amhandler   | amtype
---------+--------------+--------
 btree   | bthandler    | i
 hash    | hashhandler  | i
 GiST    | gisthandler  | i
 gin     | ginhandler   | i
 spgist  | spghandler   | i
 brin    | brinhandler  | i
(6 rows)
```

B-trees have already been discussed in great detail, but what are those other index types useful for? The following sections will outline the purpose of each index type that's available in PostgreSQL.

Note that there are some extensions out there that can be used on top of what you can see here. Additional index types that are available on the web are rum, vodka, and, in the future, cognac.

Hash indexes

Hash indexes have been around for many years. The idea is to hash the input value and store it for later lookups. Having hash indexes actually makes sense. However, before PostgreSQL 10.0, it was not advisable to use hash indexes because PostgreSQL had no WAL support for them. In PostgreSQL 10.0, this has changed. Hash indexes are now fully logged and are therefore ready for replication and considered to be 100% crash-safe.

Hash indexes are generally a bit larger than B-tree indexes. Suppose you want to index 4 million integer values. A B-tree will need around 90 MB of storage to do this. A hash index will need around 125 MB on disk. The assumption that's made by many people is that a hash is super small on disk and therefore, in many cases, the assumption can be wrong as well.

GiST indexes

Generalized Search Tree (GiST) indexes are highly important index types because they are used for a variety of different things. GiST indexes can be used to implement R-tree behavior, and it is even possible for them to act as B-trees. However, abusing GiST for B-tree indexes is not recommended.

Typical use cases for GiSTs are as follows:

- Range types
- Geometric indexes (for example, ones that are used by the highly popular PostGIS extension)
- Fuzzy searching

Understanding how GiST works

To many people, GiST is still a black box. Therefore, I have decided to add a section to this chapter outlining how GiST works internally.

Consider the following diagram:

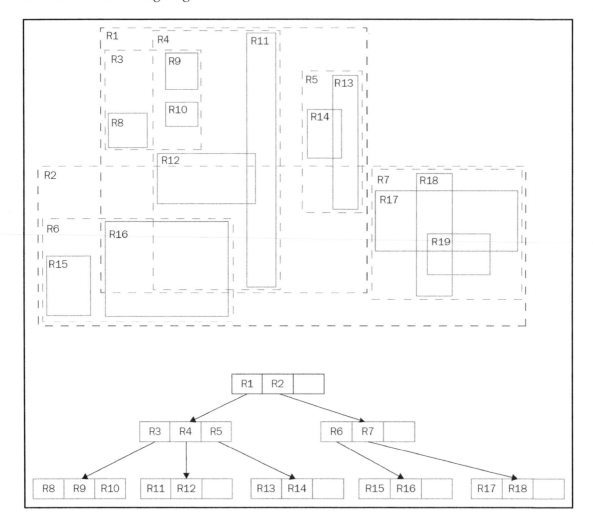

Take a look at the tree. You will see that **R1** and **R2** are on top. **R1** and **R2** are the bounding boxes that contain everything else. **R3**, **R4**, and **R5** are contained by **R1**. **R8**, **R9**, and **R10** are contained by **R3**, and so on. A GiST index is therefore hierarchically organized. What you can see in the preceding diagram is that some operations that aren't available in B-trees are supported. Some of those operations are overlaps, left of, right of, and so on. The layout of a GiST tree is ideal for geometric indexing.

Extending GiST

Of course, it is also possible to come up with your own operator classes. The following strategies are supported:

Operation	Strategy number
Strictly left of	1
Does not extend to right of	2
Overlaps	3
Does not extend to left of	4
Strictly right of	5
Same	6
Contains	7
Contained by	8
Does not extend above	9
Strictly below	10
Strictly above	11
Does not extend below	12

If you want to write operator classes for GiST, a couple of support functions have to be provided. In the case of a B-tree, there is only one function—GiST indexes provide a lot more:

Function	Description	Support function number
consistent	This determines whether a key satisfies the query qualifier. Internally, strategies are looked up and checked.	1
union	Calculates the union of a set of keys. In the case of numeric values, the upper and lower values or a range are computed. It is especially important to geometries.	2

compress	Computes a compressed representation of a key or value.	3
decompress	This is the counterpart of the compress function.	4
penalty	During insertion, the cost of inserting into the tree will be calculated. The cost determines where the new entry will go inside the tree. Therefore, a good penalty function is key to good overall performance from the index.	5
picksplit	Determines where to move entries in the case of a page split. Some entries have to stay on the old page, while others will go to the new page being created. Having a good picksplit function is essential to good index performance.	6
equal	The equal function is similar to the same function you have already seen in B-trees.	7
distance	Calculates the distance (a number) between a key and the query value. The distance function is optional and is needed if KNN search is supported.	8
fetch	Determines the original representation of a compressed key. This function is needed to handle index-only scans, as supported by the recent version of PostgreSQL.	9

Implementing operator classes for GiST indexes is usually done in C. If you are interested in a good example, I advise you to check out the btree_GiST module in the contrib directory. It shows how to index standard data types using GiST and is a good source of information, as well as inspiration.

GIN indexes

Generalized inverted (GIN) indexes are a good way to index text. Suppose you want to index 1 million text documents. A certain word may occur millions of times. In a normal B-tree, this would mean that the key is stored millions of times. This is not the case in a GIN. Each key (or word) is stored once and assigned to a document list. Keys are organized in a standard B-tree. Each entry will have a document list pointing to all the entries in the table that have the same key. A GIN index is very small and compact. However, it lacks an important feature that's found in B-trees—sorted data. In a GIN, the list of item pointers associated with a certain key is sorted by the position of the row in the table, and not by some arbitrary criteria.

Extending GIN

Just like any other index, GIN can be extended. The following strategies are available:

Operation	Strategy number
Overlap	1
Contains	2
Is contained by	3
Equal	4

On top of this, the following support functions are available:

Function	Description	Support function number
compare	This function is similar to the same function you have seen in B-trees. If two keys are compared, it returns −1 (lower), 0 (equal), or 1 (higher).	1
extractValue	Extracts keys from a value to be indexed. A value can have many keys. For example, a text value might consist of more than one word.	2
extractQuery	Extracts keys from a query condition.	3
consistent	Checks whether a value matches a query condition.	4
comparePartial	Compares a partial key from a query and a key from the index. Returns −1, 0, or 1 (similar to the same function supported by B-trees).	5
triConsistent	Determines whether a value matches a query condition (ternary variant). It is optional if the consistent function is present.	6

If you are looking for a good example of how to extend GIN, consider looking at the btree_gin module in the PostgreSQL contrib directory. It is a valuable source of information and a good way for you to start your own implementation.

If you are interested in full-text search, more information will be provided later on in this chapter.

SP-GiST indexes

Space partitioned GiST (SP-GiST) is mainly designed for in-memory use. The reason for this is that an SP-GiST stored on disk needs a fairly high number of disk hits to function. Disk hits are way more expensive than just following a couple of pointers in RAM.

The beauty is that SP-GiST can be used to implement various types of trees, such as quad-trees, k-d trees, and radix trees (tries).

The following strategies are provided:

Operation	Strategy number
Strictly left of	1
Strictly right of	5
Same	6
Contained by	8
Strictly below	10
Strictly above	11

To write your own operator classes for `SP-GiST`, a couple of functions have to be provided:

Function	Description	Support function number
config	Provides information about the `operator` class in use	1
choose	Figures out how to insert a new value into an inner tuple	2
picksplit	Figures out how to partition/split a set of values	3
inner_consistent	Determines which subpartitions need to be searched for a query	4
leaf_consistent	Determines whether the key satisfies the query qualifier	5

BRIN indexes

Block range indexes (BRINs) are of great practical use. All of the indexes we've discussed up until now need quite a lot of disk space. Although a lot of work has gone into shrinking GIN indexes and the like, they still need quite a lot of disk space because an index pointer is needed for each entry. So, if there are 10 million entries, there will be 10 million index pointers. Space is the main concern that's addressed by BRIN indexes. A BRIN does not keep an index entry for each tuple, but will store the minimum and the maximum value of 128 (default) blocks of data (1 MB). The index is therefore very small but lossy. Scanning the index will return more data than we asked for. PostgreSQL has to filter out these additional rows in a later step.

The following example demonstrates how small a BRIN index really is:

```
test=# CREATE INDEX idx_brin ON t_test USING brin(id);
CREATE INDEX
test=# \di+ idx_brin
                        List of relations
 Schema | Name      | Type  | Owner | Table  | Size
--------+-----------+-------+-------+--------+-------
 public | idx_brin  | index | hs    | t_test | 48 KB
(1 row)
```

In my example, the BRIN index is 2,000 times smaller than a standard B-tree. The question naturally arising now is, why don't we always use BRIN indexes? To answer this kind of question, it is important to reflect on the layout of BRIN; the minimum and maximum values for 1 MB are stored. If the data is sorted (high correlation), BRIN is pretty efficient because we can fetch 1 MB of data and scan it, and we are done. However, what if the data is shuffled? In this case, BRIN won't be able to exclude chunks of data anymore because it is very likely that something close to the overall high and the overall low is within 1 MB of data. Therefore, BRIN is mostly made for highly correlated data. In reality, correlated data is quite likely in data warehousing applications. Often, data is loaded every day and therefore dates can be highly correlated.

Extending BRIN indexes

BRIN supports the same strategies as a B-tree and therefore needs the same set of operators. The code can be reused nicely:

Operation	Strategy number
Less than	1
Less than or equal	2
Equal	3
Greater than or equal	4
Greater than	5

The support functions required by BRIN are as follows:

Function	Description	Support function number
opcInfo	Provides internal information about the indexed columns	1
add_value	Adds an entry to an existing summary tuple	2
consistent	Checks whether a value matches a condition	3
union	Calculates the union of two summary entries (minimum/maximum values)	4

Adding additional indexes

Since PostgreSQL 9.6, there has been an easy way to deploy entirely new index types as extensions. This is pretty cool because if those index types provided by PostgreSQL are not enough, it is possible to add additional ones that serve your purpose. The instruction to do this is CREATE ACCESS METHOD:

```
test=# \h CREATE ACCESS METHOD

Command: CREATE ACCESS METHOD
Description: define a new access method
Syntax:
CREATE ACCESS METHOD name
    TYPE access_method_type
    HANDLER handler_function

URL: https://www.postgresql.org/docs/12/sql-create-access-method.html
```

Don't worry too much about this command—if you ever deploy your own index type, it will come as a ready-to-use extension.

One of these extensions implements `bloom` filters. `bloom` filters are probabilistic data structures. They sometimes return too many rows, but never too few. Therefore, a `bloom` filter is a good way to pre-filter data.

How does it work? A `bloom` filter is defined on a couple of columns. A bitmask is calculated based on the input values, which is then compared to your query. The upside of a `bloom` filter is that you can index as many columns as you want. The downside is that the entire `bloom` filter has to be read. Of course, the `bloom` filter is smaller than the underlying data and so it is, in many cases, very beneficial.

To use the `bloom` filters, just activate the extension, which is a part of the PostgreSQL `contrib` package:

```
test=# CREATE EXTENSION bloom;
CREATE EXTENSION
```

As we stated previously, the idea behind a `bloom` filter is that it allows you to index as many columns as you want. In many real-world applications, the challenge is to index many columns without knowing which combinations the user will actually need at runtime. In the case of a large table, it is totally impossible to create standard B-tree indexes on, say, 80 fields or more. A `bloom` filter might be an alternative in this case:

```
test=# CREATE TABLE t_bloom (x1 int, x2 int, x3 int, x4 int,
                             x5 int, x6 int, x7 int);
CREATE TABLE
```

Creating the index is easy:

```
test=# CREATE INDEX idx_bloom ON t_bloom USING bloom(x1, x2, x3, x4,
                                                     x5, x6, x7);
CREATE INDEX
```

If sequential scans are turned off, the index can be seen in action:

```
test=# SET enable_seqscan TO off;
SET
test=# explain SELECT * FROM t_bloom WHERE x5 = 9 AND x3 = 7;
                            QUERY PLAN
------------------------------------------------------------------------
 Bitmap Heap Scan on t_bloom (cost=18.50..22.52 rows=1 width=28)
   Recheck Cond: ((x3 = 7) AND (x5 = 9))
   -> Bitmap Index Scan on idx_bloom (cost=0.00..18.50 rows=1 width=0)
         Index Cond: ((x3 = 7) AND (x5 = 9))
```

Note that I have queried a combination of random columns; they are not related to the actual order in the index. The `bloom` filter will still be beneficial.

Achieving better answers with fuzzy searching

Performing precise searching is not the only thing expected by users these days. Modern websites have educated users in a way that they always expect a result, regardless of the user input. If you search on Google, there will always be an answer, even if the user input is wrong, full of typos, or simply pointless. People expect good results, regardless of the input data.

Taking advantage of pg_trgm

To do fuzzy searching with PostgreSQL, you can add the `pg_trgm` extension. To activate this extension, just run the following command:

```
test=# CREATE EXTENSION pg_trgm;
CREATE EXTENSION
```

The `pg_trgm` extension is pretty powerful, and to show you what it is capable of, I have compiled some sample data consisting of 2,354 names of villages and cities here in Austria, Europe.

Our sample data can be stored in a simple table:

```
test=# CREATE TABLE t_location (name text);
CREATE TABLE
```

My company website has all the data available, and PostgreSQL allows you to load the data directly:

```
test=# COPY t_location FROM PROGRAM
        'curl https://www.cybertec-postgresql.com/secret/orte.txt';
COPY 2354
```

`curl` (a command-line tool for fetching data) has to be installed. If you don't have this tool, download the file normally and import it from your local filesystem.

Once the data has been loaded, it is possible to check out the contents of the table:

```
test=# SELECT * FROM t_location LIMIT 4;
               name
-----------------------------------
 Eisenstadt
 Rust
 Breitenbrunn am Neusiedler See
 Donnerskirchen
(4 rows)
```

If German is not your mother tongue, it will be impossible to spell the names of those locations without severe mistakes.

`pg_trgm` provides us with a distance operator that computes the distance between two strings:

```
test=# SELECT 'abcde' <-> 'abdeacb';
 ?column?
----------
 0.833333
(1 row)
```

The distance is a number between 0 and 1. The lower the number, the more similar the two strings are.

How does this work? Trigrams take a string and dissect it into sequences of three characters each:

```
test=# SELECT show_trgm('abcdef');
              show_trgm
-------------------------------------
 {" a"," ab",abc,bcd,cde,def,"ef "}
(1 row)
```

These sequences will then be used to come up with the distance you have just seen. Of course, the `distance` operator can be used inside a query to find the closest match:

```
test=# SELECT *
FROM t_location
ORDER BY name <-> 'Kramertneusiedel'
LIMIT 3;
```

```
      name
------------------
  Gramatneusiedl
  Klein-Neusiedl
  Potzneusiedl
(3 rows)
```

Gramatneusiedl is pretty close to Kramertneusiedel. It sounds similar, and using a K instead of a G is a pretty common mistake. On Google, you will sometimes see **Did you mean**. It is quite likely that Google is using n-grams here to do that.

In PostgreSQL, it is possible to use GiST to index on text using trigrams:

```
test=# CREATE INDEX idx_trgm ON t_location
       USING GiST(name GiST_trgm_ops);
CREATE INDEX
```

pg_trgm provides us with the GiST_trgm_ops operator class, which is designed to do similarity searches. The following code shows that the index is used as expected:

```
test=# explain SELECT *
  FROM t_location
  ORDER BY name <-> 'Kramertneusiedel'
  LIMIT 5;
                           QUERY PLAN
---------------------------------------------------------------
  Limit  (cost=0.14..0.58 rows=5 width=17)
    -> Index Scan using idx_trgm on t_location
          (cost=0.14..207.22 rows=2354 width=17)
          Order By: (name <-> 'Kramertneusiedel'::text)
(3 rows)
```

Speeding up LIKE queries

LIKE queries definitely cause some of the worst performance problems faced by people around the globe these days. In most database systems, LIKE is pretty slow and requires a sequential scan. In addition to this, end users quickly figure out that a fuzzy search will, in many cases, return better results than precise queries. A single type of LIKE query on a large table can, therefore, often cripple the performance of an entire database server if it is called often enough.

Fortunately, PostgreSQL offers a solution to this problem, and the solution happens to be installed already:

```
test=# explain SELECT * FROM t_location WHERE name LIKE '%neusi%';
                               QUERY PLAN
---------------------------------------------------------------------
 Bitmap Heap Scan on t_location
   (cost=4.33..19.05 rows=24 width=13)
   Recheck Cond: (name ~~ '%neusi%'::text)
   -> Bitmap Index Scan on idx_trgm (cost=0.00..4.32 rows=24 width=0)
         Index Cond: (name ~~ '%neusi%'::text)
(4 rows)
```

The trigram index that we deployed in the previous section is also suitable for speeding up LIKE. Note that the % symbols can be used at any point in the search string. This is a major advantage over standard B-trees, which just happen to speed up wildcards at the end of the query.

Handling regular expressions

However, this is still not everything. Trigram indexes are even capable of speeding up simple regular expressions. The following example shows how this can be done:

```
test=# SELECT * FROM t_location WHERE name ~ '[A-C].*neu.*';
      name
---------------
 Bruckneudorf
(1 row)
test=# explain SELECT * FROM t_location WHERE name ~ '[A-C].*neu.*';
                             QUERY PLAN
---------------------------------------------------------------------
 Index Scan using idx_trgm on t_location (cost=0.14..8.16
   rows=1 width=13)
   Index Cond: (name ~ '[A-C].*neu.*'::text)
(2 rows)
```

PostgreSQL will inspect the regular expression and use the index to answer the question.

Internally, PostgreSQL can transform the regular expression into a graph and traverse the index accordingly.

Understanding full-text search

If you are looking up names or looking for simple strings, you are usually querying the entire content of a field. In full-text search, this is different. The purpose of the full-text search is to look for words or groups of words that can be found in a text. Therefore, full-text search is more of a contains operation, as you are basically never looking for an exact string.

In PostgreSQL, full-text search can be done using GIN indexes. The idea is to dissect a text, extract valuable lexemes (= "preprocessed tokens of words"), and index those elements rather than the underlying text. To make your search even more successful, those words are preprocessed.

Here is an example:

```
test=# SELECT to_tsvector('english',
                          'A car, I want a car. I would not even mind
                           having many cars');
                          to_tsvector
-----------------------------------------------------------------
 'car':2,6,14 'even':10 'mani':13 'mind':11 'want':4 'would':8
(1 row)
```

This example shows a simple sentence. The to_tsvector function will take the string, apply English rules, and perform a stemming process. Based on the configuration (english), PostgreSQL will parse the string, throw away stop words, and stem individual words. For example, car and cars will be transformed to car. Note that this is not about finding the word stem. In the case of many, PostgreSQL will simply transform the string into mani by applying standard rules that work nicely with the English language.

Note that the output of the to_tsvector function is highly language-dependent. If you tell PostgreSQL to treat the string as dutch, the result will be totally different:

```
test=# SELECT to_tsvector('dutch', 'A car, I want a car. I would not even
mind having many cars');
                          to_tsvector
-----------------------------------------------------------------
 'a':1,5 'car':2,6,14 'even':10 'having':12 'i':3,7 'many':13
   'mind':11 'not':9 'would':8
(1 row)
```

To figure out which configurations are supported, consider running the following query:

```
SELECT cfgname FROM pg_ts_config;
```

Let's now compare the strings.

Comparing strings

After taking a brief look at the stemming process, it is time to figure out how a stemmed text can be compared to a user query. The following code snippet checks for the word wanted:

```
test=# SELECT to_tsvector('english', 'A car, I want a car. I would not even
mind having many cars') @@ to_tsquery('english', 'wanted');
 ?column?
----------
 t
(1 row)
```

Note that wanted doesn't actually show up in the original text. Still, PostgreSQL will return true. The reason is that want and wanted are both transformed into the same lexeme, so the result is true. Practically, this makes a lot of sense. Imagine that you are looking for a car on Google. If you find pages selling cars, this is totally fine. Finding common lexemes is, therefore, an intelligent idea.

Sometimes, people are not only looking for a single word, but want to find a set of words. With to_tsquery, this is possible, as shown in the following example:

```
test=# SELECT to_tsvector('english', 'A car, I want a car. I would not even
mind having many cars') @@ to_tsquery('english', 'wanted & bmw');
 ?column?
----------
 f
(1 row)
```

In this case, false is returned because bmw cannot be found in our input string. In the to_tsquery function, & means and and | means or. It is therefore easy to build complex search strings.

Defining GIN indexes

If you want to apply text search to a column or a group of columns, there are basically two choices:

- Create a functional index using GIN
- Add a column containing ready-to-use `tsvectors` and a trigger to keep them in sync

In this section, both options will be outlined. To show you how things work, I have created some sample data:

```
test=# CREATE TABLE t_fts AS SELECT comment
 FROM pg_available_extensions;
SELECT 43
```

Indexing the column directly with a functional index is definitely a slower but more space-efficient way to get things done:

```
test=# CREATE INDEX idx_fts_func ON t_fts
       USING gin(to_tsvector('english', comment));
CREATE INDEX
```

Deploying an index on the function is easy, but it can lead to some overhead. Adding a materialized column needs more space, but will lead to better runtime behavior:

```
test=# ALTER TABLE t_fts ADD COLUMN ts tsvector;
ALTER TABLE
```

The only trouble is, how do you keep this column in sync? The answer is by using a trigger:

```
test=# CREATE TRIGGER tsvectorupdate
 BEFORE INSERT OR UPDATE ON t_fts
 FOR EACH ROW
 EXECUTE PROCEDURE
 tsvector_update_trigger(somename, 'pg_catalog.english', 'comment');
```

Fortunately, PostgreSQL already provides a C function that can be used by a trigger to sync the `tsvector` column. Just pass a name, the desired language, and a couple of columns to the function, and you are already done. The `trigger` function will take care of all that is needed. Note that a trigger will always operate within the same transaction as the statement making the modification. Therefore, there is no risk of being inconsistent.

Debugging your search

Sometimes, it is not quite clear why a query matches a given search string. To debug your query, PostgreSQL offers the `ts_debug` function. From a user's point of view, it can be used just like `to_tsvector`. It reveals a lot about the inner workings of the full-text search infrastructure:

```
test=# \x
Expanded display is on.

test=# SELECT * FROM ts_debug('english', 'go to
www.postgresql-support.de');
-[ RECORD 1 ]+---------------------------
alias        | asciiword
description  | Word, all ASCII
token        | go
dictionaries | {english_stem}
dictionary   | english_stem
lexemes      | {go}
-[ RECORD 2 ]+---------------------------
alias        | blank
description  | Space symbols
token        |
dictionaries | {}
dictionary   |
lexemes      |
-[ RECORD 3 ]+---------------------------
alias        | asciiword
description  | Word, all ASCII
token        | to
dictionaries | {english_stem}
dictionary   | english_stem
lexemes      | {}
-[ RECORD 4 ]+---------------------------
alias        | blank
description  | Space symbols
token        |
dictionaries | {}
dictionary   |
lexemes      |
-[ RECORD 5 ]+---------------------------
alias        | host
description  | Host
token        | www.postgresql-support.de
dictionaries | {simple}
dictionary   | simple
lexemes      | {www.postgresql-support.de}
```

`ts_debug` will list every token found and display information about the token. You will see which token the parser found, the dictionary used, and the type of object. In my example, blanks, words, and hosts have been found. You might also see numbers, email addresses, and a lot more. Depending on the type of string, PostgreSQL will handle things differently. For example, it makes absolutely no sense to stem hostnames and email addresses.

Gathering word statistics

A full-text search can handle a lot of data. To give end users more insight into their texts, PostgreSQL offers the `pg_stat` function, which returns a list of words:

```
SELECT * FROM  ts_stat('SELECT to_tsvector(''english'', comment)
       FROM  pg_available_extensions')
       ORDER BY 2 DESC
       LIMIT 3;
  word     | ndoc | nentry
-----------+------+--------
 function  | 10   | 10
 data      | 10   | 10
 type      | 7    | 7
(3 rows)
```

The `word` column contains the stemmed words; `ndoc` tells us about the number of documents a certain word occurs in. `nentry` indicates how often a word was found altogether.

Taking advantage of exclusion operators

So far, indexes have been used to speed things up and to ensure uniqueness. However, a couple of years ago, somebody came up with the idea of using indexes for even more. As you have seen in this chapter, GiST supports operations such as intersects, overlaps, contains, and many others. So, why not use those operations to manage data integrity?

Here is an example:

```
test=# CREATE EXTENSION btree_gist;
test=# CREATE TABLE t_reservation (
       room int,
       from_to tsrange,
       EXCLUDE USING GiST (room with =,
                           from_to with &&)
);
CREATE TABLE
```

The `EXCLUDE USING GiST` clause defines additional constraints. If you are selling rooms, you might want to allow different rooms to be booked at the same time. However, you don't want to sell the same room twice during the same period. What the `EXCLUDE` clause says in my example is this: if a room is booked twice at the same time, an error should pop up (the data in `from_to` must not overlap (`&&`) if it is related to the same room).

The following two rows will not violate the constraints:

```
test=# INSERT INTO t_reservation
        VALUES (10, '["2017-01-01", "2017-03-03"]');
INSERT 0 1
test=# INSERT INTO t_reservation
        VALUES (13, '["2017-01-01", "2017-03-03"]');
INSERT 0 1
```

However, the next `INSERT` will cause a violation because the data overlaps:

```
test=# INSERT INTO t_reservation
        VALUES (13, '["2017-02-02", "2017-08-14"]');
psql: ERROR:  conflicting key value violates exclusion constraint
"t_reservation_room_from_to_excl"
DETAIL:  Key (room, from_to)=(13, ["2017-02-02 00:00:00","2017-08-14
00:00:00"]) conflicts with existing key (room, from_to)=(13, ["2017-01-01
00:00:00","2017-03-03 00:00:00"]).
```

The use of exclusion operators is very useful and can provide you with highly advanced means to handle integrity.

Summary

This chapter was all about indexes. We learned about when PostgreSQL will decide on an index and which types of indexes exist. On top of just using indexes, it is also possible to implement your own strategies to speed up your applications with custom operators and indexing strategies.

For those of you who really want to take things to the limit, PostgreSQL offers custom access methods.

In `Chapter 4`, *Handling Advanced SQL*, we will talk about advanced SQL. Many people are not aware of what SQL is really capable of, and therefore, I am going to show you some efficient, more advanced SQL techniques.

Questions

1. Do indexes always improve performance?
2. Does an index use a lot of space?
3. How can I find missing indexes?
4. Can indexes be built in parallel?

Handling Advanced SQL 4

In Chapter 3, *Making Use of Indexes*, you learned about indexing, as well as about PostgreSQL's ability to run custom indexing code to speed up queries. In this chapter, you will learn about advanced SQL. Most of the people who read this book will have some experience in using SQL. However, experience has shown that the advanced features outlined in this book are not widely known, and therefore it makes sense to cover them in this context to help people to achieve their goals faster and more efficiently. There has been a long discussion on whether the database is just a simple data store or whether the business logic should be in the database or not. Maybe this chapter will shed some light and show how capable a modern relational database really is. SQL is not what it used to be back when SQL92 was around. Over the years, the language has grown and become more and more powerful.

This chapter is about modern SQL and its features. A variety of different and sophisticated SQL features are included and presented in detail. We will cover the following topics:

- Introducing grouping sets
- Using ordered sets
- Understanding hypothetical aggregates
- Utilizing windowing functions and analytics

By the end of this chapter, you will be able to understand and use advanced SQL.

Introducing grouping sets

Every advanced user of SQL should be familiar with `GROUP BY` and `HAVING` clauses. But are they also aware of `CUBE`, `ROLLUP`, and `GROUPING SETS`? If not, this chapter is a must-read.

Loading some sample data

To make this chapter a pleasant experience for you, we will compile some sample data that has been taken from the BP energy report, which can be found at `http://www.bp.com/en/global/corporate/energy-economics/statistical-review-of-world-energy/downloads.html`.

Here is the data structure that will be used:

```
test=# CREATE TABLE t_oil (
    region      text,
    country     text,
    year        int,
    production  int,
    consumption int
);
CREATE TABLE
```

The test data can be downloaded from our website using `curl` directly:

```
test=# COPY t_oil FROM PROGRAM '
  curl https://www.cybertec-postgresql.com/secret/oil_ext.txt ';
COPY 644
```

Like we did in the previous chapter, we can download the file before importing it. On some operating systems, `curl` is not present by default or has not been installed, so downloading the file before might be an easier option for many people.

There is data for between 1965 and 2010 for 14 nations in 2 regions of the world:

```
test=# SELECT region, avg(production) FROM t_oil GROUP BY region;
    region     |        avg
---------------+----------------------
 Middle East   | 1992.6036866359447005
 North America | 4541.3623188405797101
(2 rows)
```

Applying grouping sets

The GROUP BY clause will turn many rows into one row per group. However, if you do reporting in real life, they might also be interested in the overall average. One additional line might be needed.

Here is how this can be achieved:

```
test=# SELECT region, avg(production)
   FROM t_oil
   GROUP BY ROLLUP (region);
    region      |          avg
----------------+-----------------------
 Middle East    | 1992.6036866359447005
 North America  | 4541.3623188405797101
                | 2607.5139860139860140
(3 rows)
```

ROLLUP will inject an additional line, which will contain the overall average. If you do reporting, it is highly likely that a summary line will be needed. Instead of running two queries, PostgreSQL can provide the data by running just a single query. There is also a second thing you might notice here; different versions of PostgreSQL might return data in a different order. The reason for this is that, in PostgreSQL 10.0, the way those grouping sets were implemented has improved significantly. Back in 9.6 and before, PostgreSQL had to do a lot of sorting. Starting with version 10.0, it is already possible to use hashing for those operations, which will speed things up dramatically in many cases, as shown in the following:

```
test=# explain SELECT region, avg(production)
   FROM t_oil
   GROUP BY ROLLUP (region);
                         QUERY PLAN
------------------------------------------------------------
 MixedAggregate (cost=0.00..17.31 rows=3 width=44)
   Hash Key: region
   Group Key: ()
   -> Seq Scan on t_oil  (cost=0.00..12.44 rows=644 width=16)
(4 rows)
```

If we want data to be sorted, and ensure that all of the versions return the data in exactly the same order, it is necessary to add an ORDER BY clause to the query.

Of course, this kind of operation can also be used if you are grouping by more than just one column:

```
test=# SELECT region, country, avg(production)
    FROM t_oil
    WHERE  country IN ('USA', 'Canada', 'Iran', 'Oman')
    GROUP BY ROLLUP (region, country);
    region     | country |          avg
---------------+---------+-----------------------
 Middle East   | Iran    | 3631.6956521739130435
 Middle East   | Oman    | 586.4545454545454545
 Middle East   |         | 2142.9111111111111111
 North America | Canada  | 2123.2173913043478261
 North America | USA     | 9141.3478260869565217
 North America |         | 5632.2826086956521739
               |         | 3906.7692307692307692
(7 rows)
```

In the preceding example, PostgreSQL will inject three lines into the result set. One line will be injected for the Middle East, and one line will be injected for North America. On top of that, we will get a line for the overall averages. If we are building a web application, the current result is ideal because you can easily build a GUI to drill into the result set by filtering out the null values.

ROLLUP is suitable when you instantly want to display a result. Personally, I have always used it to display final results to end users. However, if you are doing reporting, then you might want to precalculate more data to ensure more flexibility. The CUBE keyword will help you with this:

```
test=# SELECT region, country, avg(production)
   FROM t_oil
   WHERE country IN ('USA', 'Canada', 'Iran', 'Oman')
   GROUP BY CUBE (region, country);
    region     | country | avg
---------------+---------+-----------------------
 Middle East   | Iran    | 3631.6956521739130435
 Middle East   | Oman    | 586.4545454545454545
 Middle East   |         | 2142.9111111111111111
 North America | Canada  | 2123.2173913043478261
 North America | USA     | 9141.3478260869565217
 North America |         | 5632.2826086956521739
               |         | 3906.7692307692307692
               | Canada  | 2123.2173913043478261
               | Iran    | 3631.6956521739130435
```

```
                        | Oman     |  586.4545454545454545
                        | USA      | 9141.3478260869565217
(11 rows)
```

Note that even more rows have been added to the result. CUBE will create the same data as GROUP BY region, country + GROUP BY region + GROUP BY country + the overall average. So, the whole idea is to extract many results and various levels of aggregation at once. The resultant cube contains all possible combinations of groups.

ROLLUP and CUBE are really just convenience features on top of the GROUPING SETS clause. With the GROUPING SETS clause, you can explicitly list the aggregates you want:

```
test=# SELECT region, country, avg(production)
   FROM  t_oil
   WHERE country IN ('USA', 'Canada', 'Iran', 'Oman')
   GROUP BY GROUPING SETS ( (), region, country);
   region        |  country |          avg
-----------------+----------+-----------------------
 Middle East     |          | 2142.9111111111111111
 North America   |          | 5632.2826086956521739
                 |          | 3906.7692307692307692
                 | Canada   | 2123.2173913043478261
                 | Iran     | 3631.6956521739130435
                 | Oman     |  586.4545454545454545
                 | USA      | 9141.3478260869565217
(7 rows)
```

In this section, I went for three grouping sets: the overall average, GROUP BY region, and GROUP BY country. If you want regions and countries combined, use (region, country).

Investigating performance

Grouping sets is a powerful feature; they help to reduce the number of expensive queries. Internally, PostgreSQL will basically use MixedAggregate to perform the aggregation. It can perform many operations at once, which ensures efficiency, as shown in the following example:

```
test=# explain SELECT region, country, avg(production)
   FROM    t_oil
   WHERE   country IN ('USA', 'Canada', 'Iran', 'Oman')
   GROUP BY GROUPING SETS ( (), region, country);
                             QUERY PLAN
-------------------------------------------------------------------
 MixedAggregate  (cost=0.00..18.17 rows=17 width=52)
   Hash Key: region
```

```
      Hash Key: country
      Group Key: ()
      -> Seq Scan on t_oil (cost=0.00..15.66 rows=184 width=24)
            Filter: (country = ANY ('{USA,Canada,Iran,Oman}'::text[]))
 (6 rows)
```

In older versions of PostgreSQL, the system used `GroupAggregate` to perform this operation in all cases. In a more modern version, `MixedAggregate` has been added. However, you can still force the optimizer to use the old strategy using the `enable_hashagg` setting. `MixedAggregate` is essentially `HashAggregate` and therefore the same setting applies, as shown in the next example:

```
test=# SET enable_hashagg TO off;
SET
test=# explain SELECT region, country, avg(production)
    FROM    t_oil
    WHERE   country IN ('USA', 'Canada', 'Iran', 'Oman')
    GROUP BY GROUPING SETS ( (), region, country);
                               QUERY PLAN
--------------------------------------------------------------------------------
 GroupAggregate (cost=22.58..32.48 rows=17 width=52)
   Group Key: region
   Group Key: ()
   Sort Key: country
     Group Key: country
   -> Sort (cost=22.58..23.04 rows=184 width=24)
       Sort Key: region
       -> Seq Scan on t_oil (cost=0.00..15.66 rows=184 width=24)
           Filter: (country = ANY ('{USA,Canada,Iran,Oman}'::text[]))
 (9 rows)
test=# SET enable_hashagg TO on;
SET
```

In general, the hash-based version (`MixedAggregate`) is faster and is favored by the optimizer if there is enough memory to keep the hash needed for `MixedAggregate` in memory.

Combining grouping sets with the FILTER clause

In real-world applications, grouping sets can often be combined with `FILTER` clauses. The idea behind the `FILTER` clause is to be able to run partial aggregates. Here is an example:

```
test=# SELECT region,
    avg(production) AS all,
    avg(production) FILTER (WHERE year  < 1990) AS old,
```

```
    avg(production) FILTER (WHERE year  >= 1990) AS new
FROM t_oil
GROUP BY ROLLUP (region);
    region      | all             | old             | new
----------------+-----------------+-----------------+-----------------
  Middle East   | 1992.603686635  | 1747.325892857  | 2254.233333333
  North America | 4541.362318840  | 4471.653333333  | 4624.349206349
                | 2607.513986013  | 2430.685618729  | 2801.183150183
(3 rows)
```

The idea here is that not all columns will use the same data for aggregation. The FILTER clause allows you to selectively pass data to those aggregates. In this example, the second aggregate will only consider data before 1990, the third aggregate will take care of more recent data, and the first one will get all the data.

> If it is possible to move conditions to a WHERE clause, it is always more desirable, as less data has to be fetched from the table. FILTER is only useful if the data left by the WHERE clause is not needed by each aggregate.

FILTER works for all kinds of aggregates and offers a simple way to pivot your data. Also, FILTER is faster than mimicking the same behavior with CASE WHEN ... THEN NULL ... ELSE END. You can find some real performance comparisons here: https://www.cybertec-postgresql.com/en/postgresql-9-4-aggregation-filters-they-do-pay-off/.

Making use of ordered sets

Ordered sets are powerful features, but are not widely regarded as such and not widely known in the developer community. The idea is actually quite simple: data is grouped normally, and then the data inside each group is ordered given a certain condition. The calculation is then performed on this sorted data.

A classic example would be the calculation of the median.

> The median is the middle value. If you are, for example, earning the median income, the number of people earning less and more than you are identical; 50% of people do better and 50% of people do worse.

One way to get the median is to take sorted data and move 50% into the dataset. This is an example of what the WITHIN GROUP clause will ask PostgreSQL to do:

```
test=# SELECT region,
    percentile_disc(0.5) WITHIN GROUP (ORDER BY production)
FROM t_oil
GROUP BY 1;
 region          | percentile_disc
-----------------+-----------------
 Middle East     |            1082
 North  America  |            3054
(2 rows)
```

The percentile_disc function will skip 50% of the group and return the desired value.

Note that the median can significantly deviate from the average.

In economics, the deviation between the median and the average income can even be used as an indicator of social equality or inequality. The higher the median is compared to the average, the greater the income inequality. To provide more flexibility, the ANSI standard does not just propose a median function. Instead, percentile_disc allows you to use any value between 0 and 1.

The beauty is that you can even use ordered sets along with grouping sets, as shown in the following:

```
test=# SELECT region,
            percentile_disc(0.5) WITHIN GROUP (ORDER BY production)
FROM    t_oil
GROUP BY ROLLUP (1);
 region          | percentile_disc
-----------------+-----------------
 Middle East     |            1082
 North  America  |            3054
                 |            1696
(3 rows)
```

In this case, PostgreSQL will again inject additional lines into the result set.

As proposed by the ANSI SQL standard, PostgreSQL provides you with two `percentile_` functions. The `percentile_disc` function will return a value that is really contained by the dataset, while the `percentile_cont` function will interpolate a value if no exact match is found. The following example shows how this works:

```
test=# SELECT percentile_disc(0.62) WITHIN GROUP (ORDER BY id),
    percentile_cont(0.62) WITHIN GROUP (ORDER BY id)
FROM  generate_series(1, 5) AS id;
 percentile_disc | percentile_cont
-----------------+-----------------
 4               |            3.48
(1 row)
```

4 is a value that really exists—3.48 has been interpolated. The `percentile_` functions are not the only ones provided by PostgreSQL. To find the most frequent value within a group, the `mode` function is available. Before showing an example of how to use the `mode` function, I have compiled a query telling us a bit more about the contents of the table:

```
test=# SELECT production, count(*)
   FROM   t_oil
   WHERE  country = 'Other Middle East'
   GROUP  BY production
   ORDER  BY 2 DESC
   LIMIT  4;
 production | count
------------+-------
 50         |     5
 48         |     5
 52         |     5
 53         |     4

(4 rows)
```

Three different values occur exactly five times. Of course, the `mode` function can only give us one of them:

```
test=# SELECT country, mode() WITHIN GROUP (ORDER BY production)
   FROM   t_oil
   WHERE  country = 'Other Middle East'
   GROUP  BY 1;
 country             | mode
---------------------+------
 Other  Middle East  |   48
(1 row)
```

The most frequent value is returned, but SQL won't tell us how often the number actually shows up. It might be that the number only shows up once.

Understanding hypothetical aggregates

Hypothetical aggregates are pretty similar to standard ordered sets. However, they help to answer a different kind of question: what would be the result if a value was in the data? As you can see, this is not about values inside the database, but about the result if a certain value was actually there.

The only hypothetical function that's provided by PostgreSQL is rank, as shown in the following:

```
test=# SELECT region,
              rank(9000) WITHIN GROUP
                        (ORDER BY production DESC NULLS LAST)
FROM t_oil
GROUP BY ROLLUP (1);
    region      | rank
----------------+------
 Middle East    |  21
 North America  |  27
                |  47
(3 rows)
```

The preceding code tells us this: if somebody produced 9,000 barrels per day, it would be ranked the 27th best year in North America and 21st in Middle East.

> In this example, I used NULLS LAST. When data is sorted, nulls are usually at the end. However, if the sort order is reversed, nulls should still be at the end of the list. NULLS LAST ensures exactly that.

Utilizing windowing functions and analytics

Now that we have discussed ordered sets, it is time to take a look at windowing functions. Aggregates follow a fairly simple principle; take many rows and turn them into fewer, aggregated rows. A windowing function is different. It compares the current row with all rows in the group. The number of rows returned does not change. Here is an example:

```
test=# SELECT avg(production) FROM t_oil;
    avg
-----------
 2607.5139
(1 row)

test=# SELECT country, year, production,
```

```
              consumption, avg(production) OVER ()
  FROM t_oil
  LIMIT 4;
  country | year | production | consumption |    avg
  --------+------+------------+-------------+----------
  USA     | 1965 |       9014 |       11522 | 2607.5139
  USA     | 1966 |       9579 |       12100 | 2607.5139
  USA     | 1967 |      10219 |       12567 | 2607.5139
  USA     | 1968 |      10600 |       13405 | 2607.5139
  (4 rows)
```

The average production in our dataset is around 2.6 million barrels per day. The goal of this query is to add this value as a column. It is now easy to compare the current row to the overall average.

Keep in mind that the OVER clause is essential. PostgreSQL is unable to process the query without it:

```
test=# SELECT country, year, production, consumption, avg(production) FROM
t_oil;
psql: ERROR: column "t_oil.country" must  appear in the GROUP BY clause or
be used
        in an aggregate function
  LINE  1: SELECT country, year,  production, consumption, avg(productio...
```

This actually makes sense because the average has to be defined precisely. The database engine cannot just guess any value.

Other database engines can accept aggregate functions without an OVER or even a GROUP BY clause. However, from a logical point of view, this is wrong and, on top of that, a violation of SQL.

Partitioning data

So far, the same result can also easily be achieved using sub-select. However, if you want more than just the overall average, sub-select will turn your queries into nightmares due to complexity. Suppose you don't just want the overall average but the average of the country you are dealing with. A PARTITION BY clause is what you need:

```
test=# SELECT country, year, production, consumption,
            avg(production) OVER (PARTITION BY country)
  FROM t_oil;
  country  | year | production | consumption |     avg
  ---------+------+------------+-------------+-----------
```

```
Canada    | 1965 |    920    |    1108    | 2123.2173
Canada    | 2010 |    3332   |    2316    | 2123.2173
Canada    | 2009 |    3202   |    2190    | 2123.2173
...
Iran      | 1966 |    2132   |    148     | 3631.6956
Iran      | 2010 |    4352   |    1874    | 3631.6956
Iran      | 2009 |    4249   |    2012    | 3631.6956
...
```

The point here is that each country will be assigned to the average of the country. The OVER clause defines the window we are looking at. In this case, the window is the country the row belongs to. In other words, the query returns the rows compared to all rows in this country.

 The year column is not sorted. The query does not contain an explicit sort order, so it might be that data is returned in random order. Remember, SQL does not promise sorted output unless you explicitly state what you want.

Basically, a PARTITION BY clause takes any expression. Usually, most people will use a column to partition the data. Here is an example:

```
test=# SELECT year, production,
              avg(production) OVER (PARTITION BY year < 1990)
FROM   t_oil
WHERE  country = 'Canada'
ORDER  BY year;
 year | production |          avg
------+------------+------------------------
 1965 |        920 | 1631.6000000000000000
 1966 |       1012 | 1631.6000000000000000
 ...
 1990 |       1967 | 2708.4761904761904762
 1991 |       1983| 2708.4761904761904762
 1992 |       2065| 2708.4761904761904762
 ...
```

The point is that data is split using an expression. year < 1990 can return two values: true or false. Depending on the group a year is in, it will be assigned to the pre-1990 average or to the post-1990 average. PostgreSQL is really flexible here. Using functions to determine group membership is not uncommon in real-world applications.

Ordering data inside a window

A PARTITION BY clause is not the only possible thing you can put into an OVER clause. Sometimes, it is necessary to sort data inside a window. ORDER BY will provide data to your aggregate functions in a certain way. Here is an example:

```
test=# SELECT country, year, production,
              min(production) OVER (PARTITION BY country ORDER BY year)
FROM    t_oil
WHERE   year BETWEEN 1978 AND 1983
        AND country IN ('Iran', 'Oman');
country | year | production | min
--------+------+------------+------
Iran    | 1978 |       5302 | 5302
Iran    | 1979 |       3218 | 3218
Iran    | 1980 |       1479 | 1479
Iran    | 1981 |       1321 | 1321
Iran    | 1982 |       2397 | 1321
Iran    | 1983 |       2454 | 1321
Oman    | 1978 |        314 |  314
Oman    | 1979 |        295 |  295
Oman    | 1980 |        285 |  285
Oman    | 1981 |        330 |  285
. . .
```

Two countries (Iran and Oman) are chosen from our dataset for the period 1978 to 1983. Keep in mind that there was a revolution going on in Iran in 1979, so this had some impact on the production of oil. The data reflects this.

What the query does is calculate the minimum production up to a certain point in our time series. At this point, it is a good way for SQL students to remember what an ORDER BY clause does inside an OVER clause. In this example, the PARTITION BY clause will create one group for each country and order data inside the group. The min function will loop over the sorted data and provide the required minimums.

If you are new to windowing functions, there is something you should be aware of. It really does make a difference, irrespective of whether you use an ORDER BY clause or not:

```
test=# SELECT country, year, production,
          min(production) OVER (),
          min(production) OVER (ORDER BY year)
   FROM t_oil
   WHERE year BETWEEN 1978 AND 1983
         AND country = 'Iran';
 country | year | production  | min  | min
---------+------+-------------+------+------
```

```
Iran      | 1978 |          5302| 1321 | 5302
Iran      | 1979 |          3218 | 1321 | 3218
Iran      | 1980 |          1479 | 1321 | 1479
Iran      | 1981 |          1321 | 1321 | 1321
Iran      | 1982 |          2397 | 1321 | 1321
Iran      | 1983 |          2454 | 1321 | 1321
(6 rows)
```

If the aggregate is used without ORDER BY, it will automatically take the minimum of the entire dataset inside your windows. This doesn't happen if there is an ORDER BY clause. In this case, it will always be the minimum up to this point, given the order you have defined.

Using sliding windows

So far, the window we have used inside our query has been static. However, for calculations such as a moving average, this is not enough. A moving average needs a sliding window that moves along as data is processed.

Here is an example of how a moving average can be achieved:

```
test=# SELECT country, year, production,
          min(production)
          OVER (PARTITION BY country
          ORDER BY year ROWS BETWEEN 1 PRECEDING AND 1 FOLLOWING)
FROM   t_oil
WHERE year BETWEEN 1978 AND 1983
       AND country IN ('Iran', 'Oman');
country  | year  | production | min
---------+-------+------------+------
Iran     | 1978  |       5302 | 3218
Iran     | 1979  |       3218 | 1479
Iran     | 1980  |       1479 | 1321
Iran     | 1981  |       1321 | 1321
Iran     | 1982  |       2397 | 1321
Iran     | 1983  |       2454 | 2397
Oman     | 1978  |        314 | 295
Oman     | 1979  |        295 | 285
Oman     | 1980  |        285 | 285
Oman     | 1981  |        330 | 285
Oman     | 1982  |        338 | 330
Oman     | 1983  |        391 | 338
(12 rows)
```

The most important thing is that a moving window should be used with an ORDER BY clause. Otherwise, there will be major problems. PostgreSQL would actually accept the query, but the result would be totally wrong. Remember, feeding data to a sliding window without ordering it first will simply lead to random data.

ROWS BETWEEN 1 PRECEDING and 1 FOLLOWING define the window. In this example, up to three rows will be in use: the current row, the one before, and the one after the current row. To illustrate how the sliding window works, check out the following example:

```
test=# SELECT *, array_agg(id)
                    OVER (ORDER BY id ROWS BETWEEN 1 PRECEDING AND 1
FOLLOWING)
    FROM  generate_series(1, 5) AS id;
id  | array_agg
----+------------
  1 | {1,2}
  2 | {1,2,3}
  3 | {2,3,4}
  4 | {3,4,5}
  5 | {4,5}
(5 rows)
```

The array_agg function will turn a list of values into a PostgreSQL array. It will help to explain how the sliding window operates.

Actually, this trivial query has some very important aspects. What you can see is that the first array contains only two values. There is no entry before 1, and therefore the array is not full. PostgreSQL does not add null entries because they would be ignored by aggregates anyway. The same happens at the end of the data.

However, sliding windows offer more. There are a couple of keywords that can be used to specify the sliding window. Consider the following code:

```
test=# SELECT *,
          array_agg(id) OVER (ORDER BY id ROWS BETWEEN
                              UNBOUNDED PRECEDING AND 0 FOLLOWING)
FROM generate_series(1, 5) AS id;
 id |   array_agg
----+--------------
  1 | {1}
  2 | {1,2}
  3 | {1,2,3}
  4 | {1,2,3,4}
  5 | {1,2,3,4,5}
(5 rows)
```

The UNBOUNDED PRECEDING keyword means that everything before the current line will be in the window. The counterpart to UNBOUNDED PRECEDING is UNBOUNDED FOLLOWING. Let's look at the following example:

```
test=# SELECT *,
    array_agg(id) OVER (ORDER BY id
                        ROWS BETWEEN 2 FOLLOWING
                        AND UNBOUNDED FOLLOWING)
FROM generate_series(1, 5) AS id;
 id | array_agg
----+-----------
  1 | {3,4,5}
  2 | {4,5}
  3 | {5}
  4 |
  5 |
(5 rows)
```

But there is more: in some cases, you might want to exclude the current row from your calculation. To do that, SQL offers some syntactic sugar, as shown in the next example:

```
test=# SELECT    year,
                 production,
                 array_agg(production) OVER (ORDER BY year
                         ROWS BETWEEN 1 PRECEDING AND 1 FOLLOWING
                         EXCLUDE CURRENT ROW)
FROM     t_oil
WHERE    country = 'USA'
         AND year < 1970;
 year | production |    array_agg
------+------------+----------------
 1965 |       9014 | {9579}
 1966 |       9579 | {9014,10219}
 1967 |      10219 | {9579,10600}
 1968 |      10600 | {10219,10828}
 1969 |      10828 | {10600}
(5 rows)
```

As you can see, it is also possible to use a window that is in the future. PostgreSQL is very flexible here.

Understanding the subtle difference between ROWS and RANGE

So far, you have seen sliding windows using OVER ... ROWS. However, there is more. Let's take a look at the SQL specification taken directly from the PostgreSQL documentation:

```
{ RANGE | ROWS | GROUPS } frame_start [ frame_exclusion ]
{ RANGE | ROWS | GROUPS } BETWEEN frame_start AND frame_end [
frame_exclusion ]
```

There is more than just ROWS. In real life, we have seen that many people are struggling to understand the difference between RANGE and ROWS. In many cases, the result is the same, which adds even more to the confusion. To understand the problem, let's first create some simple data:

```
test=# SELECT *, x / 3 AS y FROM generate_series(1, 15) AS x;
  x | y
----+---
  1 | 0
  2 | 0
  3 | 1
  4 | 1
  5 | 1
  6 | 2
  7 | 2
  8 | 2
  9 | 3
 10 | 3
 11 | 3
 12 | 4
 13 | 4
 14 | 4
 15 | 5
(15 rows)
```

This is a simple dataset. Be particularly aware of the second column, which contains a couple of duplicates. Those will be relevant in a minute:

```
test=# SELECT *, x / 3 AS y,
          array_agg(x) OVER (ORDER BY x
                         ROWS BETWEEN 1 PRECEDING AND 1 FOLLOWING) AS
rows_1,
          array_agg(x) OVER (ORDER BY x
                         RANGE BETWEEN 1 PRECEDING AND 1 FOLLOWING) AS
range_1,
```

```
           array_agg(x/3)  OVER  (ORDER BY (x/3)
                            ROWS BETWEEN 1 PRECEDING AND 1 FOLLOWING) AS
    rows_2,
           array_agg(x/3)  OVER  (ORDER BY (x/3)
                            RANGE BETWEEN 1 PRECEDING AND 1 FOLLOWING) AS
    range_2
    FROM    generate_series(1, 15) AS x;
```

x	y	rows_1	range_1	rows_2	range_2
1	0	{1,2}	{1,2}	{0,0}	{0,0,1,1,1}
2	0	{1,2,3}	{1,2,3}	{0,0,1}	{0,0,1,1,1}
3	1	{2,3,4}	{2,3,4}	{0,1,1}	{0,0,1,1,1,2,2,2}
4	1	{3,4,5}	{3,4,5}	{1,1,1}	{0,0,1,1,1,2,2,2}
5	1	{4,5,6}	{4,5,6}	{1,1,2}	{0,0,1,1,1,2,2,2}
6	2	{5,6,7}	{5,6,7}	{1,2,2}	{1,1,1,2,2,2,3,3,3}
7	2	{6,7,8}	{6,7,8}	{2,2,2}	{1,1,1,2,2,2,3,3,3}
8	2	{7,8,9}	{7,8,9}	{2,2,3}	{1,1,1,2,2,2,3,3,3}
9	3	{8,9,10}	{8,9,10}	{2,3,3}	{2,2,2,3,3,3,4,4,4}
10	3	{9,10,11}	{9,10,11}	{3,3,3}	{2,2,2,3,3,3,4,4,4}
11	3	{10,11,12}	{10,11,12}	{3,3,4}	{2,2,2,3,3,3,4,4,4}
12	4	{11,12,13}	{11,12,13}	{3,4,4}	{3,3,3,4,4,4,5}
13	4	{12,13,14}	{12,13,14}	{4,4,4}	{3,3,3,4,4,4,5}
14	4	{13,14,15}	{13,14,15}	{4,4,5}	{3,3,3,4,4,4,5}
15	5	{14,15}	{14,15}	{4,5}	{4,4,4,5}

```
(15 rows)
```

After listing the x and y columns, I have applied windowing functions on x. As you can see, the results are the same for both columns. `rows_1` and `range_1` are absolutely identical. The situation changes if we start to use the column containing those duplicates. In the case of ROWS, PostgreSQL simply takes the previous and the next rows. In the case of RANGE, it takes the entire group of duplicates. Hence, the array is a lot longer. The entire group of identical values is taken.

Removing duplicates using EXCLUDE TIES and EXCLUDE GROUP

Sometimes, you want to make sure that duplicates don't make it into the result of your windowing function. The EXCLUDE TIES clause helps you to achieve exactly that. If a value shows up in a window twice, it will be removed. This is a neat way to avoid complicated workarounds, which can be costly and slow. The following listing contains a simple example:

```
SELECT *,
       x / 3 AS y,
```

```
       array_agg(x/3) OVER (ORDER BY x/3
                       ROWS BETWEEN 1 PRECEDING AND 1 FOLLOWING) AS rows_1,
       array_agg(x/3) OVER (ORDER BY x/3
                       ROWS BETWEEN 1 PRECEDING AND 1 FOLLOWING EXCLUDE TIES)
   AS rows_2 FROM   generate_series(1, 10) AS x;
    x | y |  rows_1  | rows_2
   ---+---+----------+--------
    1 | 0 |   {0,0}  | {0}
    2 | 0 | {0,0,1}  | {0,1}
    3 | 1 | {0,1,1}  | {0,1}
    4 | 1 | {1,1,1}  | {1}
    5 | 1 | {1,1,2}  | {1,2}
    6 | 2 | {1,2,2}  | {1,2}
    7 | 2 | {2,2,2}  | {2}
    8 | 2 | {2,2,3}  | {2,3}
    9 | 3 | {2,3,3}  | {2,3}
   10 | 3 |   {3,3}  | {3}
   (10 rows)
```

I have again used the `generate_series` function to create data. Using a simple time series is a lot easier than digging through some more complicated real-world data. `array_agg` will turn all values added to the window into an array. As you can see in the last column, however, the array is a lot shorter. Duplicates have been removed automatically.

In addition to the EXCLUDE TIES clause, PostgreSQL also supports EXCLUDE GROUP. The idea here is that you want to remove an entire set of rows from the dataset before it makes it to the aggregation function. Let's take a look at the following example. We have 4 windowing functions here. The first one is the classical ROWS BETWEEN example you have already seen. I have included this column so that it is easier to spot the differences between the standard and the EXCLUDE GROUP version. What is also important to note here is that the `array_agg` function is not the only one you can use here—avg or any other window or aggregation function works just fine. I simply used `array_agg` to make it easier to see what PostgreSQL does. In the following example, you can see that EXCLUDE GROUP removes the entire set of rows:

```
SELECT *,
       x / 3 AS y,
       array_agg(x/3) OVER (ORDER BY x/3
                       ROWS BETWEEN 1 PRECEDING AND 1 FOLLOWING) AS rows_1,
       avg(x/3) OVER (ORDER BY x/3
                       ROWS BETWEEN 1 PRECEDING AND 1 FOLLOWING) AS avg_1,
       array_agg(x/3) OVER (ORDER BY x/3
                       ROWS BETWEEN 1 PRECEDING AND 1 FOLLOWING EXCLUDE GROUP) AS
rows_2,
       avg(x/3) OVER (ORDER BY x/3
                       ROWS BETWEEN 1 PRECEDING AND 1 FOLLOWING EXCLUDE GROUP) AS
```

```
avg_2
FROM    generate_series(1, 10) AS x;
  x | y |  rows_1  |   avg_1   | rows_2 |   avg_2
----+---+---------+-----------+--------+-----------
  1 | 0 |   {0,0} | 0.000000 |        |
  2 | 0 | {0,0,1} | 0.333333 |   {1}  | 1.000000
  3 | 1 | {0,1,1} | 0.666666 |   {0}  | 0.000000
  4 | 1 | {1,1,1} | 1.000000 |        |
  5 | 1 | {1,1,2} | 1.333333 |   {2}  | 2.000000
  6 | 2 | {1,2,2} | 1.666666 |   {1}  | 1.000000
  7 | 2 | {2,2,2} | 2.000000 |        |
  8 | 2 | {2,2,3} | 2.333333 |   {3}  | 3.000000
  9 | 3 | {2,3,3} | 2.666666 |   {2}  | 2.000000
 10 | 3 |   {3,3} | 3.0000000 |        |
(10 rows)
```

The entire group containing the same value is removed. That, of course also impacts the average calculated on top of this result.

Abstracting window clauses

A windowing function allows us to add columns to the result set that has been calculated on the fly. However, it is a frequent phenomenon that many columns are based on the same window. Putting the same clauses into your queries over and over again is definitely not a good idea, because your queries will be hard to read and therefore hard to maintain.

The WINDOW clause allows developers to predefine a window and use it in various places in the query. Here is how it works:

```
SELECT country, year, production,
       min(production) OVER (w),
       max(production) OVER (w)
FROM t_oil
WHERE country = 'Canada'
      AND year BETWEEN 1980
      AND 1985
WINDOW w AS (ORDER BY year);
country | year | production | min  | max
--------+------+------------+------+------
Canada  | 1980 |       1764 | 1764 | 1764
Canada  | 1981 |       1610 | 1610 | 1764
Canada  | 1982 |       1590 | 1590 | 1764
Canada  | 1983 |       1661 | 1590 | 1764
Canada  | 1984 |       1775 | 1590 | 1775
Canada  | 1985 |       1812 | 1590 | 1812
(6 rows)
```

The preceding example shows that `min` and `max` will use the same clause.

Of course, it is possible to have more than just one `WINDOW` clause—PostgreSQL does not impose serious restrictions on users here.

Using on-board windowing functions

Having introduced you to the basic concepts, it is time to take a look at which windowing functions PostgreSQL will support out of the box. You have already seen that windowing works with all standard aggregate functions. On top of those functions, PostgreSQL offers some additional functions that are exclusive to windowing and analytics.

In this section, some highly important functions will be explained and discussed.

The rank and dense_rank functions

The `rank()` and `dense_rank()` functions are, in my judgment, the most prominent functions in SQL. The `rank()` function returns the number of the current row within its window. Counting starts at `1`.

Here is an example:

```
test=# SELECT year, production,
              rank() OVER (ORDER BY production)
FROM   t_oil
WHERE  country = 'Other Middle East'
ORDER BY rank
LIMIT 7;
 year  | production | rank
-------+------------+------
 2001  |     47     |  1
 2004  |     48     |  2
 2002  |     48     |  2
 1999  |     48     |  2
 2000  |     48     |  2
 2003  |     48     |  2
 1998  |     49     |  7
(7 rows)
```

The `rank` column will number those tuples in your dataset. Note that many rows in my sample are equal. Therefore, the rank will jump from 2 to 7 directly, because many production values are identical. If you want to avoid that, the `dense_rank()` function is the way to go about this:

```
test=# SELECT year, production,
              dense_rank() OVER (ORDER BY production)
FROM  t_oil
WHERE country = 'Other Middle East'
ORDER BY dense_rank
LIMIT 7;
 year  | production | dense_rank
-------+------------+------------
 2001  |         47 |          1
 2004  |         48 |          2
 ...
 2003  |         48 |          2
 1998  |         49 |          3
(7 rows)
```

PostgreSQL will pack the numbers more tightly. There will be no more gaps.

The ntile() function

Some applications require data to be split into ideally equal groups. The `ntile()` function will do exactly that for you.

The following example shows how data can be split into groups:

```
test=# SELECT year, production,
              ntile(4) OVER (ORDER BY production)
   FROM  t_oil
   WHERE  country = 'Iraq'
        AND year BETWEEN 2000 AND 2006;
 year  | production | ntile
-------+------------+-------
 2003  |       1344 |     1
 2005  |       1833 |     1
 2006  |       1999 |     2
 2004  |       2030 |     2
 2002  |       2116 |     3
 2001  |       2522 |     3
 2000  |       2613 |     4
(7 rows)
```

The query splits data into four groups. The trouble is that only seven rows are selected, which makes it impossible to create four even groups. As you can see, PostgreSQL will fill up the first three groups and make the last one a bit smaller. You can rely on the fact that the groups at the end will always tend to be a bit smaller than the rest.

 In this example, only a handful of rows are used. In real-world applications, millions of rows will be involved, and therefore it is no problem if groups are not perfectly equal.

The `ntile()` function is usually not used alone. Sure, it helps to assign a group ID to a row. However, in real-world applications, people want to perform calculations on top of those groups. Suppose you want to create a `quartile` distribution for your data. Here's how it works:

```
test=# SELECT grp, min(production), max(production), count(*)
FROM   (
          SELECT year, production,
                 ntile(4) OVER (ORDER BY production) AS grp
          FROM   t_oil
          WHERE  country = 'Iraq'
        ) AS x
GROUP  BY ROLLUP (1);
 grp | min  | max  | count
-----+------+------+-------
  1  | 285  | 1228 |   12
  2  | 1313 | 1977 |   12
  3  | 1999 | 2422 |   11
  4  | 2428 | 3489 |   11
     | 285  | 3489 |   46
(5 rows)
```

The most important thing is that the calculation cannot be done in one step. When I do SQL training courses here at Cybertec (https://www.cybertec-postgresql.com), I try to explain to students that whenever you don't know how to do it all at once, consider using `sub-select`. In analytics, this is usually a good idea. In this example, the first thing that's done in `sub-select` is attaching a group label to each group. Then, those groups are taken and processed in the main query.

The result is already something that could be used in a real-world application (maybe as a legend located next to a graph, and so on).

The lead() and lag() functions

While the `ntile()` function is essential for splitting a dataset into groups, the `lead()` and `lag()` functions are here to move lines within the result set. A typical use case is to calculate the difference in production from one year to the next, as shown in the following example:

```
test=# SELECT year, production,
              lag(production, 1) OVER (ORDER BY year)
       FROM  t_oil
       WHERE country = 'Mexico'
       LIMIT 5;
 year | production | lag
------+------------+-----
 1965 |        362 |
 1966 |        370 | 362
 1967 |        411 | 370
 1968 |        439 | 411
 1969 |        461 | 439
(5 rows)
```

Before actually calculating the change in production, it makes sense to sit back and see what the `lag()` function actually does. You can see that the column is moved by one row. The data moved as defined in the ORDER BY clause. In my example, this means down. An ORDER BY DESC clause would, of course, have moved the data up.

From this point on, the query is easy:

```
test=# SELECT year, production,
              production - lag(production, 1) OVER (ORDER BY year)
       FROM  t_oil
       WHERE country = 'Mexico'
       LIMIT 3;
 year | production | ?column?
------+------------+----------
 1965 |        362 |
 1966 |        370 |        8
 1967 |        411 |       41
(3 rows)
```

All you have to do is to calculate the difference like you would with any other column. Note that the `lag()` function has two parameters. The first one indicates which column is to be displayed. The second column tells PostgreSQL how many rows you want to move. Putting in 7, then, means that everything is off by seven rows.

Note that the first value is `Null` (as are all of the other lagged rows without a preceding value).

The `lead()` function is the counterpart of the `lag()` function; it will move rows up instead of down:

```
test=# SELECT year, production,
              production - lead(production, 1) OVER (ORDER BY year)
       FROM  t_oil
       WHERE country = 'Mexico'
       LIMIT 3;
 year  | production | ?column?
-------+------------+----------
 1965  |        362 |       -8
 1966  |        370 |      -41
 1967  |        411 |      -28

(3 rows)
```

Basically, PostgreSQL will also accept negative values for lead and lag columns. `lag(production, -1)` is therefore a replacement for `lead(production, 1)`. However, it is definitely cleaner to use the right function to move data in the direction you want.

So far, you have seen how to lag a single column. In most applications, lagging a single value will be the standard case used by most developers. The point is, PostgreSQL can do a lot more than that. It is possible to lag entire lines:

```
test=# \x
Expanded display is on.
test=# SELECT year, production,
              lag(t_oil, 1) OVER (ORDER BY year)
       FROM  t_oil
       WHERE country = 'USA'
       LIMIT 3;
-[ RECORD 1 ]------------------------------------
year           | 1965
production     | 9014
lag            |
-[ RECORD 2 ]------------------------------------
year           | 1966
production     | 9579
lag            | ("North America",USA,1965,9014,11522)
-[ RECORD 3 ]------------------------------------
year           | 1967
production     | 10219
lag            | ("North America",USA,1966,9579,12100)
```

The beauty here is that more than just a single value can be compared to the previous row. The trouble, though, is that PostgreSQL will return the entire row as a composite type and therefore it is hard to work with. To dissect a composite type, you can use parentheses and a star:

```
test=# SELECT year, production,
            (lag(t_oil, 1) OVER (ORDER BY year)).*
       FROM   t_oil
       WHERE country = 'USA'
       LIMIT 3;
 year | prod  | region      | country | year | prod | consumption
------+-------+-------------+---------+------+------+-------------
 1965 | 9014  |             |         |      |      |
 1966 | 9579  | N. America  |    USA  | 1965 | 9014 | 11522
 1967 | 10219 | N. America  |    USA  | 1966 | 9579 | 12100
(3 rows)
```

Why is that useful? Lagging an entire row will make it possible to see whether the data has been inserted more than once. It is pretty simple to detect duplicate rows (or close-to-duplicate rows) in your time series data.

Check out the following example:

```
test=# SELECT *
       FROM (SELECT t_oil, lag(t_oil) OVER (ORDER BY year)
             FROM   t_oil
             WHERE country = 'USA'
       ) AS x
       WHERE t_oil = lag;
 t_oil  | lag
--------+-----
(0 rows)
```

Of course, the sample data doesn't contain duplicates. However, in real-world examples, duplicates can easily happen, and it is easy to detect them, even if there is no primary key.

The `t_oil` row is really the entire row. The lag returned by `sub-select` is also a complete row. In PostgreSQL, composite types can be compared directly in case the fields are identical. PostgreSQL will simply compare one field after the other.

The first_value(), nth_value(), and last_value() functions

Sometimes, it is necessary to calculate data based on the first value of a data window. Unsurprisingly, the function to do that is `first_value()`:

```
test=# SELECT year,  production,
             first_value(production) OVER (ORDER BY year)
       FROM   t_oil
       WHERE  country = 'Canada'
       LIMIT  4;
 year | production | first_value
------+------------+-------------
 1965 |        920 |         920
 1966 |       1012 |         920
 1967 |       1106 |         920
 1968 |       1194 |         920
(4 rows)
```

Again, a sort order is needed to tell the system where the first value actually is. PostgreSQL will then put the same value into the last column. If you want to find the last value in the window, simply use the `last_value()` function instead of the `first_value()` function.

If you are not interested in the first or the last value but are looking for something in the middle, PostgreSQL provides the `nth_value()` function:

```
test=# SELECT year, production,
             nth_value(production, 3) OVER (ORDER BY year)
       FROM   t_oil
       WHERE  country = 'Canada';
 year | production | nth_value
------+------------+-----------
 1965 |        920 |
 1966 |       1012 |
 1967 |       1106 |      1106
 1968 |       1194 |      1106
 ...
```

In this case, the third value will be put into the last column. However, note that the first two rows are empty. The trouble is that, when PostgreSQL starts going through the data, the third value is not known yet. Therefore, `null` is added. The question now is, how can we make the time series more complete and replace those two null values with the data to come? Here is one way to do this:

```
test=# SELECT *, min(nth_value) OVER ()
FROM   (
           SELECT year, production,
                  nth_value(production, 3) OVER (ORDER BY year)
```

```
              FROM   t_oil
              WHERE   country = 'Canada'
          ) AS x
  LIMIT   4;
   year | production | nth_value | min
  -------+------------+-----------+------
   1965 |        920 |           | 1106
   1966 |       1012 |           | 1106
   1967 |       1106 |      1106 | 1106
   1968 |       1194 |      1106 | 1106
  (4 rows)
```

sub-select will create an incomplete time series. The SELECT clause on top of that will complete the data. The clue here is that completing the data might be more complex, and therefore sub-select might create a couple of opportunities to add more complex logic than just doing it in one step.

The row_number() function

The last function we will discuss in this section is the row_number() function, which can simply be used to return a virtual ID. Sounds simple, doesn't it? Here it is:

```
test=# SELECT country, production,
              row_number() OVER (ORDER BY production)
       FROM   t_oil
       LIMIT 3;
   country | production | row_number
  ---------+------------+------------
   Yemen   |         10 |          1
   Syria   |         21 |          2
   Yemen   |         26 |          3
  (3 rows)
```

The row_number() function simply assigns a number to the row. There are definitely no duplicates. The interesting point here is that this can be done even without an order (in case it is not relevant to you):

```
test=# SELECT country, production,
              row_number() OVER()
       FROM   t_oil
       LIMIT 3;
   country | production | row_number
  ---------+------------+------------
   USA     |       9014 |          1
   USA     |       9579 |          2
```

```
USA      |      10219 |        3
(3 rows)
```

Writing your own aggregates

In this book, you will learn about most of the on-board functions provided by PostgreSQL. However, what SQL provides might not be enough for you. The good news is that it is possible to add your own aggregates to the database engine. In this section, you will learn how that can be done.

Creating simple aggregates

For this example, the goal is to solve a very simple problem. If a customer takes a taxi, they usually have to pay for getting in the taxi—for example, €2.50. Now, let's assume that for each kilometer, the customer has to pay €2.20. The question now is, what is the total price of a trip?

Of course, this example is simple enough to solve without a custom aggregate; however, let's see how it works. First, some test data needs to be created:

```
test=# CREATE TABLE t_taxi (trip_id int, km numeric);
CREATE TABLE
test=# INSERT INTO t_taxi
  VALUES (1, 4.0), (1, 3.2), (1, 4.5), (2, 1.9), (2, 4.5);
INSERT 0 5
```

To create aggregates, PostgreSQL offers the CREATE AGGREGATE command. The syntax of this command has become so powerful and long over time that it doesn't make sense anymore to include the output of it here in this book. Instead, I recommend going to the PostgreSQL documentation, which can be found at https://www.postgresql.org/docs/devel/static/sql-createaggregate.html.

The first thing that's needed when writing an aggregate is a function, which is called for every line. It will take an intermediate value, and data that's taken from the line processed. Here is an example:

```
test=# CREATE FUNCTION taxi_per_line (numeric, numeric)
RETURNS numeric AS
$$
  BEGIN
    RAISE NOTICE 'intermediate: %, per row:  %', $1, $2;
    RETURN $1 + $2*2.2;
```

```
    END;
$$
LANGUAGE 'plpgsql';
CREATE FUNCTION
```

Now, it is already possible to create a simple aggregate:

```
test=# CREATE AGGREGATE taxi_price (numeric)
(
    INITCOND = 2.5,
    SFUNC = taxi_per_line,
    STYPE = numeric
);
CREATE AGGREGATE
```

As we stated previously, every trip starts at €2.50 for getting in the taxi, which is defined by INITCOND (the init condition). It represents the starting value for each group. Then, a function is called for each line in the group. In my example, this function is taxi_per_line and has already been defined. As you can see, it needs two parameters. The first parameter is an intermediate value. Those additional parameters are the parameters that are passed to the function by the user.

The following statement shows what data is passed, when, and how:

```
test=# SELECT trip_id, taxi_price(km) FROM t_taxi GROUP  BY 1;
psql: NOTICE:   intermediate: 2.5, per row:   4.0
psql: NOTICE:   intermediate: 11.30, per row:   3.2
psql: NOTICE:   intermediate: 18.34, per row:   4.5
psql: NOTICE:   intermediate: 2.5, per row:   1.9
psql: NOTICE:   intermediate: 6.68, per row:   4.5
psql: trip_id  | taxi_price
---------+------------
       1 |     28.24
       2 |     16.58
(2 rows)
```

The system starts with trip 1 and €2.50 (the init condition). Then, 4 kilometers are added. Overall, the price is now *2.50 + 4 x 2.2*. Then, the next line is added, which will add *3.2 x 2.2* and so on. The first trip, therefore, costs €28.24.

Then, the next trip starts. Again, there is a fresh init condition, and PostgreSQL will call one function per line.

In PostgreSQL, an aggregate can automatically be used as a windowing function too. No additional steps are needed—you can use the aggregate directly:

```
test=# SELECT *, taxi_price(km) OVER (PARTITION BY trip_id ORDER BY km)
    FROM  t_taxi;
psql: NOTICE:   intermediate: 2.5,   per row:   3.2
psql: NOTICE:   intermediate: 9.54,  per row:   4.0
psql: NOTICE:   intermediate: 18.34, per row:   4.5
psql: NOTICE:   intermediate: 2.5,   per row:   1.9
psql: NOTICE:   intermediate: 6.68,  per row:   4.5
 trip_id | km  | taxi_price
---------+-----+------------
    1    | 3.2 |        9.54
    1    | 4.0 |       18.34
    1    | 4.5 |       28.24
    2    | 1.9 |        6.68
    2    | 4.5 |       16.58

(5 rows)
```

What the query does is give us the price up to a given point on the trip.

The aggregate we have defined will call one function per line. However, how would users be able to calculate an average? Without adding a FINALFUNC function, calculations like that are not possible. To demonstrate how FINALFUNC works, we must extend our example. Suppose the customer wants to give the taxi driver a 10% tip as soon as they leave the taxi. That 10% has to be added at the end, as soon as the total price is known. This is the point where FINALFUNC kicks in. Here is how it works:

```
test=# DROP AGGREGATE taxi_price(numeric);
DROP AGGREGATE
```

First of all, the old aggregate is dropped. Then, FINALFUNC is defined. It will get the intermediate result as a parameter and do its magic:

```
test=# CREATE FUNCTION taxi_final (numeric)
            RETURNS numeric AS
$$
    SELECT $1 * 1.1;
$$
LANGUAGE sql IMMUTABLE;
CREATE FUNCTION
```

The calculation is pretty simple, in this case—as we stated previously, 10% is added to the final sum.

Once the function has been deployed, it is already possible to recreate the aggregate:

```
test=# CREATE AGGREGATE taxi_price (numeric)
(
    INITCOND = 2.5,
    SFUNC   = taxi_per_line,
    STYPE   = numeric,
    FINALFUNC = taxi_final
);
CREATE AGGREGATE
```

Finally, the price will simply be a bit higher than before:

```
test=# SELECT trip_id, taxi_price(km) FROM t_taxi GROUP BY 1;
psql: NOTICE:  intermediate: 2.5, per row: 4.0
...
 trip_id | taxi_price
---------+------------
       1 |     31.064
       2 |     18.238
(2 rows)
```

PostgreSQL takes care of all of the grouping and so on automatically.

For simple calculations, simple data types can be used for the intermediate result. However, not all operations can be done by just passing simple numbers and text around. Fortunately, PostgreSQL allows the use of composite data types, which can be used as intermediate results.

Imagine that you want to calculate an average of some data, maybe a time series. An intermediate result might look as follows:

```
test=# CREATE TYPE my_intermediate AS (c int4, s numeric);
CREATE TYPE
```

Feel free to compose any arbitrary type that serves your purpose. Just pass it as the first parameter and add data as additional parameters as needed.

Adding support for parallel queries

What you have just seen is a simple aggregate, which has no support for parallel queries and so on. To solve those challenges, the following couple of examples are all about improvements and speedups.

When creating an aggregate, you can optionally define the following things:

```
[ , PARALLEL = { SAFE   | RESTRICTED | UNSAFE } ]
```

By default, an aggregate does not support parallel queries. For performance reasons, it does make sense, however, to explicitly state what the aggregate is capable of:

- UNSAFE: In this mode, no parallel queries are allowed.
- RESTRICTED: In this mode, the aggregate can be executed in parallel mode, but the execution is limited to the parallel group leader.
- SAFE: In this mode, it provides full support for parallel queries.

If you mark a function as SAFE, you have to keep in mind that the function must not have side effects. An execution order must not have an impact on the result of the query. Only then should PostgreSQL be allowed to execute operations in parallel. Examples of functions without side effects would be sin(x) and length(s). The IMMUTABLE functions are good candidates for this since they're guaranteed to return the same result given the same inputs. The STABLE function can work if certain restrictions apply.

Improving efficiency

The aggregates we've defined so far can already achieve quite a lot. However, if you are using sliding windows, the number of function calls will simply explode. Here is what happens:

```
test=# SELECT taxi_price(x::numeric)
                    OVER (ROWS BETWEEN 0 FOLLOWING AND 3 FOLLOWING)
FROM generate_series(1, 5) AS x;
psql: NOTICE:   intermediate: 2.5,   per row:  1
psql: NOTICE:   intermediate: 4.7,   per row:  2
psql: NOTICE:   intermediate: 9.1,   per row:  3
psql: NOTICE:   intermediate: 15.7,  per row:  4
psql: NOTICE:   intermediate: 2.5,   per row:  2
psql: NOTICE:   intermediate: 6.9,   per row:  3
psql: NOTICE:   intermediate: 13.5,  per row:  4
psql: NOTICE:   intermediate: 22.3,  per row:  5
...
```

For every line, PostgreSQL will process the full window. If the sliding window is large, efficiency will fall. To fix that, our aggregates can be extended. Before that, the old aggregate can be dropped:

```
DROP AGGREGATE taxi_price(numeric);
```

Basically, two functions are needed. The `msfunc` function will add the next row in the window to the intermediate result:

```
CREATE FUNCTION taxi_msfunc(numeric, numeric)
   RETURNS numeric AS
$$
   BEGIN
        RAISE  NOTICE 'taxi_msfunc called with % and %', $1, $2;
        RETURN $1 + $2;
   END;
$$ LANGUAGE 'plpgsql' STRICT;
```

The `minvfunc` function will remove the value falling out of the window from the intermediate result:

```
CREATE FUNCTION taxi_minvfunc(numeric, numeric) RETURNS numeric AS
$$
BEGIN
   RAISE  NOTICE 'taxi_minvfunc called with % and %', $1, $2;
   RETURN $1 - $2;
END;
$$
LANGUAGE 'plpgsql' STRICT;
```

In this example, all we do is add and subtract. In a more sophisticated example, the calculation can be arbitrarily complex.

The following statement shows how the aggregate can be recreated:

```
CREATE AGGREGATE taxi_price (numeric)
(
   INITCOND = 0,
   STYPE  = numeric,
   SFUNC  = taxi_per_line,
   MSFUNC = taxi_msfunc,
   MINVFUNC = taxi_minvfunc,
   MSTYPE = numeric
);
```

Let's run the same query again now:

```
test#  SELECT taxi_price(x::numeric)
                  OVER  (ROWS  BETWEEN 0 FOLLOWING AND 3 FOLLOWING)
FROM      generate_series(1, 5) AS x;
psql: NOTICE:   taxi_msfunc called with 1 and 2
psql: NOTICE:   taxi_msfunc called with 3 and 3
psql: NOTICE:   taxi_msfunc called with 6 and 4
psql: NOTICE:   taxi_minvfunc called with 10 and 1
```

```
psql: NOTICE:   taxi_msfunc called with 9 and 5
psql: NOTICE:   taxi_minfunc called with 14 and 2
psql: NOTICE:   taxi_minfunc called with 12 and 3
psql: NOTICE:   taxi_minfunc called with 9 and 4
```

The number of function calls has decreased dramatically. Only a fixed handful of calls per row have to be performed. There is no longer any need to calculate the same frame all over again.

Writing hypothetical aggregates

Writing aggregates is not hard and can be highly beneficial for performing more complex operations. In this section, the plan is to write a hypothetical aggregate, which has already been discussed in this chapter.

Implementing hypothetical aggregates is not too different from writing normal aggregates. The really hard part is figuring out when to actually use one. To make this section as easy to understand as possible, I have decided to include a trivial example: given a specific order, what would the result be if we added abc to the end of the string?

Here is how it works:

```
CREATE AGGREGATE name   ( [ [ argmode ] [ argname ] arg_data_type [ , ... ]
]
    ORDER  BY [ argmode ] [ argname ] arg_data_type
    [ , ...])
(
    SFUNC  = sfunc,
    STYPE  = state_data_type
    [ , SSPACE = state_data_size ] [ , FINALFUNC = ffunc  ]
    [ , FINALFUNC_EXTRA ]
    [ , INITCOND = initial_condition ]
    [ , PARALLEL = { SAFE  | RESTRICTED | UNSAFE } ] [ , HYPOTHETICAL ]
)
```

Two functions will be needed. The sfunc function will be called for every line:

```
CREATE FUNCTION hypo_sfunc(text, text)
    RETURNS text  AS
$$
    BEGIN
         RAISE  NOTICE 'hypo_sfunc called with  % and %', $1, $2;
         RETURN $1 || $2;
    END;
$$ LANGUAGE 'plpgsql';
```

Two parameters will be passed to the procedure. The logic is the same as it was previously. Just like we did earlier, a final function call can be defined:

```
CREATE FUNCTION hypo_final(text, text,  text)
   RETURNS text  AS
$$
   BEGIN
        RAISE  NOTICE 'hypo_final called with  %, %, and %',
              $1, $2, $3;
        RETURN $1 || $2;
   END;
$$ LANGUAGE 'plpgsql';
```

Once these functions are in place, the hypothetical aggregate can be created:

```
CREATE AGGREGATE whatif(text ORDER  BY text)
(
   INITCOND = 'START',
   STYPE  = text,
   SFUNC  = hypo_sfunc,
   FINALFUNC = hypo_final,
   FINALFUNC_EXTRA = true,
   HYPOTHETICAL
);
```

Note that the aggregate has been marked as hypothetical so that PostgreSQL will know what kind of aggregate it actually is.

Now that the aggregate has been created, it is possible to run it:

```
test=# SELECT whatif('abc'::text) WITHIN GROUP  (ORDER BY id::text)
        FROM     generate_series(1, 3) AS id;
psql: NOTICE:  hypo_sfunc called with  START  and 1
psql: NOTICE:  hypo_sfunc called with  START1 and 2
psql: NOTICE:  hypo_sfunc called with  START12 and 3
psql: NOTICE:  hypo_final called with  START123, abc,  and <NULL>
   whatif
--------------
 START123abc
(1 row)
```

The key to understanding all of these aggregates is really to fully see when each kind of function is called and how the overall machinery works.

Summary

In this chapter, you learned about the advanced features provided by SQL. On top of simple aggregates, PostgreSQL provides ordered sets, grouping sets, windowing functions, and recursions, as well as an interface that you can use to create custom aggregates. The advantage of running aggregations in the database is that code is easy to write, and a database engine will usually have an edge when it comes to efficiency.

In Chapter 5, *Log Files and System Statistics*, we will turn our attention to more administrative tasks, such as handling log files, understanding system statistics, and implementing monitoring.

5
Log Files and System Statistics

In Chapter 4, *Handling Advanced SQL*, you learned about advanced SQL and ways of viewing SQL in a different light. However, database work doesn't only consist of hacking up fancy SQL. Sometimes, it is about keeping things running in a professional manner. To do that, it is highly important to keep an eye on system statistics, log files, and so on. Monitoring is the key to running databases professionally. Fortunately, PostgreSQL has many features that can help you monitor your databases, and you will learn how to use them in this chapter.

In this chapter, you will learn about the following topics:

- Gathering runtime statistics
- Creating log files
- Gathering important information
- Making sense of database statistics

By the end of this chapter, you will be able to configure PostgreSQL's logging infrastructure properly and take care of log files in the most professional way possible.

Gathering runtime statistics

The first thing you really have to learn about is understanding what PostgreSQL's onboard statistics have got to offer and using them. In my personal opinion, there is no way to improve performance and reliability without collecting the necessary data to make prudent decisions.

This section will guide you through PostgreSQL's runtime statistics and explain how you can extract more runtime information from your database setups.

Working with PostgreSQL system views

PostgreSQL offers a large set of system views that allow administrators and developers alike to take a deep look into what is really going on in their system. The trouble is that many people actually collect all this data but cannot make real sense out of it. The general rule is this: there is no point in drawing a graph for something you don't understand anyway. Therefore, the goal of this section is to shed some light on what PostgreSQL has to offer to hopefully make it easier for people to take advantage of what is there for them to use.

Checking live traffic

Whenever I inspect a system, there is a system view I prefer to inspect first before digging deeper. I am, of course, talking about `pg_stat_activity`. The idea behind this view is to give you a chance to figure out what is going on right now.

Here's how it works:

```
test=# \d pg_stat_activity
  View "pg_catalog.pg_stat_activity"
  Column           |           Type            | Collation | Nullable |
  Default
------------------+---------------------------+-----------+----------+------
---
 datid            | oid                       |           |          |
 datname          | name                      |           |          |
 pid              | integer                   |           |          |
 usesysid         | oid                       |           |          |
 usename          | name                      |           |          |
 application_name | text                      |           |          |
 client_addr      | inet                      |           |          |
 client_hostname  | text                      |           |          |
 client_port      | integer                   |           |          |
 backend_start    | timestamp with time zone  |           |          |
 xact_start       | timestamp with time zone  |           |          |
 query_start      | timestamp with time zone  |           |          |
 state_change     | timestamp with time zone  |           |          |
 wait_event_type  | text                      |           |          |
 wait_event       | text                      |           |          |
 state            | text                      |           |          |
 backend_xid      | xid                       |           |          |
 backend_xmin     | xid                       |           |          |
 query            | text                      |           |          |
 backend_type     | text                      |           |          |
```

Furthermore, `pg_stat_activity` will provide you with one line per active connection. You will see the internal object ID of the database (`datid`), the name of the database somebody is connected to, and the process ID serving this connection (`pid`). On top of that, PostgreSQL will tell you who is connected (`usename`; note the missing `r`) and that user's internal object ID (`usesysid`).

Then, there is a field called `application_name`, which is worth commenting on a bit more extensively. In general, `application_name` can be set freely by the end user, as follows:

```
test=# SET application_name TO 'www.cybertec-postgresql.com';
SET
test=# SHOW application_name;
   application_name
----------------------
 www.cybertec-postgresql.com
(1 row)
```

The point is this: let's assume that thousands of connections are coming from a single IP. Can you, as the administrator, tell what a specific connection is really doing right now? You may not know all the SQL stuff off by heart. If the client is kind enough to set an `application_name` parameter, it is a lot easier to see what the purpose of a connection really is. In my example, I have set the name to the domain the connection belongs to. This makes it easy to find similar connections that may cause similar problems.

The next three columns (`client_`) will tell you where a connection comes from. PostgreSQL will show IP addresses and (if it has been configured to) even hostnames.

Additionally, `backend_start` will tell you when a certain connection has started and `xact_start` indicates when a transaction has started. Then, there is `query_start` and `state_change`. Back in the dark old days, PostgreSQL would only show active queries. During a time when queries took a lot longer than today, this made sense. On modern hardware, OLTP queries may only consume a fraction of a millisecond, and therefore it is hard to catch such queries doing potential harm. The solution was to either show the active query or the previous query that was executed by the connection you are looking at.

Here's what you may see:

```
test=# SELECT pid, query_start, state_change, state, query
FROM   pg_stat_activity;
...
-[ RECORD 2 ] +----------------------------------------------
pid           | 28001
query_start   | 2018-11-05 10:03:57.575593+01
```

```
state_change | 2018-11-05 10:03:57.575595+01
state        | active
query        | SELECT pg_sleep(10000000);
```

In this case, you can see that `pg_sleep` is being executed in a second connection. As soon as this query is terminated, the output will change, as shown in the following code:

```
-[ RECORD 2 ]+--------------------------------------------
pid          | 28001
query_start  | 2018-11-05 10:03:57.575593+01
state_change | 2018-11-05 10:05:10.388522+01
state        | idle
query        | SELECT pg_sleep(10000000);
```

The query is now marked as idle. The difference between `state_change` and `query_start` is the time the query needs to execute. Therefore, `pg_stat_activity` will give you a great overview of what's going on in your system right now. The new `state_change` field makes it a lot more likely for us to spot expensive queries.

The question now is this: once you have found bad queries, how can you actually get rid of them? PostgreSQL provides two functions to take care of these things: `pg_cancel_backend` and `pg_terminate_backend`. The `pg_cancel_backend` function will terminate the query but will leave the connection in place. The `pg_terminate_backend` function is a bit more radical and will kill the entire database connection, along with the query.

If you want to disconnect all the other users but yourself, here is how you can do this:

```
test=# SELECT pg_terminate_backend(pid)
       FROM   pg_stat_activity
       WHERE pid <> pg_backend_pid()
             AND backend_type = 'client backend';

 pg_terminate_backend
----------------------
 t
 t
(2 row)
```

If you happen to be kicked out, the following message will be displayed:

```
test=# SELECT pg_sleep(10000000);
psql: FATAL: terminating connection due to administrator command server
closed the connection unexpectedly
This probably means that the server terminated abnormally before or while
processing the request. The
  connection to the server was lost. Attempting reset: succeeded.
```

Only `psql` will try to reconnect. This is not true for most other clients
– especially not for client libraries.

Inspecting databases

Once you have inspected the active database connections, you can dig deeper and inspect database-level statistics. `pg_stat_database` will return one line per database inside your PostgreSQL instance.

This is what you will find there:

```
test=# \d pg_stat_database
                      View "pg_catalog.pg_stat_database"
         Column          |           Type            | Collation | Nullable |
Default
-------------------------+---------------------------+-----------+----------+-
--------
 datid                   | oid                       |           |          |
 datname                 | name                      |           |          |
 numbackends             | integer                   |           |          |
 xact_commit             | bigint                    |           |          |
 xact_rollback           | bigint                    |           |          |
 blks_read               | bigint                    |           |          |
 blks_hit                | bigint                    |           |          |
 tup_returned            | bigint                    |           |          |
 tup_fetched             | bigint                    |           |          |
 tup_inserted            | bigint                    |           |          |
 tup_updated             | bigint                    |           |          |
 tup_deleted             | bigint                    |           |          |
 conflicts               | bigint                    |           |          |
 temp_files              | bigint                    |           |          |
 temp_bytes              | bigint                    |           |          |
 deadlocks               | bigint                    |           |          |
 checksum_failures       | bigint                    |           |          |
 checksum_last_failure   | timestamp with time zone  |           |          |
 blk_read_time           | double precision          |           |          |
 blk_write_time          | double precision          |           |          |
 stats_reset             | timestamp with time zone  |           |          |
```

Next to the database ID and the database name is a column called `numbackends`, which shows the number of database connections that are currently open.

Then, there's `xact_commit` and `xact_rollback`. These two columns indicate whether your application tends to commit or roll back. `blks_hit` and `blks_read` will tell you about cache hits and cache misses. When inspecting these two columns, keep in mind that we are mostly talking about shared buffer hits and shared buffer misses. At the database level, there is no reasonable way to distinguish between filesystem cache hits and real disk hits. At Cybertec (`https://www.cybertec-postgresql.com`), we like to see if there are disk wait and cache misses at the same time in `pg_stat_database` to get an idea of what really goes on in the system.

The `tup_` columns will tell you whether there is a lot of reading or a lot of writing going on in your system.

Then, we have `temp_files` and `temp_bytes`. These two columns are of incredible importance because they will tell you whether your database has to write temporary files to disk, which will inevitably slow down operations. What can be the reasons for high temporary file usage? The major reasons are as follows:

- **Poor settings**: If your `work_mem` settings are too low, there is no way to do anything in RAM, and therefore PostgreSQL will go to disk.
- **Stupid operations**: It happens quite frequently that people torture their system with fairly expensive and pointless queries. If you see many temporary files on an OLTP system, consider checking for expensive queries.
- **Indexing and other administrative tasks**: Once in a while, indexes may be created or people may run DDLs. These operations can lead to temporary file I/O but are not necessarily considered a problem (in many cases).

In short, temporary files can occur, even if your system is perfectly fine. However, it definitely makes sense to keep an eye on them and ensure that temporary files are not needed frequently.

Finally, there are two more important fields: `blk_read_time` and `blk_write_time`. By default, these two fields are empty and no data is collected. The idea behind these fields is to give you a way of seeing how much time was spent on I/O. The reason these fields are empty is that `track_io_timing` is off by default. This is for a good reason. Imagine that you want to check how long it takes to read 1 million blocks. To do that, you have to call the time function in your `C` library twice, which leads to 2 million additional function calls just to read 8 GB of data. It really depends on the speed of your system as to whether this will lead to a lot of overhead or not.

Fortunately, there is a tool that helps you determine how expensive the timing is, as shown in the following code block:

```
[hs@zenbook ~]$ pg_test_timing
Testing timing overhead for 3 seconds.
Per loop time including overhead: 23.16   nsec
Histogram of timing durations:
```

< usec %	of total	count
1	97.70300	126549189
2	2.29506	2972668
4	0.00024	317
8	0.00008	101
16	0.00160	2072
32	0.00000	5
64	0.00000	6
128	0.00000	4
256	0.00000	0
512	0.00000	0
1024	0.00000	4
2048	0.00000	2

In my case, the overhead of turning `track_io_timing` on for a session in the `postgresql.conf` file is around 23 nanoseconds, which is fine. Professional high-end servers can provide you with numbers as low as 14 nanoseconds, while really bad virtualization can return values of up to 1,400 nanoseconds or even 1,900 nanoseconds. If you are using a cloud service, you can expect around 100-120 nanoseconds (in most cases). If you are ever confronted with four-digit values, measuring the I/O timing may lead to real measurable overhead, which will slow down your system. The general rule is this: on real hardware, timing is not an issue; on virtual systems, check it out before you turn it on.

It is also possible to turn things on selectively by using ALTER DATABASE, ALTER USER, and so on.

Inspecting tables

Once you have gained an overview of what's going on in your databases, it may be a good idea to dig deeper and see what's going on in individual tables. Two system views are here to help you: `pg_stat_user_tables` and `pg_statio_user_tables`.

Here is the first one:

```
test=# \d pg_stat_user_tables
                    View "pg_catalog.pg_stat_user_tables"
          Column          |            Type            | Collation | Nullable |
Default
--------------------------+----------------------------+-----------+----------+---
------
 relid                    | oid                        |           |          |
 schemaname               | name                       |           |          |
 relname                  | name                       |           |          |
 seq_scan                 | bigint                     |           |          |
 seq_tup_read             | bigint                     |           |          |
 idx_scan                 | bigint                     |           |          |
 idx_tup_fetch            | bigint                     |           |          |
 n_tup_ins                | bigint                     |           |          |
 n_tup_upd                | bigint                     |           |          |
 n_tup_del                | bigint                     |           |          |
 n_tup_hot_upd            | bigint                     |           |          |
 n_live_tup               | bigint                     |           |          |
 n_dead_tup               | bigint                     |           |          |
 n_mod_since_analyze      | bigint                     |           |          |
 last_vacuum              | timestamp with time zone   |           |          |
 last_autovacuum          | timestamp with time zone   |           |          |
 last_analyze             | timestamp with time zone   |           |          |
 last_autoanalyze         | timestamp with time zone   |           |          |
 vacuum_count             | bigint                     |           |          |
 autovacuum_count         | bigint                     |           |          |
 analyze_count            | bigint                     |           |          |
 autoanalyze_count        | bigint                     |           |          |
```

By my judgment, `pg_stat_user_tables` is one of the most important but also one of the most misunderstood or even ignored system views. I have a feeling that many people read it but fail to extract the full potential of what can really be seen here. When used properly, `pg_stat_user_tables` can, in some cases, be nothing short of a revelation.

Before we dig into the interpretation of data, it is important to understand which fields are actually there. First of all, there is one entry for each table, which will show us the number of sequential scans that happened on the table (`seq_scan`). Then, we have `seq_tup_read`, which tells us how many tuples the system has to read during those sequential scans.

Remember the `seq_tup_read` column; it contains vital information that can help you find performance problems.

Then, `idx_scan` is next on the list. It will show us how often an index was used for this table. PostgreSQL will also show us how many rows those scans returned. Then, there are a couple of columns, starting with `n_tup_`. These will tell us how much we inserted, updated, and deleted. The most important thing here is related to `HOT UPDATE`. When running an `UPDATE`, PostgreSQL has to copy a row to ensure that `ROLLBACK` will work correctly. `HOT UPDATE` is pretty good because it allows PostgreSQL to ensure that a row doesn't have to leave a block.

The copy of the row stays inside the same block, which is beneficial for performance in general. A fair amount of `HOT UPDATE` indicates that you are on the right track in the case of an intense `UPDATE` workload. The perfect ratio between normal and `HOT UPDATE` cannot be stated here for all use cases. People have really got to think for themselves to figure out which workload benefits from many in-place operations. The general rule is this: the more `UPDATE`-intense your workload is, the better it is to have many `HOT UPDATE` clauses.

Finally, there are some `VACUUM` statistics, which mostly speak for themselves.

Making sense of pg_stat_user_tables

Reading all of this data may be interesting; however, unless you are able to make sense out of it, it is pretty pointless. One way to use `pg_stat_user_tables` is to detect which tables may need an index. One way to find this out is to use the following query, which has served me well over the years:

```
SELECT schemaname, relname, seq_scan, seq_tup_read,
       seq_tup_read / seq_scan AS avg, idx_scan
FROM pg_stat_user_tables
WHERE seq_scan > 0
ORDER BY seq_tup_read DESC LIMIT 25;
```

The idea is to find large tables that have been used frequently in a sequential scan. Those tables will naturally come out on the top of the list to bless us with enormously high `seq_tup_read` values, which can be mind-blowing.

> Work your way from top to bottom and look for expensive scans. Keep in mind that sequential scans are not necessarily bad. They appear naturally in backups, analytical statements, and so on without causing any harm. However, if you are running large sequential scans all the time, your performance will go down the drain.

Note that this query is really golden—it will help you spot tables with missing indexes. My practical experience, which is nearly two decades' worth, has shown again and again that missing indexes are the single most important reason for bad performance. Therefore, the query you are looking at is literally gold.

Once you are done looking for potentially missing indexes, consider taking a brief look at the caching behavior of your tables. To facilitate this, `pg_statio_user_tables` contains information about all kinds of things, such as the caching behavior of the table (`heap_blks_`), of your indexes (`idx_blks_`), and of **The Oversized-Attribute Storage Technique (TOAST)** tables. Finally, you can find out more about TID scans, which are usually irrelevant to the overall performance of the system:

```
test=# \d pg_statio_user_tables
          View "pg_catalog.pg_statio_user_tables"
      Column       |  Type   | Collation | Nullable | Default
-------------------+---------+-----------+----------+---------
 relid             | oid     |           |          |
 schemaname        | name    |           |          |
 relname           | name    |           |          |
 heap_blks_read    | bigint  |           |          |
 heap_blks_hit     | bigint  |           |          |
 idx_blks_read     | bigint  |           |          |
 idx_blks_hit      | bigint  |           |          |
 toast_blks_read   | bigint  |           |          |
 toast_blks_hit    | bigint  |           |          |
 tidx_blks_read    | bigint  |           |          |
 tidx_blks_hit     | bigint  |           |          |
```

Although `pg_statio_user_tables` contains important information, it is usually the case that `pg_stat_user_tables` is more likely to provide you with a really relevant insight (such as a missing index and so on).

Digging into indexes

While `pg_stat_user_tables` is important for spotting missing indexes, it is sometimes necessary to find indexes that shouldn't really exist. Recently, I was on a business trip to Germany and discovered a system that contained mostly pointless indexes (74% of the total storage consumption). While this may not be a problem if your database is really small, it does make a difference in the case of large systems—having hundreds of gigabytes of pointless indexes can seriously harm your overall performance.

Fortunately, `pg_stat_user_indexes` can be inspected to find those pointless indexes:

```
test=# \d pg_stat_user_indexes
          View "pg_catalog.pg_stat_user_indexes"
     Column      |  Type   | Collation | Nullable | Default
-----------------+---------+-----------+----------+---------
 relid           | oid     |           |          |
 indexrelid      | oid     |           |          |
 schemaname      | name    |           |          |
 relname         | name    |           |          |
 indexrelname    | name    |           |          |
 idx_scan        | bigint  |           |          |
 idx_tup_read    | bigint  |           |          |
 idx_tup_fetch   | bigint  |           |          |
```

The view tells us how often every index on every table in every schema has been used (`idx_scan`). To enrich this view a bit, I suggest using the following SQL query:

```
SELECT schemaname, relname, indexrelname, idx_scan,
  pg_size_pretty(pg_relation_size(indexrelid)) AS idx_size,
  pg_size_pretty(sum(pg_relation_size(indexrelid))
  OVER (ORDER BY idx_scan, indexrelid)) AS total
FROM pg_stat_user_indexes
ORDER BY 6 ;
```

The output of this statement is very useful. It doesn't only contain information about how often an index was used—it also tells us how much space has been wasted for each index. Finally, it adds up all the space consumption in column 6. You can now go through the table and rethink all of those indexes that have rarely been used. It is hard to come up with a general rule regarding when to drop an index, so some manual checking makes a lot of sense.

Don't just blindly drop indexes. In some cases, indexes are simply not used because end users use the application differently to what's expected. If an end user changes (a new secretary is hired and so on), an index may very well turn into a useful object again.

There is also a view called `pg_statio_user_indexes`, which contains caching information about an index. Although it is interesting, it usually doesn't contain information that leads to big leaps forward.

Tracking the background worker

In this section, we will take a look at the background writer statistics. As you may already know, database connections will, in many cases, not write blocks to disks directly. Instead, data is written by the background writer process or by the checkpointer.

To see how data is written, inspect the `pg_stat_bgwriter` view:

```
test=# \d pg_stat_bgwriter
                    View "pg_catalog.pg_stat_bgwriter"
         Column         |            Type             | Collation | Nullable |
Default
------------------------+-----------------------------+-----------+----------+-
--------
 checkpoints_timed      | bigint                      |           |          |
 checkpoints_req        | bigint                      |           |          |
 checkpoint_write_time  | double precision            |           |          |
 checkpoint_sync_time   | double precision            |           |          |
 buffers_checkpoint     | bigint                      |           |          |
 buffers_clean          | bigint                      |           |          |
 maxwritten_clean       | bigint                      |           |          |
 buffers_backend        | bigint                      |           |          |
 buffers_backend_fsync  | bigint                      |           |          |
 buffers_alloc          | bigint                      |           |          |
 stats_reset            | timestamp with time zone    |           |          |
```

What should first catch your attention here are the first two columns. Later in this book, you will learn that PostgreSQL will perform regular checkpoints, which are necessary to ensure that data has really made it to disk. If your checkpoints are too close to each other, `checkpoint_req` may point you in the right direction. If requested checkpoints are high, this may mean that a lot of data has been written and that checkpoints are always triggered because of high throughput. In addition to that, PostgreSQL will tell you about how much time is needed to write data during a checkpoint and the time needed to sync. In addition to that, `buffers_checkpoint` indicates how many buffers were written during the checkpoint and how many were written by the background writer (`buffers_clean`).

But there's more: `maxwritten_clean` tells us about the number of times the background writer stopped a cleaning scan because it had written too many buffers.

Finally, there's `buffers_backend` (the number of buffers directly written by a backend database connection), `buffers_backend_fsync` (the number of buffers flushed by a database connection), and `buffers_alloc` (contains the number of buffers allocated). In general, it isn't a good thing if database connections start to write their own stuff themselves.

Tracking, archiving, and streaming

In this section, we will take a look at some features related to replication and transaction log archiving. The first thing to inspect is pg_stat_archiver, which tells us about the archiver process moving the transaction log (WAL) from the main server to some backup device:

```
test=# \d pg_stat_archiver
                     View "pg_catalog.pg_stat_archiver"
        Column        |            Type          | Collation | Nullable |
Default
----------------------+--------------------------+-----------+----------+----
-----
 archived_count       | bigint                   |           |          |
 last_archived_wal    | text                     |           |          |
 last_archived_time   | timestamp with time zone |           |          |
 failed_count         | bigint                   |           |          |
 last_failed_wal      | text                     |           |          |
 last_failed_time     | timestamp with time zone |           |          |
 stats_reset          | timestamp with time zone |           |          |
```

Furthermore, pg_stat_archiver contains important information about your archiving process. First of all, it will inform you about the number of transaction log files that have been archived (archived_count). It will also know of the last file that was archived and when that happened (last_archived_wal and last_archived_time).

While knowing the number of WAL files is certainly interesting, it isn't really that important. Therefore, consider taking a look at failed_count and last_failed_wal. If your transaction log archiving failed, it will tell you about the latest file that failed and when that happened. It is recommended to keep an eye on those fields because otherwise, it may be possible that archiving will work without you even noticing.

If you are running a streaming replication, the following two views will be really important for you. The first one is called pg_stat_replication and will provide information about the streaming process from the master to the slave. One entry per WAL sender process will be visible. If there is no single entry, then this means there's no transaction log streaming going on, which may not be what you want.

Let's take a look at `pg_stat_replication`:

```
test=# \d pg_stat_replication
                  View "pg_catalog.pg_stat_replication"
        Column        |           Type           | Collation | Nullable |
Default
----------------------+--------------------------+-----------+----------+------
---
 pid                  | integer                  |           |          |
 usesysid             | oid                      |           |          |
 usename              | name                     |           |          |
 application_name     | text                     |           |          |
 client_addr          | inet                     |           |          |
 client_hostname      | text                     |           |          |
 client_port          | integer                  |           |          |
 backend_start        | timestamp with time zone |           |          |
 backend_xmin         | xid                      |           |          |
 state                | text                     |           |          |
 sent_lsn             | pg_lsn                   |           |          |
 write_lsn            | pg_lsn                   |           |          |
 flush_lsn            | pg_lsn                   |           |          |
 replay_lsn           | pg_lsn                   |           |          |
 write_lag            | interval                 |           |          |
 flush_lag            | interval                 |           |          |
 replay_lag           | interval                 |           |          |
 sync_priority        | integer                  |           |          |
 sync_state           | text                     |           |          |
```

Here, you will find columns that indicate the username that's connected via the streaming replication. Then, there's the application name, along with the connection data (`client_`). Here, PostgreSQL will tell us when the streaming connection started. In production, a young connection can point to a network problem or to something even worse (reliability issues and so on). The state column shows in which state the other side of the stream is. We will cover this in more detail in Chapter 10, *Making Sense of Backups and Replication*.

There are fields here telling us how much of the transaction log has been sent over the network connection (`sent_lsn`), how much has been sent to the kernel (`write_lsn`), how much has been flushed to disk (`flush_lsn`), and how much has already been replayed (`replay_lsn`). Finally, the sync status is listed. Since PostgreSQL 10.0, there are additional fields that already contain the time difference between the master and the slave. The `*_lag` fields contain intervals, which give some indication of the actual time difference between your servers.

While `pg_stat_replication` can be queried on the sending server of a replication setup, `pg_stat_wal_receiver` can be consulted on the receiving end. It provides similar information and allows this information to be extracted on the replica.

Here is the definition of the view:

```
test=# \d pg_stat_wal_receiver
                    View "pg_catalog.pg_stat_wal_receiver"
        Column          |            Type             | Collation | Nullable |
Default
------------------------+-----------------------------+-----------+----------+-
--------
 pid                    | integer                     |           |          |
 status                | text                        |           |          |
 receive_start_lsn      | pg_lsn                      |           |          |
 receive_start_tli      | integer                     |           |          |
 received_lsn           | pg_lsn                      |           |          |
 received_tli           | integer                     |           |          |
 last_msg_send_time     | timestamp with time zone    |           |          |
 last_msg_receipt_time  | timestamp with time zone    |           |          |
 latest_end_lsn         | pg_lsn                      |           |          |
 latest_end_time        | timestamp with time zone    |           |          |
 slot_name              | text                        |           |          |
 sender_host            | text                        |           |          |
 sender_port            | integer                     |           |          |
 conninfo               | text                        |           |          |
```

First of all, PostgreSQL will tell us the process ID of the WAL receiver process. Then, the view shows us the status of the connection in use. `receive_start_lsn` will tell us the transaction log position that was used when the WAL receiver was started. In addition to this, `receive_start_tli` contains the timeline that was in use when the WAL receiver was started. At some point, you may want to know the latest WAL position and timeline. To get those two numbers, use `received_lsn` and `received_tli`.

In the next two columns, there are two timestamps: `last_msg_send_time` and `last_msg_receipt_time`. The first one states when a message was last sent and when it was received.

`latest_end_lsn` contains the last transaction log position that was reported to the WAL sender process at `latest_end_time`. Then, there is the `slot_name` field and an obfuscated version of the connection information. In PostgreSQL 11, additional fields have been added—the `sender_host`, `sender_port`, and `conninfo` fields tell us about the host the WAL receiver is connected to.

Checking SSL connections

Many people running PostgreSQL use SSL to encrypt connections from the server to the client. More recent versions of PostgreSQL provide a view so that we can gain an overview of those encrypted connections, that is, `pg_stat_ssl`:

```
test=# \d pg_stat_ssl
              View "pg_catalog.pg_stat_ssl"
    Column     |  Type   | Collation | Nullable | Default
---------------+---------+-----------+----------+---------
 pid           | integer |           |          |
 ssl           | boolean |           |          |
 version       | text    |           |          |
 cipher        | text    |           |          |
 bits          | integer |           |          |
 compression   | boolean |           |          |
 client_dn     | text    |           |          |
 client_serial | numeric |           |          |
 issuer_dn     | text    |           |          |
```

Every process is represented by the process ID. If a connection uses SSL, the second column is set to `true`. The third and fourth columns will define the version, as well as the cipher. Finally, there's the number of bits that are used by the encryption algorithm, including an indicator of whether compression is used or not, as well as the **distinguished name (DN)** field from the client certificate.

Inspecting transactions in real time

Thus far, some statistics tables have been discussed. The idea behind all of them is to see what is going on in the entire system. But what if you are a developer who wants to inspect an individual transaction? `pg_stat_xact_user_tables` is here to help. It doesn't contain system-wide transactions; it only contains data about your current transaction. This is shown in the following code:

```
test=# \d pg_stat_xact_user_tables
          View "pg_catalog.pg_stat_xact_user_tables"
    Column     |  Type   | Collation | Nullable | Default
---------------+---------+-----------+----------+---------
 relid         | oid     |           |          |
 schemaname    | name    |           |          |
 relname       | name    |           |          |
 seq_scan      | bigint  |           |          |
 seq_tup_read  | bigint  |           |          |
 idx_scan      | bigint  |           |          |
 idx_tup_fetch | bigint  |           |          |
```

```
n_tup_ins      | bigint |           |           |
n_tup_upd      | bigint |           |           |
n_tup_del      | bigint |           |           |
n_tup_hot_upd  | bigint |           |           |
```

Therefore, developers can look into a transaction just before it commits to see whether it has caused any performance issues. It helps us distinguish the overall data from what has just been caused by our application.

The ideal way for application developers to use this view is to add a function call in the application before a commit to track what the transaction has done.

This data can then be inspected so that the output of the current transaction can be distinguished from the overall workload.

Tracking VACUUM and CREATE INDEX progress

In PostgreSQL 9.6, the community introduced a system view that many people have been waiting for. For many years, people have wanted to track the progress of a vacuum process to see how long things may take.

Due to this, pg_stat_progress_vacuum was invented to address this issue:

```
test=# \d pg_stat_progress_vacuum
        View "pg_catalog.pg_stat_progress_vacuum"
        Column       |  Type   | Collation | Nullable | Default
---------------------+---------+-----------+----------+---------
 pid                 | integer |           |          |
 datid               | oid     |           |          |
 datname             | name    |           |          |
 relid               | oid     |           |          |
 phase               | text    |           |          |
 heap_blks_total     | bigint  |           |          |
 heap_blks_scanned   | bigint  |           |          |
 heap_blks_vacuumed  | bigint  |           |          |
 index_vacuum_count  | bigint  |           |          |
 max_dead_tuples     | bigint  |           |          |
 num_dead_tuples     | bigint  |           |          |
```

Most of the columns speak for themselves and so I won't go too much into the details here. There are just a couple of things that should be kept in mind. First of all, the process is not linear—it can jump quite a bit. In addition to that, a vacuum is usually pretty fast, so progress can be rapid and hard to track.

Starting with PostgreSQL 12, there is also a way to see what CREATE INDEX is doing. pg_stat_progress_create_index is the counterpart to pg_progress_vacuum. Here is the definition of the system view:

```
test=# \d pg_stat_progress_create_index
  View "pg_catalog.pg_stat_progress_create_index"
        Column          |  Type    | Collation | Nullable | Default
------------------------+----------+-----------+----------+---------
 pid                    | integer  |           |          |
 datid                  | oid      |           |          |
 datname                | name     |           |          |
 relid                  | oid      |           |          |
 index_relid            | oid      |           |          |
 phase                  | text     |           |          |
 lockers_total          | bigint   |           |          |
 lockers_done           | bigint   |           |          |
 current_locker_pid     | bigint   |           |          |
 blocks_total           | bigint   |           |          |
 blocks_done            | bigint   |           |          |
 tuples_total           | bigint   |           |          |
 tuples_done            | bigint   |           |          |
 partitions_total       | bigint   |           |          |
 partitions_done        | bigint   |           |          |
```

The content of this table helps us get an idea of how far CREATE INDEX has proceeded. To show you what the content of this table looks like, I have created a fairly large table that can be indexed:

```
test=# CREATE TABLE t_index (x numeric);
CREATE TABLE
test=# INSERT INTO t_index
       SELECT * FROM generate_series(1, 50000000);
INSERT 0 50000000
test=# CREATE INDEX idx_numeric ON t_index (x);
CREATE INDEX
```

There are various phases during the index's creation. First, PostgreSQL has to scan the table you want to index, which is represented in the system view as follows:

```
test=# SELECT * FROM pg_stat_progress_create_index;
-[ RECORD 1 ]
------------------------+-------------------------------
 pid                    | 29191
 datid                  | 16410
 datname                | test
 relid                  | 24600
 index_relid            | 0
```

```
phase                   | building index: scanning table
lockers_total           | 0
lockers_done            | 0
current_locker_pid      | 0
blocks_total            | 221239
blocks_done             | 221239
tuples_total            | 0
tuples_done             | 0
partitions_total        | 0
partitions_done         | 0
```

Once this is done, PostgreSQL will actually build the real index, which can also be seen inside the system table, as shown in the following code listing:

```
test=# SELECT * FROM pg_stat_progress_create_index;
-[ RECORD 1 ]
-------------------+-----------------------------------------
pid                | 29191
datid              | 16410
datname            | test
relid              | 24600
index_relid        | 0
phase              | building index: loading tuples in tree
lockers_total      | 0
lockers_done       | 0
current_locker_pid | 0
blocks_total       | 0
blocks_done        | 0
tuples_total       | 50000000
tuples_done        | 4289774
partitions_total   | 0
partitions_done    | 0
```

In my listing, close to 10% of the loading process has been done, as shown in the `tuples_*` columns toward the end of the listing.

Using pg_stat_statements

Now that we've discussed the first couple of views, it's time to turn our attention to one of the most important views, which can be used to spot performance problems. I am, of course, speaking about `pg_stat_statements`. The idea is to have information about queries on your system. It helps us figure out which types of queries are slow and how often queries are called.

To use this module, we need to follow three steps:

1. Add pg_stat_statements to shared_preload_libraries in the postgresql.conf file.
2. Restart the database server.
3. Run CREATE EXTENSION pg_stat_statements in the databases of your choice.

Let's inspect the definition of the view:

```
test=# \d pg_stat_statements
                    View "public.pg_stat_statements"
        Column        |       Type       | Collation | Nullable | Default
----------------------+------------------+-----------+----------+---------
 userid               | oid              |           |          |
 dbid                 | oid              |           |          |
 queryid              | bigint           |           |          |
 query                | text             |           |          |
 calls                | bigint           |           |          |
 total_time           | double precision |           |          |
 min_time             | double precision |           |          |
 max_time             | double precision |           |          |
 mean_time            | double precision |           |          |
 stddev_time          | double precision |           |          |
 rows                 | bigint           |           |          |
 shared_blks_hit      | bigint           |           |          |
 shared_blks_read     | bigint           |           |          |
 shared_blks_dirtied  | bigint           |           |          |
 shared_blks_written  | bigint           |           |          |
 local_blks_hit       | bigint           |           |          |
 local_blks_read      | bigint           |           |          |
 local_blks_dirtied   | bigint           |           |          |
 local_blks_written   | bigint           |           |          |
 temp_blks_read       | bigint           |           |          |
 temp_blks_written    | bigint           |           |          |
 blk_read_time        | double precision |           |          |
 blk_write_time       | double precision |           |          |
```

Interestingly, pg_stat_statements provides simply fabulous information. For every user in every database, it provides one line per query. By default, it tracks 5,000 (this can be changed by setting pg_stat_statements.max).

Queries and parameters are separated. PostgreSQL will put placeholders into the query. This allows identical queries, which just use different parameters, to be aggregated. For example, SELECT ... FROM x WHERE y = 10 will be turned into SELECT ... FROM x WHERE y = ?.

For each query, PostgreSQL will tell us the total time it has consumed, along with the number of calls it has made. In more recent versions, `min_time`, `max_time`, `mean_time`, and `stddev` have been added. The standard deviation is especially noteworthy because it will tell us whether a query has stable or fluctuating runtimes. Unstable runtimes can occur for various reasons:

- If the data is not fully cached in RAM, queries that have to go to disk will take a lot longer than their cached counterparts.
- Different parameters can lead to different plans and totally different result sets.
- Concurrency and locking can have an impact.

PostgreSQL will also tell us about the caching behavior of a query. `shared_` columns shows us how many blocks came from the cache (`_hit`) or from the operating system (`_read`). If many blocks come from the operating system, the runtime of a query may fluctuate.

The next block of columns is all about local buffers. Local buffers are memory blocks that are allocated by the database connection directly.

On top of all this information, PostgreSQL provides information about temporary file I/O. Note that temporary file I/O will naturally happen when a large index is built or when some other large DDL is executed. However, temporary files are usually a very bad thing to have in OLTP as they will slow down the entire system by potentially blocking the disk. A high amount of temporary file I/O can point to some undesirable things. The following list contains my top three:

- Undesirable `work_mem` settings (OLTP)
- Suboptimal `maintenance_work_mem` settings (DDLs)
- Queries that shouldn't have been run in the first place

Finally, there are two fields containing information about I/O timing. By default, these two fields are empty. The reason for this is that measuring timing can involve quite a lot of overhead on some systems. Therefore, the default value for `track_io_timing` is `false`—remember to turn it on if you need this data.

Once the module has been enabled, PostgreSQL will be collecting data, and you can use the view.

Never run `SELECT * FROM pg_stat_statements` in front of a customer. It has been known that people have started pointing at queries. They happened to know and started to explain why, who, what, when, and so on. When you use this view, always create a sorted output so that the most relevant information can be seen instantly.

Here at Cybertec, we have found the following query very helpful for us to gain an overview of what's happening on the database server:

```
test=# SELECT round((100 * total_time / sum(total_time)
              OVER ())::numeric, 2) percent,
           round(total_time::numeric, 2) AS total,
           calls,
           round(mean_time::numeric, 2) AS mean,
           substring(query, 1, 40)
FROM  pg_stat_statements
ORDER BY total_time DESC
LIMIT 10;
 percent |   total   | calls  |  mean  | substring
---------+-----------+--------+--------+------------------------------------
   54.47 | 111289.11 | 122161 |   0.91 | UPDATE pgbench_branches SET
                                         bbalance = b
   43.01 |  87879.25 | 122161 |   0.72 | UPDATE pgbench_tellers SET
                                         tbalance = tb
    1.46 |   2981.06 | 122161 |   0.02 | UPDATE pgbench_accounts SET
                                         abalance = a
    0.50 |   1019.83 | 122161 |   0.01 | SELECT abalance FROM
                                         pgbench_accounts WH
    0.42 |    856.22 | 122161 |   0.01 | INSERT INTO pgbench_history
                                         (tid, bid, a
    0.04 |     85.63 |      1 |  85.63 | copy pgbench_accounts from
                                         stdin
    0.02 |     44.11 |      1 |  44.11 | vacuum analyze pgbench_accounts
    0.02 |     42.86 | 122161 |   0.00 | END;
    0.02 |     34.08 | 122171 |   0.00 | BEGIN;
    0.01 |     22.46 |      1 |  22.46 | alter table pgbench_accounts
                                                add primary
(10 rows)
```

The preceding code shows the top 10 queries and their runtime, including a percentage. It also makes sense to display the average execution time of the queries so that you can decide whether the runtime of those queries is too high or not.

Work your way down the list and inspect all the queries that seem to run too long on average.

Keep in mind that working through the top 1,000 queries is usually not worth it. In most cases, the first few queries are already responsible for most of the load on the system.

 In my example, I have used a substring to shorten the query so that it fits on one page. This makes no sense if you really want to see what is going on.

Remember that pg_stat_statements will, by default, cut off queries at 1024 bytes:

```
test=# SHOW track_activity_query_size;
 track_activity_query_size
---------------------------
 1024

(1 row)
```

Consider increasing this value to, say, 16,384. If your clients are running Java applications based on Hibernate, a larger value of track_activity_query_size will ensure that queries are not cut off before the interesting part is shown.

At this point, I want to use this situation to point out how important pg_stat_statements really is. It is by far the easiest way to track down performance problems. A slow query log can never be as useful as pg_stat_statements because a slow query log will only point to individual slow queries—it won't show us problems that are caused by tons of medium queries. Therefore, it is recommended to always turn this module on. The overhead is really small and in no way harms the overall performance of the system.

By default, 5,000 types of queries are tracked. In most reasonably sane applications, this will be enough.

To reset the data, consider using the following instruction:

```
test=# SELECT pg_stat_statements_reset();
 pg_stat_statements_reset
---------------------------

(1 row)
```

Creating log files

Now that we've taken a deep look at the system views provided by PostgreSQL, it's time to configure logging. Fortunately, PostgreSQL provides us with an easy way to work with log files and helps people set up a good configuration easily.

Collecting logs is important because it can point to errors and potential database problems.

The `postgresql.conf` file contains all the parameters you need so that you're provided with all the necessary information.

Configuring the postgresql.conf file

In this section, we will go through some of the most important entries in the `postgresql.conf` file that we can use in order to configure logging and see how logging can be used in the most beneficial way.

Before we get started, I want to say a few words about logging in PostgreSQL in general. On Unix systems, PostgreSQL will send log information to `stderr` by default. However, `stderr` is not a good place for logs to go because you will want to inspect the log stream at some point. Therefore, you should work through this chapter and adjust things to your needs.

Defining log destination and rotation

Let's go through the `postgresql.conf` file and see what can be done:

```
#------------------------------------------------------------------
# REPORTING AND LOGGING
#------------------------------------------------------------------

# - Where to Log -

#log_destination = 'stderr'
                        # Valid values are combinations of
                        # stderr, csvlog, syslog, and eventlog,
                        # depending on platform. csvlog
                        # requires logging_collector to be on.

# This is used when logging to stderr:
#logging_collector = off
                        # Enable capturing of stderr and csvlog
                        # into log files. Required to be on for
```

```
# csvlogs.
# (change requires restart)
```

The first configuration option defines how the log is processed. By default, it will go to stderr (on Unix). On Windows, the default is eventlog, which is the Windows onboard tool that's used to handle logging. Alternatively, you can choose to go with csvlog or syslog.

If you want to make PostgreSQL log files, you should go for stderr and turn the logging collector on. PostgreSQL will then create log files.

The logical question now is: what will the names of those log files be and where will those files be stored? Fortunately, postgresql.conf has the answer:

```
# These are only used if logging_collector is on:
#log_directory = 'pg_log'
                # directory where log files are written,
                # can be absolute or relative to PGDATA
#log_filename = 'postgresql-%Y-%m-%d_%H%M%S.log'
                # log file name pattern,
                # can include strftime() escapes
```

Furthermore, log_directory will tell the system where to store the log. If you are using an absolute path, you can explicitly configure where logs will go. If you prefer the logs to be in the PostgreSQL data directly, simply go for a relative path. The advantage of this is that the data directory will be self-contained, and you can move it without having to worry.

In the next step, you can define the filename PostgreSQL is supposed to use. PostgreSQL is very flexible and allows you to use all the shortcuts provided by strftime. To give you an idea of how powerful this feature is, a quick count on my platform reveals that strftime provides 43 (!) placeholders to create the filename. Everything people usually need is certainly possible.

Once the filename has been defined, it makes sense to briefly think about cleanup. The following settings will be available:

```
#log_truncate_on_rotation = off
#log_rotation_age = 1d
#log_rotation_size = 10MB
```

By default, PostgreSQL will keep producing log files if files are older than 1 day or larger than 10 MB. Additionally, `log_truncate_on_rotation` specifies whether you want to append data to a log file or not. Sometimes, `log_filenames` is defined in a way that it becomes cyclic. The `log_truncate_on_rotation` parameter defines whether to overwrite or append to the file that already exists. Given the default log file, this will, of course, not happen.

One way to handle auto-rotation is to use something such as `postgresql_%a.log`, along with `log_truncate_on_rotation = on`. The `%a` means that the day of the week will be used inside the log file. The advantage here is that the day of the week tends to repeat itself every seven days. Therefore, the log will be kept for a week and recycled. If you are aiming for weekly rotation, a 10 MB file size may not be enough. Consider turning the maximum file size off.

Configuring syslog

Some people prefer to use `syslog` to collect log files. PostgreSQL offers the following configuration parameters:

```
# These are relevant when logging to syslog:
#syslog_facility = 'LOCAL0'
#syslog_ident = 'postgres'
#syslog_sequence_numbers = on
#syslog_split_messages = on
```

`syslog` is pretty popular among `sys` admins. Fortunately, it is easy to configure. Basically, you set a facility and an identifier. If `log_destination` is set to `syslog`, then you don't need to do anything else.

Logging slow queries

The log can also be used to track down individual slow queries. Back in the old days, this was pretty much the only way to spot performance problems.

How does it work? Basically, `postgresql.conf` has a variable called `log_min_duration_statement`. If this is set to a value greater than 0, every query exceeding our chosen setting will make it to the log:

```
# log_min_duration_statement = -1
```

Most people see the slow query log as the ultimate source of wisdom. However, I would like to add a word of caution. There are many slow queries, and they just happen to eat up a lot of CPU: index creation, data exports, analytics, and so on.

These long-running queries are totally expected and are in many cases not the root of all evil. It is frequently the case that many shorter queries are to blame. Here is an example.

1,000 queries x 500 milliseconds is worse than 2 queries x 5 seconds. The slow query log can be misleading in some cases.

Still, it doesn't mean that it is pointless—it just means that it is *a* source of information and not *the* source of information.

Defining what and how to log

After taking a look at some basic settings, it's time to decide what to log. By default, only errors will be logged. However, this may not be enough. In this section, you will learn about what can be logged and what a logline will look like.

By default, PostgreSQL doesn't log information about checkpoints. The following setting is here to change exactly that:

```
#log_checkpoints = off
```

The same applies to connections; whenever a connection is established or properly destroyed, PostgreSQL can create log entries:

```
#log_connections = off
#log_disconnections = off
```

In most cases, it doesn't make sense to log connections since extensive logging significantly slows down the system. Analytical systems won't suffer much. However, OLTP may be seriously impacted.

If you want to see how long statements take, consider switching the following setting to on:

```
#log_duration = off
```

Let's move on to one of the most important settings. We haven't defined the layout of the messages yet, and so far, the `log` files contain errors in the following form:

```
test=# SELECT 1/0;
psql: ERROR: division by zero
```

The log will state ERROR, along with the error message. Before PostgreSQL 10.0, there wasn't a timestamp, username, and so on. You had to change the value immediately to make any sense of the logs. In PostgreSQL 10.0, the default value has changed to something much more reasonable. To change that, take a look at `log_line_prefix`:

```
#log_line_prefix = '%m [%p] '
# special values:
#    %a = application name
#    %u = user name
#    %d = database name
#    %r = remote host and port
#    %h = remote host
#    %p = process ID
#    %t = timestamp without milliseconds
#    %m = timestamp with milliseconds
#    %n = timestamp with milliseconds (as a Unix epoch)
#    %i = command tag
#    %e = SQL state
#    %c = session ID
#    %l = session line number
#    %s = session start timestamp
#    %v = virtual transaction ID
#    %x = transaction ID (0 if none)
#    %q = stop here in non-session processes
#    %% = '%'
```

Furthermore, `log_line_prefix` is pretty flexible and allows you to configure the logline to exactly match your needs. In general, it is a good idea to log a timestamp. Otherwise, it is close to impossible to see when something bad has happened. Personally, I also like to know the username, the transaction ID, and the database. However, it is up to you to decide what you really need.

Sometimes, slowness is caused by bad locking behavior. Users blocking each other can cause bad performance, and it is important to sort out those issues to ensure high throughput. In general, locking-related issues can be hard to track down.

Basically, `log_lock_waits` can help detect such issues. If a lock is held longer than `deadlock_timeout`, then a line will be sent to the log, provided that the following configuration variable is turned on:

```
#log_lock_waits = off
```

Finally, it's time to tell PostgreSQL what to actually log. So far, only errors, slow queries, and the like have been sent to the log. However, `log_statement` has four possible settings, as shown in the following block:

```
#log_statement = 'none'
        # none, ddl, mod, all
```

Note that `none` means that only errors will be logged. `ddl` means that errors, as well as DDLs (`CREATE TABLE`, `ALTER TABLE`, and so on), will be logged. `mod` will already include data changes, and `all` will send every statement to the log.

> Be aware that `all` can lead to a lot of logging information, which can slow down your system. To show you how much of an impact there can be, I have compiled a blog post. It can be found at https://www.cybertec-postgresql.com/en/logging-the-hidden-speedbrakes/.

If you want to inspect replication in more detail, consider turning the following setting on:

```
#log_replication_commands = off
```

This will send replication-related commands to the log.

> For more information on replication, visit the following website: https://www.postgresql.org/docs/current/static/protocol-replication.html.

It can frequently be the case that performance problems are caused by temporary file I/O. To see which queries cause problems, the following setting can be used:

```
#log_temp_files = -1
# log temporary files  equal  or larger
# than  the specified size  in kilobytes;
# -1 disables, 0 logs  all temp  files
```

While `pg_stat_statements` contains aggregated information, `log_temp_files` will point to specific queries causing issues. It usually makes sense to set this one to a reasonably low value. The correct value depends on your workload, but maybe 4 MB is a good start.

By default, PostgreSQL will write log files in the time zone where the server is located. However, if you are running a system that is spread all over the world, it can make sense to adjust the time zone in a way so that you can go and compare log entries, as shown in the following code:

```
log_timezone = 'Europe/Vienna'
```

Keep in mind that, on the SQL side, you will still see the time in your local time zone. However, if this variable is set, log entries will be in a different time zone.

Summary

This chapter was all about system statistics. You learned how to extract information from PostgreSQL and how to use system statistics in a beneficial way. The most important views were discussed in detail. Chapter 6, *Optimizing Queries for Good Performance*, which is the next chapter in this book, is all about query optimization. You will learn how to inspect queries and how they are optimized.

Questions

As in most of the chapters in this book, we will take a look at some of the key questions that will have risen from what has just been covered:

1. What kind of runtime statistics does PostgreSQL gather?
2. How can I spot performance problems easily?
3. How does PostgreSQL write log files?
4. Does logging have an impact on performance?

6
Optimizing Queries for Good Performance

In Chapter 5, *Log Files and System Statistics*, you learned how to read system statistics and how to make use of what PostgreSQL provides. Armed with this knowledge, this chapter is all about good query performance.

In this chapter, you will learn about the following topics:

- Learning what the optimizer does
- Understanding execution plans
- Understanding and fixing joins
- Enabling and disabling optimizer settings
- Partitioning data
- Adjusting parameters for good query performance
- Making use of parallel queries
- Introducing JIT compilation

By the end of this chapter, we will be able to write better and faster queries. If the queries still aren't very good, we should be able to understand why this is the case. We will also be able to use the new techniques we will have learned about to partition data.

Learning what the optimizer does

Before even attempting to think about query performance, it makes sense to familiarize yourself with what the query optimizer does. Having a deeper understanding of what is going on under the hood makes a lot of sense because it helps you see what the database is really up to.

Optimizations by example

To demonstrate how the optimizer works, I have compiled an example. It is something that has been used by me over the years for PostgreSQL training. Let's assume that there are three tables, as follows:

```
CREATE TABLE a (aid int, ...);      -- 100 million rows
CREATE TABLE b (bid int, ...);      -- 200 million rows
CREATE TABLE c (cid int, ...);      -- 300 million rows
```

Let's further assume that those tables contain millions, or maybe hundreds of millions, of rows. In addition to that, there are indexes:

```
CREATE INDEX idx_a ON a (aid);
CREATE INDEX idx_b ON b (bid);
CREATE INDEX idx_c ON c (cid);
CREATE VIEW v AS SELECT *
        FROM a, b
        WHERE aid = bid;
```

Finally, there is a view that's joining the first two tables together.

Let's suppose that the end user wants to run the following query. What will the optimizer do with this query? What choices does the planner have?

```
SELECT *
FROM   v, c
WHERE v.aid = c.cid
      AND cid = 4;
```

Before looking at the real optimization process, we will focus on some of the options that the planner has.

Evaluating join options

The planner has a couple of options here, so let's take this opportunity to understand what can go wrong if trivial approaches are used.

Suppose the planner just steams ahead and calculates the output of the view. What is the best way to join 100 million rows with 200 million rows?

In this section, a couple of (not all) join options will be discussed to show you what PostgreSQL is able to do.

Nested loops

One way to join two tables is to use a nested loop. The principle here is simple. Here is some pseudocode:

```
for x in table1:
    for y in table2:
        if x.field == y.field
            issue row
        else
            keep doing
```

Nested loops are often used if one of the sides is very small and contains only a limited set of data. In our example, a nested loop would lead to 100 million x 200 million iterations through the code. This is clearly not an option because the runtime would simply explode.

A nested loop is generally $O(n2)$, so it is only efficient if one side of the join is very small. In this example, this is not the case, so a nested loop can be ruled out for calculating the view.

Hash joins

The second option is a hash join. The following strategy could be applied to solve our little problem. The following listing shows how a hash join works:

```
Hash join
    Sequential scan table 1
    Sequential scan table 2
```

Both sides can be hashed and the hash keys could be compared, leaving us with the result of the join. The problem here is that all of the values have to be hashed and stored somewhere.

Merge joins

Finally, there is the merge join. The idea here is to use sorted lists to join the results. If both sides of the join are sorted, the system can just take the rows from the top and see if they match and return them. The main requirement here is that the lists are sorted. Here is a sample plan:

```
Merge join
  Sort table 1
    Sequential scan table 1
  Sort table 2
    Sequential scan table 2
```

To join these two tables (`table 1` and `table 2`), data has to be provided in a sorted order. In many cases, PostgreSQL will just sort the data. However, there are other options we can use to provide the join with sorted data. One way is to consult an index, as shown in the following example:

```
Merge join
    Index scan table 1
    Index scan table 2
```

One side of the join or both sides can use sorted data coming from lower levels of the plan. If the table is accessed directly, an index is the obvious choice for this, but only if the returned result set is significantly smaller than the entire table. Otherwise, we encounter almost double the overhead because we have to read the entire index and then the entire table. If the result set is a large portion of the table, a sequential scan is more efficient, especially if it is being accessed in the primary key order.

The beauty of a merge join is that it can handle a lot of data. The downside is that data has to be sorted or taken from an index at some point.

Sorting is $O(n * log(n))$. Therefore, sorting 300 million rows to perform the join is not attractive either.

 Note that, since the introduction of PostgreSQL 10.0, all the join options described here are also available in a parallel version. Therefore, the optimizer will not just consider those standard join options, but also evaluate whether it makes sense to perform parallel queries or not.

Applying transformations

Obviously, doing the obvious thing (joining the view first) makes no sense at all. A nested loop would send the execution time through the roof. A hash join has to hash millions of rows, and a nested loop has to sort 300 million rows. All three options are clearly unsuitable here. The way out is to apply logical transformations to make the query fast. In this section, you will learn what the planner does to speed up the query. A couple of steps will need to be performed.

Step 1: Inlining the view

The first transformation that the optimizer does is inline the views. Here's what happens:

```
SELECT *
FROM
  (
```

```
      SELECT *
      FROM a, b
      WHERE aid = bid
   ) AS v, c
   WHERE v.aid = c.cid
         AND cid = 4;
```

The view is inlined and transformed into a subselect. What does this one buy us? Actually, nothing. All it does is open the door for further optimization, which will really be a game-changer for this query.

Step 2: Flattening subselects

The next thing we need to do is flatten the subselects, which means integrating them into the main query. By getting rid of subselects, a couple more options we can use to optimize the query will appear.

Here is what the query will look like after flattening the subselects:

```
   SELECT * FROM a, b, c WHERE a.aid = c.cid AND aid = bid AND cid = 4;
```

Now, it's a normal join.

> We could have rewritten this SQL on our own, but the planner will take care of those transformations for us anyway. The optimizer can now perform further optimizations.

Applying equality constraints

The following process creates equality constraints. The idea is to detect additional constraints, join options, and filters. Let's take a deep breath and take a look at the following query: if `aid = cid` and `aid = bid`, we know that `bid = cid`. If `cid = 4` and all the others are equal, we know that `aid` and `bid` have to be 4 as well, which leads to the following query:

```
   SELECT *
   FROM a, b, c
   WHERE a.aid = c.cid
         AND aid = bid
         AND cid = 4
         AND bid = cid
         AND aid = 4
         AND bid = 4
```

The importance of this optimization cannot be stressed enough. What the planner did here was open the door for two additional indexes that weren't clearly visible in the original query.

By being able to use indexes on all three columns, the query is now a lot cheaper. The optimizer has the option to just retrieve a couple of rows from the index and use whatever join option makes sense.

Exhaustive searching

Now that those formal transformations have been done, PostgreSQL will perform an exhaustive search. It will try out all the possible plans and come up with the cheapest solution to your query. PostgreSQL knows which indexes are possible and just uses the cost model to determine how to do things in the best way possible.

During an exhaustive search, PostgreSQL will also try to determine the best join order. In the original query, the join order was fixed to $A \rightarrow B$ and $A \rightarrow C$. However, using those equality constraints, we could join $B \rightarrow C$ and join A later. All of these options are open to the planner.

Trying it all out

Now that all of the optimization options have been discussed, it is time to see what kind of execution plan is produced by PostgreSQL.

Let's try using the query with fully analyzed but empty tables first:

```
test=# explain SELECT * FROM v, c WHERE v.aid = c.cid AND cid = 4;
                            QUERY PLAN
---------------------------------------------------------------------
-----------
 Nested Loop  (cost=12.77..74.50 rows=2197 width=12)
   ->  Nested Loop  (cost=8.51..32.05 rows=169 width=8)
         ->  Bitmap Heap Scan on a  (cost=4.26..14.95 rows=13 width=4)
               Recheck Cond: (aid = 4)
               ->  Bitmap Index Scan on idx_a  (cost=0.00..4.25 rows=13
width=0)
                     Index Cond: (aid = 4)
         ->  Materialize  (cost=4.26..15.02 rows=13 width=4)
               ->  Bitmap Heap Scan on b  (cost=4.26..14.95 rows=13
width=4)
                     Recheck Cond: (bid = 4)
                     ->  Bitmap Index Scan on idx_b  (cost=0.00..4.25
```

```
rows=13 width=0)
                                Index Cond:  (bid = 4)
    ->  Materialize  (cost=4.26..15.02 rows=13 width=4)
          ->  Bitmap Heap Scan on c  (cost=4.26..14.95 rows=13 width=4)
                Recheck Cond: (cid = 4)
                  ->  Bitmap Index Scan on idx_c  (cost=0.00..4.25 rows=13
width=0)
                        Index Cond: (cid = 4)
(16 rows)
```

Now, let's do the same again after adding some data:

```
test=# INSERT INTO a SELECT * FROM generate_series(1, 1000000);
INSERT 0 1000000
test=# INSERT INTO b SELECT * FROM generate_series(1, 1000000);
INSERT 0 1000000
test=# INSERT INTO c SELECT * FROM generate_series(1, 1000000);
INSERT 0 1000000
test=# ANALYZE ;
ANALYZE
```

As shown in the following code, the plan has changed. However, what's important is that, in both plans, you will see filters being applied to all the columns in the query automatically. PostgreSQL's equality constraints have done their job:

```
test=# explain SELECT * FROM v, c WHERE v.aid = c.cid AND cid = 4;
                                QUERY PLAN
-----------------------------------------------------------------------------
-----
 Nested Loop (cost=1.27..25.35 rows=1 width=12)
    -> Nested Loop (cost=0.85..16.90 rows=1 width=8)
          -> Index Only Scan using idx_a on a (cost=0.42..8.44 rows=1
width=4)
                Index Cond: (aid = 4)
          -> Index Only Scan using idx_b on b (cost=0.42..8.44 rows=1
width=4)
                Index Cond: (bid = 4)
    -> Index Only Scan using idx_c on c (cost=0.42..8.44 rows=1 width=4)
          Index Cond: (cid = 4)
(8 rows)
```

Note that the plans shown in this chapter are not necessarily 100% identical to what you will observe. Depending on how much data you have loaded, there may be slight variations. Costs may also depend on the physical alignment of data on the disk (order on disk). Please keep this in mind when running these examples.

As you can see, PostgreSQL will use three indexes. It is also interesting to see that PostgreSQL decides to go for a nested loop to join the data. This makes perfect sense because there is virtually no data coming back from the index scans. Therefore, using a loop to join things is perfectly feasible and highly efficient.

Making the process fail

So far, you have seen what PostgreSQL can do for you and how the optimizer helps speed up queries. PostgreSQL is pretty smart, but it needs smart users. There are some cases in which the end user cripples the entire optimization process by doing stupid things. Let's drop the view by using the following command:

```
test=# DROP VIEW v;
DROP VIEW
```

Now, the view has been recreated. Note that OFFSET 0 has been added to the end of the view. Let's take a look at the following example:

```
test=# CREATE VIEW v AS SELECT *
        FROM  a, b
        WHERE aid = bid
        OFFSET 0;
CREATE VIEW
```

While this view is logically equivalent to the example that was shown previously, the optimizer has to treat things differently. Every OFFSET other than 0 will change the result, and therefore the view has to be calculated. The entire optimization process is crippled by adding things such as OFFSET.

 The PostgreSQL community didn't dare optimize this case of having an OFFSET 0 in a view. People are simply not supposed to do that. We will use this just as an example to observe how some operations can cripple performance and that we, as developers, should be aware of the underlying optimization process. However, if you happen to know how PostgreSQL works, this trick can be used for optimization.

Here is the new plan:

```
test=# EXPLAIN SELECT * FROM v, c WHERE v.aid = c.cid AND cid = 4;
                        QUERY PLAN
-------------------------------------------------------------
Nested Loop (cost=120.71..7949879.40 rows=1 width=12)
  -> Subquery Scan on v
            (cost=120.13..7949874.80 rows=1 width=8)
```

```
          Filter: (v.aid = 4)
          -> Merge Join (cost=120.13..6699874.80 rows=100000000 width=8)
                Merge Cond: (a.aid = b.bid)
                -> Index Only Scan using idx_a on a
                      (cost=0.57..2596776.57 rows=100000000 width=4)
                -> Index Only Scan using idx_b on b
                      (cost=0.57..5193532.33 rows=199999984 width=4)
    -> Index Only Scan using idx_c on c
          (cost=0.57..4.59 rows=1 width=4)
          Index Cond: (cid = 4)
 (9 rows)
```

Just take a look at the costs that have been predicted by the planner. Costs have skyrocketed from being two-digit numbers to a staggering one. Clearly, this query is going to provide you with bad performance.

There are various ways to cripple performance, but it makes sense to keep the optimization process in mind.

Constant folding

However, there are many more optimizations in PostgreSQL that take place behind the scenes and that contribute to overall good performance. One of these features is called **constant folding**. The idea is to turn expressions into constants, as shown in the following example:

```
test=# explain SELECT * FROM a WHERE aid = 3 + 1;
                     QUERY PLAN
-------------------------------------------------------------
 Index Only Scan using idx_a on a
     (cost=0.57..4.58 rows=1 width=4)
   Index Cond: (aid = 4)
 (2 rows)
```

As you can see, PostgreSQL will try to look for 4. Since aid is indexed, PostgreSQL will go for an index scan. Note that our table has just one column, so PostgreSQL even figured out that all the data it needs can be found in the index.

What happens if the expression is on the left-hand side?

```
test=# explain SELECT * FROM a WHERE aid - 1 = 3;
                     QUERY PLAN
-------------------------------------------------------------
 Seq Scan on a (cost=0.00..1942478.48 rows=500000 width=4)
   Filter: ((aid - 1) = 3)
 (2 rows)
```

In this case, the index lookup code will fail, and PostgreSQL has to go for a sequential scan. Keep in mind that this is a single-core plan. If the size of the table is large or if your PostgreSQL configuration is different, you may see a multi-core plan. For the sake of simplicity, this chapter only contains single-core plans to make reading easier.

Understanding function inlining

As we already outlined in this section, there are many optimizations that help speed up queries. One of them is called **function inlining**. PostgreSQL is able to inline immutable SQL functions. The main idea is to reduce the number of function calls that have to be made in order to speed things up.

Here is an example of a function that can be inlined by the optimizer:

```
test=# CREATE OR REPLACE FUNCTION ld(int)
RETURNS numeric AS
$$
    SELECT log(2, $1);
$$
LANGUAGE 'sql' IMMUTABLE;
CREATE FUNCTION
```

This function will calculate the logarithmus dualis of the input value:

```
test=# SELECT ld(1024);
        ld
---------------------
 10.0000000000000000
(1 row)
```

To demonstrate how things work, we will recreate the table with less content to speed up the index creation process:

```
test=# TRUNCATE a;
TRUNCATE TABLE
```

Then, data can be added again and the index can be applied:

```
test=# INSERT INTO a SELECT * FROM generate_series(1, 10000);
INSERT 0 10000
test=# CREATE INDEX idx_ld ON a (ld(aid));
CREATE INDEX
```

As expected, the index that's created on the function will be used just like any other index. However, let's take a closer look at the indexing condition:

```
test=# EXPLAIN SELECT * FROM a WHERE ld(aid) = 10;
                        QUERY PLAN
-----------------------------------------------------------------
 Index Scan using idx_ld on a (cost=0.29..8.30 rows=1 width=4)
   Index Cond: (log('2'::numeric, (aid)::numeric) = '10'::numeric)
(2 rows)
```

The important observation here is that the indexing condition actually looks for the log function instead of the `ld` function. The optimizer has completely gotten rid of the function call.

Logically, this opens the door for the following query:

```
test=# EXPLAIN SELECT * FROM a WHERE log(2, aid) = 10;
                        QUERY PLAN
-----------------------------------------------------------------
 Index Scan using idx_ld on a (cost=0.29..8.30 rows=1 width=4)
   Index Cond: (log('2'::numeric, (aid)::numeric) = '10'::numeric)
(2 rows)
```

Join pruning

PostgreSQL also provides an optimization called **join pruning**. The idea is to remove joins if they are not needed by the query. This can come in handy if queries are generated by some middleware or some ORM. If a join can be removed, it naturally speeds things up dramatically and leads to less overhead.

The question now is, how does join pruning work? Here is an example:

```
CREATE TABLE x (id int, PRIMARY KEY (id));
CREATE TABLE y (id int, PRIMARY KEY (id));
```

First of all, two tables are created. Make sure that both sides of the join condition are actually unique. Those constraints will be important in a minute.

Now, we can write a simple query:

```
test=# EXPLAIN SELECT *
FROM  x LEFT JOIN y ON (x.id = y.id)
WHERE x.id = 3;
                            QUERY PLAN
-----------------------------------------------------------------
 Nested Loop Left Join  (cost=0.31..16.36 rows=1 width=8)
```

```
      Join Filter:  (x.id = y.id)
      ->   Index Only Scan using x_pkey on x
           (cost=0.15..8.17 rows=1 width=4)
              Index Cond:  (id = 3)
      ->   Index Only Scan using y_pkey on y
           (cost=0.15..8.17 rows=1 width=4)
              Index Cond:  (id = 3)
  (6 rows)
```

As you can see, PostgreSQL will join those tables directly. So far, there are no surprises. However, the following query has been slightly modified. Instead of selecting all the columns, it only selects those columns on the left-hand side of the join:

```
test=# EXPLAIN SELECT x.*
 FROM x LEFT JOIN y ON (x.id = y.id)
 WHERE x.id = 3;
                            QUERY PLAN
-----------------------------------------------------------------
 Index Only Scan using x_pkey on x   (cost=0.15..8.17 rows=1 width=4)
    Index Cond:  (id = 3)
 (2 rows)
```

PostgreSQL will go for a direct inside scan and skip the join completely. There are two reasons why this is actually possible and logically correct:

- No columns are selected from the right-hand side of the join; thus, looking those columns up doesn't buy us anything.
- The right-hand side is unique, which means that joining cannot increase the number of rows due to duplicates on the right-hand side.

If joins can be pruned automatically, then the queries may be a magnitude faster. The beauty here is that an increase in speed can be achieved by just removing columns that may not be needed by the application anyway.

Speedup set operations

Set operations combine the results of more than one query into a single result set. They include UNION, INTERSECT, and EXCEPT. PostgreSQL implements all of them and offers many important optimizations to speed them up.

The planner is able to push restrictions down into the set operation, opening the door for fancy indexing and speedups in general. Let's take a look at the following query, which shows us how this works:

```
test=# EXPLAIN SELECT *
FROM
(
    SELECT aid AS xid
    FROM a
    UNION ALL
    SELECT bid FROM b
) AS y
WHERE xid = 3;
                            QUERY PLAN
-------------------------------------------------------------------
 Append (cost=0.29..12.89 rows=2 width=4)
   -> Index Only Scan using idx_a on a
         (cost=0.29..8.30 rows=1 width=4)
         Index Cond: (aid = 3)
   -> Index Only Scan using idx_b on b
         (cost=0.57..4.59 rows=1 width=4)
         Index Cond: (bid = 3)
(5 rows)
```

What you can see here is that two relations are added to each other. The trouble is that the only restriction is outside the subselect. However, PostgreSQL figures out that the filter can be pushed further down the plan. Therefore, `xid = 3` is attached to `aid` and `bid`, opening up the option for us to use indexes on both tables. By avoiding the sequential scan on both tables, the query will run a lot faster.

> Note that there is a distinction between the UNION clause and the UNION ALL clause. The UNION ALL clause will just blindly append the data and deliver the results of both tables.

The UNION clause is different as it will filter out duplicates. The following plan shows how that works:

```
test=# EXPLAIN SELECT *
 FROM
 (
     SELECT aid AS xid
     FROM a
     UNION SELECT bid
     FROM b
 ) AS y
```

```
WHERE xid = 3;
                              QUERY PLAN
---------------------------------------------------------------
 Unique (cost=12.92..12.93 rows=2 width=4)
   -> Sort (cost=12.92..12.93 rows=2 width=4)
         Sort Key: a.aid
         -> Append (cost=0.29..12.91 rows=2 width=4)
               -> Index Only Scan using idx_a on a
                     (cost=0.29..8.30 rows=1 width=4)
                     Index Cond: (aid = 3)
               -> Index Only Scan using idx_b on b
                     (cost=0.57..4.59 rows=1 width=4)
                     Index Cond: (bid = 3)
(8 rows)
```

PostgreSQL has to add a `Sort` node on top of the `Append` node to ensure that duplicates can be filtered later on.

> Many developers who are not fully aware of the difference between the
> `UNION` clause and the `UNION ALL` clause complain about bad performance
> because they are unaware that PostgreSQL has to filter out duplicates,
> which is especially painful in the case of large datasets.

Understanding execution plans

Now that we've dug into some important optimizations that are implemented in PostgreSQL, let's proceed to take a closer look at execution plans. You have already seen some execution plans in this book. However, in order to make full use of plans, it is important to develop a systematic approach when it comes to reading this information.

Approaching plans systematically

The first thing you have to know is that an `EXPLAIN` clause can do quite a lot for you, and I highly recommend making full use of these features.

As many of you may already know, an `EXPLAIN ANALYZE` clause will execute the query and return the plan, including real runtime information. Here is an example:

```
test=# EXPLAIN ANALYZE SELECT *
FROM
(
    SELECT *
    FROM b
```

```
     LIMIT 1000000
) AS b
ORDER BY cos(bid);
                                              QUERY PLAN
----------------------------------------------------------------------------
----------------
  Sort (cost=146173.34..148673.34 rows=1000000 width=12)
       (actual time=494.028..602.733 rows=1000000 loops=1)
    Sort Key: (cos((b.bid)::double precision))
    Sort Method: external merge Disk: 25496kB
    -> Subquery Scan on b (cost=0.00..29425.00 rows=1000000 width=12)
       (actual time=6.274..208.224 rows=1000000 loops=1)
          -> Limit (cost=0.00..14425.00 rows=1000000 width=4)
             (actual time=5.930..105.253 rows=1000000 loops=1)
                -> Seq Scan on b b_1 (cost=0.00..14425.00 rows=1000000
width=4)
                    (actual time=0.014..55.448 rows=1000000 loops=1)
  Planning Time: 0.170 ms
  JIT:
    Functions: 3
    Options: Inlining false, Optimization false, Expressions true, Deforming
true
    Timing: Generation 0.319 ms, Inlining 0.000 ms, Optimization 0.242 ms,
            Emission 5.196 ms, Total 5.757 ms
  Execution Time: 699.903 ms
(12 rows)
```

The plan looks a bit scary, but don't panic; we will go through it step by step. When reading a plan, make sure that you read it from the inside out. In our example, execution starts with a sequential scan on b. There are actually two blocks of information here: the **cost block** and the **actual time block**. While the cost block contains estimations, the actual time block is hard evidence. It shows the real execution time. What you can also see here is that in PostgreSQL 12, JIT compilation is on by default. The query is already time-consuming enough to justify JIT compilation.

 Note that the costs shown on your system may not be identical. A small difference in the optimizer's statistics can cause differences. The important thing here is the way the plan has to be read.

The data coming from the index scan is then passed on to the `Limit` node, which ensures that there is not too much data. Note that each stage of execution will also show us the number of rows involved. As you can see, PostgreSQL will only fetch 1 million rows from the table in the first place; the `Limit` node ensures that this will actually happen. However, there is a price tag at this stage since the runtime has jumped to 169 milliseconds already. Finally, the data is sorted, which takes a lot of time. The most important thing when looking at the plan is to figure out where time is actually lost. The best way to do that is to take a look at the actual time block and try to figure out where time jumps. In this example, the sequential scan takes some time, but it cannot be sped up significantly. Instead, we can see that time skyrockets as sorting starts.

Of course, the process of sorting can be sped up, but we'll cover that in more detail later in this chapter.

Making EXPLAIN more verbose

In PostgreSQL, the output of an `EXPLAIN` clause can be beefed up a little to provide you with more information. To extract as much as possible out of a plan, consider turning the following options on:

```
test=# EXPLAIN (analyze, verbose, costs, timing, buffers)
  SELECT * FROM a ORDER BY random();
                                           QUERY PLAN
-----------------------------------------------------------------------------
--------------------------
 Sort (cost=133673.34..136173.34 rows=1000000 width=12)
       (actual time=384.112..491.145 rows=1000000 loops=1)
   Output: aid, (random())
   Sort Key: (random())
   Sort Method: external merge Disk: 25496kB
   Buffers: shared hit=1255 read=3170, temp read=3902 written=3919
   -> Seq Scan on public.a (cost=0.00..16925.00 rows=1000000 width=12)
          (actual time=5.921..100.886 rows=1000000 loops=1)
          Output: aid, random()
          Buffers: shared hit=1255 read=3170
 Planning Time: 0.104 ms
 JIT:
   Functions: 2
   Options: Inlining false, Optimization false, Expressions true, Deforming
true
   Timing: Generation 0.836 ms, Inlining 0.000 ms, Optimization 0.428 ms,
   Emission 5.169 ms, Total 6.433 ms
 Execution Time: 539.782 ms
(14 rows)
```

analyze true will actually execute the query, as shown previously. verbose true will add some more information to the plan (such as column information and so on). costs true will show information about costs. timing true is equally important, as it will provide us with good runtime data so that we can see where in the plan time gets lost. Finally, there is buffers true, which can be very enlightening. In my example, it reveals that we needed to access thousands of buffers to execute the query.

Spotting problems

Given all the information that was shown in Chapter 5, *Log Files and System Statistics*, it is already possible to spot a couple of potential performance problems that are very important in real life.

Spotting changes in runtime

When looking at a plan, there are always two questions that you have got to ask yourself:

- Is the runtime shown by the EXPLAIN ANALYZE clause justified for the given query?
- If the query is slow, where does the runtime jump?

In my case, the sequential scan is rated at 2.625 milliseconds. The sort is done after 7.199 milliseconds, so the sort takes roughly 4.5 milliseconds to complete and is therefore responsible for most of the runtime that's needed by the query.

Looking for jumps in the execution time of the query will reveal what's really going on. Depending on which type of operation will burn too much time, you have to act accordingly. Some general advice is not possible here because there are simply too many things that can cause issues.

Inspecting estimates

However, there is something that should always be done: we should make sure that estimates and real numbers are reasonably close together. In some cases, the optimizer will make poor decisions because the estimates are way off for some reason. Sometimes, estimates can be off because the system statistics are not up to date. Therefore, running an ANALYZE clause is definitely a good thing to start with. However, optimizer stats are mostly taken care of by the auto-vacuum daemon, so it is definitely worth considering other options that are causing bad estimates.

Take a look at the following example, which helps us add some data to a table:

```
test=# CREATE TABLE t_estimate AS
        SELECT * FROM generate_series(1, 10000) AS id;
SELECT 10000
```

After loading `10000` rows, the optimizer statistics are created:

```
test=# ANALYZE t_estimate;
ANALYZE
```

Let's take a look at the estimates now:

```
test=# EXPLAIN ANALYZE SELECT * FROM t_estimate WHERE cos(id) < 4;
                            QUERY PLAN
------------------------------------------------------------------
 Seq Scan on t_estimate  (cost=0.00..220.00 rows=3333 width=4)
          (actual time=0.010..4.006 rows=10000 loops=1)
    Filter: (cos((id)::double precision) < '4'::double precision)
 Planning time: 0.064 ms
 Execution time: 4.701 ms
(4 rows)
```

In many cases, PostgreSQL may not be able to process the WHERE clause properly because it only has statistics on columns, not on expressions. What we can see here is a nasty underestimation of the data returned from the WHERE clause.

Of course, the amount of data can also be overestimated, as shown in the following code:

```
test=# EXPLAIN ANALYZE
SELECT *
FROM t_estimate
WHERE cos(id) > 4;
                QUERY PLAN
------------------------------------------------------------------
 Seq Scan on t_estimate  (cost=0.00..220.00 rows=3333 width=4)
      (actual time=3.802..3.802 rows=0 loops=1)
      Filter: (cos((id)::double precision) > '4'::double precision)
      Rows Removed by Filter: 10000
 Planning time: 0.037 ms
 Execution time: 3.813 ms
(5 rows)
```

If something like this happens deep inside the plan, the process may very well create a bad plan. Therefore, making sure that estimates are within a certain range makes perfect sense.

Fortunately, there is a way to get around this problem. Consider the following code block:

```
test=# CREATE INDEX idx_cosine ON t_estimate (cos(id));
CREATE INDEX
```

Creating an index will make PostgreSQL track the statistics of the expression:

```
test=# ANALYZE t_estimate;
ANALYZE
```

Apart from the fact that this plan will ensure significantly better performance, it will also fix statistics, even if the index isn't used, as shown in the following code:

```
test=# EXPLAIN ANALYZE SELECT * FROM t_estimate WHERE cos(id) > 4;
                            QUERY PLAN
-----------------------------------------------------------------
  Index Scan using idx_cosine on t_estimate
      (cost=0.29..8.30 rows=1 width=4)
      (actual time=0.002..0.002 rows=0 loops=1)
      Index Cond: (cos((id)::double precision) > '4'::double precision)
  Planning time: 0.095 ms
  Execution time: 0.011 ms
 (4 rows)
```

However, there is more to wrong estimates than meets the eye. One problem that is often underestimated is called a **cross-column correlation**. Consider a simple example involving two columns:

- 20% of people like to ski
- 20% of people are from Africa

If we want to count the number of skiers in Africa, mathematics says that the result will be $0.2 \times 0.2 = 4\%$ of the overall population. However, there is no snow in Africa and the income in this country is low. Therefore, the real result will surely be lower. The observation Africa and the observation skiing are not statistically independent. In many cases, the fact that PostgreSQL keeps column statistics that don't span more than one column can lead to bad results.

Of course, the planner does a lot to prevent these things from happening as often as possible. Still, it can be an issue.

Starting with PostgreSQL 10.0, we have multivariate statistics, which has put an end to cross-column correlation once and for all.

Inspecting buffer usage

However, the plan itself is not the only thing that can cause issues. In many cases, dangerous things are hidden on some other level. Memory and caching can lead to undesired behavior, which is often hard to understand for end users who are not trained to see the problem that was described in this section.

Here is an example that depicts the random insertion of data into the table. The query will generate some randomly ordered data and add it to a new table:

```
test=# CREATE TABLE t_random AS
        SELECT * FROM generate_series(1, 10000000) AS id ORDER BY
random();
SELECT 10000000
test=# ANALYZE t_random ;
ANALYZE
```

Now, we have generated a simple table containing 10 million rows and created the optimizer statistics.

In the next step, a simple query that's retrieving only a handful of rows is executed:

```
test=# EXPLAIN (analyze true, buffers true, costs true, timing true)
        SELECT * FROM t_random WHERE id < 1000;
                        QUERY PLAN
-----------------------------------------------------------------
 Seq Scan on t_random (cost=0.00..169248.60 rows=1000 width=4)
   (actual time=1.068..685.410 rows=999 loops=1)
   Filter: (id < 1000)
   Rows Removed by Filter: 9999001
 Buffers: shared hit=2112 read=42136
 Planning time: 0.035 ms
 Execution time: 685.551 ms
(6 rows)
```

Before inspecting the data, make sure that you have executed the query twice. Of course, it makes sense to use an index here. However, in this query, PostgreSQL has found 2112 buffers inside the cache and 421136 buffers that had to be taken from the operating system. Now, there are two things that can happen. If you are lucky, the operating system lands a couple of cache hits and the query is fast. If the filesystem cache is not lucky, those blocks have to be taken from disk. This may seem obvious; it can, however, lead to wild swings in the execution time. A query that runs entirely in the cache can be 100 times faster than a query that has to slowly collect random blocks from disk.

Let's try to outline this problem by using a simple example. Suppose we have a phone system that stores 10 billion rows (which is not uncommon for large phone carriers). Data flows in at a rapid rate, and users want to query this data. If you have 10 billion rows, the data will only partially fit into memory and therefore a lot of stuff will naturally end up coming from the disk.

Let's run a simple query to learn how PostgreSQL looks up a phone number:

```
SELECT * FROM data WHERE phone_number = '+12345678';
```

Even if you are on the phone, your data will be spread all over the place. If you end a phone call just to start the next call, thousands of people will do the same, so the odds that two of your calls will end up in the very same 8,000 block is close to zero. Just imagine for the time being that there are 100,000 calls going on at the same time. On disk, data will be randomly distributed. If your phone number shows up often, it means that for each row, at least one block has to be fetched from disk (assuming there's a very low cache hit rate). Let's say 5,000 rows are returned. Assuming that you have to go to disk 5,000 times, it leads to something such as *5,000 x 5 milliseconds = 25* seconds of execution time. Note that the execution time of this query may vary between milliseconds and, say, 30 seconds, depending on how much has been cached by the operating system or by PostgreSQL.

Keep in mind that every server restart will naturally clean out the PostgreSQL and filesystem caches, which can lead to real trouble after a node failure.

Fixing high buffer usage

The question that begs an answer is, *how can I improve this situation?* One way to do this is to run a CLUSTER clause:

```
test=# \h CLUSTER
Command: CLUSTER
Description: cluster a table according to an index
Syntax:
CLUSTER [VERBOSE] table_name [ USING index_name ]
CLUSTER [VERBOSE]

URL: https://www.postgresql.org/docs/12/sql-cluster.html
```

The CLUSTER clause will rewrite the table in the same order as a btree index. If you are running an analytical workload, this can make sense. However, in an OLTP system, the CLUSTER clause may not be feasible because a table lock is required while the table is being rewritten.

Understanding and fixing joins

Joins are important; everybody needs them on a regular basis. Consequently, joins are also relevant for maintaining or achieving good performance. To ensure that you can write good joins, we will also learn about joining in this book.

Getting joins right

Before we dive into optimizing joins, it is important to take a look at some of the most common problems that arise with joins and which of them should ring alarm bells for you.

Here is an example of a simple table structure to demonstrate how joins work:

```
test=# CREATE TABLE a (aid int);
CREATE TABLE
test=# CREATE TABLE b (bid int);
CREATE TABLE
test=# INSERT INTO a VALUES (1), (2), (3);
INSERT 0 3
test=# INSERT INTO b VALUES (2), (3), (4);
INSERT 0 3
```

The following example shows a simple outer join:

```
test=# SELECT * FROM a LEFT JOIN b ON (aid = bid);
 aid | bid
-----+-----
   1 |
   2 |   2
   3 |   3
(3 rows)
```

As you can see, PostgreSQL will take all the rows from the left-hand side and only list the ones that fit the join.

The following example may come as a surprise to many people:

```
test=# SELECT * FROM a LEFT JOIN b ON (aid = bid AND bid = 2);
 aid | bid
-----+-----
   1 |
   2 |   2
   3 |
(3 rows)
```

No, the number of rows does not decrease – it will stay constant. Most people assume that there will only be one row in the join, but this is not true and will lead to some hidden issues.

Consider the following query, which performs a simple join:

```
test=# SELECT avg(aid), avg(bid)
       FROM a LEFT JOIN b
           ON (aid = bid AND bid = 2);
        avg         |         avg
--------------------+--------------------
 2.0000000000000000 | 2.0000000000000000
(1 row)
```

Most people assume that the average is calculated based on a single row. However, as we stated earlier, this is not the case, and therefore queries such as that are often considered to be a performance problem because, for some reason, PostgreSQL doesn't index the table on the left-hand side of the join. Of course, we aren't looking at a performance problem here – we are definitely looking at a semantic issue. Often, people writing outer joins don't really know what they are asking PostgreSQL to do. So, my personal advice is to always question the semantic correctness of an outer join before attacking the performance problem that's reported by the client.

I cannot stress enough how important this kind of work is to ensure that your queries are correct and do exactly what is needed.

Processing outer joins

After verifying that your queries are actually correct from a business point of view, it makes sense to check what the optimizer can do to speed up your outer joins. The most important thing is that PostgreSQL can, in many cases, reorder inner joins to speed things up dramatically. However, in the case of outer joins, this is not always possible. Only a handful of reordering operations are actually allowed:

```
(A leftjoin B on (Pab)) innerjoin C on (Pac) = (A innerjoin C on (Pac))
leftjoin B on (Pab)
```

`Pac` is a predicate referencing A and C, and so on (in this case, clearly, `Pac` cannot reference B, otherwise the transformation is nonsensical):

- `(A leftjoin B on (Pab)) leftjoin C on (Pac) = (A leftjoin C on (Pac)) leftjoin B on (Pab)`
- `(A leftjoin B on (Pab)) leftjoin C on (Pbc) = (A leftjoin (B leftjoin C on (Pbc)) on (Pab)`

The last rule only holds true if the `Pbc` predicate must fail for all null B rows (that is, `Pbc` is strict for at least one column of B). If `Pbc` is not strict, the first form may produce some rows with non-null C columns, while the second form would make those entries null.

While some joins can be reordered, a typical type of query cannot benefit from join reordering:

```
SELECT ...
  FROM a LEFT JOIN b ON (aid = bid)
   LEFT JOIN c ON (bid = cid)
   LEFT JOIN d ON (cid = did)
...
```

The way to approach this is to check whether all the outer joins are really necessary. In many cases, it happens that people write outer joins without actually needing them. Often, the business case doesn't even need to use outer joins.

Understanding the join_collapse_limit variable

During the planning process, PostgreSQL tries to check all the possible join orders. In many cases, this can be pretty expensive because there can be many permutations, which naturally slows down the planning process.

The `join_collapse_limit` variable is here to give the developer a tool to actually work around these problems and define how a query should be processed in a more straightforward way.

To show you what this setting is all about, we will compile a little example:

```
SELECT * FROM tab1, tab2, tab3
WHERE tab1.id = tab2.id
     AND tab2.ref = tab3.id;
SELECT * FROM tab1 CROSS JOIN tab2
CROSS JOIN tab3
WHERE tab1.id = tab2.id
     AND tab2.ref = tab3.id;
```

```
SELECT * FROM tab1 JOIN (tab2 JOIN tab3
   ON (tab2.ref = tab3.id))
   ON (tab1.id = tab2.id);
```

Basically, these three queries are identical and treated by the planner in the same way. The first query consists of implicit joins. The last one only consists of explicit joins. Internally, the planner will inspect those requests and order joins accordingly to ensure the best runtime possible. The question here is, how many explicit joins will PostgreSQL plan implicitly? This is exactly what you can tell the planner by setting the `join_collapse_limit` variable. The default value is reasonably good for normal queries. However, if your query contains a very high number of joins, playing around with this setting can reduce planning time considerably. Reducing planning time can be essential to maintaining good throughput.

To see how the `join_collapse_limit` variable changes the plan, we will write this simple query:

```
test=# EXPLAIN WITH x AS
(
   SELECT *
   FROM  generate_series(1, 1000) AS id
)
SELECT *
FROM x AS a
   JOIN x AS b ON (a.id = b.id)
   JOIN x AS c ON (b.id = c.id)
   JOIN x AS d ON (c.id = d.id)
   JOIN x AS e ON (d.id = e.id)
   JOIN x AS f ON (e.id = f.id);
```

Try running the query with different settings and see how the plan changes. Unfortunately, the plan is too long to copy here, so it is impossible to include the actual changes in this section.

Enabling and disabling optimizer settings

So far, the most important optimizations that are performed by the planner have been discussed in detail. PostgreSQL has improved a lot over the years. Still, something can go south and users have to convince the planner to do the right thing.

To modify plans, PostgreSQL offers a couple of runtime variables that will have a significant impact on planning. The idea is to give the end user the chance to make certain types of nodes in the plan more expensive than others. What does that mean in practice? Here is a simple plan:

```
test=# explain SELECT *
 FROM generate_series(1, 100) AS a,
 generate_series(1, 100) AS b
 WHERE a = b;
                              QUERY PLAN
---------------------------------------------------------------------
----------
 Hash Join   (cost=2.25..4.63 rows=100 width=8)
   Hash Cond: (a.a = b.b)
   ->  Function Scan on generate_series a   (cost=0.00..1.00 rows=100
width=4)
   ->  Hash   (cost=1.00..1.00 rows=100 width=4)
         ->  Function Scan on generate_series b   (cost=0.00..1.00 rows=100
width=4)
(5 rows)
```

Here, PostgreSQL will scan the functions and perform a hash join. Let's me run the same query in PostgreSQL 11 or older and show you the execution plan:

```
                           QUERY PLAN
--------------------------------------------------------------
 Merge Join (cost=119.66..199.66 rows=5000 width=8)
   Merge Cond: (a.a = b.b)
   -> Sort (cost=59.83..62.33 rows=1000 width=4)
         Sort Key: a.a
         -> Function Scan on generate_series a
         (cost=0.00..10.00 rows=1000 width=4)
   -> Sort (cost=59.83..62.33 rows=1000 width=4)
         Sort Key: b.b
         -> Function Scan on generate_series b
         (cost=0.00..10.00 rows=1000 width=4)
 (8 rows)
```

Can you see the difference between these two plans? In PostgreSQL 12, the estimate of the set returning function is already correct. In the older version, the optimizer still estimates that a set returning function will always return 100 rows. In PostgreSQL, there are optimizer support functions that can help estimate the result set. Therefore, the plan in PostgreSQL 12 and beyond is vastly superior to the old plan.

What we can see in the new plan is that a `hashjoin` is performed, which is, of course, the most efficient way to do things. However, what if we're smarter then the optimizer? Fortunately, PostgreSQL has the means to overrule the optimizer. You can set variables in a connection that changes the default cost estimates. Here's how it works:

```
test=# SET enable_hashjoin TO off;
SET
test=# explain SELECT *
  FROM generate_series(1, 100) AS a,
       generate_series(1, 100) AS b
  WHERE a = b;
                              QUERY PLAN
-----------------------------------------------------------------------------
---------
 Merge Join (cost=8.65..10.65 rows=100 width=8)
   Merge Cond: (a.a = b.b)
   -> Sort (cost=4.32..4.57 rows=100 width=4)
         Sort Key: a.a
         -> Function Scan on generate_series a (cost=0.00..1.00 rows=100
width=4)
   -> Sort (cost=4.32..4.57 rows=100 width=4)
         Sort Key: b.b
         -> Function Scan on generate_series b (cost=0.00..1.00 rows=100
width=4)
(8 rows)
```

PostgreSQL assumes that `hashjoins` are bad and makes them infinitely expensive. Thus, is falls back to a merge join. However, we can turn merge joins off as well:

```
test=# explain SELECT *
 FROM generate_series(1, 100) AS a,
      generate_series(1, 100) AS b
 WHERE a = b;
                              QUERY PLAN
-----------------------------------------------------------------------------
---
 Nested Loop (cost=0.01..226.00 rows=100 width=8)
 Join Filter: (a.a = b.b)
 -> Function Scan on generate_series a (cost=0.00..1.00 rows=100 width=4)
 -> Function Scan on generate_series b (cost=0.00..1.00 rows=100 width=4)
(4 rows)
```

PostgreSQL is slowly running out of options. The following example shows what happens if we turn off nested loops as well:

```
test=# SET enable_nestloop TO off;
SET
test=# explain SELECT *
   FROM generate_series(1, 100) AS a,
        generate_series(1, 100) AS b
   WHERE a = b;
                              QUERY PLAN
-------------------------------------------------------------------------------
----
 Nested Loop  (cost=10000000000.00..10000000226.00 rows=100 width=8)
   Join Filter: (a.a = b.b)
   -> Function Scan on generate_series a  (cost=0.00..1.00 rows=100
width=4)
   -> Function Scan on generate_series b  (cost=0.00..1.00 rows=100
width=4)
 JIT:
   Functions: 10
   Options: Inlining true, Optimization true, Expressions true, Deforming
true
(7 rows)
```

The important thing is that turning off doesn't really mean off – it just means insanely expensive. If PostgreSQL has no cheaper options, it will fall back to the ones we turned off. Otherwise, there would be no way to execute SQL anymore.

What settings influence the planner? The following switches are available:

- enable_bitmapscan = on
- enable_hashagg = on
- enable_hashjoin = on
- enable_indexscan = on
- enable_indexonlyscan = on
- enable_material = on
- enable_mergejoin = on
- enable_nestloop = on
- enable_parallel_append = on
- enable_seqscan = on
- enable_sort = on
- enable_tidscan = on

- enable_partitionwise_join = off
- enable_partitionwise_aggregate = off
- enable_parallel_hash = on
- enable_partition_pruning = on

While these settings can definitely be beneficial, let's understand that these tweaks should be handled with care. They should only be used to speed up individual queries and not turn off things globally. Switching off options can turn against you fairly quickly and destroy performance. Therefore, it really makes sense to think twice before changing these parameters.

Understanding genetic query optimization

The result of the planning process is key to achieving superior performance. As we have seen in this chapter, planning is far from trivial and involves various complex calculations. The more tables are touched by a query, the more complicated planning will become. The more tables there are, the more choices the planner will have. Logically, the planning time will increase. At some point, planning will take so long that performing the classical exhaustive search is not feasible anymore. On top of that, the errors that occur during planning are so big that finding the theoretically best plan doesn't necessarily lead to the best plan in terms of runtime.

Genetic Query Optimization (GEQO) can come to the rescue in such cases. What is **GEQO**? The idea derives inspiration from nature and resembles the natural process of evolution.

PostgreSQL will approach this problem just like a traveling salesman problem and encode the possible joins as integer strings. For example, *4-1-3-2* means first, join *4* and *1*, then *3*, and then *2*. The numbers represent the relation's IDs.

First, the genetic optimizer will generate a random set of plans. Those plans are then inspected. The bad ones are discarded and new ones are generated based on the genes of the good ones. This way, potentially even better plans are generated. This process can be repeated as often as desired. At the end of the day, we are left with a plan that is expected to be a lot better than just using a random plan. GEQO can be turned on and off by adjusting the geqo variable, as shown in the following lines of code:

```
test=# SHOW geqo;
 geqo
------
 on
(1 row)
```

```
test=# SET geqo TO off;
SET
```

By default, the `geqo` variable kicks in if a statement exceeds a certain level of complexity, which is controlled by the following variable:

```
test=# SHOW geqo_threshold ;
 geqo_threshold
----------------
 12
(1 row)
```

If your queries are so large that you start to reach this threshold, it certainly makes sense to play with this setting to see how plans are changed by the planner if you change those variables.

As a general rule, however, I would suggest avoiding GEQO for as long as you can and try to fix things first by trying to somehow fix the join order by using the `join_collapse_limit` variable. Note that every query is different, so it certainly helps to experiment and gain more experience by learning how the planner behaves under different circumstances.

 If you want to see what a really crazy join is, consider checking out a talk I gave in Madrid
at `http://de.slideshare.net/hansjurgenschonig/postgresql-joining-1-million-tables`.

Partitioning data

Given default 8 K blocks, PostgreSQL can store up to 32 TB of data inside a single table. If you compile PostgreSQL with 32 K blocks, you can even put up to 128 TB into a single table. However, large tables such as this aren't necessarily convenient anymore, and it can make sense to partition tables to make processing easier and, in some cases, a bit faster. Starting with version 10.0, PostgreSQL offers improved partitioning, which will offer end users significantly easier handling of data partitioning.

In this chapter, the old means of partitioning, as well as the new features that are available as of PostgreSQL 12.0, will be covered. Features in partitioning are added in all areas as we speak so that people can expect more and better partitioning in all the future versions of PostgreSQL.

Creating partitions

First, we will take a closer look at the outdated method of partitioning data. Keep in mind that understanding this technique is important to gain a deeper overview of what PostgreSQL really does behind the scenes.

Before digging deeper into the advantages of partitioning, I want to show you how partitions can be created. The entire thing starts with a parent table that we can create by using the following command:

```
test=# CREATE TABLE t_data (id serial, t date, payload text);
CREATE TABLE
```

In this example, the parent table has three columns. The date column will be used for partitioning, but we'll cover more on that a bit later.

Now that the parent table is in place, the child tables can be created. This is how it works:

```
test=# CREATE TABLE t_data_2016 () INHERITS (t_data);
CREATE TABLE
test=# \d t_data_2016
                     Table "public.t_data_2016"
 Column  | Type    | Modifiers
---------+---------+--------------------------------------------------
 id      | integer | not null default
                     nextval('t_data_id_seq'::regclass)
 t       | date    |
 payload | text    |
Inherits: t_data
```

The table is called t_data_2016 and inherits from t_data. (). This means that no extra columns are added to the child table. As you can see, inheritance means that all the columns from the parents are available in the child table. Also note that the id column will inherit the sequence from the parent so that all the children can share the very same numbering.

Let's create some more tables:

```
test=# CREATE TABLE t_data_2015 () INHERITS (t_data);
CREATE TABLE
test=# CREATE TABLE t_data_2014 () INHERITS (t_data);
CREATE TABLE
```

So far, all of the tables are identical and just inherit from the parent. However, there's more: child tables can actually have more columns than parents. Adding more fields is simple:

```
test=# CREATE TABLE t_data_2013 (special text) INHERITS (t_data);
CREATE TABLE
```

In this case, a special column has been added. It has no impact on the parent; it just enriches the children and makes them capable of holding more data.

After creating a handful of tables, a row can be added:

```
test=# INSERT INTO t_data_2015 (t, payload)
        VALUES ('2015-05-04', 'some data');
INSERT 0 1
```

The most important thing now is that the parent table can be used to find all the data in the child tables:

```
test=# SELECT * FROM t_data;
 id |     t      | payload
----+------------+-----------
  1 | 2015-05-04 | some data
(1 row)
```

Querying the parent allows you to gain access to everything below the parent in a simple and efficient manner.

To understand how PostgreSQL does partitioning, it makes sense to take a look at the plan:

```
test=# EXPLAIN SELECT * FROM t_data;
                              QUERY PLAN
----------------------------------------------------------------------
 Append  (cost=0.00..84.10 rows=4411 width=40)
   -> Seq Scan on t_data  (cost=0.00..0.00 rows=1 width=40)
   -> Seq Scan on t_data_2016
         (cost=0.00..22.00 rows=1200 width=40)
   -> Seq Scan on t_data_2015
         (cost=0.00..22.00 rows=1200 width=40)
   -> Seq Scan on t_data_2014
         (cost=0.00..22.00 rows=1200 width=40)
   -> Seq Scan on t_data_2013
         (cost=0.00..18.10 rows=810 width=40)
(6 rows)
```

Actually, the process is quite simple. PostgreSQL will simply unify all the tables and show us all the content from all the tables inside and below the partition we are looking at. Note that all the tables are independent and are just connected logically through the system catalog.

Applying table constraints

What happens if filters are applied to the table? What will the optimizer decide to do in order to execute this query in the most efficient way possible? The following example shows us how the PostgreSQL planner will behave:

```
test=# EXPLAIN SELECT * FROM t_data WHERE t = '2016-01-04';
                          QUERY PLAN
-------------------------------------------------------------------
 Append  (cost=0.00..95.12 rows=23 width=40)
   -> Seq Scan on t_data  (cost=0.00..0.00 rows=1 width=40)
         Filter: (t = '2016-01-04'::date)
   -> Seq Scan on t_data_2016  (cost=0.00..25.00 rows=6 width=40)
         Filter: (t = '2016-01-04'::date)
   -> Seq Scan on t_data_2015  (cost=0.00..25.00 rows=6 width=40)
         Filter: (t = '2016-01-04'::date)
   -> Seq Scan on t_data_2014  (cost=0.00..25.00 rows=6 width=40)
         Filter: (t = '2016-01-04'::date)
   -> Seq Scan on t_data_2013  (cost=0.00..20.12 rows=4 width=40)
         Filter: (t = '2016-01-04'::date)
(11 rows)
```

PostgreSQL will apply the filter to all the partitions in the structure. It doesn't know that the table name is somehow related to the content of the tables. To the database, names are just names and have nothing to do with what we are looking for. This makes sense, of course, since there is no mathematical justification for doing anything else.

The point now is: how can we teach the database that the 2016 table only contains 2016 data, the 2015 table only contains 2015 data, and so on? Table constraints are here to do exactly that. They teach PostgreSQL about the content of those tables and therefore allow the planner to make smarter decisions than before. This feature is called constraint exclusion and helps dramatically speed up queries in many cases.

The following listing shows how table constraints can be created:

```
test=# ALTER TABLE t_data_2013
    ADD CHECK (t < '2014-01-01');
ALTER TABLE
test=# ALTER TABLE t_data_2014
    ADD CHECK (t >= '2014-01-01' AND t < '2015-01-01');
ALTER TABLE
test=# ALTER TABLE t_data_2015
    ADD CHECK (t >= '2015-01-01' AND t < '2016-01-01');
ALTER TABLE
test=# ALTER TABLE t_data_2016
    ADD CHECK (t >= '2016-01-01' AND t < '2017-01-01');
ALTER TABLE
```

For each table, a CHECK constraint can be added.

 PostgreSQL will only create the constraint if all the data in those tables is perfectly correct and if every single row satisfies the constraint. In contrast to MySQL, constraints in PostgreSQL are taken seriously and honored under any circumstance.

In PostgreSQL, these constraints can overlap – this is not forbidden and can make sense in some cases. However, it is usually better to have non-overlapping constraints because PostgreSQL has the option to prune more tables.

Here's what happens after adding those table constraints:

```
test=# EXPLAIN SELECT * FROM t_data WHERE t = '2016-01-04';
                        QUERY PLAN
--------------------------------------------------------------------
 Append  (cost=0.00..25.00 rows=7 width=40)
    -> Seq Scan on t_data  (cost=0.00..0.00 rows=1 width=40)
          Filter: (t = '2016-01-04'::date)
    -> Seq Scan on t_data_2016  (cost=0.00..25.00 rows=6 width=40)
          Filter: (t = '2016-01-04'::date)
(5 rows)
```

The planner will be able to remove many of the tables from the query and only keep those that potentially contain the data. This query can greatly benefit from a shorter and more efficient plan. In particular, if those tables are really large, removing them can boost speed considerably.

Modifying inherited structures

Once in a while, data structures have to be modified. The ALTER TABLE clause is here to do exactly that. The question here is, how can partitioned tables be modified?

Basically, all you have to do is tackle the parent table and add or remove columns. PostgreSQL will automatically propagate those changes through to the child tables and ensure that changes are made to all the relations, as follows:

```
test=# ALTER TABLE t_data ADD COLUMN x int;
ALTER TABLE
test=# \d t_data_2016
                    Table "public.t_data_2016"
 Column  |  Type   | Modifiers
---------+---------+-------------------------------------------------
      id | integer | not null default
                     nextval('t_data_id_seq'::regclass)
       t |    date |
 payload |    text |
       x | integer |
Check constraints:
    "t_data_2016_t_check"
    CHECK (t >= '2016-01-01'::date AND t < '2017-01-01'::date)
Inherits: t_data
```

As you can see, the column is added to the parent and automatically added to the child table here.

Note that this works for columns as well. Indexes are a totally different story. In an inherited structure, every table has to be indexed separately. If you add an index to the parent table, it will only be present on the parent – it won't be deployed on those child tables. Indexing all of those columns in all of those tables is your task, and PostgreSQL isn't going to make those decisions for you. Of course, this can be seen as a feature or as a limitation. On the upside, you could say that PostgreSQL gives you the flexibility to index things separately and therefore potentially more efficiently. However, people may also argue that deploying all those indexes one by one is a lot more work.

Moving tables in and out of partitioned structures

Suppose you have an inherited structure. Data is partitioned by date, and you want to provide the most recent years to the end user. At some point, you may want to remove some data from the scope of the user without actually touching it. You may want to put data into some sort of archive.

PostgreSQL provides a simple means to achieve exactly that. First, a new parent can be created:

```
test=# CREATE TABLE t_history (LIKE t_data);
CREATE TABLE
```

The LIKE keyword allows you to create a table that has exactly the same layout as the t_data table. If you have forgotten which columns the t_data table actually has, this may come in handy as it saves you a lot of work. It is also possible to include indexes, constraints, and defaults.

Then, the table can be moved away from the old parent table and put below the new one. Here's how it works:

```
test=# ALTER TABLE t_data_2013 NO INHERIT t_data;
ALTER TABLE
test=# ALTER TABLE t_data_2013 INHERIT t_history;
ALTER TABLE
```

The entire process can, of course, be done in a single transaction to assure that the operation stays atomic.

Cleaning up data

One advantage of partitioned tables is the ability to clean data up quickly. Let's assume that we want to delete an entire year. If the data is partitioned accordingly, a simple DROP TABLE clause can do the job:

```
test=# DROP TABLE t_data_2014;
DROP TABLE
```

As you can see, dropping a child table is easy. But what about the parent table? There are depending objects and so PostgreSQL naturally errors out to make sure that nothing unexpected happens:

```
test=# DROP TABLE t_data;
ERROR: cannot drop table t_data because other objects depend on it
DETAIL: default for table t_data_2013 column id depends on
    sequence t_data_id_seq
table t_data_2016 depends on table t_data
table t_data_2015 depends on table t_data
HINT: Use DROP ... CASCADE to drop the dependent objects too.
```

The DROP TABLE clause will warn us that there are depending objects and will refuse to drop those tables. The following example shows us how to use a cascaded DROP TABLE:

```
test=# DROP TABLE t_data CASCADE;
NOTICE:  drop  cascades to 3 other  objects
DETAIL:  drop  cascades to default for table  t_data_2013 column id drop
cascades to table  t_data_2016
drop  cascades to table  t_data_2015
DROP TABLE
```

The CASCADE clause is needed to force PostgreSQL to actually remove those objects, along with the parent table.

Understanding PostgreSQL 12.0 partitioning

A lot of what has been added in PostgreSQL 10, 11, and 12 will make sure that what you have seen in the "old world" is automated. This is especially true for indexing, tuple routing on insertion, and so on. However, let's go through those things in a more organized way.

For many years, the PostgreSQL community has been working on built-in partitioning. Finally, PostgreSQL 10.0 now offers the first implementation of in-core partitioning, which will be covered in this chapter. In PostgreSQL 10, the partitioning functionality was still pretty basic and therefore a lot of stuff has been improved in PostgreSQL 11 and 12 to make life even easier for people who want to use this important feature.

To show you how partitioning works, I have compiled a simple example featuring range partitioning, as follows:

```
CREATE TABLE data (
    payload  integer
)  PARTITION BY RANGE (payload);

CREATE TABLE negatives PARTITION
   OF data FOR VALUES FROM (MINVALUE) TO (0);
CREATE TABLE positives PARTITION
   OF data FOR VALUES FROM (0) TO (MAXVALUE);
```

In this example, one partition will hold all the negative values, while the other one will take care of the positive values. While creating the parent table, you can simply specify which way you want to partition data.

Once the parent table has been created, it is time to create the partitions. To do that, the PARTITION OF clause has to be added. At this point, there are still some limitations (as of PostgreSQL 10). The most important one is that a tuple (a row) cannot move from one partition to the other, as follows

```
UPDATE data SET payload = -10 WHERE id = 5
```

Fortunately, this restriction has been lifted, and PostgreSQL 11 is able to move a row from one partition to the other. However, keep in mind that moving data between partitions may not be the best of ideas in general.

Let's take a look and see what happens under the hood:

```
test=# INSERT INTO data VALUES (5);
INSERT 0 1
test=# SELECT * FROM data;
 payload
---------
       5
(1 row)
test=# SELECT * FROM positives;
 payload
---------
       5
(1 row)
```

The data is moved to the correct partition. If we change the value, you will see that the partition also changes. The following listing shows an example of this:

```
test=# UPDATE data
              SET       payload = -10
              WHERE     payload = 5
              RETURNING *;
 payload
---------
     -10
(1 row)
UPDATE 1
test=# SELECT * FROM negatives;
 payload
---------
     -10
(1 row)
```

The next important aspect is related to indexing: in PostgreSQL 10, every table (every partition) had to be indexed separately. This isn't true in PostgreSQL 11 anymore. Let's try this out and see what happens:

```
test=# CREATE INDEX idx_payload ON data (payload);
CREATE INDEX
test=# \d positives
 Table "public.positives"
  Column | Type    | Collation | Nullable | Default
---------+---------+-----------+----------+---------
 payload | integer |           |          |
Partition of: data FOR VALUES FROM (0) TO (MAXVALUE)
Indexes:
 "positives_payload_idx" btree (payload)
```

What you can see here is that the index has also been added to the child table automatically, which is a really important feature of PostgreSQL 11 and which has widely been appreciated by users moving their applications to PostgreSQL 11 and 12 already.

Another important feature is the ability to create a default partition. To show you how that works, we can drop one of our two partitions:

```
test=# DROP TABLE negatives;
DROP TABLE
```

Then, a default partition for the `data` table can be created easily:

```
test=# CREATE TABLE p_def PARTITION OF data DEFAULT;
CREATE TABLE
```

All the data that doesn't fit anywhere will end up in this default partition, which ensures that creating the right partition can never be forgotten. Experience has shown that the existence of a default partition makes applications a lot more reliable as time goes by.

Adjusting parameters for good query performance

Writing good queries is the first step to achieving good performance. Without a good query, you will most likely suffer from bad performance. Therefore, writing good and intelligent code will give you the greatest edge possible. Once your queries have been optimized from a logical and semantical point of view, good memory settings can provide you with a final nice speedup.

In this section, we will learn what more memory can do for you and how PostgreSQL can use it for your benefit. Again, this section assumes that we are using single-core queries to make the plans more readable. To ensure that there is always just one core at work, use the following command:

```
test=# SET max_parallel_workers_per_gather TO 0;
SET
```

Here is a simple example demonstrating what memory parameters can do for you:

```
test=# CREATE TABLE t_test (id serial, name text);
CREATE TABLE
test=# INSERT INTO t_test (name)
    SELECT 'hans' FROM generate_series(1, 100000);
INSERT 0 100000
test=# INSERT INTO t_test (name)
    SELECT 'paul' FROM generate_series(1, 100000);
INSERT 0 100000
```

1 million rows containing `hans` will be added to the table. Then, 1 million rows containing `paul` will be loaded. Altogether, there will be 2 million unique IDs, but just two different names.

Let's run a simple query by using PostgreSQL's default memory settings:

```
test=# SELECT name, count(*) FROM t_test GROUP BY 1;
 name  | count
-------+--------
 hans  | 100000
 paul  | 100000
(2 rows)
```

Two rows will be returned, which should not come as a surprise. The important thing here is not the result, but what PostgreSQL is doing behind the scenes:

```
test=# EXPLAIN ANALYZE SELECT name, count(*)
   FROM t_test
   GROUP BY 1;
                             QUERY PLAN
-------------------------------------------------------------------
 HashAggregate (cost=4082.00..4082.01 rows=1 width=13)
   (actual time=51.448..51.448 rows=2 loops=1)
             Group Key: name
   -> Seq Scan on t_test
         (cost=0.00..3082.00 rows=200000 width=5)
         (actual time=0.007..14.150 rows=200000 loops=1)
 Planning time: 0.032 ms
```

```
    Execution time: 51.471 ms
  (5 rows)
```

PostgreSQL figured out that the number of groups is actually very small. Therefore, it creates a hash, adds one hash entry per group, and starts to count. Due to the low number of groups, the hash is really small and PostgreSQL can quickly do the count by incrementing the numbers for each group.

What happens if we group by ID and not by name? The number of groups will skyrocket, as shown in the following code:

```
test=# EXPLAIN ANALYZE SELECT id, count(*) FROM t_test GROUP BY 1;
                              QUERY PLAN
-----------------------------------------------------------------
  GroupAggregate (cost=23428.64..26928.64 rows=200000 width=12)
      (actual time=97.128..154.205 rows=200000 loops=1)
      Group Key: id
      -> Sort (cost=23428.64..23928.64 rows=200000 width=4)
          (actual time=97.120..113.017 rows=200000 loops=1)
          Sort Key: id
          Sort Method: external sort Disk: 2736kB
          -> Seq Scan on t_test
              (cost=0.00..3082.00 rows=200000 width=4)
              (actual time=0.017..19.469 rows=200000 loops=1)
  Planning time: 0.128 ms
  Execution time: 160.589 ms
  (8 rows)
```

PostgreSQL figures out that the number of groups is now a lot larger and quickly changes its strategy. The problem is that a hash containing so many entries doesn't fit into memory:

```
test=# SHOW work_mem ;
  work_mem
  ----------
  4MB
  (1 row)
```

As we can see, the `work_mem` variable governs the size of the hash that's used by the GROUP BY clause. Since there are too many entries, PostgreSQL has to find a strategy that doesn't require that we hold the entire dataset in memory. The solution is to sort the data by ID and group it. Once the data has been sorted, PostgreSQL can move down the list and form one group after the other. If the first type of value is counted, the partial result is read and can be emitted. Then, the next group can be processed. Once the value in the sorted list changes when moving down, it will never show up again; thus, the system knows that a partial result is ready.

To speed up the query, a higher value for the `work_mem` variable can be set on the fly (and, of course, globally):

```
test=# SET work_mem TO '1 GB';
SET
```

Now, the plan will, once again, feature a fast and efficient hash aggregate:

```
test=# EXPLAIN ANALYZE SELECT id, count(*) FROM t_test GROUP BY 1;
                            QUERY PLAN
-----------------------------------------------------------------
 HashAggregate  (cost=4082.00..6082.00 rows=200000 width=12)
    (actual time=76.967..118.926 rows=200000 loops=1)
    Group Key: id
    -> Seq Scan on t_test
        (cost=0.00..3082.00 rows=200000 width=4)
        (actual time=0.008..13.570 rows=200000 loops=1)
 Planning time: 0.073 ms
 Execution time: 126.456 ms
(5 rows)
```

PostgreSQL knows (or at least assumes) that data will fit into memory and switch to the faster plan. As you can see, the execution time is lower. The query won't be as fast as in the GROUP BY name case because many more hash values have to be calculated, but you will be able to see a nice and reliable benefit in the vast majority of cases.

Speeding up sorting

The `work_mem` variable doesn't only speed up grouping. It can also have a very nice impact on simple things such as sorting, which is an essential mechanism that's been mastered by every database system in the world.

The following query shows a simple operation using the default setting of 4 MB:

```
test=# SET work_mem TO default;
SET
test=# EXPLAIN ANALYZE SELECT * FROM t_test ORDER BY name, id;
                        QUERY PLAN
-----------------------------------------------------------------
 Sort  (cost=24111.14..24611.14 rows=200000 width=9)
        (actual time=219.298..235.008 rows=200000 loops=1)
        Sort Key: name, id
        Sort Method: external sort  Disk: 3712kB
        -> Seq Scan on t_test
            (cost=0.00..3082.00 rows=200000 width=9)
```

```
                  (actual time=0.006..13.807 rows=200000 loops=1)
   Planning time: 0.064 ms
   Execution time: 241.375 ms
 (6 rows)
```

PostgreSQL needs 13.8 milliseconds to read the data and over 200 milliseconds to sort the data. Due to the low amount of memory available, sorting has to be performed using temporary files. The external sort Disk method only needs small amounts of RAM but has to send intermediate data to a comparatively slow storage device, which of course leads to poor throughput.

Increasing the work_mem variable setting will make PostgreSQL use more memory for sorting:

```
 test=# SET work_mem TO '1 GB';
 SET
 test=# EXPLAIN ANALYZE SELECT * FROM t_test ORDER  BY name, id;
                             QUERY PLAN
 --------------------------------------------------------------
  Sort (cost=20691.64..21191.64 rows=200000 width=9)
         (actual time=36.481..47.899 rows=200000 loops=1)
         Sort Key: name, id
         Sort Method: quicksort Memory: 15520kB
         -> Seq Scan on t_test
            (cost=0.00..3082.00 rows=200000 width=9)
            (actual time=0.010..14.232 rows=200000 loops=1)
   Planning time: 0.037 ms
   Execution time: 55.520 ms
 (6 rows)
```

Since there is enough memory now, the database will do all the sorting in memory and therefore speed up the process dramatically. The sort takes just 33 milliseconds now, which is a seven-times improvement compared to the query we had previously. More memory will lead to faster sorting and will speed up the system.

So far, you have seen two mechanisms that can be used to sort data: external sort Disk and quicksort Memory. In addition to these two mechanisms, there is also a third algorithm, that is, top-N heapsort Memory. It can be used to provide you with only the top-N rows:

```
 test=# EXPLAIN ANALYZE SELECT * FROM t_test ORDER BY name, id LIMIT 10;
                             QUERY PLAN
 --------------------------------------------------------------
  Limit (cost=7403.93..7403.95 rows=10 width=9)
         (actual time=31.837..31.838 rows=10 loops=1)
         -> Sort (cost=7403.93..7903.93 rows=200000 width=9)
```

```
        (actual time=31.836..31.837 rows=10 loops=1)
        Sort Key: name, id
        Sort Method: top-N heapsort Memory: 25kB
        -> Seq Scan on t_test
           (cost=0.00..3082.00 rows=200000 width=9)
           (actual time=0.011..13.645 rows=200000 loops=1)
 Planning time: 0.053 ms
 Execution time: 31.856 ms
(7 rows)
```

The algorithm is lightning fast, and the entire query will be done in just over 30 milliseconds. The sorting part is now only 18 milliseconds and is therefore almost as fast as reading the data in the first place.

Note that the `work_mem` variable is allocated per operation. Theoretically, a query may need the `work_mem` variable more than once. It is not a global setting – it is really per operation. Therefore, you have to set it in a careful way.

The one thing that we need to keep in mind is that there are many books that claim that setting the `work_mem` variable too high on an OLTP system may cause your server to run out of memory. Yes; if 1,000 people sort 100 MB at the same time, this can result in memory failures. However, do you expect the disk to be able to handle that? I doubt it. The solution can only be to rethink what you are doing. Sorting 100 MB 1,000 times concurrently is not what should happen in an OLTP system anyway. Consider deploying proper indexes, writing better queries, or simply rethinking your requirements. Under any circumstances, sorting so much data so often concurrently is a bad idea – stop before those things stop your application.

Speeding up administrative tasks

There are more operations that actually have to do some sorting or memory allocation of some kind. The administrative ones such as the CREATE INDEX clause don't rely on the `work_mem` variable and use the `maintenance_work_mem` variable instead. Here is how it works:

```
test=# SET maintenance_work_mem TO '1 MB';
SET
test=# \timing
Timing is on.
test=# CREATE INDEX idx_id ON t_test (id);
CREATE INDEX
Time: 104.268 ms
```

As you can see, creating an index on 2 million rows takes around 100 milliseconds, which is really slow. Therefore, the `maintenance_work_mem` variable can be used to speed up sorting, which is essentially what the `CREATE INDEX` clause does:

```
test=# SET maintenance_work_mem TO '1 GB';
SET
test=# CREATE INDEX idx_id2 ON t_test (id);
CREATE INDEX
Time:   46.774 ms
```

The speed has now doubled just because sorting has been improved so much.

There are more administrative jobs that can benefit from more memory. The most prominent ones are the `VACUUM` clause (to clean out indexes) and the `ALTER TABLE` clause. The rules for the `maintenance_work_mem` variable are the same as they are for the `work_mem` variable. The setting is per operation, and only the required memory is allocated on the fly.

In PostgreSQL 11, an additional feature was added to the database engine: PostgreSQL is now able to build `btree` indexes in parallel, which can dramatically speed up the indexing of large tables. The parameter that's in charge of configuring parallelism is as follows:

```
test=# SHOW max_parallel_maintenance_workers;
 max_parallel_maintenance_workers
-----------------------------------
 2
(1 row)
```

`max_parallel_maintenance_workers` controls the maximum number of worker processes that can be used by `CREATE INDEX`. As for every parallel operation, PostgreSQL will determine the number of workers based on table sizes. When indexing large tables, index creation can see drastic improvements. Here at Cybertec, I did some extensive testing and summarized my findings in one of my blog posts: `https://www.cybertec-postgresql.com/en/postgresql-parallel-create-index-for-better-performance/`.

Making use of parallel queries

Starting with version 9.6, PostgreSQL supports parallel queries. This support for parallelism has been improved gradually over time, and version 11 has added even more functionality to this important feature. In this section, we will take a look at how parallelism works and what can be done to speed up things.

Before digging into the details, it is necessary to create some sample data, as follows:

```
test=# CREATE TABLE t_parallel AS
  SELECT * FROM generate_series(1, 25000000) AS id;
SELECT 25000000
```

After loading the initial data, we can run our first parallel query. A simple count will show what a parallel query looks like in general:

```
test=# explain SELECT count(*) FROM t_parallel;
  QUERY PLAN
----------------------------------------------------------------------
----------
  Finalize Aggregate (cost=258537.40..258537.41 rows=1 width=8)
  -> Gather (cost=258537.19..258537.40 rows=2 width=8)
  Workers Planned: 2
  -> Partial Aggregate (cost=257537.19..257537.20 rows=1 width=8)
  -> Parallel Seq Scan on t_parallel (cost=0.00..228153.75 rows=11753375
width=0)
  (5 rows)
```

Let's take a detailed look at the execution plan of the query. First, PostgreSQL performs a parallel sequential scan. This implies that PostgreSQL will use more than 1 CPU to process the table (block by block) and it will create partial aggregates. The job of the gather node is to collect the data and to pass it on to do the final aggregation. The gather node is the end of parallelism. It is important to mention that parallelism is (currently) never nested. There can never be a gather node inside another gather node. In this example, PostgreSQL has decided on two worker processes. Why is that?

Let's consider the following variable:

```
test=# SHOW max_parallel_workers_per_gather;
  max_parallel_workers_per_gather
-----------------------------------
  2
(1 row)
```

max_parallel_workers_per_gather limits the number of worker processes allowed below the gather node to two. The important thing is this: if a table is small, it will never use parallelism. The size of a table has to be at least 8 MB, as defined by the following config setting:

```
test=# SHOW min_parallel_table_scan_size;
  min_parallel_table_scan_size
-----------------------------------
  8MB
(1 row)
```

Now, the rule for parallelism is as follows: the size of the table has to triple in order for PostgreSQL to add one more worker process. In other words, to get four additional workers, you need at least 81 times as much data. This makes sense because the size of your database goes up 100 times, and the storage system is usually not 100 times faster. Therefore, the number of useful cores is somewhat limited.

However, our table is fairly large:

```
test=# \d+
 List of relations
 Schema | Name       | Type  | Owner | Size   | Description
--------+------------+-------+-------+--------+-------------
 public | t_parallel | table | hs    | 864 MB |
(1 row)
```

In this example, `max_parallel_workers_per_gather` limits the number of cores. If we change this setting, PostgreSQL will decide on more cores:

```
test=# SET max_parallel_workers_per_gather TO 10;
SET
test=# explain SELECT count(*) FROM t_parallel;
                                            QUERY PLAN
--------------------------------------------------------------------------------
--------------------
 Finalize Aggregate (cost=174119.72..174119.73 rows=1 width=8)
   -> Gather (cost=174119.20..174119.71 rows=5 width=8)
         Workers Planned: 5
         -> Partial Aggregate (cost=173119.20..173119.21 rows=1 width=8)
               -> Parallel Seq Scan on t_parallel (cost=0.00..160619.36
rows=4999936 width=0)
 JIT:
   Functions: 4
   Options: Inlining false, Optimization false, Expressions true, Deforming
true
(8 rows)
```

In this case, we get 5 workers (just as expected).

However, there are cases in which you'll want the number of cores being used for a certain table to be a lot higher. Just imagine a 200 GB database, 1 TB of RAM, and only a single user. This user could use up all the CPU without harming anybody else. ALTER TABLE can be used to overrule what we have just discussed:

```
test=# ALTER TABLE t_parallel SET (parallel_workers = 9);
ALTER TABLE
```

If you want to overrule the x3 rule to determine the number of desired CPUs, you can use `ALTER TABLE` to hardware the number of CPUs explicitly.

Note that `max_parallel_workers_per_gather` will still be effective and serve as the upper limit.

If you look at the plan, you will see that the number of cores will actually be considered:

```
test=# explain SELECT count(*) FROM t_parallel;
                                            QUERY PLAN
-----------------------------------------------------------------------------
----------------------
 Finalize Aggregate  (cost=146342.71..146342.72 rows=1 width=8)
   -> Gather  (cost=146341.77..146342.68 rows=9 width=8)
         Workers Planned: 9
         -> Partial Aggregate  (cost=145341.77..145341.79 rows=1 width=8)
               -> Parallel Seq Scan on t_parallel  (cost=0.00..138397.42
rows=2777742 width=0)
 JIT:
   Functions: 4
   Options: Inlining false, Optimization false, Expressions true, Deforming
true
(8 rows)

Time: 2.454 ms
```

However, that doesn't mean that those cores are actually used as well:

```
test=# explain analyze SELECT count(*) FROM t_parallel;
                                            QUERY PLAN
-----------------------------------------------------------------------------
----------------------
 Finalize Aggregate  (cost=146342.71..146342.72 rows=1 width=8)
                     (actual time=1164.445..1164.445 rows=1 loops=1)
   -> Gather  (cost=146341.77..146342.68 rows=9 width=8)
            (actual time=1164.427..1164.533 rows=8 loops=1)
         Workers Planned: 9
         Workers Launched: 7
         -> Partial Aggregate  (cost=145341.77..145341.79 rows=1 width=8)
                               (actual time=1128.530..1128.530 rows=1
loops=8)
               -> Parallel Seq Scan on t_parallel  (cost=0.00..138397.42
rows=2777742 width=0)
                               (actual time=0.218..1023.449 rows=3125000
loops=8)
 Planning Time: 0.028 ms
 JIT:
   Functions: 18
```

```
   Options: Inlining false, Optimization false, Expressions true, Deforming
true
   Timing: Generation 1.703 ms, Inlining 0.000 ms, Optimization 1.119 ms,
      Emission 14.707 ms, Total 17.529 ms
 Execution Time: 1164.922 ms
(12 rows)
```

As you can see, only seven cores were launched, despite the fact that nine processes were planned. What's the reason for this? In this example, two more variables come into play:

```
test=# SHOW max_worker_processes;
 max_worker_processes
----------------------
 8
(1 row)

test=# SHOW max_parallel_workers;
 max_parallel_workers
----------------------
 8
(1 row)
```

The first process tells PostgreSQL how many worker processes are generally available. `max_parallel_workers` states how many workers are available for parallel queries. Why are there two parameters? Background processes aren't only used by the parallel query infrastructure – they can also be used for other purposes and therefore most developers decide to use two parameters.

In general, we at Cybertec (`https://www.cybertec-postgresql.com`) tend to set `max_worker_processes` to the number of CPUs in the server. It seems that using more is usually not beneficial.

What is PostgreSQL able to do in parallel?

As we've already mentioned in this section, the support for parallelism has been gradually improved since PostgreSQL 9.6. In every version, new stuff is added.

The following are the most important operations that can be done in parallel:

- Parallel sequential scans
- Parallel index scans (btrees only)
- Parallel bitmap heap scans
- Parallel joins (all types of joins)

- Parallel btree creation (CREATE INDEX)
- Parallel aggregation
- Parallel append

In PostgreSQL 11, the support for parallel index creation has been added. Normal sort operations are not fully parallel yet – so far, only btree creation can be done in parallel. To control the amount of parallelism, we need to apply the following parameter:

```
test=# SHOW max_parallel_maintenance_workers;
 max_parallel_maintenance_workers
----------------------------------
 2
(1 row)
```

The rules for parallelism are basically the same as they are for normal operations.

If you want to speed up your index creation, consider checking out one of my blog posts about index creation and performance: https://www.cybertec-postgresql.com/en/postgresql-parallel-create-index-for-better-performance/.

Parallelism in practice

Now that we've introduced the basics of parallelism, we have to learn what it means in the real world. Let's take a look at the following query:

```
test=# explain SELECT * FROM t_parallel;
                          QUERY PLAN
---------------------------------------------------------------------
 Seq Scan on t_parallel (cost=0.00..360621.20 rows=25000120 width=4)
(1 row)
```

Why does PostgreSQL not use a parallel query? The table is sufficiently large and the worker PostgreSQL is available, so why doesn't it use a parallel query? The answer is that interprocess communication is really expensive. If PostgreSQL has to ship rows between processes, a query can actually be slower than in single-process mode. The optimizer uses cost parameters to punish interprocess communication:

```
#parallel_tuple_cost = 0.1
```

Every time a tuple is moved between processes, 0.1 points will be added to the calculation. To see how PostgreSQL would run parallel queries in case it is forced to, I have included the following example:

```
test=# SET force_parallel_mode TO on;
SET
test=# explain SELECT * FROM t_parallel;
                              QUERY PLAN
-----------------------------------------------------------------------
-
 Gather (cost=1000.00..2861633.20 rows=25000120 width=4)
    Workers Planned: 1
    Single Copy: true
    -> Seq Scan on t_parallel (cost=0.00..360621.20 rows=25000120 width=4)
(4 rows)
```

As you can see, the costs are higher than in single-core mode. In the real world, this is an important issue because many people are wondering why PostgreSQL is going for a single core.

In a real example, it is also important to see that more cores doesn't automatically lead to more speed. A delicate balancing act is required to find the perfect number of cores.

Introducing JIT compilation

JIT compilation has been one of **the** hot topics in PostgreSQL 11. It has been a major undertaking, and the first results look promising. However, let's start with the fundamentals: what is JIT compilation all about? When you run a query, PostgreSQL has to figure out a lot of stuff at runtime. When PostgreSQL itself is compiled, it doesn't know which kind of query you will run next, so it has to be prepared for all kinds of scenarios.

The core is generic, meaning that it can do all kinds of stuff. However, when you are in a query, you just want to execute the current query as fast as possible – not some other random stuff. The point is, at runtime, you know a lot more about what you have to do than at compile time (that is, when PostgreSQL is compiled). That is exactly the point: when JIT compilation is enabled, PostgreSQL will check your query, and if it happens to be time-consuming enough, highly optimized code for your query will be created on the fly (just-in-time).

Configuring JIT

To use JIT, it has to be added at compile time. The following configure options are available:

```
--with-llvm build with LLVM based JIT support
...
LLVM_CONFIG path to llvm-config command
```

Some Linux distributions ship an extra package containing support for JIT. If you want to make use of JIT, make sure those packages are installed.

Once you have made sure that JIT is available, the following configuration parameters will be available so that you can fine-tune JIT compilation for your queries:

```
#jit = on                            # allow JIT compilation
#jit_provider = 'llvmjit'            # JIT implementation to use
#jit_above_cost = 100000             # perform JIT compilation if
available
                                     # and query more expensive, -1
disables
#jit_optimize_above_cost = 500000    # optimize JITed functions if query
is
                                     # more expensive, -1 disables
#jit_inline_above_cost = 500000      # attempt to inline operators and
                                     # functions if query is more
expensive,
                                     # -1 disables
```

jit_above_cost means that JIT is only considered if the expected cost is at least 100,000. Why is that relevant? If a query isn't sufficiently long, the overhead of compilation can be a lot higher than the potential gain. Therefore, optimization is only attempted. However, there are two more parameters: really deep optimizations are attempted if the query is considered to be more expensive than 500,000. In this case, function calls will be inlined.

At this point, PostgreSQL only supports LLVM as a JIT backend. Maybe additional backends will be available in the future as well. For now, LLVM does a really good job and covers most of the environments that are used in professional environments.

Running queries

To show you how JIT works, we shall compile a simple example. Let's begin by creating a big table – one that contains a lot of data. Remember, JIT compilation is only useful if the operation is sufficiently large. For beginners, 50 million rows should suffice. The following example shows how to populate the table:

```
jit=# CREATE TABLE t_jit AS
        SELECT (random()*10000)::int AS x, (random()*100000)::int AS y,
(random()*1000000)::int AS z
        FROM generate_series(1, 50000000) AS id;
SELECT 50000000
jit=# VACUUM ANALYZE t_jit;
VACUUM
```

In this case, we will use the random function to generate some data. To show you how JIT works and to make execution plans easier to read, you can turn off parallel queries. JIT works fine with parallel queries, but execution plans tend to be a lot longer:

```
jit=# SET max_parallel_workers_per_gather TO 0;
SET
jit=# SET jit TO off;
SET
jit=# explain (analyze, verbose) SELECT avg(z+y-pi()), avg(y-pi()),
max(x/pi())
                FROM    t_jit
                WHERE   ((y+z))>((y-x)*0.000001);
                                                QUERY PLAN
-----------------------------------------------------------------------------
-------------------------------
 Aggregate  (cost=1936901.68..1936901.69 rows=1 width=24)
            (actual time=20617.425..20617.425 rows=1 loops=1)
   Output: avg((((z + y))::double precision - '3.14159265358979'::double
precision)),
           avg(((y)::double precision - '3.14159265358979'::double
precision)),
           max(((x)::double precision / '3.14159265358979'::double
precision))
        -> Seq Scan on public.t_jit  (cost=0.00..1520244.00 rows=16666307
width=12)
           (actual time=0.061..15322.555 rows=50000000 loops=1)
           Output: x, y, z
           Filter: (((t_jit.y + t_jit.z))::numeric > (((t_jit.y -
t_jit.x))::numeric * 0.000001))
 Planning Time: 0.078 ms
 Execution Time: 20617.473 ms
(7 rows)
```

In this case, the query took 20 seconds.

I have used a VACUUM to ensure that all the hint bits and so on have been properly set to ensure a fair comparison between a jitted query and a normal query.

Let's repeat this test with JIT enabled:

```
jit=# SET jit TO on;
SET
jit=# explain (analyze, verbose) SELECT avg(z+y-pi()), avg(y-pi()),
max(x/pi())
                FROM    t_jit
                WHERE   ((y+z))>((y-x)*0.000001);
                                                QUERY PLAN
----------------------------------------------------------------------------
---------------------------
 Aggregate  (cost=1936901.68..1936901.69 rows=1 width=24)
           (actual time=15585.788..15585.789 rows=1 loops=1)
   Output: avg(((((z + y))::double precision - '3.14159265358979'::double
precision)),
           avg(((y)::double precision - '3.14159265358979'::double
precision)),
           max(((x)::double precision / '3.14159265358979'::double
precision))
       -> Seq Scan on public.t_jit  (cost=0.00..1520244.00 rows=16666307
width=12)
           (actual time=81.991..13396.227 rows=50000000 loops=1)
           Output: x, y, z
           Filter: (((t_jit.y + t_jit.z))::numeric > (((t_jit.y -
t_jit.x))::numeric * 0.000001))
 Planning Time: 0.135 ms
 JIT:
    Functions: 5
 Options: Inlining true, Optimization true, Expressions true, Deforming
true
           Timing: Generation 2.942 ms, Inlining 15.717 ms, Optimization
40.806 ms,
           Emission 25.233 ms,
           Total 84.698 ms
 Execution Time: 15588.851 ms
(11 rows)
```

In this case, you can see that the query is a lot faster than before, which is already significant. In some cases, the benefits can be even bigger. However, keep in mind that recompiling code is also associated with some additional effort, so it doesn't make sense for every kind of query.

Summary

In this chapter, a number of query optimizations were discussed. You learned about the optimizer and about various internal optimizations, such as constant folding, view inlining, joins, and much more. All of these optimizations contribute to good performance and help speed things up considerably.

Now that we've covered this introduction to optimizations, in the next chapter, Chapter 7, *Writing Stored Procedures*, we will talk about stored procedures. You will learn about all the options PostgreSQL has so that we can handle user-defined code.

Writing Stored Procedures

7

In Chapter 6, *Optimizing Queries for Good Performance*, we learned a lot about the optimizer, as well as the optimizations going on in the system. This chapter is going to be about stored procedures and how to use them efficiently and easily. You will learn what a stored procedure is made up of, which languages are available, and how you can speed things up nicely. On top of that, you will be introduced to some of the more advanced features of PL/pgSQL.

The following topics will be covered in this chapter:

- Understanding stored procedure languages
- Understanding various stored procedure languages
- Improving functions
- Using functions for various purposes

By the end of this chapter, you will be able to write good, efficient procedures.

Understanding stored procedure languages

When it comes to stored procedures and functions, PostgreSQL differs quite significantly from other database systems. Most database engines force you to use a certain programming language to write server-side code. Microsoft SQL Server offers Transact-SQL, while Oracle encourages you to use PL/SQL. PostgreSQL doesn't force you to use a certain language; instead, it allows you to decide on what you know and like the best.

The reason PostgreSQL is so flexible is actually quite interesting in a historical sense, too. Many years ago, one of the most well-known PostgreSQL developers, Jan Wieck, who had written countless patches back in its early days, came up with the idea of using **Tool Command Language** (**Tcl**) as the server-side programming language. The trouble was that nobody wanted to use Tcl and nobody wanted to have this stuff in the database engine. The solution to the problem was to make the language interface so flexible that basically any language can be easily integrated with PostgreSQL. At this point, the CREATE LANGUAGE clause was born. Here is the syntax of CREATE LANGUAGE:

```
test=# \h CREATE LANGUAGE
Command: CREATE LANGUAGE
Description: define a new procedural language
Syntax:
CREATE [ OR REPLACE ] [ PROCEDURAL ] LANGUAGE name
CREATE [ OR REPLACE ] [ TRUSTED ] [ PROCEDURAL ] LANGUAGE name
    HANDLER call_handler [ INLINE inline_handler ] [ VALIDATOR valfunction
]

URL: https://www.postgresql.org/docs/12/sql-createlanguage.html
```

Nowadays, many different languages can be used to write functions and stored procedures. The flexibility that's been added to PostgreSQL has really paid off; we can now choose from a rich set of programming languages.

How exactly does PostgreSQL handle languages? If we take a look at the syntax of the CREATE LANGUAGE clause, we will see a few keywords:

- HANDLER: This function is actually the glue between PostgreSQL and any external language that you want to use. It is in charge of mapping PostgreSQL data structures to whatever is needed by the language, and it helps pass the code around.
- VALIDATOR: This is the police officer of the infrastructure. If it is available, it will be in charge of delivering tasty syntax errors to the end user. Many languages are able to parse code before actually executing it. PostgreSQL can use that and tell you whether a function is correct or not when you create it. Unfortunately, not all languages can do this, so in some cases, you will still be left with problems showing up at runtime.
- INLINE: If this is present, PostgreSQL will be able to run anonymous code blocks utilizing this handler function.

Understanding fundamentals – stored procedures versus functions

Before we dig into the anatomy of a stored procedure, it is important to talk about functions and procedures in general. The term stored procedure has traditionally been used to actually talk about a function. Thus, it is essential that we understand the difference between a function and a procedure.

A function is part of a normal SQL statement, and is not allowed to start or commit transactions. Here is an example:

```
SELECT func(id) FROM large_table;
```

Suppose `func(id)` is called 50 million times. If you use the function called `commit`, what exactly should happen? It is impossible to simply end a transaction in the middle of a query and launch a new one. The entire concept of transactional integrity, consistency, and so on would be violated.

A procedure, in contrast, is able to control transactions and even run multiple transactions one after the other. However, you cannot run it inside a `SELECT` statement. Instead, you have to invoke `CALL`. The following listing shows the syntax of the `CALL` command:

```
test=# \h CALL
Command: CALL
Description: invoke a procedure
Syntax:
CALL name ( [ argument ] [, ...] )

URL: https://www.postgresql.org/docs/12/sql-call.html
```

Therefore, there is a fundamental distinction between functions and procedures. The terminology that you will find on the internet is not always clear. However, you have to be aware of those important differences. In PostgreSQL, functions have been around since the very beginning. However, the concept of a procedure, as outlined in this section, is new and has only been introduced in PostgreSQL 11. In this chapter, we will take a look at functions and procedures in detail.

The anatomy of a function

Before we dig into a specific language, we will look at the anatomy of a typical function. For demonstration purposes, let's look at the following function, which just adds two numbers:

```
test=# CREATE OR REPLACE FUNCTION mysum(int, int)
RETURNS int AS
'
   SELECT $1 + $2;
' LANGUAGE 'sql';
CREATE FUNCTION
```

The first thing to observe is that this function is written in SQL. PostgreSQL needs to know which language we are using, so we have to specify that in the definition.

Note that the code of the function is passed to PostgreSQL as a string ('). This is somewhat noteworthy because it allows a function to become a black box to the execution machinery.

In other database engines, the code of the function is not a string, but is directly attached to the statement. This simple abstraction layer is what gives the PostgreSQL function manager all its power. Inside the string, you can basically use all that the programming language of your choice has to offer.

In this example, we will simply add up two numbers that have been passed to the function. Two integer variables are in use. The important part here is that PostgreSQL provides you with function overloading. In other words, the mysum(int, int) function is not the same as the mysum(int8, int8) function.

PostgreSQL sees these things as two distinct functions. Function overloading is a good feature; however, you have to be very careful not to accidentally deploy too many functions if your parameter list happens to change from time to time. Always make sure that functions that are not needed anymore are really deleted.

The CREATE OR REPLACE FUNCTION clause will not change the parameter list. You can, therefore, use it only if the signature does not change. It will either error out or simply deploy a new function.

Let's run the `mysum` function:

```
test=# SELECT mysum(10, 20);
 mysum
-------
 30
(1 row)
```

The result here is `30`, which is not really surprising. After this introduction to functions, it is important to focus on the next major topic: quoting.

Introducing dollar quoting

Passing code to PostgreSQL as a string is very flexible. However, using single quotes can be an issue. In many programming languages, single quotes show up frequently. To be able to use these quotes, people have to escape them when passing the string to PostgreSQL. For many years, this has been the standard procedure. Fortunately, those old times have passed by, and new means of passing the code to PostgreSQL are available. One of these is dollar quoting, as shown in the following code:

```
test=# CREATE OR REPLACE FUNCTION mysum(int, int)
RETURNS int AS
$$
    SELECT $1 + $2;
$$ LANGUAGE 'sql';
CREATE FUNCTION
```

Instead of using quotes to start and end strings, you can simply use $$. Currently, there are two languages that have assigned a meaning to $$. In Perl, as well as in bash scripts, $$ represents the process ID. To overcome this little obstacle, we can use $ before almost anything to start and end the string. The following example shows how that works:

```
test=# CREATE OR REPLACE FUNCTION mysum(int, int) RETURNS int AS
$body$
    SELECT $1 + $2;
$body$ LANGUAGE 'sql';
CREATE FUNCTION
```

All this flexibility allows you to overcome the problem of quoting once and for all. As long as the start string and the end string match, there won't be any problems at all.

Making use of anonymous code blocks

So far, we have written the most simple stored procedures possible, and also learned how to execute code. However, there is more to code execution than just full-blown functions. In addition to functions, PostgreSQL allows the use of anonymous code blocks. The idea is to run code that is needed only once. This kind of code execution is especially useful for dealing with administrative tasks. Anonymous code blocks don't take parameters and are not permanently stored in the database, since they don't have names.

Here is a simple example showing an anonymous code block in action:

```
test=# DO
$$
    BEGIN
            RAISE NOTICE 'current time: %', now();
    END;
$$ LANGUAGE 'plpgsql';
NOTICE: current time: 2016-12-12 15:25:50.678922+01
CONTEXT: PL/pgSQL function inline_code_block line 3 at RAISE
DO
```

In this example, the code only issues a message and quits. Again, the code block has to know which language it uses. This string is passed to PostgreSQL using simple dollar quoting.

Using functions and transactions

As you know, everything that PostgreSQL exposes in user land is a transaction. The same, of course, applies if you are writing functions. A function is always part of the transaction you are in. It is not autonomous, just like an operator or any other operation.

Here is an example:

```
test=# SELECT now(), mysum(id, id) FROM generate_series(1, 3) AS id;

 now                            | mysum
--------------------------------+-------
 2017-10-12 15:54:32.287027+01 |    2
 2017-10-12 15:54:32.287027+01 |    4
 2017-10-12 15:54:32.287027+01 |    6
(3 rows)
```

All three function calls happen in the same transaction. This is important to understand because it implies that you cannot do too much transactional flow control inside a function. What happens when the second function call commits? It just cannot work.

However, Oracle has a mechanism that allows for autonomous transactions. The idea is that even if a transaction rolls back, some parts might still be needed, and they should be kept. A classic example is as follows:

1. Start a function to look up secret data.
2. Add a log line to the document to state that somebody has modified this important secret data.
3. Commit the log line but roll back the change.
4. Preserve the information, stating that an attempt has been made to change data.

To solve problems such as this one, autonomous transactions can be used. The idea is to be able to commit a transaction inside the main transaction independently. In this case, the entry in the log table will prevail, while the change will be rolled back.

As of PostgreSQL 11.0, autonomous transactions are not implemented. However, there are already patches floating around that implement this feature. It is still to be seen as to when these features will make it to the core.

To give you an impression of how things will most likely work, here is a code snippet, based on the first patches:

```
...
AS
$$
DECLARE
   PRAGMA AUTONOMOUS_TRANSACTION;
BEGIN
   FOR i IN 0..9  LOOP
     START  TRANSACTION;
     INSERT INTO  test1  VALUES (i);
     IF i % 2 = 0 THEN
       COMMIT;
     ELSE
       ROLLBACK;
     END IF;
   END LOOP;
   RETURN 42;
END;
$$;
...
```

The point of this example is to show you that we can decide whether to commit or to roll back the autonomous transaction on the fly.

Understanding various stored procedure languages

As we've already stated in this chapter, PostgreSQL gives you the power to write functions and store procedures in various languages. The following options are available, and are shipped along with the PostgreSQL core:

- SQL
- PL/pgSQL
- PL/Perl and PL/PerlU
- PL/Python
- PL/Tcl and PL/TclU

SQL is the obvious choice for writing functions and it should be used whenever possible, as it gives the most freedom to the optimizer. However, if you want to write slightly more complex code, PL/pgSQL might be the language of your choice.

PL/pgSQL offers flow control and much more. In this chapter, some of the more advanced and lesser-known features of PL/pgSQL will be shown, but do keep in mind that this chapter is not meant to be a complete tutorial on PL/pgSQL.

The core contains code to run server-side functions in Perl. Basically, the logic is the same here. Code will be passed as a string and executed by Perl. Remember that PostgreSQL does not speak Perl; it merely has the code to pass things on to the external programming language.

Maybe you have noticed that Perl and Tcl are available in two flavors: trusted (PL/Perl and PL/Tcl) and untrusted (PL/PerlU and PL/TclU). The difference between a trusted and an untrusted language is actually an important one. In PostgreSQL, a language is loaded directly into the database connection. Therefore, the language is able to do quite a lot of nasty stuff. To get rid of security problems, the concept of trusted languages was invented. The idea is that a trusted language is restricted to the very core of the language. It is not possible to do the following:

- Include libraries
- Open network sockets
- Perform system calls of any kind, which would include opening files, and so on

Perl offers something called **taint mode**, which is used to implement this feature in PostgreSQL. Perl will automatically restrict itself to trusted mode, and error out if a security violation is about to happen. In untrusted mode, everything is possible, and therefore only the superuser is allowed to run untrusted code.

If you want to run trusted as well as untrusted code, you have to activate both languages, that is, `plperl` and `plperlu` (`pltcl` and `pltclu`, respectively).

Python is currently only available as an untrusted language; therefore, administrators have to be very careful when it comes to security in general, as a function running in untrusted mode can bypass all the security mechanisms that are enforced by PostgreSQL. Just keep in mind that Python is running as part of your database connection, and is in no way responsible for security.

Let's get started with the most awaited topic of this chapter.

Introducing PL/pgSQL

In this section, you will be introduced to some of the more advanced features of PL/pgSQL, which are important for writing proper and highly efficient code.

Note that this is not a beginner's introduction to programming, or to PL/pgSQL in general.

Handling quoting and the string format

One of the most important things in database programming is quoting. If you don't use proper quoting, you will surely get into trouble with SQL injection and open unacceptable security holes.

What is SQL injection? Let's consider the following example:

```
CREATE FUNCTION broken(text) RETURNS void AS
$$
DECLARE
  v_sql text;
BEGIN
  v_sql := 'SELECT schemaname
            FROM pg_tables
            WHERE tablename = ''' || $1 || '''';
  RAISE NOTICE 'v_sql: %', v_sql;
```

```
    RETURN;
END;
$$ LANGUAGE 'plpgsql';
```

In this example, the SQL code is simply pasted together without ever worrying about security. All we are doing here is using the | | operator to concatenate strings. This works fine if people run normal queries. Consider the following example, showing some broken code:

```
SELECT broken('t_test');
```

However, we have to be prepared for people who try to exploit your systems. Consider the following example:

```
SELECT broken('''; DROP  TABLE  t_test; ');
```

Running the function with this parameter will show a problem. The following code shows classical SQL injection:

```
NOTICE: v_sql: SELECT schemaname FROM  pg_tables
WHERE tablename = ''; DROP TABLE t_test; '
CONTEXT: PL/pgSQL function broken(text) line  6 at RAISE
 broken
--------

(1 row)
```

Dropping a table when you just want to do a lookup is not a desirable thing to do. It is definitely not acceptable to make the security of your application depend on the parameters that are passed to your statements.

To avoid SQL injection, PostgreSQL offers various functions; these should be used at all times to ensure that your security stays intact:

```
test=# SELECT quote_literal(E'o''reilly'), quote_ident(E'o''reilly');
 quote_literal  | quote_ident
----------------+-------------
 'o''reilly'    | "o'reilly" (1 row)
```

The quote_literal function will escape a string in such a way that nothing bad can happen anymore. It will add all the quotes around the string, and will escape problematic characters inside the string. Therefore, there is no need to start and end the string manually.

The second function that's shown here is `quote_ident`. It can be used to quote object names properly. Note that double quotes are used, which is exactly what is needed to handle table names. The following example shows how to use complex names:

```
test=# CREATE TABLE "Some  stupid name" ("ID" int);
CREATE TABLE
test=# \d "Some stupid name" Table "public.Some stupid name";
 Column  |  Type   | Modifiers
---------+---------+-----------
 ID      | integer |
```

Normally, all of the table names in PostgreSQL are lowercase. However, if double quotes are used, object names can contain capitalized letters. In general, it is not a good idea to use this kind of trickery, as you would have to use double quotes all the time, which can be a bit inconvenient.

Now that you've had a basic introduction to quoting, it is important to take a look at how NULL values are handled. The following code shows how NULL is treated by the `quote_literal` function:

```
test=# SELECT quote_literal(NULL);
 quote_literal
---------------


(1 row)
```

If you call the `quote_literal` function on a NULL value, it will simply return NULL. There is no need to take care of quoting in this case.

PostgreSQL provides even more functions to explicitly take care of a NULL value:

```
test=# SELECT quote_nullable(123), quote_nullable(NULL);
 quote_nullable  | quote_nullable
-----------------+----------------
 '123'           | NULL (1 row)
```

It is not only possible to quote strings and object names, but to also use PL/pgSQL onboard to format and prepare entire queries. The beauty here is that you can use the `format` function to add parameters to a statement. Here is how it works:

```
CREATE FUNCTION simple_format() RETURNS text AS
$$
DECLARE
  v_string text;
  v_result text;
BEGIN
```

```
    v_string := format('SELECT schemaname|| '' .'' || tablename
                        FROM pg_tables
                        WHERE %I = $1
                          AND %I = $2', 'schemaname', 'tablename');
    EXECUTE v_string USING 'public', 't_test' INTO v_result;
    RAISE NOTICE 'result: %', v_result;
    RETURN v_string;
END;
$$ LANGUAGE 'plpgsql';
```

The names of the fields are passed to the format function. Finally, the USING clause of the EXECUTE statement is there to add the parameters to the query, which is then executed. Again, the beauty here is that no SQL injection can happen.

Here is what happens when the simple_format function is called:

```
test=# SELECT simple_format ();
NOTICE: result: public .t_test
                    simple_format
------------------------------------------------
 SELECT schemaname|| ' .' || tablename        +
                    FROM pg_tables            +
                    WHERE schemaname = $1+
                      AND tablename = $2
(1 row)
```

As you can see, the debug message correctly displays the table, including the schema, and correctly returns the query. However, the format function can do a lot more. Here are some examples:

```
test=# SELECT format('Hello, %s %s','PostgreSQL', 12);
        format
---------------------
 Hello, PostgreSQL 12
(1 row)

test=# SELECT format('Hello, %s %10s','PostgreSQL', 12);
        format
---------------------
 Hello, PostgreSQL 12
(1 row)
```

`format` is able to use format options as shown in the example. `%10s` means that the string we want to add will be padded. Blanks are added.

In some cases it can be necessary to use a variable more than once. The following example shows two parameters, which are added more than once to the string that we want to create. What you can do is to use $1, $2, and so on to identify the entries in the argument list:

```
test=# SELECT format('%1$s, %1$s, %2$s', 'one', 'two');
    format
----------------
 one, one, two
(1 row)
```

`format` is a very powerful function, which is super important when you want to avoid SQL injection, and you should make good use of this powerful feature.

Managing scopes

After dealing with quoting and basic security (SQL injection) in general, we will focus on another important topic: scopes.

Just like most popular programming languages, PL/pgSQL uses variables, depending on their context. Variables are defined in the `DECLARE` statement of a function. However, PL/pgSQL allows you to nest a `DECLARE` statement:

```
CREATE FUNCTION scope_test () RETURNS int AS
$$
DECLARE
  i int := 0;
BEGIN
  RAISE NOTICE 'i1: %', i;
  DECLARE
    i int;
    BEGIN
      RAISE NOTICE 'i2: %', i;
    END;
  RETURN i;
END;
$$ LANGUAGE 'plpgsql';
```

In the DECLARE statement, the i variable is defined and a value is assigned to it. Then, i is displayed. The output will, of course, be 0. Then, a second DECLARE statement starts. It contains an additional incarnation of i, which is not assigned a value. Therefore, the value will be NULL. Note that PostgreSQL will now display the inner i. Here is what happens:

```
test=# SELECT scope_test();
NOTICE:   i1: 0
NOTICE:   i2: <NULL>
 scope_test
------------
   0
(1 row)
```

As expected, the debug messages will show 0 and NULL.

> PostgreSQL allows you to use all kinds of tricks. However, it is strongly recommended that you keep your code simple and easy to read.

Understanding advanced error handling

For programming languages, in every program, and in every module, error handling is an important thing. Everything is expected to go wrong once in a while, and therefore it is vital, and of key importance, to handle errors properly and professionally. In PL/pgSQL, you can use EXCEPTION blocks to handle errors. The idea is that if the BEGIN block does something wrong, the EXCEPTION block will take care of it, and handle the problem correctly. Just like many other languages, such as Java, you can react to different types of errors and catch them separately.

In the following example, the code might run into a division-by-zero problem. The goal is to catch this error and react accordingly:

```
CREATE FUNCTION error_test1(int, int) RETURNS int AS
$$
BEGIN
  RAISE  NOTICE 'debug message: % / %', $1, $2;
  BEGIN
    RETURN $1 / $2;
  EXCEPTION
    WHEN division_by_zero THEN
      RAISE NOTICE 'division by zero  detected: %', sqlerrm;
    WHEN others THEN
      RAISE NOTICE 'some other error: %', sqlerrm;
```

```
    END;
    RAISE  NOTICE 'all errors handled';
    RETURN 0;
END;
$$ LANGUAGE 'plpgsql';
```

The BEGIN block can clearly throw an error because there can be a division by zero. However, the EXCEPTION block catches the error that we are looking at and also takes care of all other potential problems that can unexpectedly pop up.

Technically, this is more or less the same as savepoint, and therefore the error does not cause the entire transaction to fail completely. Only the block that is causing the error will be subject to a mini rollback.

By inspecting the sqlerrm variable, you can also have direct access to the error message itself. Let's run the code:

```
test=# SELECT error_test1(9, 0);
NOTICE:  debug message: 9 / 0
NOTICE:  division by zero  detected: division by zero
NOTICE:  all errors handled
 error_test1
-------------
          0
(1 row)
```

PostgreSQL catches the exception and shows the message in the EXCEPTION block. It is kind enough to show us the line that is the error. This makes it a whole lot easier to debug and fix the code if it is broken.

In some cases, it also makes sense to raise your own exception. As you might expect, this is quite easy to do:

```
RAISE unique_violation
USING MESSAGE = 'Duplicate user  ID: ' || user_id;
```

Apart from this, PostgreSQL offers many predefined error codes and exceptions. The following page contains a complete list of these error messages:
https://www.postgresql.org/docs/10/static/errcodes-appendix.html.

Making use of GET DIAGNOSTICS

Many people who have used Oracle in the past might be familiar with the GET DIAGNOSTICS clause. The idea behind the GET DIAGNOSTICS clause is to allow users to see what is going on in the system. While the syntax might appear a bit strange to people who are used to modern code, it is still a valuable tool that can make your applications better.

From my point of view, there are two main tasks that the GET DIAGNOSTICS clause can be used for:

- Inspecting the row count
- Fetching context information and getting a backtrace

Inspecting the row count is definitely something that you will need during everyday programming. Extracting context information will be useful if you want to debug applications.

The following example shows how the GET DIAGNOSTICS clause can be used inside your code:

```
CREATE FUNCTION get_diag() RETURNS int AS
$$
DECLARE
  rc  int;
  _sqlstate text;
  _message text;
  _context text;
BEGIN
  EXECUTE 'SELECT * FROM generate_series(1, 10)';
  GET DIAGNOSTICS rc = ROW_COUNT;
  RAISE NOTICE 'row count: %', rc;
  SELECT rc / 0;
EXCEPTION
  WHEN OTHERS THEN
    GET STACKED DIAGNOSTICS
    _sqlstate = returned_sqlstate,
    _message = message_text,
    _context = pg_exception_context;
    RAISE NOTICE 'sqlstate: %, message: %, context: [%]',
                _sqlstate,
                _message,
                replace( _context, E'n', ' <- ' );
  RETURN rc;
END;
$$ LANGUAGE 'plpgsql';
```

The first thing after declaring those variables is to execute a SQL statement and ask the GET DIAGNOSTICS clause for a row count, which is then displayed in a debug message. Then, the function forces PL/pgSQL to error out. Once this happens, we will use the GET DIAGNOSTICS clause to extract information from the server to display it.

Here is what happens when we call the get_diag function:

```
test=# SELECT get_diag();
NOTICE:  row count: 10
CONTEXT:   PL/pgSQL function get_diag() line  12 at RAISE
NOTICE:  sqlstate: 22012,
message: division by zero,
context: [SQL  statement "SELECT rc / 0"
<- PL/pgSQL function get_diag() line  14 at
SQL statement]
CONTEXT:  PL/pgSQL function get_diag() line  22 at RAISE
 get_diag
----------
 10
(1 row)
```

As you can see, the GET DIAGNOSTICS clause gives us detailed information about the activities in the system.

Using cursors to fetch data in chunks

If you execute SQL, the database will calculate the result and send it to your application. Once the entire result set has been sent to the client, the application can continue doing its job. The problem is this: what happens if the result set is so large that it doesn't fit into the memory anymore? What if the database returns 10 billion rows? The client application usually cannot handle so much data at once, and actually, it shouldn't. The solution to this problem is a cursor. The idea behind a cursor is that data is generated only when it is needed (when FETCH is called). Therefore, the application can already start to consume data while it is actually being generated by the database. On top of that, much less memory is required to perform this operation.

When it comes to PL/pgSQL, cursors also play a major role. Whenever you loop over a result set, PostgreSQL will automatically use a cursor internally. The advantage is that the memory consumption of your applications will be reduced dramatically, and there is hardly a chance of ever running out of memory, due to the large amounts of data that are processed. There are various ways to use cursors.

Here is the most simplistic example of a cursor inside a function:

```
CREATE OR REPLACE FUNCTION c(int)
  RETURNS setof text AS
$$
DECLARE
  v_rec record;
BEGIN
  FOR v_rec IN SELECT tablename
               FROM pg_tables
               LIMIT $1
  LOOP
    RETURN NEXT v_rec.tablename;
  END LOOP;
  RETURN;
END;
$$ LANGUAGE 'plpgsql';
```

This code is interesting for two reasons. First of all, it is a **set returning function (SRF)**. It produces an entire column and not just a single row. The way to achieve this is to use the set of variables instead of just the data type. The RETURN NEXT clause will build up the result set, until we have reached the end. The RETURN clause will tell PostgreSQL that we want to leave the function and that we have the results.

The second important issue is that looping over the cursor will automatically create an internal cursor. In other words, there is no need to be afraid that you could potentially run out of memory. PostgreSQL will optimize the query in a way that it tries to produce the first 10% of the data (defined by the cursor_tuple_fraction variable) as fast as possible. Here is what the query will return:

```
test=# SELECT * FROM c(3);
  c
---------------
 t_test
 pg_statistic
 pg_type
(3 rows)
```

In this example, there will simply be a list of random tables. If the result differs on your side, this is somewhat expected.

What you have just seen is, in my opinion, the most frequent and most common way to use implicit cursors in PL/pgSQL.

The following example shows an older mechanism that many people from Oracle might know of:

```
CREATE OR REPLACE FUNCTION d(int)
  RETURNS setof text AS
$$
DECLARE
  v_cur refcursor;
  v_data text;
BEGIN
  OPEN v_cur FOR
    SELECT tablename
    FROM pg_tables
    LIMIT $1;
  WHILE true LOOP
    FETCH v_cur INTO v_data;
    IF FOUND THEN
      RETURN NEXT v_data;
    ELSE
      RETURN;
    END IF;
  END LOOP;
END;
$$ LANGUAGE 'plpgsql';
```

In this example, the cursor is explicitly declared and opened. Inside, the loop data is then explicitly fetched and returned to the caller. Basically, the query does exactly the same thing. It is merely a matter of taste in regard to what syntax developers actually prefer.

Do you still have the feeling that you don't know enough about cursors yet? There's more; here is a third option to do exactly the same thing:

```
CREATE OR REPLACE FUNCTION e(int)
  RETURNS setof text AS
$$
DECLARE
  v_cur CURSOR (param1 int) FOR
        SELECT tablename
        FROM pg_tables
        LIMIT param1;
  v_data text;
BEGIN
  OPEN v_cur ($1);
  WHILE true LOOP
    FETCH v_cur INTO v_data;
    IF FOUND THEN
      RETURN NEXT v_data;
    ELSE
```

```
        RETURN;
      END IF;
    END LOOP;
END;
$$ LANGUAGE 'plpgsql';
```

In this case, the cursor is fed with an `integer` parameter, which comes directly from the function call (`$1`).

Sometimes, a cursor is not used up by the stored procedure itself, but returned for later use. In this case, you can return a simple use `refcursor` as the return value:

```
CREATE OR REPLACE FUNCTION cursor_test(c refcursor)
  RETURNS refcursor AS
$$
BEGIN
  OPEN c FOR SELECT *
            FROM generate_series(1, 10) AS id;
  RETURN c;
END;
$$ LANGUAGE plpgsql;
```

The logic here is quite simple. The name of the cursor is passed to the function. Then, the cursor is opened and returned. The beauty here is that the query behind the cursor can be created on the fly and compiled dynamically.

The application can fetch from the cursor just like from any other application. Here is how it works:

```
test=# BEGIN;
BEGIN
test=# SELECT cursor_test('mytest');
 cursor_test
-------------
 mytest
(1 row)
 test=# FETCH NEXT FROM mytest;
 id
----
 1
(1 row)
test=# FETCH NEXT FROM mytest;
 id
----
 2
(1 row)
```

Note that it works only when a transaction block is used.

In this section, we have learned that cursors will only produce data as it is consumed. This holds true for most queries. However, there is a catch to this example; whenever an SRF is used, the entire result has to be materialized. It is not created on the fly, but instead, at once. The reason for this is that SQL must be able to rescan a relation, which is easily possible in the case of a normal table. However, for functions, the situation is different. Therefore, an SRF is always calculated and materialized, making the cursor in this example totally useless. In other words, we need to be careful while writing functions. In some cases, danger is hidden in the nifty details.

Utilizing composite types

In most other database systems, stored procedures are only used with primitive data types, such as `integers`, `numeric`, `varchar`, and so on. However, PostgreSQL is very different. We can use all the data types that are available to us. This includes primitive, composite, and custom types of data. There are simply no restrictions as far as data types are concerned. To unleash the full power of PostgreSQL, composite types are highly important, and are often used by extensions that are found on the internet. The following example shows how a composite type can be passed to a function, and how it can be used internally. Finally, the composite type will be returned again:

```
CREATE TYPE my_cool_type AS (s text, t text);

CREATE FUNCTION f(my_cool_type)
  RETURNS my_cool_type AS
$$
DECLARE
    v_row my_cool_type;
BEGIN
  RAISE NOTICE 'schema: (%) / table: (%)'
            , $1.s, $1.t;
  SELECT schemaname, tablename
  INTO v_row
  FROM pg_tables
  WHERE tablename = trim($1.t)
        AND schemaname = trim($1.s)
  LIMIT 1;
  RETURN v_row;
END;
$$ LANGUAGE 'plpgsql';
```

The main issue here is that you can simply use `$1.field_name` in order to access the composite type. Returning the composite type is not difficult, either.

You just have to assemble the composite type variable on the fly and return it, just like any other data type. You can even easily use arrays, or even more complex structures.

The following code shows what PostgreSQL will return:

```
test=# SELECT (f).s, (f).t
  FROM f ('("public", "t_test")'::my_cool_type);
NOTICE:  schema: (public) / table: ( t_test)
    s    |    t
--------+---------
 public | t_test
(1 row)
```

Writing triggers in PL/pgSQL

Server-side code is especially popular if you want to react to certain events that are happening in the database. A trigger allows you to call a function if an INSERT, UPDATE, DELETE, or TRUNCATE clause happens on a table. The function that is called by the trigger can then modify the data that's changed in your table, or simply perform a necessary operation.

In PostgreSQL, triggers have become more powerful over the years, and they now provide a rich set of features:

```
test=# \h CREATE TRIGGER
Command: CREATE TRIGGER
Description: define a new trigger
Syntax:
CREATE [ CONSTRAINT ] TRIGGER name { BEFORE | AFTER | INSTEAD OF } { event
[ OR ... ] }
    ON table_name
    [ FROM referenced_table_name ]
    [ NOT DEFERRABLE | [ DEFERRABLE ] [ INITIALLY IMMEDIATE | INITIALLY
DEFERRED ] ]
    [ REFERENCING { { OLD | NEW } TABLE [ AS ] transition_relation_name } [
... ] ]
    [ FOR [ EACH ] { ROW | STATEMENT } ]
    [ WHEN ( condition ) ]
    EXECUTE { FUNCTION | PROCEDURE } function_name ( arguments )

where event can be one of:

    INSERT
```

```
UPDATE [ OF column_name [, ... ] ]
DELETE
TRUNCATE
```

URL: https://www.postgresql.org/docs/12/sql-createtrigger.html

The first thing to observe is that a trigger is always fired for a table or a view, and calls a function. It has a name, and it can happen before or after an event. The beauty of PostgreSQL is that you can have umpteen number of triggers on a single table. While this will not come as a surprise to hardcore PostgreSQL users, I want to point out that this is not possible in many expensive commercial database engines that are still in use around the world.

If there is more than one trigger on the same table, then the following rule, which was introduced many years ago in PostgreSQL 7.3, will be useful: triggers are fired in alphabetical order. First, all of those BEFORE triggers happen in alphabetical order. Then, PostgreSQL performs the row operation that the trigger has been fired for, and continues executing after the triggers in alphabetical order. In other words, the execution order of triggers is absolutely deterministic, and the number of triggers is basically unlimited.

Triggers can modify data before or after the actual modification has happened. In general, this is a good way to verify data and to error out if some custom restrictions are violated. The following example shows a trigger that is fired in the INSERT clause, and which changes the data that's added to the table:

```
CREATE TABLE t_sensor (
        id serial,
        ts timestamp,
        temperature numeric
);
```

Our table just stores a couple of values. The goal now is to call a function as soon as a row is inserted:

```
CREATE OR REPLACE FUNCTION trig_func()
RETURNS trigger AS
$$
        BEGIN
                IF NEW.temperature < -273
                THEN
                        NEW.temperature := 0;
                END IF;

                RETURN NEW;
        END;
$$ LANGUAGE 'plpgsql';
```

As we stated previously, the trigger will always call a function, which allows you to use nicely abstract code. The important thing here is that the trigger function has to return a trigger. To access the row that you are about to insert, you can access the NEW variable.

The INSERT and UPDATE triggers always provide a NEW variable. UPDATE and DELETE will offer a variable called OLD. These variables contain the row that you are about to modify.

In my example, the code checks whether the temperature is too low. If it is, the value is not okay; it is dynamically adjusted. To ensure that the modified row can be used, NEW is simply returned. If there is a second trigger called after this one, the next function call will already see the modified row.

In the next step, the trigger can be created by using the CREATE TRIGGER command:

```
CREATE TRIGGER sensor_trig
  BEFORE INSERT ON t_sensor
  FOR EACH  ROW
  EXECUTE PROCEDURE trig_func();
```

Here is what the trigger will do:

```
test=# INSERT INTO t_sensor (ts,  temperature)
  VALUES ('2017-05-04 14:43', -300) RETURNING *;
 id  |    ts                 | temperature
-----+---------------------+--------------
 1   | 2017-05-04 14:43:00 |   0
(1 row)

INSERT 0 1
```

As you can see, the value has been adjusted correctly. The content of the table shows 0 for the temperature.

If you are using triggers, you should be aware of the fact that a trigger knows a lot about itself. It can access a couple of variables that allow you to write more sophisticated code, and therefore achieve better abstraction.

Let's drop the trigger first:

```
test=# DROP TRIGGER sensor_trig ON t_sensor;
DROP TRIGGER
```

Then, a new function can be added:

```
CREATE OR REPLACE FUNCTION trig_demo()
  RETURNS trigger AS
$$
BEGIN
  RAISE NOTICE 'TG_NAME: %', TG_NAME;
  RAISE NOTICE 'TG_RELNAME: %', TG_RELNAME;
  RAISE NOTICE 'TG_TABLE_SCHEMA: %', TG_TABLE_SCHEMA;
  RAISE NOTICE 'TG_TABLE_NAME: %', TG_TABLE_NAME;
  RAISE NOTICE 'TG_WHEN: %', TG_WHEN;
  RAISE NOTICE 'TG_LEVEL: %', TG_LEVEL;
  RAISE NOTICE 'TG_OP: %', TG_OP;
  RAISE NOTICE 'TG_NARGS: %', TG_NARGS;
-- RAISE  NOTICE 'TG_ARGV: %', TG_NAME;
  RETURN NEW;
END;
$$ LANGUAGE 'plpgsql';

CREATE TRIGGER sensor_trig
    BEFORE INSERT ON t_sensor
    FOR EACH ROW
    EXECUTE PROCEDURE trig_demo();
```

All of the variables that are used here are predefined, and are available by default. All our code does is display them, so that we can see their content:

```
test=# INSERT INTO t_sensor (ts, temperature)
           VALUES ('2017-05-04 14:43', -300) RETURNING *;

NOTICE: TG_NAME: demo_trigger
NOTICE: TG_RELNAME: t_sensor
NOTICE: TG_TABLE_SCHEMA: public
NOTICE: TG_TABLE_NAME: t_sensor
NOTICE: TG_WHEN: BEFORE
NOTICE: TG_LEVEL: ROW
NOTICE: TG_OP: INSERT
NOTICE: TG_NARGS: 0

 id | ts                  | temperature
----+---------------------+-------------
  2 | 2017-05-04 14:43:00 | -300
(1 row)

INSERT 0 1
```

What we see here is that the trigger knows its name, the table it has been fired for, and a lot more. To apply similar actions on various tables, these variables help to avoid duplicate code by just writing a single function. This can then be used for all the tables that we are interested in.

So far, we have seen simple row-level triggers, which are fired once per statement. However, with the introduction of PostgreSQL 10.0, there are a couple of new features. Statement-level triggers have been around for a while already. However, it wasn't possible to access the data that's changed by a trigger. This has been fixed in PostgreSQL 10.0, and it is now possible to make use of transition tables, which contain all the changes that were made.

The following code contains a complete example, showing how a transition table can be used:

```sql
CREATE OR REPLACE FUNCTION transition_trigger()
  RETURNS TRIGGER AS $$
    DECLARE
  v_record   record;
    BEGIN
        IF  (TG_OP = 'INSERT') THEN
    RAISE NOTICE 'new data: ';
    FOR v_record IN SELECT * FROM new_table
    LOOP
      RAISE NOTICE '%', v_record;
    END LOOP;
        ELSE
    RAISE NOTICE 'old data: ';
    FOR v_record IN SELECT * FROM old_table
    LOOP
      RAISE NOTICE '%', v_record;
    END LOOP;
        END IF;
        RETURN NULL; -- result is ignored since this is an AFTER trigger
    END;
$$ LANGUAGE plpgsql;

CREATE TRIGGER transition_test_trigger_ins
    AFTER INSERT ON t_sensor
    REFERENCING NEW TABLE AS new_table
    FOR EACH STATEMENT EXECUTE PROCEDURE transition_trigger();

CREATE TRIGGER transition_test_trigger_del
    AFTER DELETE ON t_sensor
    REFERENCING OLD TABLE AS old_table
    FOR EACH STATEMENT EXECUTE PROCEDURE transition_trigger();
```

In this case, we need two trigger definitions, because we cannot just squeeze everything into just one definition. Inside the `trigger` function, the transition table is easy to use: it can be accessed just like a normal table.

Let's test the code of the trigger by inserting some data:

```
INSERT INTO t_sensor
  SELECT   *, now(), random() * 20
  FROM   generate_series(1, 5);

DELETE FROM t_sensor;
```

In my example, the code will simply issue NOTICE for each entry in the transition table:

```
NOTICE: new data:
NOTICE: (1,"2017-10-04 15:47:14.129151",10.4552665632218)
NOTICE: (2,"2017-10-04 15:47:14.129151",12.8670312650502)
NOTICE: (3,"2017-10-04 15:47:14.129151",14.3934494629502)
NOTICE: (4,"2017-10-04 15:47:14.129151",4.35718866065145)
NOTICE: (5,"2017-10-04 15:47:14.129151",10.9121138229966)
INSERT 0 5

NOTICE: old data:
NOTICE: (1,"2017-10-04 15:47:14.129151",10.4552665632218)
NOTICE: (2,"2017-10-04 15:47:14.129151",12.8670312650502)
NOTICE: (3,"2017-10-04 15:47:14.129151",14.3934494629502)
NOTICE: (4,"2017-10-04 15:47:14.129151",4.35718866065145)
NOTICE: (5,"2017-10-04 15:47:14.129151",10.9121138229966)
DELETE 5
```

Keep in mind that it is not necessarily a good idea to use transition tables for billions of rows. PostgreSQL really is scalable, but at some point, it is necessary to see that there are performance implications as well.

Writing stored procedures in PL/pgSQL

Now, let's move on, and learn how to write procedures. In this section, you will learn how to write real stored procedures, which were introduced in PostgreSQL 11. To create a procedure, you have to use CREATE PROCEDURE. The syntax of this command is remarkably similar to CREATE FUNCTION. There are just a few minor differences:

```
test=# \h CREATE PROCEDURE
Command: CREATE PROCEDURE
Description: define a new procedure
Syntax:
```

```
CREATE [ OR REPLACE ] PROCEDURE
    name ( [ [ argmode ] [ argname ] argtype [ { DEFAULT | = } default_expr
] [, ...] ] )
  { LANGUAGE lang_name
    | TRANSFORM { FOR TYPE type_name } [, ... ]
    | [ EXTERNAL ] SECURITY INVOKER | [ EXTERNAL ] SECURITY DEFINER
    | SET configuration_parameter { TO value | = value | FROM CURRENT }
    | AS 'definition'
    | AS 'obj_file', 'link_symbol'
  } ...
URL: https://www.postgresql.org/docs/12/sql-createprocedure.html
```

The following example shows a stored procedure that runs two transactions. The first transaction will COMMIT, and therefore create two tables. The second procedure will ROLLBACK:

```
test=# CREATE PROCEDURE test_proc()
       LANGUAGE plpgsql
AS $$
  BEGIN
    CREATE TABLE a (aid int);
    CREATE TABLE b (bid int);
    COMMIT;
    CREATE TABLE c (cid int);
    ROLLBACK;
  END;
$$;
CREATE PROCEDURE
```

As we can see, a procedure is able to do explicit transaction handling. The idea behind a procedure is to be able to run batch jobs and other operations, which are hard to do in a function.

To run the procedure, you have to use CALL, as shown in the following example:

```
test=# CALL test_proc();
CALL
```

The first two tables were committed. The third table hasn't been created, because of the rollback inside the procedure:

```
test=# \d
List of relations
 Schema | Name | Type  | Owner
--------+------+-------+-------
 public | a    | table | hs
 public | b    | table | hs
(2 rows)
```

Procedures are one of the most important features that were introduced in PostgreSQL 11, and they make a significant contribution to the efficiency of software development.

Introducing PL/Perl

There is a lot more to say about PL/pgSQL. However, not everything can be covered in one book, so it is time to move on to the next procedural language. PL/Perl has been adopted by many people as the ideal language for string crunching. As you might know, Perl is famous for its string manipulation capabilities, and is therefore still fairly popular after all these years.

To enable PL/Perl, you have two choices:

```
test=# create extension plperl;
CREATE EXTENSION

test=# create extension plperlu;
CREATE EXTENSION
```

You can deploy trusted or untrusted Perl. If you want both, you have to enable both languages.

To show you how PL/Perl works, I have implemented a function that simply parses an email address and returns true or false. Here is how it works:

```
test=# CREATE OR REPLACE FUNCTION verify_email(text)
RETURNS boolean AS
$$
if   ($_[0] =~ /^[a-z0-9.]+@[a-z0-9.-]+$/)
{
  return true;
}
return false;
$$ LANGUAGE 'plperl'; CREATE FUNCTION
```

A text parameter is passed to the function. Inside the function, all those input parameters can be accessed using $_. In this example, the regular expression is executed, and the function is returned.

The function can be called, just like any other procedure written in any other language:

```
test=# SELECT verify_email('hs@cybertec.at');
 verify_email
--------------
 t
(1 row)

test=# SELECT verify_email('totally wrong');
 verify_email
--------------
 f
(1 row)
```

Keep in mind that you cannot load packages, and so on, if you are inside a trusted function. For example, if you want to use the w command to find words, Perl will internally load utf8.pm, which, of course, is not allowed.

Using PL/Perl for data type abstraction

As stated already in this chapter, functions in PostgreSQL are pretty universal, and can be used in many different contexts. If you want to use functions to improve your data quality, you can use a CREATE DOMAIN clause:

```
test=# \h CREATE DOMAIN
Command: CREATE DOMAIN
Description: define a new domain
Syntax:
CREATE DOMAIN name [ AS ] data_type
    [ COLLATE collation ]
    [ DEFAULT expression ]
    [ constraint [ ... ] ]

where constraint is:

[ CONSTRAINT constraint_name ]
{ NOT NULL | NULL | CHECK (expression) }

URL: https://www.postgresql.org/docs/12/sql-createdomain.html
```

In this example, the PL/Perl function will be used to create a domain called email, which, in turn, can be used as a data type.

The following code shows how the domain can be created:

```
test=# CREATE DOMAIN email AS text
        CHECK (verify_email(VALUE) = true);
CREATE DOMAIN
```

As we mentioned previously, the domain functions just like a normal data type:

```
test=# CREATE TABLE t_email (id serial, data  email);
CREATE TABLE
```

The Perl function ensures that nothing that violates our checks can be inserted into the database, as the following example demonstrates successfully:

```
test=# INSERT INTO t_email (data)
        VALUES ('somewhere@example.com');
INSERT 0 1
test=# INSERT INTO  t_email (data)
        VALUES ('somewhere_wrong_example.com');
ERROR:  value  for domain email  violates check       constraint
"email_check"
```

Perl might be a good option to do string crunching but, as always, you have to decide whether you want this code directly in the database, or not.

Deciding between PL/Perl and PL/PerlU

So far, the Perl code has not caused any security-related problems, because all we did was use regular expressions. The question here is, what if somebody tries to do something nasty inside the Perl function? As we've stated already, PL/Perl will simply error out:

```
test=# CREATE OR REPLACE FUNCTION test_security()
RETURNS boolean AS
$$
use strict;
my $fp = open("/etc/password", "r");

return false;
$$ LANGUAGE 'plperl';
ERROR:  'open' trapped by operation mask  at line
CONTEXT:  compilation of PL/Perl function "test_security"
```

PL/Perl will complain as soon as you try to create the function. An error will be displayed instantly.

If you really want to run untrusted code in Perl, you have to use PL/PerlU:

```
test=# CREATE OR REPLACE FUNCTION first_line()
RETURNS text AS
$$
open(my $fh, '<:encoding(UTF-8)', "/etc/passwd")
   or elog(NOTICE, "Could not open  file  '$filename' $!");

my $row  = <$fh>;
close($fh);

return $row;
$$ LANGUAGE 'plperlu';
CREATE FUNCTION
```

The procedure stays the same. It returns a string. However, it is allowed to do everything. The only difference is that the function is marked as plperlu.

The result is somewhat unsurprising:

```
test=# SELECT first_line();
 first_line
-----------------------------------
 root:x:0:0:root:/root:/bin/bash+

(1 row)
```

Making use of the SPI interface

Once in a while, your Perl procedure has to carry out some database work. Remember, the function is part of the database connection. Therefore, it is pointless to actually create a database connection. To talk to the database, the PostgreSQL server infrastructure provides the **Server Programming Interface** (**SPI**), which is a C interface that you can use to talk to database internals. All procedural languages that help you to run server-side code use this interface to expose functionality to you. PL/Perl does the same, and in this section, you will learn how to use the Perl wrapper around the SPI interface.

The most important thing that you might want to do is simply run SQL, and retrieve the number of rows that have been fetched. The spi_exec_query function is here to do exactly that. The first parameter that's passed to the function is the query parameter. The second parameter has the number of rows that you actually want to retrieve. For simplicity, I decided to fetch all of them. The following code shows an example of this:

```
test=# CREATE OR REPLACE FUNCTION spi_sample(int)
RETURNS void AS
```

```
$$
my $rv = spi_exec_query(" SELECT *
  FROM  generate_series(1, $_[0])", $_[0]
);
elog(NOTICE, "rows  fetched: " . $rv->{processed});
elog(NOTICE, "status: " . $rv->{status});

return;
$$ LANGUAGE 'plperl';
```

SPI will execute the query and display the number of rows. The important thing here is that all of the stored procedure languages provide a means to send log messages. In the case of PL/Perl, this function is called `elog`, and it takes two parameters. The first one defines the importance of the message (INFO, NOTICE, WARNING, ERROR, and so on), and the second parameter contains the actual message.

The following message shows what the query returns:

```
test=# SELECT spi_sample(9);
NOTICE:   rows   fetched: 9
NOTICE:   status: SPI_OK_SELECT
 spi_sample
------------

(1 row)
```

Using SPI for set-returning functions

In many cases, you don't just want to execute some SQL and forget about it. In most cases, a procedure will loop over the result and do something with it. The following example will show how you can loop over the output of a query. On top of that, I decided to beef up the example a bit, and make the function return a composite data type. Working with composite types in Perl is very easy, because you can simply stuff the data into a hash and return it.

The `return_next` function will gradually build up the result set until the function is terminated with a simple return statement.

The example in the following code generates a table consisting of random values:

```
CREATE TYPE random_type AS  (a float8, b float8);

CREATE OR REPLACE FUNCTION spi_srf_perl(int)
  RETURNS setof random_type AS
$$
```

```
my $rv = spi_query("SELECT random() AS a,
                           random() AS b
                    FROM generate_series(1, $_[0])");
while (defined (my $row = spi_fetchrow($rv)))
{
  elog(NOTICE, "data: " .
       $row->{a} . " / " . $row->{b});
  return_next({a => $row->{a},
               b => $row->{b}});
}

return;
$$ LANGUAGE 'plperl';

CREATE FUNCTION
```

First, the `spi_query` function is executed, and a loop using the `spi_fetchrow` function is started. Inside the loop, the composite type will be assembled and stuffed into the result set.

As expected, the function will return a set of random values:

```
test=# SELECT * FROM  spi_srf_perl(3);
NOTICE:   data:  0.154673356097192 / 0.278830723837018
CONTEXT:  PL/Perl function "spi_srf_perl"
NOTICE:   data:  0.615888888947666 / 0.632620786316693
CONTEXT:  PL/Perl function "spi_srf_perl"
NOTICE:   data:  0.910436692181975 / 0.753427186980844
CONTEXT:  PL/Perl function "spi_srf_perl"
 a_col               |  b_col
---------------------+--------------------
 0.154673356097192   | 0.278830723837018
 0.615888888947666   | 0.632620786316693
 0.910436692181975   | 0.753427186980844
(3 rows)
```

Keep in mind that set-returning functions have to be materialized so that the entire result set can be stored in-memory.

Escaping in PL/Perl and support functions

So far, we have only used integers, so SQL injection or special table names were not an issue. Basically, the following functions are available:

- `quote_literal`: This returns a string quote as a string literal.
- `quote_nullable`: This quotes a string.

- `quote_ident`: This quotes SQL identifiers (object names, and so on).
- `decode_bytea`: This decodes a PostgreSQL byte array field.
- `encode_bytea`: This encodes data, and turns it into a byte array.
- `encode_literal_array`: This encodes an array of literals.
- `encode_typed_literal`: This converts a Perl variable into the value of the data type that's passed as a second argument, and returns a string representation of this value.
- `encode_array_constructor`: This returns the content of the referenced array as a string in array constructor format.
- `looks_like_number`: This returns true if a string looks like a number.
- `is_array_ref`: This returns true if something is an array reference.

These functions are always available, and they can be called directly without having to include a library.

Sharing data across function calls

Sometimes, it is necessary to share data across calls. The infrastructure has the means to actually do that. In Perl, a hash can be used to store whatever data is needed. Take a look at the following example:

```
CREATE FUNCTION perl_shared(text) RETURNS int AS
$$
if ( !defined $_SHARED{$_[0]} )
{
   $_SHARED{$_[0]} = 0;
}
else
{
   $_SHARED{$_[0]}++;
}
return $_SHARED{$_[0]};
$$ LANGUAGE 'plperl';
```

The `$_SHARED` variable will be initialized with 0 as soon as we figure out that the key that's been passed to the function is not there yet. For every other call, 1 is added to the counter, leaving us with the following output:

```
test=# SELECT perl_shared('some_key') FROM  generate_series(1, 3);
 perl_shared
-------------
           0
```

```
                    1
                    2
      (3 rows)
```

In the case of a more complex statement, the developer usually doesn't know what order the functions will be called in. It is important to keep that in mind. In most cases, you cannot rely on an execution order.

Writing triggers in Perl

Every stored procedure language that is shipped with the core of PostgreSQL allows you to write triggers in that language. The same, of course, applies to Perl. Since the length of this chapter is limited, I have decided not to include an example of a trigger written in Perl, but instead to point you to the official PostgreSQL documentation: `https://www.postgresql.org/docs/10/static/plperl-triggers.html`. Basically, writing a trigger in Perl doesn't differ from writing one in PL/pgSQL. All predefined variables are in place, and as far as return values are concerned, the rules apply in every stored procedure language.

Introducing PL/Python

If you don't happen to be a Perl expert, PL/Python might be the right thing for you. Python has been part of the PostgreSQL infrastructure for a long time, and is therefore a solid, well-tested implementation.

When it comes to PL/Python, there is one thing that you have to keep in mind: PL/Python is only available as an untrusted language. From a security point of view, it is important to keep that in mind at all times.

To enable PL/Python, you can run the following line from your command line, and `test` is the name of the database that you want to use with PL/Python:

```
    createlang plpythonu test
```

Once the language is enabled, it is possible to write code.

Alternatively, you can use a `CREATE LANGUAGE` clause. Also, keep in mind that in order to use server-side languages, PostgreSQL packages that contain those languages are needed (`postgresql-plpython-$(VERSIONNUMBER)`, and so on).

Writing simple PL/Python code

In this section, you will learn how to write simple Python procedures. The example that we'll discuss here is quite simple: if you are visiting a client by car in Austria, you can deduct 42 Euro cents per kilometer in expenses, in order to reduce your income tax. So, what the function does is take the number of kilometers, and return the amount of money that we can deduct from our tax bill. Here is how it works:

```
CREATE OR REPLACE FUNCTION calculate_deduction(km float)
  RETURNS numeric AS
$$
if   km <= 0:
  elog(ERROR, 'invalid number of kilometers')
else:

    return km * 0.42

$$ LANGUAGE 'plpythonu';
```

The function ensures that only positive values are accepted. Finally, the result is calculated and returned. As you can see, the way that a Python function is passed to PostgreSQL doesn't really differ from Perl or PL/pgSQL.

Using the SPI interface

Like all procedural languages, PL/Python gives you access to the SPI interface. The following example shows how numbers can be added up:

```
CREATE FUNCTION add_numbers(rows_desired integer)
  RETURNS integer AS
$$
mysum  = 0

cursor = plpy.cursor("SELECT * FROM
  generate_series(1, %d) AS id" % (rows_desired))

while  True:
  rows  = cursor.fetch(rows_desired)
  if not rows:
    break

  for row in rows:
    mysum  += row['id']
return mysum
$$ LANGUAGE 'plpythonu';
```

When you try this example out, make sure that the call to the cursor is actually a single line. Python is all about indentation, so it does make a difference if your code consists of one or two lines.

Once the cursor has been created, we can loop over it and add up those numbers. The columns inside those rows can easily be referenced using column names.

Calling the function will return the desired result:

```
test=# SELECT add_numbers(10);
 add_numbers
-------------
          55
(1 row)
```

If you want to inspect the result set of a SQL statement, PL/Python offers various functions, allowing you to retrieve more information from the result. Again, those functions are wrappers around what SPI offers on the C level.

The following function inspects a result more closely:

```
CREATE OR REPLACE FUNCTION result_diag(rows_desired integer)
   RETURNS integer AS
$$
rv = plpy.execute("SELECT *
   FROM  generate_series(1, %d) AS id" % (rows_desired))
plpy.notice(rv.nrows())
plpy.notice(rv.status())
plpy.notice(rv.colnames())
plpy.notice(rv.coltypes())
plpy.notice(rv.coltypmods())
plpy.notice(rv.  str   ())

return 0
$$ LANGUAGE 'plpythonu';
```

The nrows() function will display the number of rows. The status() function tells us whether everything worked out fine. The colnames() function returns a list of columns. The coltypes() function returns the object IDs of the data types in the result set. 23 is the internal number of integers, as shown in the following code:

```
test=# SELECT typname FROM pg_type WHERE oid = 23;
 typname
---------
   int4
(1 row)
```

Then comes `typmod`. Consider something like `varchar(20)`: the configuration part of the type is what `typmod` is all about.

Finally, there is a function to return the entire thing as a string for debugging purposes. Calling the function will return the following result:

```
test=# SELECT result_diag(3);
NOTICE:   3
NOTICE:   5
NOTICE:   ['id']
NOTICE:   [23]
NOTICE:   [-1]
NOTICE:   <PLyResult status=5 nrows=3 rows=[{'id': 1},
    {'id': 2}, {'id': 3}]>
result_diag
-------------
          0
(1 row)
```

There are many more functions in the SPI interface that can help you execute SQL.

Handling errors

Once in a while, you might have to catch an error. Of course, this is also possible in Python. The following example shows how this works:

```
CREATE OR REPLACE FUNCTION trial_error()
  RETURNS text   AS
$$
try:
  rv = plpy.execute("SELECT surely_a_syntax_error")
except plpy.SPIError:
  return "we caught the error" else:
else:
  return "all fine"
$$ LANGUAGE 'plpythonu';
```

You can use a normal `try` or `except` block, and access `plpy` to treat the error that you want to catch. The function can then return normally without destroying your transaction, as follows:

```
test=# SELECT trial_error();
 trial_error
----------------------
 we caught the error
(1 row)
```

Remember, PL/Python has full access to the internals of PostgreSQL. Therefore, it can also expose all kinds of errors to your procedure. Here is an example:

```
except spiexceptions.DivisionByZero:
  return "found a division by zero"
except spiexceptions.UniqueViolation:
  return "found a unique violation"
except plpy.SPIError, e:
  return "other error, SQLSTATE %s" % e.sqlstate
```

Catching errors in Python is really easy, and can help prevent your functions from failing.

Improving functions

So far, you have seen how to write basic functions and triggers in various languages. Of course, many more languages are supported. Some of the most prominent ones are PL/R (R is a powerful statistics package) and PL/v8 (which is based on the Google JavaScript engine). However, those languages are beyond the scope of this chapter (regardless of their usefulness).

In this section, we will focus on improving the performance of a function. There are a few ways in which we can speed up processing:

- Reducing the number of function calls
- Using cached plans
- Giving hints to the optimizer

In this chapter, all three of these areas will be discussed.

Reducing the number of function calls

In many cases, performance is bad because functions are called way too often. In my personal opinion—and I cannot stress this point enough—calling things too often is the main reason for bad performance. When you create a function, you can choose from three types of functions: `volatile`, `stable`, and `immutable`. Here is an example:

```
test=# SELECT random(), random();
 random             |  random
--------------------+--------------------
 0.276252629235387  | 0.710661871358752
(1 row)
```

```
test=# SELECT now(), now();
              now              |             now
------------------------------+------------------------------
 2016-12-16 12:57:17.135751+01 | 2016-12-16 12:57:17.135751+01
(1 row)

test=# SELECT pi();
        pi
------------------
 3.14159265358979
(1 row)
```

A `volatile` function means that the function cannot be optimized away. It has to be executed over and over again. A `volatile` function can also be the reason why a certain index is not used. By default, every function is considered to be volatile. A `stable` function will always return the same data within the same transaction. It can be optimized and calls can be removed. The `now()` function is a good example of a `stable` function; within the same transaction, it returns the same data. `Immutable` functions are the gold standard because they allow for most optimizations, which is because they always return the same result if they are given the same input. As a first step to optimizing functions, always make sure that they are marked correctly by adding volatile, stable, or immutable to the end of the definition.

Using cached plans

In PostgreSQL, a query is executed using four stages:

1. **Parser**: This checks the syntax
2. **Rewrite system**: This take cares of rules
3. **Optimizer/planner**: This optimizes the query
4. **Executor**: This executes the plan that is provided by the planner

If the query is short, the first three steps are relatively time-consuming compared to the real execution time. Therefore, it makes sense to cache execution plans. PL/pgSQL basically does all the plan caching for you automatically behind the scenes. You don't have to worry about it. PL/Perl and PL/Python will give you the choice.

The SPI interface provides functions so that you can handle and run prepared queries, so the programmer has the choice regarding whether a query should be prepared, or not. In the case of long queries, it actually makes sense to use unprepared queries. Short queries should always be prepared in order to reduce internal overheads.

Assigning costs to functions

From the optimizer's point of view, a function is basically just like an operator. PostgreSQL will also treat the costs in the same way as if it was a standard operator. The problem is this: adding two numbers is usually cheaper than intersecting costlines using a PostGIS-provided function. The thing is that the optimizer doesn't know whether a function is cheap or expensive.

Fortunately, we can tell the optimizer to make functions cheaper or more expensive:

```
test=# \h CREATE FUNCTION
Command: CREATE FUNCTION
Description: Define a new function
Syntax:
CREATE [ OR REPLACE ] FUNCTION
...
| COST   execution_cost
| ROWS   result_rows
...
```

The COST parameter indicates how much more expensive than a standard operator your operator really is. It is a multiplier for cpu_operator_cost, and is not a static value. In general, the default value is 100 unless the function has been written in C. Now that we have learned all about functions, let's explore more about them in the following section.

Using functions for various purposes

In PostgreSQL, stored procedures can be used for pretty much everything. In this chapter, you have already learned about the CREATE DOMAIN clause, and so on, but it is also possible to create your own operators, type casts, and even collations.

In this section, you will see how a simple type cast can be created, and how it can be used to your advantage. To define a type cast, consider taking a look at the CREATE CAST clause. The syntax of this command is shown in the following code:

```
test=# \h CREATE CAST
Command: CREATE CAST
Description: define a new cast
Syntax:
CREATE CAST (source_type AS target_type)
    WITH FUNCTION function_name [ (argument_type [, ...]) ]
    [ AS ASSIGNMENT | AS IMPLICIT ]

CREATE CAST (source_type AS target_type)
```

```
WITHOUT FUNCTION
    [ AS ASSIGNMENT | AS IMPLICIT ]

CREATE CAST (source_type AS target_type)
    WITH INOUT
    [ AS ASSIGNMENT | AS IMPLICIT ]
```

URL: https://www.postgresql.org/docs/12/sql-createcast.html

Using this stuff is very simple. You simply tell PostgreSQL which procedure it is supposed to call in order to cast whatever type to your desired data type.

In standard PostgreSQL, you cannot cast an IP address to a Boolean. Therefore, it makes for a good example. First, the stored procedure has to be defined:

```
CREATE FUNCTION inet_to_boolean(inet)
RETURNS boolean AS
$$
        BEGIN
                RETURN true;
        END;
$$ LANGUAGE 'plpgsql';
```

For simplicity, it returns `true`. However, you can use any code in any language to do the actual transformation.

In the next step, it is already possible to define the CAST type:

```
CREATE CAST (inet  AS boolean)
WITH FUNCTION inet_to_boolean(inet) AS IMPLICIT;
```

The first thing we need to do is tell PostgreSQL that we want to cast `inet` to `boolean`. Then, the function is listed and we tell PostgreSQL that we prefer an implicit cast.

It is a simple and straightforward process, and we can test the cast as follows:

```
test=# SELECT '192.168.0.34'::inet::boolean;
 bool
------
 t
(1 row)
```

Basically, the same logic can also be applied to define collations. Again, a stored procedure can be used to perform whatever has to be done:

```
test=# \h CREATE COLLATION
Command: CREATE COLLATION
Description: define a new collation
Syntax:
CREATE COLLATION [ IF NOT EXISTS ] name (
    [ LOCALE = locale, ]
    [ LC_COLLATE = lc_collate, ]
    [ LC_CTYPE = lc_ctype, ]
    [ PROVIDER = provider, ]
    [ DETERMINISTIC = boolean, ]
    [ VERSION = version ]
)
CREATE COLLATION [ IF NOT EXISTS ] name FROM existing_collation

URL: https://www.postgresql.org/docs/12/sql-createcollation.html
```

Summary

In this chapter, you have learned how to write stored procedures. After a theoretical introduction, our attention was focused on some selected features of PL/pgSQL. In addition to that, you learned how to use PL/Perl and PL/Python, which are two important languages that are provided by PostgreSQL. Of course, there are many more languages available. However, due to the limitations of the scope of this book, those could not be covered in detail. If you want to know more, check out the following website: https://wiki.postgresql.org/wiki/PL_Matrix. We also learned how to improve function calls, and how we can use them for various other purposes.

In Chapter 8, *Managing PostgreSQL Security*, you will learn about PostgreSQL security. You will learn how to manage users and permissions in general. On top of that, you will also learn about network security.

Questions

1. What is the difference between a function and a stored procedure?
2. What is the difference between a trusted and an untrusted language?
3. In general, are functions good or bad?
4. Which server-side languages are available in PostgreSQL?
5. What is a trigger?
6. Which languages can be used to write functions?
7. Which language is fastest?

Managing PostgreSQL Security

8

In `Chapter 7`, *Writing Stored Procedures*, we learned about stored procedures and writing server-side code. After being introduced to many important topics, it is now time to shift to PostgreSQL security. Here, we will learn how to secure a server and configure permissions.

The following topics will be covered in this chapter:

- Managing network security
- Digging into RLS
- Inspecting permissions
- Reassigning objects and dropping users

By the end of the chapter, we will be able to professionally configure PostgreSQL security. Let's now start off with managing network security.

Managing network security

Before moving on to real-world, practical examples, let's briefly focus on the various layers of security that we will be dealing with. When dealing with security, it makes sense to keep these levels in mind in order to approach security-related issues in an organized way.

Here is my mental model:

- **Bind addresses**: `listen_addresses` in the `postgresql.conf` file
- **Host-based access control**: The `pg_hba.conf` file
- **Instance-level permissions**: Users, roles, database creation, login, and replication
- **Database-level permissions**: Connecting, creating schemas, and more
- **Schema-level permissions**: Using schema and creating objects inside a schema
- **Table-level permissions**: Selecting, inserting, updating, and more
- **Column-level permissions**: Allowing or restricting access to columns
- **RLS**: Restricting access to rows

In order to read a value, PostgreSQL has to ensure that we have sufficient permissions on every level. The entire chain of permissions has to be correct.

Understanding bind addresses and connections

When configuring a PostgreSQL server, one of the first things that you need to do is define the remote access. By default, PostgreSQL does not accept remote connections. The important thing here is that PostgreSQL does not even reject the connection, because it simply does not listen on the port. If we try to connect, the error message will actually come from the operating system, because PostgreSQL does not care at all.

Assuming that there is a database server using the default configuration on `192.168.0.123`, the following will happen:

```
iMac:~ hs$ telnet 192.168.0.123 5432
Trying 192.168.0.123...
telnet: connect to address 192.168.0.123: Connection refused
telnet: Unable to connect to remote host
```

Telnet tries to create a connection on port `5432`, and is instantly rejected by the remote box. From the outside, it looks as if PostgreSQL is not running at all.

The key to success can be found in the `postgresql.conf` file:

```
# - Connection Settings -

# listen_addresses = 'localhost'
    # what IP address(es) to listen on;
    # comma-separated list of addresses;
    # defaults to 'localhost'; use '*' for all
    # (change requires restart)
```

The `listen_addresses` setting will tell PostgreSQL which addresses to listen on. Technically speaking, those addresses are bind addresses. What does that actually mean? Suppose that we have four network cards in our machine. We can listen on, say, three of those **Internet Protocol (IP)** addresses. PostgreSQL takes requests to those three cards into account and does not listen on the fourth one. The port is simply closed.

We have to put our server's IP address into `listen_addresses`, and not the IPs of the clients.

If we put * in PostgreSQL, we will listen to every IP assigned to your machine.

Keep in mind that changing `listen_addresses` requires a PostgreSQL service restart. It cannot be changed on the fly without a restart.

However, there are more settings related to connection management that are very important to understand. They are as follows:

```
#port = 5432
                # (change requires restart)
max_connections = 100
                # (change requires restart)
# Note: Increasing max_connections costs ~400 bytes of
# shared memory per
# connection slot, plus lock space
# (see max_locks_per_transaction)
#superuser_reserved_connections = 3
                # (change requires restart)
#unix_socket_directories = '/tmp'
                # comma-separated list of directories
                # (change requires restart)
#unix_socket_group = ''
                # (change requires restart)
#unix_socket_permissions = 0777
                # begin with 0 to use octal notation
                # (change requires restart)
```

First of all, PostgreSQL listens to a single **Transmission Control Protocol** (**TCP**) port, the default value of which is `5432`. Keep in mind that PostgreSQL will listen on a single port only. Whenever a request comes in, the postmaster will fork and create a new process to handle the connection. By default, up to 100 normal connections are allowed. On top of that, 3 additional connections are reserved for superusers. This means that we can either have 97 connections, plus 3 superusers, or 100 superuser connections.

Note that these connection-related settings will also need a restart. The reason for this is that a static amount of memory is allocated to shared memory, which cannot be changed on the fly.

Inspecting connections and performance

While consulting, many people ask me whether raising the connection limit will have an impact on performance in general. The answer is: not much, as there is always some overhead due to context switches. It makes little difference as to how many connections there are. However, what does make a difference is the number of open snapshots. The more open snapshots there are, the more the overhead on the database side. In other words, we can increase `max_connections` cheaply.

> If you are interested in some real-world data, consider taking a look at one of my older blog posts at `https://www.cybertec-postgresql.com/max_connections-performance-impacts/`.

Living in a world without TCP

In some cases, we might not want to use a network. It often happens that a database will only talk to a local application anyway. Maybe our PostgreSQL database has been shipped along with our application, or maybe we just don't want the risk of using a network; in this case, Unix sockets are what you need. Unix sockets are a network-free means of communication. Your application can connect through a Unix socket locally without exposing anything to the outside world.

What we need, however, is a directory. By default, PostgreSQL will use the `/tmp` directory. However, if more than one database server is running per machine, each one will need a separate data directory to live in.

Apart from security, there are various reasons why not using a network might be a good idea. One of these reasons is performance. Using Unix sockets is a lot faster than going through the loopback device (`127.0.0.1`). If that sounds surprising, don't worry; it is for many people. However, the overhead of a real network connection should not be underestimated if you are only running very small queries.

To depict what this really means, I have included a simple benchmark.

We will create a `script.sql` file. This is a simple script that creates a random number and selects it. It is the most simplistic statement possible. There is nothing simpler than fetching a number.

So, let's run this simple benchmark on a normal laptop. To do so, we shall write a small thing called `script.sql`. It will be used by the following benchmark:

```
[hs@linuxpc ~]$ cat /tmp/script.sql
SELECT 1
```

Then, we can simply run `pgbench` to execute the SQL over and over again. The `-f` option allows us to pass the name of the SQL to the script. `-c 10` means that we want 10 concurrent connections to be active for 5 seconds (`-T 5`). The benchmark is running as the `postgres` user and is supposed to use the `postgres` database, which should be there by default. Note that the following examples will work on **Red Hat Enterprise Linux (RHEL)** derivatives. Debian-based systems will use different paths:

```
[hs@linuxpc ~]$ pgbench -f /tmp/script.sql
                -c 10 -T 5
                -U postgres postgres 2>
/dev/null transaction type: /tmp/script.sql
scaling factor: 1
query mode: simple
number of clients: 10
number of threads: 1
duration: 5 s
number of transactions actually processed: 871407
latency average = 0.057 ms
tps = 174278.158426 (including connections establishing)
tps = 174377.935625 (excluding connections establishing)
```

As we can see, no hostname is passed to `pgbench`, so the tool connects locally to the Unix socket and runs the script as fast as possible. On this four-core Intel box, the system was able to achieve around 174,000 transactions per second.

What happens if the `-h` localhost is added? The performance will change, as you can see in the next code snippet:

```
[hs@linuxpc ~]$ pgbench -f /tmp/script.sql
                -h localhost -c 10 -T 5
                -U postgres postgres 2>
/dev/null transaction type: /tmp/script.sql
scaling factor: 1
query mode: simple
number of clients: 10
number of threads: 1
duration: 5 s
number of transactions actually processed: 535251
```

```
latency average = 0.093 ms
tps = 107000.872598 (including connections establishing)
tps = 107046.943632 (excluding connections establishing)
```

The throughput will drop like a stone to `107000` transactions per second. The difference is clearly related to the networking overhead.

 By using the `-j` option (the number of threads assigned to `pgbench`), we can squeeze some more transactions out of our systems. However, it does not change the overall picture of the benchmark in our situation. In other tests, it does, because `pgbench` can be a real bottleneck if you don't provide enough CPU power.

As we can see, networking can not only be a security issue, but also a performance issue.

Managing pg_hba.conf

After configuring bind addresses, we can move on to the next level. The `pg_hba.conf` file will tell PostgreSQL how to authenticate people coming over the network. In general, the `pg_hba.conf` file entries have the following layout:

```
# local DATABASE USER METHOD [OPTIONS]
# host DATABASE USER ADDRESS METHOD [OPTIONS]
# hostssl DATABASE USER ADDRESS METHOD [OPTIONS]
# hostnossl DATABASE USER ADDRESS METHOD [OPTIONS]
```

There are four types of rules that can be put into the `pg_hba.conf` file:

- `local`: This can be used to configure local Unix socket connections.
- `host`: This can be used for **Secure Socket Layer (SSL)** and non-SSL connections.
- `hostssl`: This is only valid for SSL connections. To make use of this option, SSL must be compiled into the server, which is the case if we are using prepackaged versions of PostgreSQL. In addition to that, `ssl = on` has to be set in the `postgresql.conf` file. This file is called when the server is started.
- `hostnossl`: This works for non-SSL connections.

A list of rules can be put into the `pg_hba.conf` file. Here is an example:

```
# TYPE DATABASE USER ADDRESS METHOD
# "local" is for Unix domain socket connections only
local all all trust

# IPv4 local connections:
```

```
host all all 127.0.0.1/32 trust

# IPv6 local connections:
host all all ::1/128 trust
```

You can see three simple rules:

- The local record says that all users from local Unix sockets for all databases are to be trusted. The `trust` method means that no password has to be sent to the server and people can log in directly.
- The other two rules say that the same applies to connections from the `127.0.0.1` localhost and `::1/128`, which is an IPv6 address.

As connecting without a password is certainly not the best choice for remote access, PostgreSQL provides various authentication methods that can be used to configure the `pg_hba.conf` file flexibly. Here is a list of possible authentication methods:

- `trust`: This allows authentication without providing a password. The desired user has to be available on the PostgreSQL side.
- `reject`: The connection will be rejected.
- `md5` and `password`: The connections can be created using a password. `md5` means that the password is encrypted when it is sent over the wire. In the case of passwords, the credentials are sent in plain text, which should not be done on a modern system anymore. `md5` is not considered safe anymore. You should use `scram-sha-256` instead in PostgreSQL 10 and beyond.
- `scram-sha-256`: This setting is the successor of `md5`, and uses a far more secure hash than the previous version.
- `gss` and `sspi`: This uses **Generic Security Service Application Program Interface (GSSAPI)** or **Security Support Provider Interface (SSPI)** authentication. This is only possible for TCP/IP connections. The idea here is to allow for single sign-on.
- `ident`: This obtains the operating system username of the client by contacting the `ident` server of the client and checking whether it matches the requested database username.
- `peer`: Suppose we are logged in as `abc` on Unix. If `peer` is enabled, we can only log in to PostgreSQL as `abc`. If we try to change the username, we will be rejected. The beauty is that `abc` won't need a password in order to authenticate. The idea here is that only the database administrator can log in to the database on a Unix system and not somebody else who just has the password or a Unix account on the same machine. This only works for local connections.

- `pam`: This uses the **Pluggable Authentication Module (PAM)**. This is especially important if you want to use a means of authentication that is not provided by PostgreSQL out of the box. To use the PAM, create a file called `/etc/pam.d/postgresql` on your Linux system, and put the desired PAM modules that you are planning to use into the config file. Using the PAM, we can even authenticate against less common components. However, it can also be used to connect to Active Directory and so on.
- `ldap`: This configuration allows you to authenticate using **lightweight directory access protocol (LDAP)**. Note that PostgreSQL will only ask LDAP for authentication; if a user is present only on the LDAP side but not on the PostgreSQL side, you cannot log in. You should also note that PostgreSQL has to know where your LDAP server is. All of this information has to be stored in the `pg_hba.conf` file, as outlined in the official documentation at `https://www.postgresql.org/docs/10/static/auth-methods.html#AUTH-LDAP`.
- `radius`: The **Remote Authentication Dial-In User Service (RADIUS)** is a means of performing single sign-on. Again, parameters are passed using configuration options.
- `cert`: This authentication method uses SSL client certificates to perform authentication, and therefore it is possible only if SSL is used. The advantage here is that no password has to be sent. The `CN` attribute of the certificate will be compared to the requested database username, and, if they match, the login will be allowed. A map can be used to allow user mapping.

Rules can simply be listed one after the other. The important thing here is that the order does make a difference, as shown in the following example:

```
host    all    all    192.168.1.0/24     scram-sha-256
host    all    all    192.168.1.54/32    reject
```

When PostgreSQL walks through the `pg_hba.conf` file, it will use the first rule that matches. So, if our request is coming from `192.168.1.54`, the first rule will always match before we make it to the second one. This means that `192.168.1.54` will be able to log in if the password and user are correct; therefore, the second rule is pointless.

If we want to exclude the IP, we need to ensure that those two rules are swapped.

Handling SSL

PostgreSQL allows us to encrypt the transfer between the server and the client. Encryption is highly beneficial, especially if we are communicating over long distances. SSL offers a simple and secure way to ensure that nobody is able to listen to your communication.

In this section, we will learn how to set up SSL:

1. The first thing to do is to set the `ssl` parameter to `on` in the `postgresql.conf` file when the server starts. In the next step, we can put SSL certificates into the `$PGDATA` directory. If we don't want the certificates to be in some other directory, we need to change the following parameters:

   ```
   #ssl_cert_file = 'server.crt'      # (change requires restart)
   #ssl_key_file = 'server.key'       # (change requires restart)
   #ssl_ca_file = ''                  # (change requires restart)
   #ssl_crl_file = ''                 # (change requires restart)
   ```

2. If we want to use self-signed certificates, we need to perform the following step:

   ```
   openssl req -new -text -out server.req
   ```

   Answer the questions that are asked by OpenSSL. Make sure that we enter the local hostname as the common name. We can leave the password empty. This call will generate a key that is passphrase protected; it will not accept a passphrase that is less than four characters long.

3. To remove the passphrase (as you must if you want an automatic startup of the server), run the following code:

   ```
   openssl rsa -in privkey.pem -out server.key
   rm privkey.pem
   ```

4. Enter the old passphrase to unlock the existing key. Now, use the following code to turn the certificate into a self-signed certificate and to copy the key and certificate to where the server will look for them:

   ```
   openssl req -x509 -in server.req -text
     -key server.key -out server.crt
   ```

5. After doing this, make sure that the files have the right set of permissions:

   ```
   chmod og-rwx server.key
   ```

6. Once the proper rules have been put into the `pg_hba.conf` file, we can use SSL to connect to your server. To verify that we are using SSL, consider checking out the `pg_stat_ssl` function. It will tell us about every connection and whether it uses SSL or not, and it will provide some important information about encryption:

```
test=# \d pg_stat_sslView   "pg_catalog.pg_stat_ssl"

   Column      |    Type    | Modifiers
-------------+----------+-----------
 pid         | integer  |
 ssl         | boolean  |
 version     | text     |
 cipher      | text     |
 bits        | integer  |
 compression | boolean  |
 clientdn    | text     |
```

7. If the `ssl` field for a process contains `true`, PostgreSQL does what we would expect it to do:

```
postgres=# select * from pg_stat_ssl;
-[ RECORD 1 ]
-----------------------------
pid         | 20075
ssl         | t
version     | TLSv1.2
cipher      | ECDHE-RSA-AES256-GCM-SHA384
bits        | 256
compression | f
clientdn    |
```

Handling instance-level security

So far, we have configured bind addresses and we have told PostgreSQL which means of authentication to use for which IP ranges. Up until now, the configuration has been purely network-related.

In the next step, we can shift our attention to permissions at the instance level. The most important thing to know is if users in PostgreSQL exist at the instance level. If we create a user, it is not just visible inside one database; it can be seen by all the databases. A user might have permissions to access just a single database, but users are essentially created at the instance level.

To those of you who are new to PostgreSQL, there is one more thing you should keep in mind: users and roles are the same thing. The CREATE ROLE and CREATE USER clauses have different default values (the only difference is that roles do not get the LOGIN attribute by default), but, at the end of the day, users and roles are the same. Therefore, the CREATE ROLE and CREATE USER clauses support the very same syntax:

```
test=# \h CREATE USER
Command: CREATE USER
Description: define a new database role
Syntax:
CREATE USER name [ [ WITH ] option [ ... ] ]

where option can be:

      SUPERUSER | NOSUPERUSER
    | CREATEDB | NOCREATEDB
    | CREATEROLE | NOCREATEROLE
    | INHERIT | NOINHERIT
    | LOGIN | NOLOGIN
    | REPLICATION | NOREPLICATION
    | BYPASSRLS | NOBYPASSRLS
    | CONNECTION LIMIT connlimit
    | [ ENCRYPTED ] PASSWORD 'password' | PASSWORD NULL
    | VALID UNTIL 'timestamp'
    | IN ROLE role_name [, ...]
    | IN GROUP role_name [, ...]
    | ROLE role_name [, ...]
    | ADMIN role_name [, ...]
    | USER role_name [, ...]
    | SYSID uid

URL: https://www.postgresql.org/docs/12/sql-createuser.html
```

Let's discuss those syntax elements one by one. The first thing that we can see is that a user can be a superuser or a normal user. If somebody is marked as SUPERUSER, there are no longer any restrictions that a normal user has to face. SUPERUSER can drop objects (for example, databases) as they wish.

The next important thing is that it takes permissions on the instance level to create a new database.

Note that when somebody creates a database, this user will automatically be the owner of the database.

The rule is this: the creator is always automatically the owner of an object (unless specified otherwise, as can be done with the CREATE DATABASE clause). The beauty of this is that object owners can also drop an object again.

> The CREATEROLE or NOCREATEROLE clause defines whether somebody is allowed to create new users/roles or not.

The next important thing is the INHERIT or NOINHERIT clause. If the INHERIT clause is set (which is the default value), a user can inherit permissions from some other user. Using inherited permissions allows us to use roles, which is a good way to abstract permissions. For example, we can create the role of bookkeeper, and make many other roles inherit from bookkeeper. The idea is that we only have to tell PostgreSQL once what a bookkeeper role is allowed to do, even if we have many people working in accounting.

The LOGIN, or NOLOGIN, clause defines whether a role is allowed to log in to the instance.

> Note that the LOGIN clause is not enough to actually connect to a database. To do that, more permissions are needed.

At this point, we are trying to make it into the instance, which is the gate to all the databases inside the instance. Let's get back to our example: bookkeeper might be marked as NOLOGIN, because we want people to log in with their real name. All your accountants (say, Joe and Jane) might be marked as the LOGIN clause, but can inherit all the permissions from the bookkeeper role. A structure such as this makes it easy to ensure that all bookkeepers will have the same permissions, while ensuring their individual activity is operated and logged under their separate identities.

If we are planning to run PostgreSQL with streaming replication, we can do all the transaction log streaming as a superuser. However, this is not recommended from a security point of view. As an assurance that we don't have to be a superuser to stream XLog, PostgreSQL allows us to give replication rights to a normal user, which can then be used to do the streaming. It is common practice to create a special user just for the purpose of managing streaming.

As we will see later in this chapter, PostgreSQL provides a feature called RLS. The idea is that we can exclude rows from the scope of a user. If a user is explicitly supposed to bypass RLS, set this value to BYPASSRLS. The default value is NOBYPASSRLS.

Sometimes, it makes sense to restrict the number of connections allowed for a user. CONNECTION LIMIT allows us to do exactly that. Note that, overall, there can never be more connections than defined in the postgresql.conf file (max_connections). However, we can always restrict certain users to a lower value.

By default, PostgreSQL will store encrypted passwords in the system table, which is a good default behavior. However, suppose you are doing a training course, and 10 students are attending and everybody is connected to your box. You can be 100% certain that one of those people will forget his or her password once in a while. As your setup is not security critical, you might decide to store the password in plain text so that you can easily look it up and give it to a student. This feature might also come in handy if you are testing software.

Often, we already know that somebody will leave the organization fairly soon. The VALID UNTIL clause allows us to automatically lock out a specific user if his or her account has expired.

The IN ROLE clause lists one or more existing roles to which the new role will be immediately added as a new member. It helps to avoid additional manual steps. An alternative to IN ROLE is IN GROUP.

The ROLE clause will define the roles that are automatically added as members of the new role.

The ADMIN clause is the same as the ROLE clause, but it adds WITH ADMIN OPTION.

Finally, we can use the SYSID clause to set a specific ID for the user (this is similar to what some Unix administrators do for usernames at the operating system level).

Creating and modifying users

After this theoretical introduction, it is time to actually create users and see how things can be used in a practical example:

```
test=# CREATE ROLE  bookkeeper NOLOGIN;
CREATE ROLE
test=# CREATE ROLE  joe LOGIN;
CREATE ROLE
test=# GRANT  bookkeeper TO joe;
GRANT ROLE
```

The first thing that has been done here is that a role called bookkeeper has been created.

Note that we don't want people to log in as `bookkeeper`, so the role is marked as `NOLOGIN`.

> You should also note that `NOLOGIN` is the default value if you use the `CREATE ROLE` clause. If you prefer the `CREATE USER` clause, the default setting is `LOGIN`.

Then, the `joe` role is created and marked as `LOGIN`. Finally, the `bookkeeper` role is assigned to the `joe` role, so that he can do everything `bookkeeper` is actually allowed to do.

Once the users are in place, we can test what we have so far:

```
[hs@zenbook ~]$ psql test -U bookkeeper
psql: FATAL:  role "bookkeeper" is not permitted to log in
```

As expected, the `bookkeeper` role is not allowed to log in to the system. What happens if the `joe` role tries to log in? Have a look at the following code snippet:

```
[hs@zenbook ~]$ psql test -U joe
...
test=>
```

This will actually work as expected. However, note that Command Prompt has changed. This is just a way for PostgreSQL to show you that you are not logged in as a superuser.

Once a user has been created, it might be necessary to modify it. One thing we might want to change is the password. In PostgreSQL, users are allowed to change their own passwords. Here is how it works:

```
test=> ALTER   ROLE   joe PASSWORD 'abc';
ALTER   ROLE
test=> SELECT current_user;
 current_user
--------------
 joe
(1 row)
```

> Be aware of the fact that `ALTER ROLE` changes the attributes of a role. `PASSWORD` will actually make the password show up in the logfile if **Data Definition Language (DDL)** logging has been configured. This is not too desirable. It is better to change the password using a visual tool. In this case there is some protocol support, which ensures that the password is never sent over the wire in plain text. Using `ALTER ROLE` directly to change the password is not a good idea at all.

The ALTER ROLE clause (or ALTER USER) will allow us to change most of the settings that can be set during user creation. However, there is even more to managing users. In many cases, we want to assign special parameters to a user. The ALTER USER clause gives us the means to do that:

```
ALTER ROLE { role_specification | ALL }
    [ IN DATABASE database_name ]
            SET configuration_parameter { TO | = } { value | DEFAULT }
ALTER ROLE { role_specification | ALL }
    [ IN DATABASE database_name ]
            SET configuration_parameter FROM CURRENT
ALTER ROLE { role_specification | ALL }
    [ IN DATABASE database_name ] RESET configuration_parameter
ALTER ROLE { role_specification | ALL }
    [ IN DATABASE database_name ] RESET ALL
```

The syntax is fairly simple and pretty straightforward. To depict why this is really useful, I have added a real-world example. Let's suppose that Joe happens to live on the island of Mauritius. When he logs in, he wants to be in his own time zone, even if his database server is located in Europe:

```
test=> ALTER   ROLE   joe SET TimeZone = 'UTC-4';
ALTER   ROLE
test=> SELECT now();
            now
-------------------------------
2017-01-09 20:36:48.571584+01
(1 row)

test=> q
[hs@zenbook ~]$ psql   test   -U joe
. . .
test=> SELECT now();
            now
-------------------------------
2017-01-09 23:36:53.357845+04
(1 row)
```

The ALTER ROLE clause will modify the user. As soon as joe reconnects, the time zone will already be set for him.

The time zone is not changed immediately. You should either reconnect, or use a SET ... TO DEFAULT clause.

The important thing here is that this is also possible for some memory parameters, such as `work_mem`, which have already been covered earlier in this book.

Defining database-level security

After configuring users at the instance level, it is possible to dig deeper and see what can be done at the database level. The first major question that arises is this: we explicitly allowed Joe to log in to the database instance, but who or what allowed Joe to actually connect to one of the databases? Maybe you don't want Joe to access all the databases in your system. Restricting access to certain databases is exactly what we can achieve at this level.

For databases, the following permissions can be set using a GRANT clause:

```
GRANT { { CREATE | CONNECT | TEMPORARY | TEMP } [, ...]
    | ALL [ PRIVILEGES ] }
    ON DATABASE database_name [, ...]
    TO role_specification [, ...] [ WITH GRANT OPTION ]
```

There are two major permissions on the database level that deserve close attention:

- CREATE: This allows somebody to create a schema inside the database. Note that a CREATE clause does not allow for the creation of tables; it is about schemas. In PostgreSQL, a table resides inside a schema, so you have to get to the schema level first in order to be able to create a table.
- CONNECT: This allows somebody to connect to a database.

The question now is this: nobody has explicitly assigned any CONNECT permissions to the joe role, so where do those permissions actually come from? The answer is this: there is a thing called `public`, which is similar to the Unix world. If the world is allowed to do something, so is joe, who is part of the general public.

The main thing is that `public` is not a role in the sense that it can be dropped and renamed. We can simply see it as the equivalent of everybody on the system.

So, to ensure that not everybody can connect to any database at any time, CONNECT may have to be revoked from the general public. To do so, we can connect as a superuser and fix the problem:

```
[hs@zenbook ~]$ psql  test  -U postgres
...
test=# REVOKE ALL ON DATABASE test FROM public;
REVOKE
test=# \q
```

```
[hs@zenbook ~]$ psql test -U joe
psql:  FATAL:  permission denied for database "test"
DETAIL:  User does not have CONNECT privilege.
```

As we can see, the `joe` role is not allowed to connect anymore. At this point, only superusers have access to `test`.

In general, it is a good idea to revoke permissions from the `postgres` database even before other databases are created. The idea behind this concept is that those permissions won't be in all those newly created databases anymore. If somebody needs access to a certain database, the rights have to be explicitly granted. The rights are not automatically there anymore.

If we want to allow the `joe` role to connect to the test database, try the following line as a superuser:

```
[hs@zenbook ~]$ psql test -U postgres
. . .
test=# GRANT CONNECT ON DATABASE test TO bookkeeper;
GRANT
test=# \q
[hs@zenbook ~]$ psql test -U joe
. . .
test=>
```

There are two choices here:

- We can allow the `joe` role directly, so that only the `joe` role will be able to connect.
- Alternatively, we can grant permissions to the `bookkeeper` role. Remember, the `joe` role will inherit all the permissions from the `bookkeeper` role, so if we want all accountants to be able to connect to the database, assigning permissions to the `bookkeeper` role seems to be an attractive idea.

It is not risky if we grant permissions to the `bookkeeper` role, because the role is not allowed to log in to the instance in the first place, so it purely serves as a source of permissions.

Adjusting schema-level permissions

Once we are done configuring the database level, it makes sense to take a look at the schema level.

Before actually taking a look at the schema, let's run a small test:

```
test=> CREATE DATABASE test;
ERROR:  permission denied to create database test=>
CREATE USER  xy;
ERROR:  permission denied to create role test=>
CREATE SCHEMA sales;
ERROR:  permission denied for database test
```

As we can see, Joe is having a bad day and nothing but connecting to the database is allowed.

However, there is a small exception, and it comes as a surprise to many people:

```
test=> CREATE TABLE t_broken (id int);
CREATE TABLE
test=> \d
          List  of relations
 Schema  |   Name    | Type   | Owner
---------+-----------+--------+-------
 public | t_broken | table  | joe
(1 rows)
```

By default, `public` is allowed to work with the public schema, which is always around. If we are seriously interested in securing our database, make sure that this problem is taken care of. Otherwise, normal users will potentially spam your public schema with all kinds of tables and the entire setup might suffer. You should also keep in mind that if somebody is allowed to create an object, that person is also its owner. Ownership means that all permissions are automatically available to the creator, including the destruction of the object.

To take those permissions away from `public`, run the following line as a superuser:

```
test=# REVOKE ALL ON SCHEMA public FROM public;
REVOKE
```

From now on, nobody can put things into your public schema without the correct permissions any more. The next listing is proof of that:

```
[hs@zenbook ~]$ psql test -U joe
...
test=> CREATE TABLE  t_data (id int);
ERROR:  no schema has been selected to create in
LINE  1: CREATE TABLE t_data (id int);
```

As we can see, the command will fail. The important thing here is the error message that will be displayed; PostgreSQL does not know where to put these tables. By default, it will try to put the table into one of the following schema:

```
test=> SHOW search_path ;
 search_path
-----------------
 "$user", public
(1 row)
```

As there is no schema called `joe`, it is not an option, so PostgreSQL will try the public schema. As there are no permissions, it will complain that it does not know where to put the table.

If the table is explicitly prefixed, the situation will change instantly:

```
test=> CREATE TABLE  public.t_data (id int);
ERROR:  permission denied for schema public
LINE  1: CREATE TABLE  public.t_data (id int);
```

In this case, we will get the error message that you expect. PostgreSQL denies access to the public schema.

The next logical question now is this: which permissions can be set at the schema level to give some more power to the `joe` role:

```
GRANT  { { CREATE | USAGE  } [, ...]  | ALL [ PRIVILEGES ] }
   ON SCHEMA schema_name [, ...]
TO role_specification [, ...]  [ WITH  GRANT  OPTION ]
```

CREATE means that somebody can put objects into a schema. USAGE means that somebody is allowed to enter the schema. Note that entering the schema does not mean that something inside the schema can actually be used; those permissions have not been defined yet. This just means that the user can see the system catalog for this schema.

To allow the joe role to access the table it has created previously, the following line will be necessary (executed as a superuser):

```
test=# GRANT USAGE ON SCHEMA public TO bookkeeper;
GRANT
```

The joe role is now able to read its table as expected:

```
[hs@zenbook ~]$ psql test -U joe
test=> SELECT count(*) FROM t_broken;
 count
-------
     0
(1 row)
```

The joe role is also able to add and modify rows, because it happens to be the owner of the table. However, although it can do quite a lot of things already, the joe role is not yet almighty. Consider the following statement:

```
test=> ALTER TABLE t_broken RENAME TO t_useful;
ERROR:  permission denied for schema public
```

Let's take a closer look at the actual error message. As we can see, the message complains about the permissions on the schema, not about the permissions on the table itself (remember, the joe role owns the table). To fix the problem, it has to be tackled on the schema level and not on the table level. Run the following line as a superuser:

```
test=# GRANT CREATE ON SCHEMA public TO bookkeeper;
GRANT
```

The joe role can now change the name of its table to a more useful name:

```
[hs@zenbook ~]$ psql test -U joe
test=> ALTER TABLE t_broken RENAME TO t_useful;
ALTER TABLE
```

Keep in mind that this is necessary if DDLs are used. In my daily work as a PostgreSQL support service provider, I have seen a couple of issues where this turned out to be a problem.

Working with tables

After taking care of bind addresses, network authentication, users, databases, and schema, we have finally made it to the table level. The following snippet shows which permissions can be set for a table:

```
GRANT { { SELECT | INSERT | UPDATE | DELETE | TRUNCATE
            | REFERENCES | TRIGGER }
    [, ...] | ALL [ PRIVILEGES ] }
    ON { [ TABLE ] table_name [, ...]
        | ALL TABLES IN SCHEMA schema_name [, ...] }
    TO role_specification [, ...] [ WITH GRANT OPTION ]
```

Let me explain these permissions one by one:

- SELECT: This allows you to read a table.
- INSERT: This allows you to add rows to the table (this also includes copy and so on; it is not only about the INSERT clause). Note that if you are allowed to insert, you are not automatically allowed to read. The SELECT and INSERT clauses are needed to be able to read the data that you have inserted.
- UPDATE: This modifies the content of a table.
- DELETE: This is used to remove rows from a table.
- TRUNCATE: This allows you to use the TRUNCATE clause. Note that the DELETE and TRUNCATE clauses are two separate permissions, because the TRUNCATE clause will lock the table, which is not done by the DELETE clause (not even if there is no WHERE condition).
- REFERENCES: This allows the creation of foreign keys. It is necessary to have this privilege on both the referencing and referenced columns, otherwise the creation of the key won't work.
- TRIGGER: This allows for the creation of triggers.

> The nice thing about the GRANT clause is that we can set permissions on all tables in a schema at the same time.

This greatly simplifies the process of adjusting permissions. It is also possible to use the WITH GRANT OPTION clause. The idea is to ensure that normal users can pass on permissions to others, which has the advantage of being able to reduce the workload of the administrators by quite a bit. Just imagine a system that provides access to hundreds of users; it can start to be a lot of work to manage all those people, and therefore administrators can appoint people to manage a subset of the data themselves.

Handling column-level security

In some cases, not everybody is allowed to see all the data. Just imagine a bank. Some people might see the entire information about a bank account, while others might be limited to only a subset of the data. In a real-world situation, somebody might not be allowed to read the balance column while somebody else might not see the interest rates of people's loans.

Another example would be that people are allowed to see people's profiles, but not their pictures or some other private information. The question now is this: how can column-level security be used?

To demonstrate this, we will add a column to the existing table belonging to the `joe` role:

```
test=> ALTER TABLE t_useful ADD COLUMN name text;
ALTER TABLE
```

The table now consists of two columns. The goal of the example is to ensure that a user can see only one of those columns:

```
test=> \d t_useful
       Table  "public.t_useful"
  Column |   Type    | Modifiers
 --------+----------+-----------
  id     | integer  |
  name   | text     |
```

As a superuser, let's create a user and give it access to the schema containing our table:

```
test=# CREATE ROLE paul LOGIN;
CREATE ROLE
test=# GRANT CONNECT ON DATABASE test TO paul;
GRANT
test=# GRANT USAGE ON SCHEMA public TO paul;
GRANT
```

Do not forget to give CONNECT rights to the new guy, because earlier in the chapter, CONNECT was revoked from `public`. Explicit granting is therefore absolutely necessary to ensure that we can get to the table.

The SELECT permissions can be given to the `paul` role:

```
test=# GRANT  SELECT (id)  ON t_useful TO paul;
GRANT
```

This is already enough. It is already possible to connect to the database as the `paul` user and read the column:

```
[hs@zenbook ~]$ psql test -U paul
...
test=> SELECT id FROM t_useful;
 id
----
(0 rows)
```

If we are using column-level permissions, there is an important thing to keep in mind; we should stop using SELECT *, as it will not work anymore:

```
test=> SELECT * FROM t_useful;
ERROR:  permission denied for relation t_useful
```

* still means all columns, but as there is no way to access all columns, things will error out instantly.

Configuring default privileges

So far, a lot of stuff has already been configured. The trouble is, what happens if new tables are added to the system? It can be quite painful and risky to process these tables one by one, and to set the proper permissions. Wouldn't it be nice if those things would just happen automatically? This is exactly what the ALTER DEFAULT PRIVILEGES clause does. The idea is to give users an option to make PostgreSQL automatically set the desired permissions, as soon as an object comes into existence. It is now impossible to simply forget to set those rights.

The following listing shows the first part of the syntax specification:

```
postgres=# \h ALTER DEFAULT PRIVILEGES
Command: ALTER DEFAULT PRIVILEGES
Description: define default access privileges
Syntax:
ALTER DEFAULT PRIVILEGES
    [ FOR { ROLE | USER } target_role [, ...] ]
    [ IN SCHEMA schema_name [, ...] ]
    abbreviated_grant_or_revoke

where abbreviated_grant_or_revoke is one of:

GRANT { { SELECT | INSERT | UPDATE | DELETE | TRUNCATE | REFERENCES |
TRIGGER }
    [, ...] | ALL [ PRIVILEGES ] }
```

```
    ON TABLES
    TO { [ GROUP ] role_name | PUBLIC } [, ...] [ WITH GRANT OPTION ]
...
```

The syntax works similarly to the GRANT clause, and is therefore easy and intuitive to use. To show us how it works, I compiled a simple example. The idea is that if the joe role creates a table, the paul role will automatically be able to use it:

```
test=# ALTER DEFAULT PRIVILEGES FOR ROLE joe
        IN SCHEMA public GRANT ALL ON TABLES TO paul;
ALTER DEFAULT PRIVILEGES
```

Let's connect as the joe role now and create a table:

```
[hs@zenbook ~]$ psql  test  -U joe
...
test=> CREATE TABLE  t_user (id serial, name  text,  passwd text);
CREATE TABLE
```

Connecting as the paul role will prove that the table has been assigned to the proper set of permissions:

```
[hs@zenbook ~]$ psql test -U paul
...
test=> SELECT * FROM  t_user;
 id | name | passwd
----+------+--------
(0 rows)
```

Digging into RLS

Up to this point, a table has always been shown as a whole. When the table contained 1 million rows, it was possible to retrieve 1 million rows from it. If somebody had the rights to read a table, it was all about the entire table. In many cases, this is not enough. It is often desirable that a user is not allowed to see all the rows.

Consider the following real-world example, where an accountant is doing accounting work for many people. The table containing tax rates should really be visible to everybody, as everybody has to pay the same rates. However, when it comes to the actual transactions, the accountant might want to ensure that everybody is only allowed to see his or her own transactions. Person *A* should not be allowed to see person *B*'s data. In addition to that, it might also make sense that the boss of a division is allowed to see all the data in their part of the company.

RLS has been designed to do exactly this, and enables you to build multi-tenant systems in a fast and simple way. The way to configure those permissions is to come up with policies. The CREATE POLICY command is here to provide us with a means to write these rules:

```
test=# \h CREATE POLICY
Command: CREATE POLICY
Description: define a new row level security policy for a table
Syntax:
CREATE POLICY name ON table_name
    [ AS { PERMISSIVE | RESTRICTIVE } ]
    [ FOR { ALL | SELECT | INSERT | UPDATE | DELETE } ]
    [ TO { role_name | PUBLIC | CURRENT_USER | SESSION_USER } [, ...] ]
    [ USING ( using_expression ) ]
    [ WITH CHECK ( check_expression ) ]

URL: https://www.postgresql.org/docs/12/sql-createpolicy.html
```

To depict how a policy can be written, let's first log in as a superuser and create a table containing a couple of entries:

```
test=# CREATE TABLE t_person (gender text, name text);
CREATE TABLE
test=# INSERT INTO t_person
  VALUES     ('male', 'joe'),
             ('male', 'paul'),
             ('female', 'sarah'),
             (NULL, 'R2- D2');
INSERT 0 4
```

Access is then granted to the joe role:

```
test=# GRANT ALL ON t_person TO joe;
GRANT
```

So far, everything is pretty normal, and the joe role will be able to actually read the entire table, as there is no RLS in place. But let's see what happens if ROW LEVEL SECURITY is enabled for the table:

```
test=# ALTER TABLE t_person ENABLE ROW LEVEL SECURITY;
ALTER TABLE
```

There is a deny, and all default policies are in place, so the `joe` role will actually get an empty table:

```
test=> SELECT * FROM t_person;
 gender | name
--------+------
(0 rows)
```

The default policy makes a lot of sense, as users are forced to explicitly set permissions.

Now that the table is under RLS control, policies can be written as a superuser:

```
test=# CREATE POLICY joe_pol_1
   ON t_person
   FOR SELECT TO joe
   USING  (gender = 'male');
CREATE POLICY
```

Logging in as the `joe` role and selecting all the data will return just two rows:

```
test=> SELECT * FROM  t_person;
 gender  | name
---------+------
 male    | joe
 male    | paul
(2 rows)
```

Let's inspect the policy we have just created in a more detailed way. The first thing that we can see is that the policy actually has a name. It is also connected to a table and allows for certain operations (in this case, the SELECT clause). Then comes the USING clause. This defines what the `joe` role will be allowed to see. The USING clause is, therefore, a mandatory filter attached to every query to only select the rows that our user is supposed to see.

There is also one important side note, where, if there is more than just a single policy, PostgreSQL will use an OR condition. In short, more policies will make you see more data by default. In PostgreSQL 9.6, this was always the case. However, with the introduction of PostgreSQL 10.0, the user can choose whether conditions should be OR or AND connected:

```
PERMISSIVE | RESTRICTIVE
```

By default, PostgreSQL is PERMISSIVE, so OR connections are at work. If we decide to use RESTRICTIVE, then those clauses will be connected with AND.

Now suppose that, for some reason, it has been decided that the joe role is also allowed to see robots. There are two choices to achieve our goal. The first option is to simply use the ALTER POLICY clause to change the existing policy:

```
test=# \h ALTER POLICY
Command: ALTER POLICY
Description: change the definition of a row level security policy
Syntax:
ALTER POLICY name ON table_name RENAME TO new_name

ALTER POLICY name ON table_name
    [ TO { role_name | PUBLIC | CURRENT_USER | SESSION_USER } [, ...] ]
    [ USING ( using_expression ) ]
    [ WITH CHECK ( check_expression ) ]

URL: https://www.postgresql.org/docs/12/sql-alterpolicy.html
```

The second option is to create a second policy, as shown in the next example:

```
test=# CREATE POLICY joe_pol_2
  ON t_person
  FOR SELECT TO joe
  USING  (gender IS NULL);
CREATE POLICY
```

The beauty is that those policies are simply connected using an OR condition as stated before, unless RESTRICTIVE is used. Therefore, PostgreSQL will now return three rows instead of two:

```
test=> SELECT * FROM  t_person;
 gender  | name
---------+-------
 male    | joe
 male    | paul
         | R2-D2
(3 rows)
```

The R2-D2 role is now also included in the result, as it matches the second policy.

To depict how PostgreSQL runs the query, I have decided to include an execution plan of the query:

```
test=> explain SELECT * FROM t_person;
                   QUERY PLAN
----------------------------------------------------------
 Seq Scan on t_person (cost=0.00..21.00 rows=9 width=64)
   Filter: ((gender IS NULL) OR (gender = 'male'::text))
(2 rows)
```

As we can see, both the USING clauses have been added as mandatory filters to the query. We might have noticed in the syntax definition that there are two types of clauses:

- USING: This clause filters rows that already exist. This is relevant to the SELECT and UPDATE clauses, and so on.
- CHECK: This clause filters new rows that are about to be created, so they are relevant to the INSERT and UPDATE clauses, and so on.

Here is what happens if we try to insert a row:

```
test=> INSERT INTO t_person VALUES ('male', 'kaarel');
ERROR:  new row violates row-level security policy for table "t_person"
```

As there is no policy for the INSERT clause, the statement will naturally error out. Here is the policy to allow insertions:

```
test=# CREATE POLICY joe_pol_3
          ON t_person
          FOR INSERT TO joe
          WITH CHECK (gender IN ('male', 'female'));
CREATE POLICY
```

The joe role is allowed to add males and females to the table, which is shown in the following listing:

```
test=> INSERT INTO t_person VALUES ('female', 'maria');
INSERT 0 1
```

However, there is also a catch; consider the following example:

```
test=> INSERT INTO  t_person VALUES ('female', 'maria') RETURNING *;
ERROR:  new row violates row-level security policy for table "t_person"
```

Remember, there is only a policy to select males. The trouble here is that the statement will return a woman, which is not allowed, because the joe role is under a male-only policy.

The `RETURNING *` clause will only work for men:

```
test=> INSERT INTO  t_person VALUES ('male', 'max') RETURNING *;
 gender  | name
---------+------
 male    | max
(1 row)
INSERT 0 1
```

If we don't want this behavior, we have to write a policy that actually contains a proper `USING` clause.

Inspecting permissions

When all of the permissions have been set, it is sometimes necessary to know who has which permissions. It is vital for administrators to find out who is allowed to do what. Unfortunately, this process is not so easy, and requires a bit of knowledge. Usually, I am a big fan of command-line usage. However, in the case of the permission system, it can really make sense to use a graphical user interface to do things.

Before I show you how to read PostgreSQL permissions, let's assign rights to the `joe` role, so that we can inspect them in the next step:

```
test=# GRANT ALL ON t_person TO joe;
GRANT
```

Retrieving information about permissions can be done using the z command in `psql`:

```
test=# \x
Expanded display is on.
test=# \z t_person
Access privileges
-[ RECORD 1 ]-----+-----------------------------------------------------------
----
Schema            | public
Name              | t_person
Type              | table
Access privileges | postgres=arwdDxt/postgres
+
                  | joe=arwdDxt/postgres
Column privileges |
Policies          | joe_pol_1 (r):
+                 | (u):  (gender = 'male'::text)
+                 | to: joe
+                 | joe_pol_2 (r):
```

```
+                      | (u): (gender IS NULL)
+                      | to: joe
+                      | joe_pol_3 (a):
+                      | (c): (gender = ANY (ARRAY['male'::text,
'female'::text]))
+                      | to: joe
```

This will return all those policies, along with information about access privileges. Unfortunately, those shortcuts are hard to read, and I have a feeling that they are not widely understood by administrators. In this example, the `joe` role has gotten `arwdDxt` from PostgreSQL. What do those shortcuts actually mean? Let's see:

- `a`: This appends for the `INSERT` clause.
- `r`: This reads for the `SELECT` clause.
- `w`: This writes for the `UPDATE` clause.
- `d`: This deletes for the `DELETE` clause.
- `D`: This is used for the `TRUNCATE` clause (when this was introduced, `t` was already taken).
- `x`: This is used for references.
- `t`: This is used for triggers.

If you don't know this code, there is also a second way to make things more readable. Consider the following function call:

```
test=# SELECT * FROM  aclexplode('{joe=arwdDxt/postgres}');
 grantor | grantee | privilege_type | is_grantable
---------+---------+----------------+--------------
      10 |   18481 | INSERT         | f
      10 |   18481 | SELECT         | f
      10 |   18481 | UPDATE         | f
      10 |   18481 | DELETE         | f
      10 |   18481 | TRUNCATE       | f
      10 |   18481 | REFERENCES     | f
      10 |   18481 | TRIGGER        | f
(7 rows)
```

As we can see, the set of permissions is returned as a simple table, which makes life really easy. To those of you who still consider inspecting permissions in PostgreSQL somewhat cumbersome, there is an additional solution (https://www.cybertec-postgresql.com) that we have implemented recently: `pg_permission`. The idea is to provide you with simple views to inspect the security system more deeply.

To download pg_permission, visit our GitHub repository page: https://github.com/cybertec-postgresql/pg_permission.

You can easily clone the repository as shown in the next listing:

```
git clone https://github.com/cybertec-postgresql/pg_permission.git
Cloning into 'pg_permission'...
remote: Enumerating objects: 111, done.
remote: Total 111 (delta 0), reused 0 (delta 0), pack-reused 111
Receiving objects: 100% (111/111), 33.08 KiB | 292.00 KiB/s, done.
Resolving deltas: 100% (52/52), done.
```

Once that is done, enter the directory and just run make install. Those two things are already enough to deploy the extension:

```
test=# CREATE EXTENSION pg_permissions;
CREATE EXTENSION
```

pg_permission will deploy a handful of views, which are all structured identically:

```
test=# \d all_permissions
 View "public.all_permissions"
    Column    |   Type    | Collation | Nullable | Default
--------------+-----------+-----------+----------+---------
 object_type  | obj_type  |           |          |
 role_name    | name      |           |          |
 schema_name  | name      |           |          |
 object_name  | text      | C         |          |
 column_name  | name      |           |          |
 permission   | perm_type |           |          |
 granted      | boolean   |           |          |
Triggers:
 permissions_trigger INSTEAD OF UPDATE ON all_permissions
                     FOR EACH ROW EXECUTE FUNCTION
permissions_trigger_func()
```

all_permissions is simply a view that provides you with an overall view of all permissions. You can simply filter by object type, and so on, to dig into the details. What is also interesting is that there is a trigger on this view, so if you want to change permissions, you can simply run UPDATE on all those views, and pg_permissions will change the permissions on the system for you.

Reassigning objects and dropping users

After assigning permissions and restricting access, it can happen that users will be dropped from the system. Unsurprisingly, the commands to do that are the DROP ROLE and DROP USER commands:

```
test=# \h DROP ROLE
Command: DROP ROLE
Description: remove a database role
Syntax:
DROP ROLE [ IF EXISTS ] name [, ...]

URL: https://www.postgresql.org/docs/12/sql-droprole.html
```

Let's give it a try. The following listing shows how this works:

```
test=# DROP ROLE joe;
ERROR:  role  "joe"  cannot be dropped because some  objects depend on it
DETAIL:  target of policy joe_pol_3 on table t_person
target of policy joe_pol_2 on table t_person
target of policy joe_pol_1 on table t_person
privileges for table t_person
owner of table t_user
owner of sequence t_user_id_seq
owner of default privileges on new relations belonging to role joe in
schema public
owner of table t_useful
```

PostgreSQL will issue error messages, because a user can only be removed if everything has been taken away from them. This makes sense for the following reason: just suppose that somebody owns a table. What should PostgreSQL do with that table? Somebody has to own them.

To reassign tables from one user to the next, consider taking a look at the REASSIGN clause:

```
test=# \h REASSIGN
Command: REASSIGN OWNED
Description: change the ownership of database objects owned by a database
role
Syntax:
REASSIGN OWNED BY { old_role | CURRENT_USER | SESSION_USER } [, ...]
                TO { new_role | CURRENT_USER | SESSION_USER }

URL: https://www.postgresql.org/docs/12/sql-reassign-owned.html
```

The syntax is, again, quite simple, and helps to simplify the process of handing over. Here is an example:

```
test=# REASSIGN OWNED  BY joe TO postgres;
REASSIGN OWNED
```

So, let's try to drop the joe role again:

```
test=# DROP ROLE joe;
ERROR:  role "joe" cannot be dropped because some objects depend on it
DETAIL:  target of policy joe_pol_3 on table t_person target of policy
joe_pol_2 on table t_person
target of policy joe_pol_1 on table t_person privileges for table t_person
owner of default privileges on new relations belonging to role joe in
schema public
```

As we can see, the list of problems has been reduced significantly. What we can do now is resolve all of those problems one after the other, and then drop the role. There is no shortcut that I am aware of. The only way to make this more efficient is to make sure that as few permissions as possible are assigned to real people. Try to abstract as much as you can into roles, which, in turn, can be used by many people. If individual permissions are not assigned to real people, things tend to be easier in general.

Summary

Database security is a wide field, and a 30-page chapter can hardly cover all of the aspects of PostgreSQL security. Many things, such as SELinux and SECURITY DEFINER/INVOKER, were left untouched. However, in this chapter, we learned the most common things that we will face as PostgreSQL developers and database administrators. We also learned how to avoid the basic pitfalls, and how to make our systems more secure.

In Chapter 9, *Handling Backup and Recovery*, we will learn about PostgreSQL streaming replication and incremental backups. The chapter will also cover failover scenarios.

Questions

1. How can you configure network access to PostgreSQL?
2. What is a user and what is a role?
3. How can a password be changed?
4. What is RLS?

Handling Backup and Recovery

In Chapter 8, *Managing PostgreSQL Security*, we took a look at all that we need to know about securing PostgreSQL in the most simplistic and most beneficial way possible. The topics that we will cover in this chapter are backup and recovery. Performing backups should be a regular task, and every administrator should keep an eye on this vital exercise. Fortunately, PostgreSQL provides an easy means for creating backups.

Therefore, in this chapter, we will cover the following topics:

- Performing simple dumps
- Handling various formats
- Relaying backups
- Handling global data

By the end of this chapter, you will be able to set up proper backup mechanisms.

Performing simple dumps

If you are running a PostgreSQL setup, there are basically two major methods to perform backups:

- Logical dumps (extract a SQL script representing your data)
- Transaction log shipping

The idea behind transaction log shipping is to archive binary changes made to the database. Most people claim that transaction log shipping is the only real way to create backups. However, in my opinion, this is not necessarily true.

Many people rely on `pg_dump` to simply extract a textual representation of the data. Interestingly, `pg_dump` is also the oldest method of creating a backup and has been around since the very early days of the PostgreSQL project (transaction log shipping was added much later). Every PostgreSQL administrator will become familiar with `pg_dump` sooner or later, so it is important to know how it really works and what it does.

Running pg_dump

The first thing we want to do is create a simple textual dump:

```
[hs@linuxpc ~]$ pg_dump test > /tmp/dump.sql
```

This is the most simplistic backup you can imagine. Basically, `pg_dump` logs in to the local database instance, connects to a database test, and starts to extract all of the data, which will then be sent to `stdout` and redirected to the file. The beauty here is that the standard output gives you all of the flexibility of a Unix system. You can easily compress the data using a pipe or do whatever you want to do with it.

In some cases, you might want to run `pg_dump` as a different user. All PostgreSQL client programs support a consistent set of command-line parameters to pass user information. If you just want to set the user, use the `-U` flag, as follows:

```
[hs@linuxpc ~]$ pg_dump -U whatever_powerful_user test > /tmp/dump.sql
```

The following set of parameters can be found in all PostgreSQL client programs:

```
...
Connection options:
 -d, --dbname=DBNAME database to dump
  -h, --host=HOSTNAME database server host or
                      socket directory
  -p, --port=PORT database server port number
  -U, --username=NAME connect as specified database user
  -w, --no-password never prompt for password
  -W, --password force password prompt (should
                      happen automatically)
  --role=ROLENAME do SET ROLE before dump
...
```

You can just pass the information you want to pg_dump, and if you have enough permissions, PostgreSQL will fetch the data. The important thing here is to see how the program really works. Basically, pg_dump connects to the database and opens a large repeatable read transaction that simply reads all of the data. Remember, a repeatable read ensures that PostgreSQL creates a consistent snapshot of the data, which does not change throughout the transactions. In other words, a dump is always consistent—no foreign keys will be violated. The output is a snapshot of data as it was when the dump started. Consistency is a key factor here. It also implies that changes made to the data while the dump is running won't make it to the backup anymore.

 A dump simply reads everything—therefore, there are no separate permissions to be able to dump something. As long as you can read it, you can back it up.

Also, note that the backup is in a textual format by default. This means that you can safely extract data from, say, Solaris, and move it to some other CPU architecture. In the case of binary copies, this is clearly not possible as the on-disk format depends on your CPU architecture.

Passing passwords and connection information

If you take a close look at the connection parameters shown in the previous section, you will notice that there is no way to pass a password to pg_dump. You can enforce a password prompt, but you cannot pass the parameter to pg_dump using a command-line option.

The reason for this is simply because the password might show up in the process table and be visible to other people. The question now is: if pg_hba.conf, which is on the server, enforces a password, how can the client program provide it?

There are various means of doing this. Here are three:

- Making use of environment variables
- Making use of .pgpass
- Using service files

In this section, we will learn about all three methods.

Using environment variables

One way to pass all kinds of parameters is to use environment variables. If information is not explicitly passed to pg_dump, it will look for the missing information in predefined environment variables. A list of all potential settings can be found at https://www.postgresql.org/docs/11/static/libpq-envars.html.

The following overview shows some of the environment variables that are commonly needed for backups:

- PGHOST: This tells the system which host to connect to.
- PGPORT: This defines the TCP port to be used.
- PGUSER: This tells a client program about the desired user.
- PGPASSWORD: This contains the password to be used.
- PGDATABASE: This is the name of the database to connect to.

The advantage of these environments is that the password won't show up in the process table. However, there's more. Consider the following example:

```
psql  -U ... -h ... -p ... -d ...
```

Given that you are a system administrator, would you really want to type a long piece of code such as this a couple of times every day? If you are working with the very same host again and again, just set those environment variables and connect with plain SQL. The following listing shows how to connect:

```
[hs@linuxpc ~]$ export PGHOST=localhost
[hs@linuxpc ~]$ export PGUSER=hs
[hs@linuxpc ~]$ export PGPASSWORD=abc
[hs@linuxpc ~]$ export PGPORT=5432
[hs@linuxpc ~]$ export PGDATABASE=test
[hs@linuxpc ~]$ psql
psql (11.0)
Type "help" for help.
```

As you can see, there are no command-line parameters anymore. Just type psql and you are in.

All applications based on the standard PostgreSQL C language client library (libpq) will understand these environment variables, so you can use them not only for psql and pg_dump, but for many other applications.

Making use of .pgpass

A very common way to store login information is via the use of .pgpass files. The idea is simple: put a file called .pgpass into your home directory and put your login information there. The format is simple:

```
hostname:port:database:username:password
```

An example would be the following:

```
192.168.0.45:5432:mydb:xy:abc
```

PostgreSQL offers some nice additional functionality, where most fields can contain *. Here is an example:

```
*:*:*:xy:abc
```

The * character implies that on every host, on every port, for every database, the user called xy will use abc as the password. To make PostgreSQL use the .pgpass file, make sure that the right file permissions are in place:

```
chmod 0600 ~/.pgpass
```

Furthermore, .pgpass can also be used on a Windows system. In this case, the file can be found in the %APPDATA%\postgresql\pgpass.conf path.

Using service files

However, .pgpass is not the only file you can use. You can also make use of service files. Here's how it works: if you want to connect to the very same servers over and over again, you can create a .pg_service.conf file. It will hold all of the connection information you need.

Here is an example of a .pg_service.conf file:

```
Mac:~  hs$ cat .pg_service.conf
# a sample service
[hansservice]
host=localhost
port=5432
dbname=test
user=hs
password=abc

[paulservice]
```

```
host=192.168.0.45
port=5432
dbname=xyz
user=paul
password=cde
```

To connect to one of the services, just set the environment and connect:

```
iMac:~ hs$ export PGSERVICE=hansservice
```

A connection can now be established without passing parameters to `psql`:

```
iMac:~ hs$ psql
psql (12.0)
Type "help" for help.
test=#
```

Alternatively, you can use the following command:

```
psql service=hansservice
```

Extracting subsets of data

Up until now, we have seen how to dump an entire database. However, this may not be what we want to do. In many cases, we just want to extract a subset of tables or schemas. Fortunately, `pg_dump` can help us to do that while also providing several switches:

- `-a`: This only dumps the data and does not dump the data structure.
- `-s`: This dumps the data structure but skips the data.
- `-n`: This only dumps a certain schema.
- `-N`: This dumps everything but excludes certain schemas.
- `-t`: This only dumps certain tables.
- `-T`: This dumps everything but certain tables (this makes sense if you want to exclude logging tables and so on).

Partial dumps can be very useful to speed things up considerably. Now that we have learned how to perform simple dumps, let's learn how to handle various file formats.

Handling various formats

So far, we have seen that pg_dump can be used to create text files. The problem here is that a text file can only be replayed completely. If we have saved an entire database, we can only replay the entire thing. In most cases, this is not what we want. Therefore, PostgreSQL has additional formats that offer more functionality.

At this point, four formats are supported:

```
-F, --format=c|d|t|p  output file  format (custom, directory, tar, plain
text  (default))
```

We have already seen plaintext, which is just normal text. On top of that, we can use a custom format. The idea behind a custom format is to have a compressed dump, including a table of contents. Here are two ways to create a custom format dump:

```
[hs@linuxpc ~]$ pg_dump -Fc test > /tmp/dump.fc
[hs@linuxpc ~]$ pg_dump -Fc test -f /tmp/dump.fc
```

In addition to the table of contents, the compressed dump has one more advantage: it is a lot smaller. The rule of thumb is that a custom format dump is around 90% smaller than the database instance you are about to back up. Of course, this is highly dependent on the number of indexes, but for many database applications, this rough estimation will hold true.

Once the backup is created, we can inspect the backup file:

```
[hs@linuxpc ~]$ pg_restore --list /tmp/dump.fc
;
; Archive created at 2018-11-04 15:44:56 CET
;     dbname: test
;     TOC Entries: 18
;     Compression: -1
;     Dump Version: 1.12-0
;     Format: CUSTOM
;     Integer: 4 bytes
;     Offset: 8 bytes
;     Dumped from database version: 12.0
;     Dumped by pg_dump version: 12.0
;
; Selected TOC Entries:
;
3103;  1262  16384  DATABASE - test  hs
3; 2615  2200  SCHEMA - public hs
3104;   0 0 COMMENT - SCHEMA public hs
1; 3079  13350  EXTENSION - plpgsql
```

```
3105;   0 0 COMMENT - EXTENSION plpgsql
187;   1259  16391   TABLE  public t_test hs
. . .
```

Note that `pg_restore --list` will return the table of contents of the backup.

Using a custom format is a good idea as the backup will shrink in size. However, there's more: the `-Fd` command will create a backup in the directory format. Instead of a single file, you will now get a directory containing a couple of files:

```
[hs@linuxpc ~]$ mkdir /tmp/backup
[hs@linuxpc ~]$ pg_dump -Fd test -f /tmp/backup/
[hs@linuxpc ~]$ cd /tmp/backup/
[hs@linuxpc backup]$ ls -lh total  86M
-rw-rw-r--. 1 hs hs   85M Jan   4 15:54  3095.dat.gz
-rw-rw-r--. 1 hs hs   107 Jan   4 15:54  3096.dat.gz
-rw-rw-r--. 1 hs hs 740K  Jan   4 15:54  3097.dat.gz
-rw-rw-r--. 1 hs hs    39 Jan   4 15:54  3098.dat.gz
-rw-rw-r--. 1 hs hs 4.3K  Jan   4 15:54  toc.dat
```

One advantage of the directory format is that we can use more than one core to perform the backup. In the case of a plain or custom format, only one process will be used by `pg_dump`. The directory format changes that rule. The following example shows how we can tell `pg_dump` to use four cores (jobs):

```
[hs@linuxpc backup]$ rm -rf *
[hs@linuxpc backup]$ pg_dump -Fd test -f /tmp/backup/ -j 4
```

 The more objects in our database, the more of a chance there is for a potential speedup.

Replaying backups

Having a backup is pointless unless you have tried to actually replay it. Fortunately, this is easy to do. If you have created a plaintext backup, simply take the SQL file and execute it. The following example shows how that can be done:

```
psql your_db < your_file.sql
```

A plaintext backup is simply a text file containing everything. We can always simply replay a text file.

If you have decided on a custom format or directory format, you can use `pg_restore` to replay the backup. Additionally, `pg_restore` allows you to do all kinds of fancy things, such as replaying just part of a database and so on. In most cases, however, you will simply replay the entire database. In this example, we will create an empty database and just replay a custom format dump:

```
[hs@linuxpc backup]$ createdb new_db
[hs@linuxpc backup]$ pg_restore -d new_db -j 4 /tmp/dump.fc
```

Note that `pg_restore` will add data to an existing database. If your database is not empty, `pg_restore` might error out but continue.

Again, `-j` is used to throw up more than one process. In this example, four cores are used to replay the data; however, this only works when more than one table is being replayed.

> If you are using a directory format, you can simply pass the name of the directory instead of the file.

As far as performance is concerned, dumps are a good solution if you are working with small or medium amounts of data. There are two major downsides:

- We will get a snapshot, so everything since the last snapshot will be lost.
- Rebuilding a dump from scratch is comparatively slow compared to binary copies because all of the indexes have to be rebuilt.

We will take a look at binary backups in Chapter 10, *Making Sense of Backups and Replication*.

Handling global data

In the previous sections, we learned about `pg_dump` and `pg_restore`, which are two vital programs when it comes to creating backups. The thing is, `pg_dump` creates database dumps—it works on the database level. If we want to back up an entire instance, we have to make use of `pg_dumpall` or dump all of the databases separately. Before we dig into that, it makes sense to see how `pg_dumpall` works:

```
pg_dumpall > /tmp/all.sql
```

Let's see: `pg_dumpall` will connect to one database after the other and send stuff to `stdout`, where you can process it with Unix. Note that `pg_dumpall` can be used just like `pg_dump`. However, it has some downsides. It does not support a custom or directory format, and therefore does not offer multi-core support. This means that we will be stuck with one thread.

However, there is more to `pg_dumpall`. Keep in mind that users live on the instance level. If you create a normal database dump, you will get all of the permissions, but you won't get all of the CREATE USER statements. `globals` are not included in a normal dump—they will only be extracted by `pg_dumpall`.

If we only want `globals`, we can run `pg_dumpall` using the `-g` option:

```
pg_dumpall -g > /tmp/globals.sql
```

In most cases, you might want to run `pg_dumpall -g`, along with a custom or directory format dump to extract your instances. A simple backup script might look like this:

```
#!/bin/sh
BACKUP_DIR=/tmp/
pg_dumpall -g > $BACKUP_DIR/globals.sql
for x in $(psql -c "SELECT datname FROM  pg_database
    WHERE  datname NOT IN ('postgres', 'template0', 'template1')" postgres -
A -t)
do
pg_dump -Fc $x > $BACKUP_DIR/$x.fc done
```

It will first dump `globals` and then loop through the list of databases to extract them one by one in a custom format.

Summary

In this chapter, we learned about creating backups and dumps in general. So far, binary backups have not been covered, but you are already able to extract textual backups from the server so that you can save and replay your data in the most simplistic way possible.

In `Chapter 10`, *Making Sense of Backups and Replication*, you will learn about transaction log shipping, streaming replication, and binary backups. You will also learn how to use PostgreSQL's onboard tools to replicate instances.

Questions

1. Should everybody create dumps?
2. Why are dumps so small?
3. Do you have to dump the globals too?
4. Is it safe to have a `.pgpass` file?

10
Making Sense of Backups and Replication

In Chapter 9, *Handling Backup and Recovery*, we learned a lot about backup and recovery, which is essential for administration. So far, only logical backups have been covered; I am about to change that in this chapter.

This chapter is all about PostgreSQL's transaction log and what we can do with it to improve our setup and to make things more secure.

In this chapter, we will cover the following topics:

- Understanding the transaction log
- Transaction log archiving and recovery
- Setting up asynchronous replication
- Upgrading to synchronous replication
- Making use of replication slots
- Making use of CREATE PUBLICATION and CREATE SUBSCRIPTION

By the end of this chapter, you will be able to set up transaction log archiving and replication. Keep in mind that this chapter could never be a comprehensive guide to replication; it is only a short introduction. Full coverage of replication would require around 500 pages. Just for a comparison, *PostgreSQL Replication* by Packt Publishing alone is close to 400 pages long. This chapter will cover the most essential things in a more compact form.

Understanding the transaction log

Every modern database system provides functionality to make sure that the system can survive a crash in case something goes wrong or somebody pulls the plug. This is true for filesystems and database systems alike.

PostgreSQL also provides a means to ensure that a crash cannot harm the data's integrity or the data itself. It is guaranteed that if the power cuts out, the system will always be able to come back on again and do its job.

The means of providing this kind of security is achieved by the **Write Ahead Log (WAL)**, or **xlog**. The idea is to not write into the data file directly, but instead write to the log first. Why is this important? Imagine that we are writing some data, as follows:

```
INSERT INTO data ... VALUES ('12345678');
```

Let's assume that data was written directly to the data file. If the operation fails midway, the data file would be corrupted. It might contain half-written rows, columns without index pointers, missing commit information, and so on. Since hardware doesn't really guarantee atomic writes of large chunks of data, a way has to be found to make this more robust. By writing to the log instead of writing to the file directly, this problem can be solved.

 In PostgreSQL, the transaction log consists of records.

A single write can consist of various records that all have a checksum and are chained together. A single transaction might contain a B-tree, index, storage manager, commit records, and a lot more. Each type of object has its own WAL entries and ensures that the object can survive a crash. If there is a crash, PostgreSQL will start up and repair the data files based on the transaction log to ensure that no permanent corruption is allowed to happen.

Looking at the transaction log

In PostgreSQL, WAL can usually be found in the pg_wal directory in the data directory, unless specified otherwise on initdb. In older versions of PostgreSQL, the WAL directory was called pg_xlog, but with the introduction of PostgreSQL 10.0, the directory has been renamed.

The reason for this is that, more often than not, people would delete the content of the pg_xlog directory, which of course led to serious issues and potential database corruption. The community has therefore taken the unprecedented step of renaming a directory inside a PostgreSQL instance. The hope is to make the name scary enough that nobody dares to delete the content again.

The following listing shows what the pg_wal directory looks like:

```
[postgres@zenbook pg_wal]$ pwd
/var/lib/pgsql/12/data/pg_wal
[postgres@zenbook pg_wal]$ ls -l
total 688132
-rw-------. 1 postgres postgres 16777216 Jan 19 07:58
000000010000000000000000CD
-rw-------. 1 postgres postgres 16777216 Jan 13 17:04
000000010000000000000000CE
-rw-------. 1 postgres postgres 16777216 Jan 13 17:04
000000010000000000000000CF
-rw-------. 1 postgres postgres 16777216 Jan 13 17:04
000000010000000000000000D0
-rw-------. 1 postgres postgres 16777216 Jan 13 17:04
000000010000000000000000D1
-rw-------. 1 postgres postgres 16777216 Jan 13 17:04
000000010000000000000000D2
```

What we can see is that the transaction log is a 16 MB file that consists of 24 digits. The numbering is hexadecimal. As we can see, CF is followed by D0. The files are always a fixed size.

One thing to note is that, in PostgreSQL, the number of transaction log files is not related to the size of a transaction. You can have a very small set of transaction log files and still run a multi-TB transaction easily.

Traditionally, the WAL directory typically consists of 16 MB files. However, since the introduction of PostgreSQL, the size of a WAL segment can now be set at initdb. In some cases, this can speed things up. Here's how it works. The following example shows us how the WAL file's size can be changed to 32 MB:

```
initdb -D /pgdata --wal-segsize=32
```

Understanding checkpoints

As I mentioned earlier, every change is written to WAL in binary format (it does not contain SQL). The problem is this—the database server cannot keep writing to WAL forever as it will consume more and more space over time. So, at some point, the transaction log has to be recycled. This is done by a **checkpoint**, which happens automatically in the background.

The idea is that, when data is written, it first goes to the transaction log, and then a dirty buffer is put into shared buffers. Those dirty buffers have to go to disk and are written out to the data files by the background writer or during a checkpoint. As soon as all of the dirty buffers up to that point have been written, the transaction log can be deleted.

 Please, never *ever* delete transaction log files manually. In the event of a crash, the database server will not be able to start up again, and the amount of disk space needed will be reclaimed anyway as new transactions come in. Never touch the transaction log manually. PostgreSQL takes care of things on its own, and doing things in there is really harmful.

Optimizing the transaction log

Checkpoints happen automatically and are triggered by the server. However, there are configuration settings that decide when a checkpoint is initiated. The following parameters in the postgresql.conf file are in charge of handling checkpoints:

```
#checkpoint_timeout = 5min          # range 30s-1d
#max_wal_size = 1GB
#min_wal_size = 80MB
```

There are two reasons to initiate a checkpoint:

- We can run out of time or we can run out of space.
- The maximum time between two checkpoints is defined by the checkpoint_timeout variables.

The amount of space provided to store transaction logs will vary between the min_wal_size and max_wal_size variables. PostgreSQL will automatically trigger checkpoints in a way that the amount of space really needed will be between those two numbers.

The `max_wal_size` variable is a soft limit and PostgreSQL may (under heavy load) temporarily need a bit more space. In other words, if our transaction log is on a separate disk, it makes sense to make sure that there is actually a bit more space available to store `WAL`.

How can somebody tune the transaction log in PostgreSQL 9.6 and 12.0? In 9.6, some changes have been made to the background writer and checkpointing machinery. In older versions, there were some use cases where smaller checkpoint distances could actually make sense from a performance point of view. In 9.6 and beyond, this has pretty much changed, and wider checkpoint distances are basically always highly favorable because many optimizations can be applied at the database and OS level to speed things up. The most noteworthy optimization is that blocks are sorted before they are written out, which greatly reduces random I/O on mechanical disks.

But there's more. Large checkpoint distances will actually decrease the amount of `WAL` created. Yes, that's right—larger checkpoint distances will lead to less `WAL`.

The reason for this is simple. Whenever a block is touched after a checkpoint for the first time, it has to be sent to `WAL` completely. If the block is changed more often, only the changes make it to the log. Larger distances basically cause fewer full-page writes, which in turn reduces the amount of `WAL` created in the first place. The difference can be quite substantial, as can be seen in one of my blog posts at `https://www.postgresql-support.com/checkpoint-distance-and-amount-of-wal/`.

PostgreSQL also allows us to configure whether checkpoints should be short and intense or whether they should be spread out over a longer period. The default value is `0.5`, which means that the checkpoint should be done in a way that the process has finished halfway between the current and the next checkpoint. The following listing shows `checkpoint_completion_target`:

```
#checkpoint_completion_target = 0.5
```

Increasing this value basically means that the checkpoint is stretched out and less intensive. In many cases, a higher value has proven beneficial for flattening out I/O spikes caused by intense checkpointing.

Transaction log archiving and recovery

After our brief introduction to the transaction log in general, it is time to focus on the process of transaction log archiving. As we have already seen, the transaction log contains a sequence of binary changes that are made to the storage system. So, why not use it to replicate database instances and do a lot of other cool stuff, such as archiving?

Configuring for archiving

The first thing we want to do in this chapter is create a configuration to perform standard **point-in-time recovery (PITR)**. There are a couple of advantages of using PITR over ordinary dumps:

- We will lose less data because we can restore the data to a certain point in time and not just to the fixed backup point.
- Restoring will be faster because indexes don't have to be created from scratch. They are just copied over and are ready to use.

Configuring for PITR is easy. Just a handful of changes have to be made in the `postgresql.conf` file:

```
wal_level = replica      # used to be "hot_standby" in older versions
max_wal_senders = 10     # at least 2, better at least 2
```

The `wal_level` variable says that the server is supposed to produce enough transaction logs to allow for PITR. If the `wal_level` variable is set to `minimal` (which is the default value up to PostgreSQL 9.6), the transaction log will only contain enough information to recover a single node setup—it is not rich enough to handle replication. In PostgreSQL 10.0, the default value is already correct and there is no longer a need to change most settings.

The `max_wal_senders` variable will allow us to stream `WAL` from the server. It will allow us to use `pg_basebackup` to create an initial backup instead of traditional file-based copying. The advantage here is that `pg_basebackup` is a lot easier to use. Again, the default value in 10.0 has been changed in a way that, for 90% of all setups, no changes are needed.

The idea behind `WAL` streaming is that the transaction log that's created is copied to a safe place for storage. Basically, there are two means of transporting `WAL`:

- Using `pg_receivewal` (up to 9.6, this is known as `pg_receivexlog`)
- Using the filesystem as a means to archive

In this section, we will look at how to set up the second option. During normal operations, PostgreSQL keeps writing to those WAL files. When `archive_mode = on` in the `postgresql.conf` file, PostgreSQL will call the `archive_command` variable for every single file.

A configuration might look as follows. First, a directory storing those transaction log files can be created:

```
mkdir /archive
chown postgres.postgres archive
```

The following entries can be changed in the `postgresql.conf` file:

```
archive_mode = on
archive_command = 'cp %p /archive/%f'
```

A restart will enable archiving, but let's configure the `pg_hba.conf` file first to reduce downtime to an absolute minimum.

> Note that we can put any command into the `archive_command` variable.

Many people use `rsync`, `scp`, and others to transport their WAL files to a safe location. If our script returns 0, PostgreSQL will assume that the file has been archived. If anything else is returned, PostgreSQL will try to archive the file again. This is necessary because the database engine has to ensure that no files are lost. To perform the recovery process, we have to have every file available; not a single file is allowed to go missing.

Configuring the pg_hba.conf file

Now that the `postgresql.conf` file has been configured successfully, it is necessary to configure the `pg_hba.conf` file for streaming. Note that this is only necessary if we are planning to use `pg_basebackup`, which is the state-of-the-art tool for creating base backups.

Basically, the options we have in the `pg_hba.conf` file are the same ones that we already saw in `Chapter 8`, *Managing PostgreSQL Security*. There is just one major issue to keep in mind:

```
# Allow replication connections from localhost, by a user with the
# replication privilege.
local   replication   postgres                   trust
host    replication   postgres   127.0.0.1/32    trust
host    replication   postgres   ::1/128         trust
```

We can define standard `pg_hba.conf` file rules. The important thing is that the second column says `replication`. Normal rules are not enough—it is really important to add explicit replication permissions. Also, keep in mind that we don't have to do this as a superuser. We can create a specific user who is only allowed to perform login and replication.

Again, PostgreSQL 10 and later versions are already configured in the way we have outlined in this section. Local replication works when out-of-the-box remote IPs have to be added to `pg_hba.conf`.

Now that the `pg_hba.conf` file has been configured correctly, PostgreSQL can be restarted.

Creating base backups

After teaching PostgreSQL how to archive those `WAL` files, it is time to create a first backup. The idea is to have a backup and replay `WAL` files based on that backup to reach any point in time.

To create an initial backup, we can turn to `pg_basebackup`, which is a command-line tool used to perform backups. Let's call `pg_basebackup` and see how it works:

```
pg_basebackup -D /some_target_dir
        -h localhost
        --checkpoint=fast
        --wal-method=stream
```

As we can see, we will use four parameters here:

- `-D`: Where do we want the base backup to live? PostgreSQL requires an empty directory. At the end of the backup, we will see a copy of the server's data directory (destination).
- `-h`: This indicates the IP address or the name of the master (source). This is the server you want to back up.

- `--checkpoint=fast`: Usually, `pg_basebackup` waits for the master to checkpoint. The reason for this is that the replay process has to start somewhere. A checkpoint ensures that data has been written up to a certain point and so PostgreSQL can safely jump in there and start the replay process. Basically, it can also be done without the `--checkpoint=fast` parameter. However, it might take a while before `pg_basebackup` starts to copy data in this case. Checkpoints can be up to 1 hour apart, which can delay our backups unnecessarily.

- `--wal-method=stream`: By default, `pg_basebackup` connects to the master server and starts copying files over. Now, keep in mind that those files are modified while they are copied. The data reaching the backup is therefore inconsistent. This inconsistency can be repaired during the recovery process using `WAL`. The backup itself, however, is not consistent. By adding the `--wal-method=stream` parameter, it is possible to create a self-contained backup; it can be started directly without replaying the transaction log. This is a nice method if we just want to clone an instance and not use PITR. Fortunately, `-wal-method=stream` is actually already the default in PostgreSQL 10.0 or higher. However, in 9.6 or earlier, it is recommended to use the predecessor, named `-xlog-method=stream`. In short: there is no need to set this explicitly in PostgreSQL 12.0 anymore.

Reducing the bandwidth of a backup

When `pg_basebackup` starts, it tries to finish its work as quickly as possible. If we have a good network connection, `pg_basebackup` is definitely able to fetch hundreds of megabytes a second from the remote server. If our server has a weak I/O system, it could mean that `pg_basebackup` could suck up all the resources easily, and end users might experience bad performance because their I/O requests are simply too slow.

To control the maximum transfer rate, `pg_basebackup` offers the following:

```
-r, --max-rate=RATE
      maximum transfer rate to transfer data directory
      (in kB/s, or use suffix "k" or "M")
```

When we create a base backup, we need to make sure that the disk system on the master can actually stand the load. Adjusting our transfer rate can, therefore, make a lot of sense.

Mapping tablespaces

Usually, `pg_basebackup` can be called directly if we are using an identical filesystem layout on the target system. If this is not the case, `pg_basebackup` allows you to map the master's filesystem layout to the desired layout:

```
-T, --tablespace-mapping=OLDDIR=NEWDIR
            relocate tablespace in OLDDIR to NEWDIR
```

> If your system is small, it could be a good idea to keep everything in one
> `tablespace`.

This holds true if I/O is not the problem (maybe because you are only managing a few gigabytes of data).

Using different formats

The `pg_basebackup` command-line tool can create various formats. By default, it will put data in an empty directory. Essentially, it will connect to the source server and create a `.tar` file over a network connection and put the data into the desired directory.

The trouble with this approach is that `pg_basebackup` will create many files, which is not suitable if we want to move the backup to an external backup solution such as Tivoli Storage Manager. The following listing shows the valid output formats supported by pg_basebackup:

```
-F, --format=p|t              output format (plain (default), tar)
```

To create a single file, we can use the `-F=t` option. By default, it will create a file called `base.tar`, which can then be managed more easily. The downside, of course, is that we have to inflate the file again before performing PITR.

Testing transaction log archiving

Before we dive into the actual replay process, it makes sense to actually check archiving to make sure that it is working perfectly and as expected by using a simple `ls` command, as shown in the following code:

```
[hs@zenbook archive]$ ls -l
total 212996
-rw------- 1 hs hs 16777216 Jan 30 09:04 000000010000000000000001
```

```
-rw------- 1 hs hs 16777216 Jan 30 09:04 000000010000000000000002
-rw------- 1 hs hs 302       Jan 30 09:04
000000010000000000000002.00000028.backup
-rw------- 1 hs hs 16777216 Jan 30 09:20 000000010000000000000003
-rw------- 1 hs hs 16777216 Jan 30 09:20 000000010000000000000004
-rw------- 1 hs hs 16777216 Jan 30 09:20 000000010000000000000005
-rw------- 1 hs hs 16777216 Jan 30 09:20 000000010000000000000006
. . .
```

As soon as there is serious activity in the database, WAL files should be sent to the archive.

In addition to just checking for files, the following view can be useful:

```
test=# \d pg_stat_archiver
            View "pg_catalog.pg_stat_archiver"
      Column       |            Type            | Modifiers
-------------------+----------------------------+-----------
 archived_count    | bigint                     |
 last_archived_wal | text                       |
 last_archived_time| timestamp with time zone   |
 failed_count      | bigint                     |
 last_failed_wal   | text                       |
 last_failed_time  | timestamp with time zone   |
 stats_reset       | timestamp with time zone   |
```

The pg_stat_archiver system view is very useful for figuring out if and when archiving has stalled for whatever reason. It will tell us about the number of files already archived (archived_count). We can also see which file was the last one and when the event happened. Finally, the pg_stat_archiver system view can tell us when archiving has gone wrong, which is vital information. Unfortunately, the error code or the error message is not shown in the table, but since archive_command can be an arbitrary command, it is easy to log.

There is one more thing to see in the archive. As we described previously, it is important to see that those files are actually archived. But there's more. When the pg_basebackup command-line tool is called, we will see a .backup file in the stream of WAL files. It is small and contains only some information about the base backup itself—it is purely informative and is not needed by the replay process. However, it gives us some vital clues. When we start to replay the transaction log later on, we can delete all WAL files that are older than the .backup file. In this case, our backup file is called 000000010000000000000002.00000028.backup. This means that the replay process starts somewhere within file . . .0002 (at position . . .28). It also means that we can delete all files older than . . .0002. Older WAL files won't be needed for recovery anymore. Keep in mind that we can keep more than just one backup around, so I am only referring to the current backup.

Now that archiving works, we can turn our attention to the replay process.

Replaying the transaction log

Let's sum up the process so far. We have adjusted the `postgresql.conf` file (`wal_level`, `max_wal_senders`, `archive_mode`, and `archive_command`) and we have allowed for the `pg_basebackup` command in the `pg_hba.conf` file. Then, the database was restarted and a base backup was successfully produced.

Keep in mind that base backups can only happen while the database is fully operational—only a brief restart to change the `max_wal_sender` and `wal_level` variables is needed.

Now that the system is working properly, we might face a crash that we will want to recover from. Therefore, we can perform PITR to restore as much data as possible. The first thing we've got to do is take the base backup and put it in the desired location.

 It can be a good idea to save the old database cluster. Even if it is broken, our PostgreSQL support company might need it to track down the reason for the crash. You can still delete it later on, once you've got everything up and running again.

Given the preceding filesystem layout, we might want to do something like the following:

```
cd /some_target_dir
cp -Rv * /data
```

We're assuming that the new database server will be located in the `/data` directory. Make sure that the directory is empty before you copy the base backup over.

In PostgreSQL 12, some things have changed: in older versions, we had to configure `recovery.conf` to control the behavior of a replica or PITR in general. All config settings to control those things have been moved to the main configuration file, `postgresql.conf`. If you are running old setups it is, therefore, time to change to the new interfaces to make sure that your automation is not broken.

So, let's see how to configure the replay process. Try to put `restore_command` and `recovery_target_time` into `postgresql.conf`:

```
restore_command = 'cp /archive/%f %p'
recovery_target_time = '2019-11-05 11:43:12'
```

After fixing the `postgresql.conf` file, we can simply start up our server. The output might look as follows:

```
waiting for server to start....2019-11-05 10:35:17.130 CET [106353] LOG:
starting PostgreSQL 12.0 on x86_64-pc-linux-gnu, compiled by gcc (GCC)
9.2.1 20190827 (Red Hat 9.2.1-1), 64-bit
2019-11-05 10:35:17.130 CET [106353] LOG: listening on IPv6 address "::1",
port 5433
2019-11-05 10:35:17.130 CET [106353] LOG: listening on IPv4 address
"127.0.0.1", port 5433
2019-11-05 10:35:17.130 CET [106353] LOG: listening on Unix socket
"/tmp/.s.PGSQL.5433"
2019-11-05 10:35:17.141 CET [106361] LOG: database system was interrupted;
last known up at 2019-11-05 10:25:16 CET
cp: cannot stat '/tmp/archive/00000002.history': No such file or directory
2019-11-05 10:35:17.154 CET [106361] LOG: entering standby mode
2019-11-05 10:35:17.168 CET [106361] LOG: restored log file
"000000010000000000000006" from archive
2019-11-05 10:35:17.170 CET [106361] LOG: redo starts at 0/60000D8
2019-11-05 10:35:17.170 CET [106361] LOG: consistent recovery state reached
at 0/60001B0
2019-11-05 10:35:17.171 CET [106353] LOG: database system is ready to
accept read only connections
cp: cannot stat '/tmp/archive/000000010000000000000007': No such file or
directory
2019-11-05 10:35:17.175 CET [106394] LOG: started streaming WAL from
primary at 0/7000000 on timeline 1
 done
server started
```

When the server is started, there are a couple of messages to look for to ensure that our recovery works perfectly. `consistent_state_reached` is the most important one to look for. Once you have reached this point, you can be sure that your database is consistent and is not corrupted. Depending on the timestamp you have chosen, you might have lost some transactions at the end (if desired) but in general, your database is consistent (there are no key violations and so on).

If you have used a timestamp in the future, PostgreSQL will complain that it could not find the next `WAL` file and terminate the replay process. If you are using a timestamp between the end of the base backup and somewhere before the crash, you will, of course, not see this kind of message.

Once the process is done, the server will successfully start up.

Finding the right timestamp

So far, we have progressed under the assumption that we know the timestamp we want to recover, or that we simply want to replay the whole transaction log to reduce data loss. However, what if we don't want to replay everything? What if we don't know which point in time to recover to? In everyday life, this is actually a very common scenario. One of our developers loses some data in the morning and we are supposed to make things fine again. The trouble is this: at what time in the morning? Once the recovery has ended, it cannot be restarted easily. Once recovery is completed, the system will be promoted, and once it has been promoted, we cannot continue to replay `WAL`.

However, what we can do is pause recovery without promotion, check what is inside the database, and continue.

Doing that is easy. The first thing we have to make sure of is that the `hot_standby` variable is set to `on` in the `postgresql.conf` file. This will make sure that the database is readable while it is still in recovery mode. Then, set the following variable in `postgresql.conf`:

```
recovery_target_action = 'pause'
```

There are various `recovery_target_action` settings. If we use `pause`, PostgreSQL will pause at the desired time and let us check what has already been replayed. We can adjust the time we want, restart, and try again. Alternatively, we can set the value to promote or shut down.

There is also a second way to pause transaction log replay. Basically, it can also be used when performing PITR. However, in most cases, it is used with streaming replication. Here is what can be done during `WAL` replay:

```
postgres=# \x
Expanded display is on.
postgres=# \df *pause*
List of functions
-[ RECORD 1 ]-------+--------------------------
Schema              | pg_catalog
Name                | pg_is_wal_replay_paused
Result data type    | boolean
Argument data types |
Type                | normal
-[ RECORD 2 ]-------+--------------------------
Schema              | pg_catalog
Name                | pg_wal_replay_pause
Result data type    | void
Argument data types |
```

```
Type                   | normal

postgres=# \df *resume*
List of functions
-[ RECORD 1 ]-------+----------------------
Schema                 | pg_catalog
Name                   | pg_wal_replay_resume
Result data type       | void
Argument data types    |
Type                   | normal
```

We can call the SELECT pg_wal_replay_pause(); command to halt WAL replay until we call the SELECT pg_wal_replay_resume(); command.

The idea is to figure out how much WAL has already been replayed and to continue as necessary. However, keep this in mind: once a server has been promoted, we cannot just continue to replay WAL without further precautions.

As we have already seen, it can be pretty tricky to figure out how far we need to recover. Therefore, PostgreSQL provides us with some help. Consider the following real-world example: at midnight, we are running a nightly process that ends at some point that is usually not known. The goal is to recover exactly to the end of the nightly process. The trouble is this: how do we know when the process has ended? In most cases, this is hard to figure out. So, why not add a marker to the transaction log? The code for this is as follows:

```
postgres=# SELECT pg_create_restore_point('my_daily_process_ended');
 pg_create_restore_point
-------------------------
 1F/E574A7B8
(1 row)
```

If our process calls this SQL statement as soon as it ends, it will be possible to use this label in the transaction log to recover exactly to this point in time by adding the following directive to the postgresql.conf file:

```
recovery_target_name = 'my_daily_process_ended'
```

By using this setting instead of recovery_target_time, the replay process will beam us exactly to the end of the nightly process.

Of course, we can also replay up to a certain transaction ID. However, in real life, this has proven to be difficult as the exact transaction ID is rarely ever known to the administrator, and therefore, there is not much practical value in this.

Cleaning up the transaction log archive

So far, data is being written to the archive all of the time and no attention has been paid to cleaning out the archive again to free up space in the filesystem. PostgreSQL cannot do this job for us because it has no idea whether we want to use the archive again. Therefore, we are in charge of cleaning up the transaction log. Of course, we can also use a backup tool—however, it is important to know that PostgreSQL has no chance of doing the cleanup for us.

Suppose we want to clean up an old transaction log that is not needed anymore. Maybe we want to keep several base backups around and clean out all transaction logs that won't be needed anymore to restore one of those backups.

In this case, the `pg_archivecleanup` command-line tool is exactly what we need. We can simply pass the archive directory and the name of the backup file to the `pg_archivecleanup` command, and it will make sure that files are removed from disk. Using this tool makes life easier for us because we don't have to figure out which transaction log files to keep on our own. Here's how it works:

```
pg_archivecleanup removes older WAL files from PostgreSQL archives.
Usage:
  pg_archivecleanup [OPTION]... ARCHIVELOCATION OLDESTKEPTWALFILE
Options:
  -d              generate debug output (verbose mode)
  -n              dry run, show the names of the files that would be removed
  -V, --version   output version information, then exit
  -x EXT          clean up files if they have this extension
  -?, --help      show this help, then exit
For use as archive_cleanup_command in postgresql.conf:
  archive_cleanup_command = 'pg_archivecleanup [OPTION]... ARCHIVELOCATION
%r'
e.g.
  archive_cleanup_command = 'pg_archivecleanup /mnt/server/archiverdir %r'
Or for use as a standalone archive cleaner:
e.g.
  pg_archivecleanup /mnt/server/archiverdir
000000010000000000000010.00000020.backup

Report bugs to <pgsql-bugs@lists.postgresql.org>.
```

This tool can be used with ease and is available on all platforms.

Now that we've taken a look at transaction log archiving and PITR, we can focus our attention on one of the most widely used features in the PostgreSQL world today: streaming replication.

Setting up asynchronous replication

The idea behind streaming replication is simple. After an initial base backup, the secondary can connect to the master and fetch a transaction log in real time and apply it. Transaction log replay is not a single operation anymore, but rather a continuous process that is supposed to keep running as long as the cluster exists.

Performing a basic setup

In this section, we will learn how to set up asynchronous replication quickly and easily. The goal is to set up a system that consists of two nodes.

Basically, most of the work has already been done for `WAL` archiving. However, to make it easy to understand, we will look at the entire process of setting up streaming because we cannot assume that `WAL` shipping is really already set up as needed.

The first thing to do is to go to the `postgresql.conf` file and adjust the following parameters:

```
wal_level = replica
max_wal_senders = 10          # or whatever value >= 2
hot_standby = on              # in already a default setting
```

 Some of these are already the default options starting with PostgreSQL 10.0.

Just as we have done previously, the `wal_level` variable has to be adjusted to ensure that PostgreSQL produces enough transaction logs to sustain a slave. Then, we have to configure the `max_wal_senders` variable. When a slave is up and running or when a base backup is created, a `WAL` sender process will talk to a `WAL` receiver process on the client side. The `max_wal_senders` setting allows PostgreSQL to create enough processes to serve those clients.

 Theoretically, it is enough to have just one `WAL` sender process. However, it is pretty inconvenient. A base backup that uses the `--wal-method=stream` parameter will already need two `WAL` sender processes. If you want to run a slave and perform a base backup at the same time, there are already three processes in use. So, make sure that you allow PostgreSQL to create enough processes to prevent pointless restarts.

Then, there's the `hot_standby` variable. Basically, a master ignores the `hot_standby` variable and does not take it into consideration. All it does is make the slave readable during `WAL` replay. So, why do we care? Keep in mind that the `pg_basebackup` command will clone the entire server, including its configuration. This means that if we have already set the value on the master, the slaves will automatically get it when the `data` directory is cloned.

After setting the `postgresql.conf` file, we can turn our attention to the `pg_hba.conf` file: just allow the slave to perform replication by adding rules. Basically, those rules are the same as we have already seen for PITR.

Then, restart the database server, just like you did for PITR.

Now, the `pg_basebackup` command can be called on the slave. Before we do that, make sure that the `/target` directory is empty. If we are using RPM packages, ensure that you shut down a potentially running instance and empty the directory (for example, `/var/lib/pgsql/data`):

```
pg_basebackup -D /target
        -h master.example.com
        --checkpoint=fast
        --wal-method=stream -R
```

Just replace the `/target` directory with your desired destination directory and replace `master.example.com` with the IP or DNS name of your master. The `--checkpoint=fast` parameter will trigger an instant checkpoint. Then, there is the `--wal-method=stream` parameter; it will open two streams. One will copy the data, while the other one will fetch the `WAL`, which is created while the backup is running.

Finally, there is the `-R` flag:

```
-R, --write-recovery-conf     # write configuration for replication
```

The `-R` flag is a really good feature. The `pg_basebackup` command can automatically create the slave configuration. In old versions, it will add various entries to the `recovery.conf` file. In PostgreSQL 12 and higher, it will make the changes automatically to `postgresql.conf`:

```
standby_mode = on primary_conninfo = ' ...'
```

The first setting says that PostgreSQL should keep replaying `WAL` all of the time—if the whole transaction log has been replayed, it should wait for a new `WAL` directory to arrive. The second setting will tell PostgreSQL where the master is. It is a normal database connection.

Slaves can also connect to other slaves to stream transaction logs. It is possible to cascade replication by simply creating base backups from a slave. So, *master* really means source server in this context.

After running the pg_basebackup command, the services can be started. The first thing we should check is whether the master shows WAL sender process:

```
[hs@zenbook ~]$ ps ax | grep sender
17873 ? Ss 0:00 postgres: wal sender process
                       ah ::1(57596) streaming 1F/E9000060
```

If it does, the slave will also carry WAL receiver process:

```
17872 ? Ss 0:00 postgres: wal receiver process
                         streaming 1F/E9000060
```

If those processes are there, we are already on the right track, and replication is working as expected. Both sides are now talking to each other and WAL flows from the master to the slave.

Improving security

So far, we have seen that data is streamed as a superuser. However, it is not a good idea to allow superuser access from a remote site. Fortunately, PostgreSQL allows us to create a user that is only allowed to consume the transaction log stream, but cannot do anything else.

Creating a user just for streaming is easy:

```
test=# CREATE USER repl LOGIN REPLICATION;
CREATE ROLE
```

By assigning replication to the user, it is possible to use it just for streaming—everything else is forbidden.

It is highly recommended to not use your superuser account to set up streaming. Simply change the configuration file to the newly created user. Not exposing superuser accounts will dramatically improve security, just like giving the replication user a password.

Halting and resuming replication

Once streaming replication has been set up, it works flawlessly without too much administrator intervention. However, in some cases, it might make sense to halt replication and resume it at a later point. Why would anybody want to do that?

Consider the following use case: you are in charge of a master/slave setup, which is running a rubbish **content management system (CMS)** or some dubious forum software. Suppose you want to update your application from the awful CMS 1.0 to the dreadful CMS 2.0. Some changes will be executed in your database, which will instantly be replicated to the slave database. What if the upgrade process does something wrong? The error will be instantly replicated to both nodes due to streaming.

To avoid instant replication, we can halt replication and resume as needed. In the case of our CMS update, we could simply do the following things:

1. Halt replication.
2. Perform the app update on the master.
3. Check that our application still works. If yes, resume replication. If not, failover to the replica, which still has the old data.

With this mechanism, we can protect our data because we can fall back to the data as it was before the problem. Later in this chapter, we will learn how to promote a slave to become the new master server.

The main question now is this: how can we halt replication? Here's how it works. Execute the following line on the standby:

```
test=# SELECT pg_wal_replay_pause();
```

This line will halt replication. Note that the transaction log will still flow from the master to the slave—only the replay process is halted. Your data is still protected as it is persisted on the slave. In the case of a server crash, no data will be lost.

Keep in mind that the replay process has to be halted on the slave. Otherwise, an error will be thrown by PostgreSQL:

```
ERROR: recovery is not in progress
HINT: Recovery control functions can only be executed during recovery.
```

Once replication is to be resumed, the following line will be needed on the slave:

```
SELECT pg_wal_replay_resume();
```

PostgreSQL will start to replay WAL again.

Checking replication to ensure availability

One of the core jobs of every administrator is to ensure that replication stays up and running at all times. If replication is down, it is possible that data could be lost if the master crashes. Therefore, keeping an eye on replication is absolutely necessary.

Fortunately, PostgreSQL provides system views, which allow us to take a deep look at what is going on. One of those views is `pg_stat_replication`:

```
\d pg_stat_replication
                    View "pg_catalog.pg_stat_replication"
       Column       | Type                     | Collation | Nullable |
Default
--------------------+--------------------------+-----------+----------+------
---
 pid                | integer                  |           |          |
 usesysid           | oid                      |           |          |
 usename            | name                     |           |          |
 application_name   | text                     |           |          |
 client_addr        | inet                     |           |          |
 client_hostname    | text                     |           |          |
 client_port        | integer                  |           |          |
 backend_start      | timestamp with time zone |           |          |
 backend_xmin       | xid                      |           |          |
 state              | text                     |           |          |
 sent_lsn           | pg_lsn                   |           |          |
 write_lsn          | pg_lsn                   |           |          |
 flush_lsn          | pg_lsn                   |           |          |
 replay_lsn         | pg_lsn                   |           |          |
 write_lag          | interval                 |           |          |
 flush_lag          | interval                 |           |          |
 replay_lag         | interval                 |           |          |
 sync_priority      | integer                  |           |          |
 sync_state         | text                     |           |          |
```

The `pg_stat_replication` view will contain information about the sender. I don't want to use the word *master* here because slaves can be connected to some other slave. It is possible to build a tree of servers. In the case of a tree of servers, the master will only have information about the slaves it is directly connected to.

The first thing we will see in this view is the process ID of the WAL sender process. It helps us to identify the process in case something goes wrong. This is usually not the case. Then, we will see the username the slave uses to connect to its sending server. The `client_*` fields will indicate where the slaves are. We will be able to extract network information from those fields. The `backend_start` field shows when the slaves started to stream from our server.

Then, there is the magical `backend_xmin` field. Suppose you are running a master/slave setup. It is possible to tell the slave to report its transaction ID to the master. The idea behind this is to delay cleanup on the master so that data is not taken from a transaction running on the slave.

The `state` field informs us about the state of the server. If our system is fine, the field will contain streaming. Otherwise, closer inspection is needed.

The next four fields are really important. The `sent_lsn` field, formerly the `sent_location` field, indicates how much WAL has already reached the other side, which implies that they have been accepted by the WAL receiver. We can use it to figure out how much data has already made it to the slave. Then, there is the `write_lsn` field, formerly the `write_location` field. Once WAL has been accepted, it is passed on to the OS. The `write_lsn` field will tell us that the WAL position has safely made it to the OS already. The `flush_lsn` field, formerly the `flush_location` field, will know how much WAL the database has already flushed to disk.

Finally, there is `replay_lsn`, formerly the `replay_location` field. The fact that WAL has made it to the disk on the standby does not mean that PostgreSQL has already replayed or been made visible to the end user yet. Suppose that replication is paused. Data will still flow to the standby. However, it will be applied later. The `replay_lsn` field will tell us how much data is already visible.

In PostgreSQL 10.0, more fields have been added to `pg_stat_replication`; the `*_lag` fields indicate the delay of the slave and offer a convenient way to see how far a slave is behind.

The fields are at different intervals so that we can see the time difference directly.

Finally, PostgreSQL tells us whether replication is synchronous or asynchronous.

If we are still on PostgreSQL 9.6, we might find it useful to calculate the difference between the sending and the receiving servers in bytes. The `*_lag` fields don't do this for 9.6 yet, so having the difference in bytes can be very beneficial. Here's how it works:

```
SELECT client_addr, pg_current_wal_location() - sent_location AS diff
    FROM  pg_stat_replication;
```

When running this on the master, the `pg_current_wal_location()` function returns the current transaction log position. PostgreSQL 9.6 has a special datatype for transaction log positions, called `pg_lsn`. It features a couple of operators, which are used here to subtract the slave's WAL position from the master's WAL position. The view outlined here, therefore, returns the difference between two servers in bytes (replication delay).

 Note that this statement only works in PostgreSQL 10. The function used to be called `pg_current_xlog_location()` in older releases.

While the `pg_stat_replication` system view contains information on the sending side, the `pg_stat_wal_receiver` system view will provide us with similar information on the receiving side:

```
test=# \d pg_stat_wal_receiver
                    View "pg_catalog.pg_stat_wal_receiver"
        Column          |           Type           | Collation | Nullable |
Default
------------------------+--------------------------+-----------+----------+-
--------
 pid                    | integer                  |           |          |
 status                 | text                     |           |          |
 receive_start_lsn      | pg_lsn                   |           |          |
 receive_start_tli      | integer                  |           |          |
 received_lsn           | pg_lsn                   |           |          |
 received_tli           | integer                  |           |          |
 last_msg_send_time     | timestamp with time zone |           |          |
 last_msg_receipt_time  | timestamp with time zone |           |          |
 latest_end_lsn         | pg_lsn                   |           |          |
 latest_end_time        | timestamp with time zone |           |          |
 slot_name              | text                     |           |          |
 sender_host            | text                     |           |          |
 sender_port            | integer                  |           |          |
 conninfo               | text                     |           |          |
```

After the process ID of the WAL receiver process, PostgreSQL will provide you with the status of the process. Then, the `receive_start_lsn` field will tell you about the transaction log position the WAL receiver started at, while the `receive_start_tli` field will inform you about the timeline used when the WAL receiver was started.

The `received_lsn` field contains information about the `WAL` position, which was already received and flushed to disk. Then, we've got some information about the time, as well as information about slots and connections.

In general, many people find it easier to read the `pg_stat_replication` system view than the `pg_stat_wal_receiver` view, and most tools are built around the `pg_stat_replication` view.

Performing failovers and understanding timelines

Once a master/slave setup has been created, it usually works flawlessly for a very long time. However, everything can fail, and therefore it is important to understand how a failed server can be replaced with a backup system.

PostgreSQL makes failovers and promotion easy. Basically, all we have to do is use the `pg_ctl` parameter to tell a replica to promote itself:

```
pg_ctl -D data_dir promote
```

The server will disconnect itself from the master and perform the promotion instantly. Remember, the slave might already support thousands of read-only connections while being promoted. One nice feature of PostgreSQL is that all open connections will be turned into read/write connections during promotion—there is not even any need to reconnect.

> Note that PostgreSQL 12 is also able to promote the database from slave to master using plain SQL. Just use `SELECT pg_promote();`.

When promoting a server, PostgreSQL will increment the timeline: if you set up a brand new server, it will be in timeline 1. If a slave is cloned from that server, it will be in the same timeline as its master. So, both boxes will be in timeline 1. If the slave is promoted to an independent master, it will move on to timeline 2.

Timelines are especially important to PITR. Suppose we create a base backup around midnight. At 12:00 A.M., the slave is promoted. At 3:00 P.M., something crashes and we want to recover to 2:00 P.M. We will replay the transaction log that was created after the base backup and follow the `WAL` stream of our desired server, as those two nodes started to diverge at 12.00 A.M.

The timeline change will also be visible in the name of the transaction log files. Here's an example of a WAL file in timeline 1:

```
000000010000000000000F5
```

If the timeline switches to 2, the new filename will be as follows:

```
000000020000000000000F5
```

As you can see, WAL files from different timelines could theoretically exist in the same archive directory.

Managing conflicts

So far, we have learned a lot about replication. However, it is important to take a look at replication conflicts. The main question that arises is this: how can a conflict ever happen in the first place?

Consider the following example:

Master	Slave
	BEGIN;
	SELECT ... FROM tab WHERE ...
DROP TABLE tab;	... running ...
	... conflict happens ...
	... transaction is allowed to continue for 30 seconds ...
	... conflict is resolved or ends before timeout ...

The problem here is that the master does not know that there is a transaction happening on the slave. Therefore, the DROP TABLE command does not block until the reading transaction is gone. If those two transactions happened on the same node, this would, of course, be the case. However, we are looking at two servers here. The DROP TABLE command will execute normally, and a request to kill those data files on disk will reach the slave through the transaction log. The slave is not in trouble: if the table is removed from disk, the SELECT clause has to die—if the slave waits for the SELECT clause to complete before applying WAL, it might fall hopelessly behind.

The ideal solution is a compromise that can be controlled using a configuration variable:

```
max_standby_streaming_delay = 30s
        # max delay before canceling queries
        # when reading streaming WAL;
```

The idea is to wait for 30 seconds before resolving the conflict by killing the query on the slave. Depending on our application, we might want to change this variable to a more or less aggressive setting. Note that 30 seconds is for the entire replication stream and not for a single query. It might be that a single query is killed a lot earlier because some other query has already waited for some time.

While the DROP TABLE command is clearly a conflict, there are some operations that are less obvious. Here is an example:

```
BEGIN;
...
DELETE FROM tab WHERE id < 10000;
COMMIT;
...
VACUUM tab;
```

Once again, let's assume that there is a long-running SELECT clause happening on the slave. The DELETE clause is clearly not the problem here as it only flags the row as deleted—it doesn't actually remove it. The commit isn't a problem either, because it simply marks the transaction as done. Physically, the row is still there.

The problem starts when an operation such as VACUUM kicks in. It will destroy the row on disk. Of course, these changes will make it to WAL and eventually reach the slave, which will then be in trouble.

To prevent typical problems caused by standard OLTP workloads, the PostgreSQL development team has introduced a config variable:

```
hot_standby_feedback = off
        # send info from standby to prevent
        # query conflicts
```

If this setting is on, the slave will periodically send the oldest transaction ID to the master. VACUUM will then know that there is an older transaction going on somewhere in the system and defer the cleanup age to a later point when it is safe to clean out those rows. In fact, the hot_standby_feedback parameter causes the same effect as a long transaction on the master.

As we can see, the `hot_standby_feedback` parameter is `off` by default. Why is that the case? Well, there is a good reason for this: if it is `off`, a slave does not have a real impact on the master. Transaction log streaming does not consume a lot of CPU power, making streaming replication cheap and efficient. However, if a slave (which might not even be under our control) keeps transactions open for too long, our master might suffer from table bloat due to late cleanup. In a default setup, this is less desirable than reduced conflicts.

Having `hot_standby_feedback = on` will usually avoid 99% of all OLTP-related conflicts, which is especially important if your transactions take longer than just a couple of milliseconds.

Making replication more reliable

In this chapter, we have already seen that setting up replication is easy and doesn't require a lot of effort. However, there are always some corner cases that can cause operational challenges. One of those corner cases is all about transaction log retention.

Consider the following scenario:

- A base backup is fetched.
- After the backup, nothing happens for 1 hour.
- The slave is started.

Keep in mind that the master does not care too much about the existence of the slave. Therefore, the transaction log needed for the slave to start up might not exist on the master anymore as it might have been removed by checkpoints already. The problem is that a resync is needed to be able to fire up the slave. In the case of a multi-TB database, this is clearly a problem.

A potential solution to this problem is to use the `wal_keep_segments` setting:

```
wal_keep_segments = 0      # in logfile segments, 16MB each; 0 disables
```

By default, PostgreSQL keeps enough transaction logs around to survive an unexpected crash, but not much more. With the `wal_keep_segments` setting, we can tell the server to preserve more data so that a slave can catch up, even if it falls behind.

It is important to keep in mind that servers not only fall behind because they are too slow or too busy—in many cases, a delay happens because the network is too slow. Suppose you are creating an index on a 1 TB table: PostgreSQL will sort the data, and when the index is actually built, it is also sent to the transaction log. Just imagine what happens when hundreds of megabytes of WAL is sent over a wire that can maybe only handle 1 GB or so. The loss of many gigabytes of data might be the consequence of this, and will happen within seconds. Therefore, adjusting the wal_keep_segments setting should not focus on the typical delay but on the highest delay tolerable to the administrator (maybe some margin of safety).

Investing in a reasonably high setting for the wal_keep_segments setting makes a lot of sense, and I recommend ensuring that there is always enough data around.

An alternative solution to the problem of running out of transaction logs is replication slots, which will be covered later in this chapter.

Upgrading to synchronous replication

So far, asynchronous replication has been covered in reasonable detail. However, asynchronous replication means that a commit on the slave is allowed to happen after the commit on the master. If a master crashes, data that has not made it to the slave yet might be lost even if replication is occurring.

Synchronous replication is here to solve the problem—if PostgreSQL replicates synchronously, a commit has to be flushed to disk by at least one replica to go through on the master. Therefore, synchronous replication basically reduces the odds of data loss substantially.

In PostgreSQL, configuring synchronous replication is easy. Only two things have to be done:

- Adjust the synchronous_standby_names setting in the postgresql.conf file on the master.
- Add an application_name setting to the primary_conninfo parameter in the config file in the replica.

Let's get started with the `postgresql.conf` file on the master:

```
synchronous_standby_names = ''
            # standby servers that provide sync rep
            # number of sync standbys and comma-separated
            # list of application_name
            # from standby(s); '*' = all
```

If we put in `'*'`, all nodes will be considered synchronous candidates. However, in real-life scenarios, it is more likely that only a couple of nodes will be listed. Here is an example:

```
synchronous_standby_names = 'slave1, slave2, slave3'
```

Now, we have to change the `config` file and add `application_name`:

```
primary_conninfo = '... application_name=slave2'
```

The replica will now connect to the master as `slave2`. The master will check its configuration and figure out that `slave2` is the first one in the list that makes a viable slave. PostgreSQL will, therefore, ensure that a commit on the master will only be successful if the slave confirms that the transaction is there.

Now, let's assume that `slave2` goes down for some reason: PostgreSQL will try to turn one of the other two nodes into a synchronous standby. The problem is this: what if there is no other server?

In this case, PostgreSQL will wait on commit forever if a transaction is supposed to be synchronous. PostgreSQL will not continue to commit unless there are at least two viable nodes available. Remember, we have asked PostgreSQL to store data on at least two nodes—if we cannot provide enough hosts at any given point in time, it is our fault. In reality, this means that synchronous replication is best achieved with at least three nodes—one master and two slaves—as there is always a chance that one host will be lost.

Talking about host failures, there is an important thing to note at this point—if a synchronous partner dies while a commit is going in, PostgreSQL will wait for it to return. Alternatively, the synchronous commit can happen with some other potential synchronous partner. The end user might not even notice that the synchronous partners have changed.

In some cases, storing data on just two nodes might not be enough: maybe we want to improve safety even more and store data on even more nodes. To achieve that, we can make use of the following syntax in PostgreSQL 9.6 or higher:

```
synchronous_standby_names =
    '4(slave1, slave2, slave3, slave4, slave5, slave6)'
```

In this case, data is supposed to end up on four out of six nodes before the commit is confirmed by the master.

Of course, this comes with a price tag—keep in mind that speed will go down if we add more and more synchronous replicas. There is no such thing as a free lunch. PostgreSQL provides a couple of ways to keep the performance overhead under control, which we'll discuss in the following section.

In PostgreSQL 10.0, even more functionality has been added:

```
[FIRST] num_sync ( standby_name [, ...] )
ANY num_sync ( standby_name [, ...] )
standby_name [, ...]
```

The `ANY` and `FIRST` keywords have been introduced. `FIRST` allows you to set the priorities of your servers, while `ANY` gives PostgreSQL a bit more flexibility when it commits a synchronous transaction.

Adjusting durability

In this chapter, we have seen that data is either replicated synchronously or asynchronously. However, this is not a global thing. To ensure good performance, PostgreSQL allows us to configure things in a very flexible way. It is possible to replicate everything synchronously or asynchronously, but in many cases we might want to do things in a more fine-grained way. This is exactly when the `synchronous_commit` setting is needed.

Assuming that synchronous replication, the `application_name` setting, as well as the `synchronous_standby_names` setting in the `postgresql.conf` file have been configured, the `synchronous_commit` setting will offer the following options:

- `off`: This is basically a asynchronous replication. `WAL` won't be flushed to disk on the master instantly and the master won't wait for the slave to write everything to disk. If the master fails, some data might be lost (up to three times—`wal_writer_delay`).
- `local`: The transaction log is flushed to disk on commit of the master. However, the master does not wait on the slave (asynchronous replication).

- `remote_write`: The `remote_write` setting already makes PostgreSQL replicate synchronously. However, only the master saves data to disk. For the slave, it is enough to send the data to the operating system. The idea is to not wait for the second disk flush to speed things up. It is very unlikely that both storage systems will crash at exactly the same time. Therefore, the risk of data loss is close to zero.
- `on`: In this case, a transaction is OK if the master and the slaves have successfully flushed the transaction to disk. The application will not receive a commit unless data is safely stored on two servers (or more, depending on the configuration).
- `remote_apply`: While `on` ensures that data is safely stored on two nodes, it does not guarantee that we can simply load balance right away. The fact that data is flushed on the disk does not ensure that the user can already see the data. For example, if there is a conflict, a slave will halt transaction replay—however, a transaction log is still sent to the slave during a conflict and flushed to disk. In short, data may be flushed on the slave, even if it is not visible to the end user yet. The `remote_apply` option fixes this problem. It ensures that data must be visible on the replica so that the next read request can be safely executed on the slave, which can already see the changes made to the master and expose them to the end user. The `remote_apply` option is, of course, the slowest way to replicate data because it requires the slave to already expose the data to the end user.

In PostgreSQL, the `synchronous_commit` parameter is not a global value. It can be adjusted on various levels, just like many other settings. We might want to do something such as the following:

```
test=# ALTER DATABASE test SET synchronous_commit TO off;
ALTER DATABASE
```

Sometimes, only a single database should replicate in a certain way. It is also possible to just synchronously replicate if we are connected as a specific user. Last but not least, it is also possible to tell a single transaction how to commit. By adjusting the `synchronous_commit` parameter on the fly, it is even possible to control things on a per-transaction level.

For example, consider the following two scenarios:

- Writing to a log table where we might want to use an asynchronous commit because we want to be quick
- Storing a credit card payment where we want to be safe, so a synchronous transaction might be the desired thing

As we can see, the very same database might have different requirements, depending on which data is modified. Therefore, changing data at the transaction level is very useful and helps to improve speed.

Making use of replication slots

After that introduction to synchronous replication and dynamically adjustable durability, I want to focus on a feature called the replication slots.

What is the purpose of a replication slot? Let's consider the following example: There is a master and a slave. On the master, a large transaction is executed and the network connection is not fast enough to ship all of the data in time. At some point, the master removes its transaction log (checkpoint). If the slave is too far behind, a resync is needed. As we have already seen, the `wal_keep_segments` setting can be used to reduce the risk of failing replication. The question is this: what is the best value for the `wal_keep_segments` setting? Sure, more is better, but how much is best?

Replication slots will solve this problem for us: if we are using a replication slot, a master can only recycle the transaction log once it has been consumed by all replicas. The advantage here is that a slave can never fall behind so much that a resync is needed.

The trouble is, what if we shut down a replica without telling the master about it? The master would keep a transaction log forever and the disk on the primary server would eventually fill up, causing unnecessary downtime.

To reduce this risk for the master, replication slots should only be used in conjunction with proper monitoring and alerting. It is simply necessary to keep an eye on open replication slots that could potentially cause issues or might not be in use anymore.

In PostgreSQL, there are two types of replication slot:

- Physical replication slots
- Logical replication slots

Physical replication slots can be used for standard streaming replication. They will make sure that data is not recycled too early. Logical replication slots do the same thing. However, they are used for logical decoding. The idea behind logical decoding is to give users a chance to attach to the transaction log and decode it with a plugin. A logical transaction slot is, therefore, some sort of tail `-f` for database instances. It allows the user to extract changes made to the database—and therefore to the transaction log—in any format and for any purpose. In many cases, a logical replication slot is used for logical replication.

Handling physical replication slots

To make use of replication slots, changes have to be made to the `postgresql.conf` file:

```
wal_level = logical
max_replication_slots = 5     # or whatever number is needed
```

With physical slots, `logical` is not necessary—a replica is enough. However, for logical slots, we need a higher `wal_level` setting. Then, the `max_replication_slots` setting has to be changed if we are using PostgreSQL 9.6 or below. PostgreSQL 10.0 already has an improved default setting. Basically, just put in a number that serves our purpose. My recommendation is to add some spare slots so that we can easily attach more consumers without restarting the server along the way.

After a restart, the slot can be created:

```
test=# \x
Expanded display is on.
test=# \df *create*physicalslot
 List of functions
-[ RECORD 1 ]-------+------------------------------------------------
------------------
Schema              | pg_catalog
Name                | pg_create_physical_replication_slot
Result data type    | record
Argument data types | slot_name name, immediately_reserve boolean DEFAULT
false,
                      temporary boolean DEFAULT false, OUT slot_name name,
OUT lsn pg_lsn
Type                | func
```

The `pg_create_physical_replication_slot` function is here to help us to create the slot. It can be called with one of two parameters: if only a slot name is passed, the slot will be active when it is used for the first time. If `true` is passed as the second parameter, the slot will immediately start to conserve the transaction log:

```
test=# SELECT * FROM pg_create_physical_replication_slot('some_slot_name',
true);
 slot_name       | lsn
-----------------+---------------
 some_slot_name  | 0/EF8AD1D8

(1 row)
```

To see which slots are active on the master, consider running the following SQL statement:

```
test=# \x
Expanded display is on.
test=# SELECT * FROM pg_replication_slots;
-[ RECORD 1 ]-------+----------------
slot_name           | some_slot_name
plugin              |
slot_type           | physical
datoid              |
database            |
temporary           | f
active              | f
active_pid          |
xmin                |
catalog_xmin        |
restart_lsn         | 0/1653398
confirmed_flush_lsn |
```

The view will tell us a lot about the slot. It contains information about the type of slot in use, the transaction log positions, and more.

To make use of the slot, all we have to do is add it to the configuration file:

```
primary_slot_name = 'some_slot_name'
```

Once streaming is restarted, the slot will be used directly and protect replication. If we don't want our slot anymore, we can drop it easily:

```
test=# \df *drop*slot*
List of functions
-[ RECORD 1 ]-------+--------------------------
Schema              | pg_catalog
Name                | pg_drop_replication_slot
Result data type    | void
Argument data types | name
Type                | normal
```

When a slot is dropped, there is no distinction between a logical and a physical slot anymore. Just pass the name of the slot to the function and execute it.

> Nobody is allowed to use the slot when it is dropped. Otherwise, PostgreSQL will error out with good reason.

Handling logical replication slots

Logical replication slots are essential to logical replication. Due to space limitations in this chapter, it is unfortunately not possible to cover all aspects of logical replication. However, I want to outline some of the basic concepts that are essential for logical decoding and, therefore, also for logical replication.

If we want to create a replication slot, here's how it works. The function that's needed here takes two parameters: the first one will define the name of the replication slot, while the second one will carry the plugin that will be used to decode the transaction log. It will determine the format PostgreSQL is going to use to return the data:

```
test=# SELECT *
        FROM pg_create_logical_replication_slot('logical_slot',
'test_decoding');
 slot_name      | lsn
----------------+----------------
 logical_slot   | 0/EF8AD4B0

(1 row)
```

We can check for the existence of the slot using the same command that we used earlier. To check what a slot really does, a small test can be created:

```
test=# CREATE TABLE t_demo (id int, name text, payload text);
CREATE TABLE
test=#BEGIN;
BEGIN
test=# INSERT INTO t_demo
VALUES (1, 'hans', 'some data');
INSERT 0 1
test=# INSERT INTO t_demo VALUES (2, 'paul', 'some more data');
INSERT 0 1
test=# COMMIT;
COMMIT
test=# INSERT INTO t_demo VALUES (3, 'joe', 'less data');
INSERT 0 1
```

Note that two transactions were executed. The changes made to those transactions can now be extracted from the slot:

```
test=# SELECT pg_logical_slot_get_changes('logical_slot', NULL, NULL);
                    pg_logical_slot_get_changes
-------------------------------------------------------------------
 (0/EF8AF5B0,606546,"BEGIN 606546")
 (0/EF8CCCA0,606546,"COMMIT 606546")
 (0/EF8CCCD8,606547,"BEGIN 606547")
```

```
(0/EF8CCCD8,606547,"table public.t_demo: INSERT: id[integer]:1
    name[text]:'hans' payload[text]:'some data'")
(0/EF8CCD60,606547,"table public.t_demo: INSERT: id[integer]:2
    name[text]:'paul' payload[text]:'some more data'")
(0/EF8CCDE0,606547,"COMMIT 606547")
(0/EF8CCE18,606548,"BEGIN 606548")
(0/EF8CCE18,606548,"table public.t_demo: INSERT: id[integer]:3
    name[text]:'joe' payload[text]:'less data'")
(0/EF8CCE98,606548,"COMMIT 606548")
(9 rows)
```

The format that's used here depends on the output plugin we chose previously. There are various output plugins for PostgreSQL, such as `wal2json`.

> If default values are used, the logical stream will contain real values and not just functions. The logical stream has the data that ended up in the underlying tables.

Also, keep in mind that the slot does not return data anymore once it is consumed:

```
test=# SELECT pg_logical_slot_get_changes('logical_slot', NULL, NULL);
 pg_logical_slot_get_changes
-----------------------------
(0 rows)
```

The result set on the second call is therefore empty. If we want to fetch data repeatedly, PostgreSQL offers the `pg_logical_slot_peek_changes` function. It works just like the `pg_logical_slot_get_changes` function but assures that data will still be available in the slot.

Using plain SQL is, of course, not the only way to consume a transaction log. There is also a command-line tool called `pg_recvlogical`. It can be compared to doing tail `-f` on an entire database instance and receives the flow of data in real time.

Let's start the `pg_recvlogical` command:

```
[hs@zenbook ~]$ pg_recvlogical -S logical_slot -P test_decoding
                -d test -U postgres --start -f -
```

In this case, the tool connects to the test database and consumes data from `logical_slot`. `-f` means that the stream will be sent to `stdout`. Let's kill some data:

```
test=# DELETE FROM t_demo WHERE id < random()*10;
DELETE 3
```

The changes will make it into the transaction log. However, by default, the database only cares about what the table will look like after the deletion. It knows which blocks have to be touched and so on, but it doesn't know what it was previously:

```
BEGIN 606549
table public.t_demo: DELETE: (no-tuple-data)
table public.t_demo: DELETE: (no-tuple-data)
table public.t_demo: DELETE: (no-tuple-data)
COMMIT 606549
```

Therefore, the output is pretty pointless. To fix that, the following line comes to the rescue:

```
test=# ALTER TABLE t_demo REPLICA IDENTITY FULL;
ALTER TABLE
```

If the table is repopulated with data and deleted again, the transaction log stream will look as follows:

```
BEGIN 606558
table public.t_demo: DELETE: id[integer]:1 name[text]:'hans'
    payload[text]:'some data'
table public.t_demo: DELETE: id[integer]:2 name[text]:'paul'
    payload[text]:'some more data'
table public.t_demo: DELETE: id[integer]:3 name[text]:'joe'
    payload[text]:'less data'
COMMIT 606558
```

Now, all of the changes are in.

Use cases of logical slots

There are various use cases of replication slots. The most simplistic use case is the one shown here. Data can be fetched from the server in the desired format and used to audit, debug, or simply monitor a database instance.

The next logical step is to take this stream of changes and use it for replication. Solutions such as **bi-directional replication (BDR)** are totally based on logical decoding because changes at the binary level would not work with multi-master replication.

Finally, there is the need to upgrade without downtime. Remember, the binary transaction log stream cannot be used to replicate between different versions of PostgreSQL. Therefore, future versions of PostgreSQL will support a tool called `pglogical`, which helps to upgrade without downtime.

Making use of CREATE PUBLICATION and CREATE SUBSCRIPTION

For version 10.0, the PostgreSQL community created two new commands: CREATE PUBLICATION and CREATE SUBSCRIPTION. These can be used for logical replication, which means that you can now selectively replicate data and achieve close-to-zero downtime upgrades. So far, binary replication and transaction log replication has been fully covered. However, sometimes, we might not want to replicate an entire database instance—replicating a table or two might be enough. This is exactly when logical replication is the right thing to use.

Before getting started, the first thing to do is change wal_level to logical in postgresql.conf and restart:

```
wal_level = logical
```

Then, we can create a simple table:

```
test=# CREATE TABLE t_test (a int, b int);
CREATE TABLE
```

The same table layout has to exist in the second database as well to make this work. PostgreSQL will not automatically create those tables for us:

```
test=# CREATE DATABASE repl;
CREATE DATABASE
```

After creating the database, the identical table can be added:

```
repl=# CREATE TABLE t_test (a int, b int);
CREATE TABLE
```

The goal here is to publish the contents of the t_test table in the test database to somewhere else. In this case, it will simply be replicated into a database on the same instance. To publish those changes, PostgreSQL offers the CREATE PUBLICATION command:

```
test=# \h CREATE PUBLICATION
 Command: CREATE PUBLICATION
 Description: define a new publication
 Syntax:
   CREATE PUBLICATION name
       [ FOR TABLE [ ONLY ] table_name [ * ] [, ...]
```

```
| FOR ALL TABLES ]
[ WITH ( publication_parameter [= value] [, ... ] ) ]
```

URL: https://www.postgresql.org/docs/12/sql-createpublication.html

The syntax is actually pretty easy. All we need is a name and a list of all the tables that the system is supposed to replicate:

```
test=# CREATE PUBLICATION pub1 FOR TABLE t_test;
CREATE PUBLICATION
```

Now, the subscription can be created. The syntax is, again, pretty simple and really straightforward:

```
test=# \h CREATE SUBSCRIPTION
Command: CREATE SUBSCRIPTION
Description: define a new subscription
Syntax:
  CREATE SUBSCRIPTION subscription_name
  CONNECTION 'conninfo'
  PUBLICATION publication_name [, ...]
  [ WITH ( subscription_parameter [= value] [, ... ] ) ]
```

URL: https://www.postgresql.org/docs/12/sql-createsubscription.html

Basically, creating a subscription directly is absolutely no problem. However, if we play this game inside the same instance from the test database to the repl database, it is necessary to create the replication slot in use manually. Otherwise, CREATE SUBSCRIPTION will never finish:

```
test=# SELECT pg_create_logical_replication_slot('sub1', 'pgoutput');
 pg_create_logical_replication_slot
-------------------------------------
(sub1,0/27E2B2D0)
(1 row)
```

In this case, the name of the slot that's created on the master database is called sub1. Then, we need to connect to the target database and run the following command:

```
repl=# CREATE SUBSCRIPTION sub1
       CONNECTION 'host=localhost dbname=test user=postgres'
       PUBLICATION pub1
       WITH (create_slot = false);
CREATE SUBSCRIPTION
```

Of course, we have to adjust our database CONNECTION parameters. Then, PostgreSQL will sync the data, and we will be done.

Note that `create_slot = false` is only used because the test is running inside the same database server instance. If we happen to use different databases, there is no need to manually create the slot and no need for `create_slot = false`.

Summary

In this chapter, we learned about the most important features of PostgreSQL replication, such as streaming replication and replication conflicts. We then learned about PITR, as well as replication slots. Note that a book on replication is never complete unless it spans around 400 pages or so, but we have learned the most important things that every administrator should know.

Chapter 11, *Deciding on Useful Extensions*, is about useful extensions to PostgreSQL. We will learn about extensions that have been widely adopted by the industry and that provide even more functionality.

Questions

1. What is the purpose of logical replication?
2. What is the performance impact of synchronous replication?
3. Why not always use synchronous replication?

Deciding on Useful Extensions

11

In Chapter 10, *Making Sense of Backups and Replication*, our focus was on replication, transaction log shipping, and logical decoding. After looking at mostly administration-related topics, the goal now is to aim at a broader topic. In the PostgreSQL world, many things are done through extensions. The advantage of extensions is that functionality can be added without bloating the PostgreSQL core. People can choose from competing extensions and find what is best for them. The philosophy is to keep the core slim, relatively easy to maintain, and ready for the future.

In this chapter, some of the most widespread extensions for PostgreSQL will be discussed. However, before digging deeper into this issue, I want to state that this chapter only features a list of extensions that I personally find useful. There are so many modules out there these days that it is impossible to cover them all in a reasonable way. Information is published every day, and it is sometimes even hard for a professional to be aware of everything out there. New extensions are being published as we speak, and it may be a good idea to take a look at **PostgreSQL Extention Network (PGXN)** (https://pgxn.org/), which contains a large variety of extensions for PostgreSQL.

In this chapter, we will cover the following topics:

- Understanding how extensions work
- Making use of contrib modules
- Other useful extensions

Note that only the most important extensions will be covered.

Understanding how extensions work

Before digging into the extensions that are available, it is a good idea to take a look at how extensions work in the first place. Understanding the inner workings of the extension machinery can be quite beneficial.

Let's take a look at the syntax first:

```
test=# \h CREATE EXTENSION
Command:     CREATE EXTENSION
Description: install an extension
Syntax:
CREATE EXTENSION [ IF NOT EXISTS ] extension_name
    [ WITH ] [ SCHEMA schema_name ]
             [ VERSION version ]
             [ FROM old_version ]
             [ CASCADE ]
URL: https://www.postgresql.org/docs/12/sql-createextension.html
```

When you want to deploy an extension, simply call the CREATE EXTENSION command. It will check for the extension and load it into your database. Note that the extension will be loaded into a database and not into the entire database instance.

If we are loading an extension, we can decide on the schema that we want to use. Many extensions can be relocated so that the user can choose which schema to use. Then, it is possible to decide on a specific version of the extension. Often, we don't want to deploy the latest version of an extension because the client may be running outdated software. In such cases, it may be handy to be able to deploy any version that's available on the system.

The FROM old_version clause requires some more attention. Back in the old days, PostgreSQL didn't support extensions, so a lot of unpackaged code is still around. This option causes the CREATE EXTENSION clause to run an alternative installation script that absorbs existing objects into the extension, instead of creating new objects. Make sure that the SCHEMA clause specifies the schema containing these preexisting objects. Only use it when you have old modules around.

Finally, there is the CASCADE clause. Some extensions depend on other extensions. The CASCADE option will automatically deploy those software packages, too. The following is an example:

```
test=# CREATE EXTENSION earthdistance;
ERROR: required extension "cube" is not installed
HINT: Use CREATE EXTENSION ... CASCADE to install required extensions too.
```

The `earthdistance` module implements great-circle distance calculations. As you may already know, the shortest distance between two points on the Earth cannot be followed in a straight line; instead, a pilot has to adjust his/her course constantly to find the fastest route when flying from one point to the other. The thing is, the `earthdistance` extension depends on the `cube` extension, which allows you to perform operations on a sphere.

To automatically deploy this dependency, the `CASCADE` clause can be used, as we described previously:

```
test=# CREATE EXTENSION earthdistance CASCADE;
NOTICE: installing required extension "cube" CREATE EXTENSION
```

In this case, both extensions will be deployed.

Checking for available extensions

PostgreSQL offers various views so that we can figure out which extensions are on the system and which ones are actually deployed. One of those views is `pg_available_extensions`:

```
test=# \d pg_available_extensions
        View "pg_catalog.pg_available_extensions"
     Column         | Type  | Collation | Nullable | Default
--------------------+-------+-----------+----------+---------
 name               | name  |           |          |
 default_version    | text  |           |          |
 installed_version  | text  | C         |          |
 comment            | text  |           |          |
```

This contains a list of all of the extensions that are available, including their names, their default version, and the version that's currently installed. To make this easier for the end user, there is also a description available, telling us more about the extension.

The following listing contains two lines that have been taken from `pg_available_extensions`:

```
test=# \x
Expanded display is on.
test=# SELECT * FROM pg_available_extensions LIMIT 2;
-[ RECORD 1 ]-----+-------------------------------------------------
name              | unaccent
default_version   | 1.1
installed_version |
comment           | text search dictionary that removes accents
-[ RECORD 2 ]-----+-------------------------------------------------
```

```
name              | tsm_system_time
default_version   | 1.0
installed_version |
comment           | TABLESAMPLE method which accepts time in milliseconds
as a limit
```

As you can see, the earthdistance and plpgsql extensions are both enabled in my database. The plpgsql extension is there by default and earthdistance was added too. The beauty of this view is that you can quickly get an overview of what is installed and what can be installed.

However, in some cases, extensions are available in more than just one version. To find out more about versioning, check out the following view:

```
test=# \d pg_available_extension_versions
View "pg_catalog.pg_available_extension_versions"
   Column      |  Type    | Modifiers
---------------+----------+-----------
 name          | name     |
 version       | text     |
 installed     | boolean  |
 superuser     | boolean  |
 relocatable   | boolean  |
 schema        | name     |
 requires      | name[]   |
 comment       | text     |
```

Some more detailed information is available here, as shown in the following listing:

```
test=# SELECT * FROM pg_available_extension_versions LIMIT 1;
-[ RECORD 1 ]-----------------------------------------------
name        | earthdistance
version     | 1.1
installed   | t
superuser   | t
relocatable | t
schema      |
requires    | {cube}
comment     | calculate great-circle distances on the surface of the Earth
```

PostgreSQL will also tell you whether the extension can be relocated, which schema it has been deployed in, and what other extensions are needed. Then, there is the comment describing the extension, which was shown previously.

You may be wondering where PostgreSQL finds all of this information about extensions on the system. Assuming that you have deployed PostgreSQL 10.0 from the official PostgreSQL RPM repository, the /usr/pgsql-11/share/extension directory will contain a couple of files:

```
...
-bash-4.3$ ls -l citext*
ls -l citext*
-rw-r--r--. 1 hs hs 1028 Sep 11 19:53 citext--1.0--1.1.sql
-rw-r--r--. 1 hs hs 2748 Sep 11 19:53 citext--1.1--1.2.sql
-rw-r--r--. 1 hs hs 307 Sep 11 19:53 citext--1.2--1.3.sql
-rw-r--r--. 1 hs hs 668 Sep 11 19:53 citext--1.3--1.4.sql
-rw-r--r--. 1 hs hs 2284 Sep 11 19:53 citext--1.4--1.5.sql
-rw-r--r--. 1 hs hs 13466 Sep 11 19:53 citext--1.4.sql
-rw-r--r--. 1 hs hs 158 Sep 11 19:53 citext.control
-rw-r--r--. 1 hs hs 9781 Sep 11 19:53 citext--unpackaged--1.0.sql

...
```

The default version of the citext (case-insensitive text) extension is 1.4, so there's a file called citext--1.3.sql. In addition to that, there are files that are used to move from one version to the next (1.0 → 1.1, 1.1 → 1.2, and so on).

Then, there is the .control file:

```
-bash-4.3$ cat citext.control
# citext extension
comment = 'data type for case-insensitive character strings'
default_version = '1.4'
module_pathname = '$libdir/citext'
relocatable = true
```

This file contains all of the metadata related to the extension; the first entry contains the comment. Note that this content is what will be shown in the system views we just discussed. When you access those views, PostgreSQL will go to this directory and read all of the .control files. Then, there is the default version and the path to the binaries.

If you are installing a typical extension from RPM, the directory is going to be $libdir, which is inside your PostgreSQL binary directory. However, if you have written your own commercial extension, it may very well reside somewhere else.

The last setting will tell PostgreSQL whether the extension can reside in any schema or whether it has to be in a fixed, predefined schema.

Finally, there is the unpackaged file. Following is an extract from it:

```
...
ALTER EXTENSION citext ADD type citext;
ALTER EXTENSION citext ADD function citextin(cstring);
ALTER EXTENSION citext ADD function citextout(citext);
ALTER EXTENSION citext ADD function citextrecv(internal);
...
```

The unpackaged file will turn any existing code into an extension. Therefore, it is important to consolidate existing code in your database.

Making use of contrib modules

Now that we have had a look at a theoretical introduction to extensions, it is time to take a look at some of the most important extensions. In this section, you will learn about modules that are provided to you as part of the PostgreSQL `contrib` module. When you install PostgreSQL, I recommend that you always install these `contrib` modules as they contain vital extensions that can really make your life easier.

In the upcoming section, you will be guided through some extensions that I find the most interesting and the most useful for various reasons (for debugging, performance tuning, and so on).

Using the adminpack module

The idea behind the `adminpack` module is to give administrators a way to access the filesystem without SSH access. The package contains a couple of functions to make this possible.

To load the module into the database, run the following command:

```
test=# CREATE EXTENSION adminpack;
CREATE EXTENSION
```

One of the most interesting features of the `adminpack` module is the ability to inspect log files. The `pg_logdir_ls` function checks out the `log` directory and returns a list of log files:

```
test=# SELECT * FROM pg_catalog.pg_logdir_ls() AS (a timestamp, b text);
ERROR: the log_filename parameter must equal 'postgresql-%Y-%m-
%d_%H%M%S.log'
```

The important thing here is that the `log_filename` parameter has to be adjusted to the `adminpack` module's needs. If you happen to run RPMs that have been downloaded from the PostgreSQL repositories, the `log_filename` parameter is defined as `postgresql-%a`, which has to be changed so that errors can be avoided.

After making this change, a list of log filenames is returned:

```
test=# SELECT * FROM pg_catalog.pg_logdir_ls() AS (a timestamp, b text);
         a           |                        b
---------------------+------------------------------------------------
 2017-03-03 16:32:58 | pg_log/postgresql-2017-03-03_163258.log

(1 row)
```

It is also possible to determine the size of a file on disk. Following is an example:

```
test=# SELECT b, pg_catalog.pg_file_length(b)
  FROM pg_catalog.pg_logdir_ls() AS (a timestamp, b text);
            b                            | pg_file_length
-----------------------------------------+----------------
 pg_log/postgresql-2017-03-03_163258.log | 1525

(1 row)
```

In addition to these features, there are some more functions that are provided by the module:

```
test=# SELECT proname FROM pg_proc WHERE proname ~ 'pg_file_.*';
    proname
----------------
 pg_file_write
 pg_file_rename
 pg_file_unlink
 pg_file_read
 pg_file_length
(5 rows)
```

Here, you can read, write, rename, or simply delete files.

These functions can, of course, only be called by **superusers**.

Applying bloom filters

Since PostgreSQL 9.6, it has been possible to add index types on the fly using extensions. The new `CREATE ACCESS METHOD` command, along with some additional features, has made it possible for us to create fully functional and transaction-logged index types on the fly.

The bloom extension provides PostgreSQL users with bloom filters, which are prefilters that help us efficiently reduce the amount of data as soon as possible. The idea behind a bloom filter is that we can calculate a bitmask and compare the bitmask with the query. The bloom filter may produce some false positives, but it will still reduce the amount of data dramatically.

This is especially useful when a table consists of hundreds of columns and millions of rows. It isn't possible to index hundreds of columns with B-trees, so a bloom filter is a good alternative because it allows us to index everything at once.

To understand how things work, we will install the extension:

```
test=# CREATE EXTENSION bloom;
CREATE EXTENSION
```

Now, we need to create a table containing various columns:

```
test=# CREATE TABLE t_bloom
(
        id serial,
        col1 int4 DEFAULT random() * 1000,
        col2 int4 DEFAULT random() * 1000,
        col3 int4 DEFAULT random() * 1000,
        col4 int4 DEFAULT random() * 1000,
        col5 int4 DEFAULT random() * 1000,
        col6 int4 DEFAULT random() * 1000,
        col7 int4 DEFAULT random() * 1000,
        col8 int4 DEFAULT random() * 1000,
        col9 int4 DEFAULT random() * 1000
);
CREATE TABLE
```

To make this easier, these columns have a default value so that data can easily be added using a simple `SELECT` clause:

```
test=# INSERT INTO t_bloom (id)
        SELECT * FROM generate_series(1, 1000000);
INSERT 0 1000000
```

The preceding query adds 1 million rows to the table. Now, the table can be indexed:

```
test=# CREATE INDEX idx_bloom ON t_bloom
        USING bloom(col1, col2, col3, col4, col5, col6, col7, col8, col9);
CREATE INDEX
```

Note that the index contains nine columns at a time. In contrast to a B-tree, the order of those columns doesn't really make a difference.

 Note that the table we just created is around 65 MB without indexes.

The index adds another 15 MB to the storage footprint:

```
test=# \di+ idx_bloom
                          List of relations
  Schema | Name       | Type  | Owner | Table    | Size  | Description
 --------+------------+-------+-------+----------+-------+--------------
  public | idx_bloom  | index | hs    | t_bloom  | 15 MB |
 (1 row)
```

The beauty of the `bloom` filter is that it is possible to look for any combination of columns:

```
test=# SET max_parallel_workers_per_gather TO 0;
SET

test=# explain SELECT count(*)
    FROM   t_bloom
    WHERE col4 = 454 AND col3 = 354 AND col9 = 423;
                                QUERY PLAN
 ----------------------------------------------------------------------
  Aggregate  (cost=20352.02..20352.03 rows=1 width=8)
    -> Bitmap Heap Scan on t_bloom
          (cost=20348.00..20352.02 rows=1 width=0)
          Recheck Cond: ((col3 = 354) AND (col4 = 454) AND (col9 = 423))
          -> Bitmap Index Scan on idx_bloom
                (cost=0.00..20348.00 rows=1 width=0)
                Index Cond: ((col3 = 354) AND (col4 = 454)
                                AND (col9 = 423))
 (5 rows)
```

What you have seen so far feels exceptional. A natural question that might arise is: Why not always use a bloom filter? The reason is simple—the database has to read the entire `bloom` filter in order to use it. In the case of, say, a B-tree, this is not necessary.

In the future, more index types will likely be added to ensure that even more use cases can be covered with PostgreSQL.

 If you want to read more about `bloom` filters, consider reading our blog post at `https://www.cybertec-postgresql.com/en/trying-out-postgres-bloom-indexes/`.

Deploying btree_gist and btree_gin

There are even more indexing-related features that can be added. In PostgreSQL, there is the concept of operator classes, which we discussed in Chapter 3, *Making Use of Indexes*.

The `contrib` module offers two extensions (namely, `btree_gist` and `btree_gin`) so that we can add B-tree functionality to GiST and GIN indexes. Why is this so useful? GiST indexes offer various features that are not supported by B-trees. One of those features is the ability to perform a **k-nearest neighbor** (**KNN**) search.

Why is this relevant? Imagine that somebody is looking for data that was added yesterday, around noon. So, when was that? In some cases, it may be hard to come up with boundaries, for example, if somebody is looking for a product that costs around 70 euros. KNN can come to the rescue here. Following is an example:

```
test=# CREATE TABLE t_test (id int);
CREATE TABLE
```

Now, some simple data needs to be added:

```
test=# INSERT INTO t_test SELECT * FROM generate_series(1, 100000);
INSERT 0 100000
```

Now, the extension can be added:

```
test=# CREATE EXTENSION btree_gist;
CREATE EXTENSION
```

Adding a `gist` index to the column is easy; just use the `USING gist` clause. Note that adding a `gist` index to an integer column only works if the extension is present. Otherwise, PostgreSQL will report that there is no suitable operator class:

```
test=# CREATE INDEX idx_id ON t_test USING gist(id);
CREATE INDEX
```

Once the index has been deployed, it is possible to order by distance:

```
test=# SELECT *
 FROM t_test
 ORDER BY id <-> 100
 LIMIT 6;
 id
------
 100
 101
 99
 102
 98
 97
(6 rows)
```

As you can see, the first row is an exact match. The matches that follow are already less precise and are getting worse. The query will always return a fixed number of rows.

The important thing here is the execution plan:

```
test=# explain SELECT *
  FROM   t_test
  ORDER BY id <-> 100
  LIMIT 6;
                               QUERY PLAN
---------------------------------------------------------------------
 Limit (cost=0.28..0.64 rows=6 width=8)
   -> Index Only Scan using idx_id on t_test
               (cost=0.28..5968.28 rows=100000 width=8)
         Order By: (id <-> 100)
(3 rows)
```

As you can see, PostgreSQL goes straight for an index scan, which speeds up the query significantly.

In future versions of PostgreSQL, B-trees will most likely also support KNN searches. A patch to add this feature has already been added to the development mailing list. Maybe it will eventually make it to the core. Having KNN as a B-tree feature could eventually lead to fewer GiST indexes on standard datatypes.

dblink – considering phasing out

The desire to use database links has been around for many years. However, around the turn of the century, PostgreSQL foreign data wrappers weren't even on the horizon, and a traditional database link implementation was definitely not in sight either. Around this time, a PostgreSQL developer from California (**Joe Conway**) pioneered work on database connectivity by introducing the concept of dblink to PostgreSQL. While dblink served people well over the years, it is no longer state of the art.

Therefore, it is recommended we move away from dblink to the more modern SQL/MED implementation (which is a specification that defines the way external data can be integrated with a relational database). The postgres_fdw extension has been built on top of SQL/MED and offers more than just database connectivity as it allows you to connect to basically any data source.

Fetching files with file_fdw

In some cases, it can make sense to read a file from disk and expose it to PostgreSQL as a table. This is exactly what you can achieve with the file_fdw extension. The idea is to have a module that allows you to read data from a disk and query it using SQL.

Installing the module works as expected:

```
CREATE EXTENSION file_fdw;
```

Now, we need to create a virtual server:

```
CREATE SERVER file_server
  FOREIGN DATA WRAPPER file_fdw;
```

file_server is based on the file_fdw extension foreign data wrapper, which tells PostgreSQL how to access the file.

To expose a file as a table, use the following command:

```
CREATE FOREIGN TABLE t_passwd
(
    username    text,
    passwd      text,
    uid         int,
    gid         int,
    gecos       text,
    dir         text,
    shell       text
```

```
) SERVER file_server
OPTIONS (format 'text', filename '/etc/passwd', header 'false', delimiter
':');
```

In this example, the /etc/passwd file will be exposed. All the fields have to be listed and the data types have to be mapped accordingly. All of the additional important information is passed to the module using options. In this example, PostgreSQL has to know the type of the file (text), the name and path of the file, as well as the delimiter. It is also possible to tell PostgreSQL whether there is a header. If the setting is true, the first line will be skipped and deemed not important. Skipping headers is especially important if you happen to load a CSV file.

Once the table has been created, it is possible to read data:

```
SELECT * FROM t_passwd;
```

Unsurprisingly, PostgreSQL returns the content of /etc/passwd:

```
test=# \x
Expanded display is on.
test=# SELECT * FROM t_passwd LIMIT 1;
-[ RECORD 1 ]-------
username | root
passwd   | x
uid      | 0
gid      | 0
gecos    | root
dir      | /root
shell    | /bin/bash
```

When looking at the execution plan, you will see that PostgreSQL uses what is known as a **foreign scan** to fetch the data from the file:

```
test=# explain (verbose true, analyze true) SELECT * FROM t_passwd;
                              QUERY PLAN
--------------------------------------------------------------------
 Foreign Scan on public.t_passwd (cost=0.00..2.80 rows=18 width=168)
             (actual time=0.022..0.072 rows=61 loops=1)
   Output: username, passwd, uid, gid, gecos, dir, shell
   Foreign File: /etc/passwd
   Foreign File Size: 3484
 Planning time: 0.058 ms
 Execution time: 0.138 ms
(6 rows)
```

The execution plan also tells us about the file's size and so on. Since we're talking about the planner, there is a side note that is worth mentioning: PostgreSQL will even fetch statistics for the file. The planner checks the file size and assigns the same costs to the file, just like it would to a normal PostgreSQL table of the same size.

Inspecting storage using pageinspect

If you are facing storage corruption or some other storage-related problem that may be related to bad blocks in a table, the pageinspect extension may be the module you are looking for. We will begin by creating the extension, as shown in the following example:

```
test=# CREATE EXTENSION pageinspect;
CREATE EXTENSION
```

The idea behind pageinspect is to provide you with a module that allows you to inspect a table on the binary level.

When using this module, the most important thing to do is fetch a block:

```
test=# SELECT * FROM get_raw_page('pg_class', 0);
...
```

This function will return a single block. In the preceding example, it is the first block in the pg_class parameter, which is a system table. Of course, it is up to the user to pick any other table.

Next, you can extract the page header:

```
test=# \x
Expanded display is on.

test=# SELECT * FROM page_header(get_raw_page('pg_class', 0));
-[ RECORD    1 ]---------
lsn         | 1/35CAE5B8
checksum    | 0
flags       | 1
lower       | 240
upper       | 1288
special     | 8192
pagesize    | 8192
version     | 4
prune_xid   | 606562
```

The page header already contains a lot of information about the page. If you want to find out more, you can call the `heap_page_items` function, which dissects the page and returns one row per tuple:

```
test=# SELECT * FROM heap_page_items(get_raw_page('pg_class', 0))
   LIMIT 1;
-[ RECORD 1 ]---
lp          | 1
lp_off      | 49
lp_flags    | 2
lp_len      | 0
t_xmin      |
t_xmax      |
t_field3    |
t_ctid      |
t_infomask2 |
t_infomask  |
t_hoff      |
t_bits      |
t_oid       |
t_data      | ...
```

You can also split the data into various tuples:

```
test=# SELECT tuple_data_split('pg_class'::regclass,
                               t_data, t_infomask, t_infomask2, t_bits)
   FROM heap_page_items(get_raw_page('pg_class', 0))
   LIMIT 2;
-[ RECORD 1 ]----+----------------------------------
tuple_data_split |
-[ RECORD 2 ]----+----------------------------------
tuple_data_split |
{"\\x610000000000000000000000000000000000000000000000000000000000000000
00000000000000000000000000000000000000000000000000000000","\\x98080000","
\\x50ac0c00","\\x00000000","\\x01400000","\\x00000000","\\x4eac0c00","\\x00
000000","\\xbb010000","\\x0050c347","\\x00000000","\\x00000000","\\x01","\\
x00","\\x70","\\x72","\\x0100","\\x0000","\\x00","\\x00","\\x00","\\x00","\
\x00","\\x00","\\x00","\\x01","\\x64","\\xc3400900","\\x01000000",NULL,NULL
}
```

To read the data, we have to familiarize ourselves with the on-disk format of PostgreSQL. Otherwise, the data may appear to be pretty obscure.

`pageinspect` provides functions for all possible access methods (tables, indexes, and so on) and allows us to dissect storage so that more details can be provided.

Investigating caching with pg_buffercache

After this brief introduction to the `pageinspect` extension, we will turn our attention to the `pg_buffercache` extension, which allows you to take a detailed look at the contents of your I/O cache:

```
test=# CREATE EXTENSION pg_buffercache;
CREATE EXTENSION
```

The `pg_buffercache` extension provides you with a view containing the following fields:

```
test=# \d pg_buffercache
View "public.pg_buffercache"
  Column           | Type     | Modifiers
-------------------+----------+-----------
 bufferid          | integer  |
 relfilenode       | oid      |
 reltablespace     |oid       |
 reldatabase       |oid       |
 relforknumber     |smallint  |
 relblocknumber    |bigint    |
 isdirty           |boolean   |
 usagecount        |smallint  |
 pinning_backends  |integer   |
```

The `bufferid` field is just a number; it identifies the buffer. Then, there's the `relfilenode` field, which points to the file on disk. If we want to look up which table a file belongs to, we can check out the `pg_class` module, which also contains a field called `relfilenode`. Then, there are the `reldatabase` and `reltablespace` fields. Note that all the fields are defined as being the `oid` type, so to extract data in a more useful way, it is necessary to join system tables together.

The `relforknumber` field tells us which part of the table is cached. It could be the heap, the free space map, or some other component, such as the visibility map. In the future, there will surely be more types of relation fork.

The next field, `relblocknumber`, tells us which block has been cached. Finally, there is the `isdirty` flag, which tells us that a block has been modified, as well as about the usage counter and the number of backends pinning the block.

If you want to make sense of the `pg_buffercache` extension, it is important to add additional information. To figure out which database uses caching the most, the following query may help:

```
test=# SELECT datname,
              count(*),
              count(*) FILTER (WHERE isdirty = true) AS dirty
       FROM pg_buffercache AS b, pg_database AS d
       WHERE d.oid = b.reldatabase
       GROUP BY ROLLUP (1);
  datname   | count | dirty
------------+-------+-------
  abc       | 132   | 1
  postgres  | 30    | 0
  test      | 11975 | 53
            | 12137 | 54
 (4 rows)
```

In this case, the `pg_database` extension has to be joined. As we can see, `oid` is the join criterion, which may not be obvious to people who are new to PostgreSQL.

Sometimes, we may want to know which blocks in the database that are connected to us are cached:

```
test=# SELECT relname,
              relkind,
              count(*),
              count(*) FILTER (WHERE isdirty = true) AS dirty
       FROM pg_buffercache AS b, pg_database AS d, pg_class AS c
       WHERE d.oid = b.reldatabase
              AND c.relfilenode = b.relfilenode
              AND datname = 'test'
       GROUP BY 1, 2
       ORDER BY 3 DESC
       LIMIT 7;
  relname                   | relkind| count| dirty
----------------------------+--------+------+-------
  t_bloom                   | r      | 8338 | 0
  idx_bloom                 | i      | 1962 | 0
  idx_id                    | i      | 549  | 0
  t_test                    | r      | 445  | 0
  pg_statistic              | r      | 90   | 0
  pg_depend                 | r      | 60   | 0
  pg_depend_reference_index | i      | 34   | 0
 (7 rows)
```

In this case, we filtered the current database and joined with the `pg_class` module, which contains the list of objects. The `relkind` column is especially noteworthy: `r` refers to table (relation) and `i` refers to index. This tells us which object we are looking at.

Encrypting data with pgcrypto

One of the most powerful modules in the entire `contrib` module section is `pgcrypto`. It was originally written by one of the Skype sysadmins and offers countless functions so that we can encrypt and `decrypt` data.

It offers functions for symmetric as well as asymmetric encryption. Due to the large number of functions that are available, it is definitely recommended to check out the documentation page at `https://www.postgresql.org/docs/current/static/pgcrypto.html`.

Due to the limited scope of this chapter, it is impossible to dig into all of the details of the `pgcrypto` module.

Prewarming caches with pg_prewarm

When PostgreSQL operates normally, it tries to cache important data. The `shared_buffers` variable is important as it defines the size of the cache that's managed by PostgreSQL. The problem now is this: if you restart the database server, the cache managed by PostgreSQL will be lost. Maybe the operating system still has some data to reduce the impact on disk wait, but in many cases, this won't be enough. The solution to this problem is called the `pg_prewarm` extension:

```
test=# CREATE EXTENSION pg_prewarm;
CREATE EXTENSION
```

This extension deploys a function that allows us to explicitly `prewarm` the cache whenever this is needed:

```
test=# \x
Expanded display is on.
test=# \df *prewa*
List of functions
-[ RECORD 1 ]
Schema             | public
Name               | autoprewarm_dump_now
Result data type   | bigint
Argument data types |
Type               | func
```

```
-[ RECORD 2 ]
Schema               | public
Name                 | autoprewarm_start_worker
Result data type     | void
Argument data types  |
Type                 | func
-[ RECORD 3 ]
Schema               | public
Name                 | pg_prewarm
Result data type     | bigint
Argument data types  | regclass, mode text DEFAULT 'buffer'::text,
                       fork text DEFAULT 'main'::text,
                       first_block bigint DEFAULT NULL::bigint,
                       last_block bigint DEFAULT NULL::bigint
Type                 | func
```

The easiest and most common way to call the `pg_prewarm` extension is to ask it to cache an entire object:

```
test=# SELECT pg_prewarm('t_test');
 pg_prewarm
------------
        443
(1 row)
```

 Note that, if the table is so large that it doesn't fit into the cache, only parts of the table will stay in the cache, which is fine in most cases.

The function returns the number of 8 KB blocks that were processed by the function call.

If you don't want to cache all of the blocks of an object, you can also select a specific range inside the table. In the following example, we can see that blocks 10 to 30 are cached in the main fork:

```
test=# SELECT pg_prewarm('t_test', 'buffer', 'main', 10, 30);
 pg_prewarm
------------
         21
(1 row)
```

Here, it's clear that 21 blocks were cached.

Inspecting performance with pg_stat_statements

pg_stat_statements is the most important contrib module that's available. It should always be enabled and is there to provide superior performance data. Without the pg_stat_statements module, it is really hard to track down performance problems.

Inspecting storage with pgstattuple

Sometimes, it may be the case that tables in PostgreSQL grow out of proportion. The technical term for a table that has grown too much is **table bloat**. The question that arises now is: Which tables have bloated and how much bloat is there? The pgstattuple extension will help us answer those questions:

```
test=# CREATE EXTENSION pgstattuple;
CREATE EXTENSION
```

As we stated previously, the module deploys a couple of functions. In the case of the pgstattuple extension, those functions return a row consisting of a composite type. Therefore, the function has to be called in the FROM clause to ensure a readable result:

```
test=# \x
Expanded display is on.

test=# SELECT * FROM pgstattuple('t_test');
-[ RECORD 1 ]
--------------------+--------------
 table_len          | 3629056
 tuple_count        | 100000
 tuple_len          | 2800000
 tuple_percent      | 77.16
 dead_tuple_count   | 0
 dead_tuple_len     | 0
 dead_tuple_percent | 0
 free_space         | 16652
 free_percent       | 0.46
```

In this example, the table that was used for testing seems to be in a pretty good state: the table is 3.6 MB in size and doesn't contain any dead rows. Free space is also limited. If access to your table is slowed down by table bloat, then this means that the number of dead rows and the amount of free space will have grown out of proportion. Some free space and a handful of dead rows are normal; however, if the table has grown so much that it mostly consists of dead rows and free space, decisive action is needed to bring the situation under control again.

The `pgstattuple` extension also provides a function that we can use inspect indexes:

```
test=# CREATE INDEX idx_id ON t_test (id);
CREATE INDEX
```

The `pgstattindex` function returns a lot of information about the index we want to inspect:

```
test=# SELECT * FROM pgstatindex('idx_id');
-[ RECORD 1 ]
--------------------+---------------
version             | 2
tree_level          | 1
index_size          | 2260992
root_block_no       | 3
internal_pages      | 1
leaf_pages          | 274
empty_pages         | 0
deleted_pages       | 0
avg_leaf_density    | 89.83
leaf_fragmentation  | 0
```

Our index is pretty dense (89%). This is a good sign. The default FILLFACTOR setting for an index is 90%, so a value close to 90% indicates that the index is very good.

Sometimes, you don't want to check a single table; instead, you want to check all of them or just all of the tables in a schema. How can this be achieved? Normally, the list of objects you want to process is in the FROM clause. However, in my example, the function is already in the FROM clause, so how can we make PostgreSQL loop over a list of tables? The answer is to use a LATERAL join.

Keep in mind that `pgstattuple` has to read the entire object. If our database is large, it can take quite a long time to process. Therefore, it can be a good idea to store the results of the query we have just seen so that we can inspect them thoroughly without having to rerun the query again and again.

Fuzzy searching with pg_trgm

The `pg_trgm` module allows you to perform fuzzy searching. This module was discussed in Chapter 3, *Making Use of Indexes*.

Connecting to remote servers using postgres_fdw

Data is not always in just one location. More often than not, data is spread all over the infrastructure, and it may be that data residing in various places has to be integrated.

The solution to this problem is a foreign data wrapper, as defined by the SQL/MED standard.

In this section, the postgres_fdw extension will be discussed. It is a module that allows us to dynamically fetch data from a PostgreSQL data source. The first thing we need to do is deploy the foreign data wrapper:

```
test=# \h CREATE FOREIGN DATA WRAPPER
Command: CREATE FOREIGN DATA WRAPPER
Description: define a new foreign-data wrapper
Syntax:
CREATE FOREIGN DATA WRAPPER name
    [ HANDLER handler_function | NO HANDLER ]
    [ VALIDATOR validator_function | NO VALIDATOR ]
    OPTIONS ( option 'value' [, ... ] ) ]
```

Fortunately, the CREATE FOREIGN DATA WRAPPER command is hidden inside an extension; it can easily be installed using the normal process, as follows:

```
test=# CREATE EXTENSION postgres_fdw;
CREATE EXTENSION
```

Now, a virtual server has to be defined. It will point to the other host and tell PostgreSQL where to get the data. At the end of the data, PostgreSQL has to build a complete connect string—the server data is the first thing PostgreSQL has to know about. User information will be added later on. The server will only contain the host, port, and so on. Following is the syntax of CREATE SERVER:

```
test=# \h CREATE SERVER
Command:     CREATE SERVER
Description: define a new foreign server
Syntax:
CREATE SERVER [ IF NOT EXISTS ] server_name [ TYPE 'server_type' ] [
VERSION 'server_version' ]
    FOREIGN DATA WRAPPER fdw_name
    [ OPTIONS ( option 'value' [, ... ] ) ]

URL: https://www.postgresql.org/docs/12/sql-createserver.html
```

To understand how this works, we will create a second database on the same host and create a server:

```
[hs@zenbook~]$ createdb customer
[hs@zenbook~]$ psql customer
customer=# CREATE TABLE t_customer (id int, name text);
CREATE TABLE
customer=# CREATE TABLE t_company (
    country        text,
    name           text,
    active         text
);
CREATE TABLE

customer=# \d
List of relations
 Schema    | Name        | Type    | Owner
-----------+-------------+---------+-------
 public    | t_company   | table   |
 hs public | t_customer  | table   | hs

(2 rows)
```

Now, the server should be added to the standard test database:

```
test=# CREATE SERVER customer_server
        FOREIGN DATA WRAPPER postgres_fdw
        OPTIONS (host 'localhost', dbname 'customer', port '5432');
CREATE SERVER
```

Note that all the important information is stored as an OPTIONS clause. This is somewhat important because it gives users a lot of flexibility. There are many different foreign data wrappers, and each of them will need different options.

Once the server has been defined, it is time to map users. If we connect from one server to the other, we may not have the same user in both locations. Therefore, foreign data wrappers require people to define the actual user mapping:

```
test=# \h CREATE USER MAPPING
Command:      CREATE USER MAPPING
Description: define a new mapping of a user to a foreign server
Syntax:
CREATE USER MAPPING [ IF NOT EXISTS ] FOR { user_name | USER | CURRENT_USER
| PUBLIC }
    SERVER server_name
    [ OPTIONS ( option 'value' [ , ... ] ) ]
URL: https://www.postgresql.org/docs/12/sql-createusermapping.html
```

The syntax is pretty simple and can be used easily:

```
test=# CREATE USER MAPPING
        FOR CURRENT_USER SERVER customer_server
        OPTIONS (user 'hs', password 'abc');
CREATE USER MAPPING
```

Again, all of the important information is hidden in the OPTIONS clause. Depending on the type of foreign data wrapper, the list of options will differ. Note that we have to use proper user data here, which will work for our setup. In this case, we will simply use local users.

Once the infrastructure is in place, we can create foreign tables. The syntax to create a foreign table is pretty similar to how we would create a normal local table. All of the columns have to be listed, including their data types:

```
test=# CREATE FOREIGN TABLE f_customer (id int, name text)
        SERVER customer_server
        OPTIONS (schema_name 'public', table_name 't_customer');
CREATE FOREIGN TABLE
```

All of the columns are listed, just like in the case of a normal CREATE TABLE clause. The special thing here is that the foreign table points to a table on the remote side. The name of the schema and the name of the table have to be specified in the OPTIONS clause.

Once it has been created, the table can be used:

```
test=# SELECT * FROM f_customer ;
 id  | name
-----+------
(0 rows)
```

To check what PostgreSQL does internally, it is a good idea to run the EXPLAIN clause with the analyze parameter. It will reveal some information about what's really going on in the server:

```
test=# EXPLAIN (analyze true, verbose true)
        SELECT * FROM f_customer ;
                            QUERY PLAN
----------------------------------------------------------------------
 Foreign Scan on public.f_customer
     (cost=100.00..150.95 rows=1365 width=36)
     (actual time=0.221..0.221 rows=0 loops=1)
   Output: id, name
   Remote SQL: SELECT id, name FROM public.t_customer
 Planning time: 0.067 ms
 Execution time: 0.451 ms
(5 rows)
```

The important part here is Remote SQL. The foreign data wrapper will send a query to the other side and fetch as little data as possible, since as many restrictions as possible are executed on the remote side to ensure that not much data is processed locally. Filter conditions, joins, and even aggregates can be performed remotely (as of PostgreSQL 10.0).

While the CREATE FOREIGN TABLE clause is surely a nice thing to use, it can be quite cumbersome to list all of those columns over and over again.

The solution to this problem is the IMPORT clause. This allows us to quickly and easily import entire schemas onto a local database, as well as create foreign tables:

```
test=# \h IMPORT
Command:     IMPORT FOREIGN SCHEMA
Description: import table definitions from a foreign server
Syntax:
IMPORT FOREIGN SCHEMA remote_schema
    [ { LIMIT TO | EXCEPT } ( table_name [, ...] ) ]
    FROM SERVER server_name
    INTO local_schema
    [ OPTIONS ( option 'value' [, ... ] ) ]

URL: https://www.postgresql.org/docs/12/sql-importforeignschema.html
```

IMPORT allows us to link large sets of tables easily. It also reduces the chances of typos and mistakes since all of the information is fetched directly from the remote data source.

The following is how it works:

```
test=# IMPORT FOREIGN SCHEMA public
        FROM SERVER customer_server INTO public;
IMPORT FOREIGN SCHEMA
```

In this case, all of the tables that were created previously in the public schema are linked directly. As we can see, all of the remote tables are now available:

```
test=# \det
List of foreign tables
 Schema  | Table      | Server
---------+------------+-----------------
 public  | f_customer | customer_server
 public  | t_company  | customer_server
 public  | t_customer | customer_server

(3 rows)
```

Handling mistakes and typos

Creating foreign tables isn't really hard—however, it sometimes happens that people make mistakes, or maybe the passwords that have been used simply change. To handle such issues, PostgreSQL offers two commands: ALTER SERVER and ALTER USER MAPPING.

ALTER SERVER allows you to modify a server:

```
test=# \h ALTER SERVER
Command:   ALTER SERVER
Description: change the definition of a foreign server
Syntax:
ALTER SERVER name [ VERSION 'new_version' ]
    [ OPTIONS ( [ ADD | SET | DROP ] option ['value'] [, ... ] ) ]
ALTER SERVER name OWNER TO { new_owner | CURRENT_USER | SESSION_USER }
ALTER SERVER name RENAME TO new_name

URL: https://www.postgresql.org/docs/12/sql-alterserver.html
```

We can use this command to add and remove options for a specific server, which is a good thing if we have forgotten something.

To modify user information, we can alter the user mapping as well:

```
test=# \h ALTER USER MAPPING
Command:    ALTER USER MAPPING
Description: change the definition of a user mapping
Syntax:
ALTER USER MAPPING FOR { user_name | USER | CURRENT_USER | SESSION_USER |
PUBLIC }
    SERVER server_name
      OPTIONS ( [ ADD | SET | DROP ] option ['value'] [, ... ] )

URL: https://www.postgresql.org/docs/12/sql-alterusermapping.html
```

The SQL/MED interface is regularly improved and, at the time of writing, features are being added. In the future, even more optimizations will make it to the core, making the SQL/MED interface a good choice for improving scalability.

Other useful extensions

The extensions that we have described so far are all part of the PostgreSQL `contrib` package, which is shipped as part of the PostgreSQL source code. However, the packages that we've looked at here aren't the only ones that are available in the PostgreSQL community. There are many more packages that allow us to do all kinds of things.

Unfortunately, this chapter is too short to dig into everything that is currently out there. The number of modules is growing day by day, and it is impossible to cover them all. Therefore, I only want to point out the ones I find the most important.

PostGIS (`http://postgis.net/`) is the **geographical information systems (GIS)** database interface in the open source world. It has been adopted around the Globe and is a de facto standard in the relational open source database world. It is a professional and extremely powerful solution.

If you are looking for geospatial routing, `pgRouting` is what you might be looking for. It offers various algorithms that you can use to find the best connections between locations and works on top of PostgreSQL.

In this chapter, we have already learned about the `postgres_fdw` extension, which allows us to connect to some other PostgreSQL databases. There are many more foreign data wrappers around. One of the most famous and most professional ones is the `oracle_fdw` extension. It allows you to integrate with Oracle and fetch data over the wire, which can be done with the `postgres_fdw` extension.

In some cases, you may also be interested in testing the stability of your infrastructure with `pg_crash` (`https://github.com/cybertec-postgresql/pg_crash`). The idea is to have a module that constantly crashes your database. The `pg_crash` module is an excellent choice for testing and debugging connection pools and allows you to reconnect to a failing database. The `pg_crash` module will periodically run amok and kill database sessions or corrupt memory. It is ideal for long-term testing.

Summary

In this chapter, we learned about some of the most promising modules that are shipped with the PostgreSQL standard distribution. These modules are pretty diverse and offer everything from database connectivity to case-insensitive text and modules so that we can inspect the server.

Now that we have dealt with extensions, in the next chapter we will shift our attention to migration. There, we will learn how we can move to PostgreSQL in the most simplistic way.

Troubleshooting PostgreSQL 12

In Chapter 11, *Deciding on Useful Extensions*, we learned about some useful extensions that are widely adopted and that can give your deployment a real boost. Following this up, you will now be introduced to PostgreSQL troubleshooting. The idea is to give you a systematic approach to inspecting and fixing your system.

In this chapter, the following topics will be covered:

- Approaching an unknown database
- Inspecting pg_stat_activity
- Checking for slow queries
- Inspecting the log
- Checking for missing indexes
- Checking for memory and I/O
- Understanding noteworthy error scenarios

Keep in mind that many things can go wrong, so it is important to professionally monitor the database.

Approaching an unknown database

If you happen to administer a large-scale system, you might not know what the system is actually doing. Managing hundreds of systems implies that you won't know what is going on with each of them.

The most important thing when it comes to troubleshooting boils down to a single word: **data**. If there is not enough data, there is no way to fix things. Therefore, the first step to troubleshooting is to always set up a monitoring tool, such as pgwatch2 (available at https://www.cybertec-postgresql.com/en/products/pgwatch2/), which gives you some insights into your database server.

Once the reporting tool has told you about a situation that is worth checking, it means it has been proven useful to approach the system in an organized way.

Inspecting pg_stat_activity

The first thing that will be checked is `pg_stat_statements`. Now answer the following questions:

- How many concurrent queries are currently being executed on your system?
- Do you see similar types of queries showing up in the query column all the time?
- Do you see queries that have been running for a long time?
- Are there any locks that have not been granted?
- Do you see connections from suspicious hosts?

The `pg_stat_activity` view should always be checked first, because it will give us an idea of what is happening on the system. Of course, graphical monitoring is supposed to give you a first impression of the system. However, at the end of the day, it really boils down to the queries that are actually running on the server. Therefore, a good overview of the system that's provided by `pg_stat_activity` is more than vital for tracking down issues.

To make it easier for you, I have compiled a couple of queries that I find useful for spotting problems as quickly as possible.

Querying pg_stat_activity

The following query shows you how many queries are currently being executed on your database:

```
test=# SELECT datname,
         count(*) AS open,
         count(*) FILTER (WHERE state = 'active') AS active,
         count(*) FILTER (WHERE state = 'idle') AS idle,
         count(*) FILTER (WHERE state = 'idle in transaction')
                  AS idle_in_trans
FROM pg_stat_activity
WHERE backend_type = 'client backend'
GROUP BY ROLLUP(1);
 datname | open | active | idle | idle_in_trans
---------+------+--------+------+---------------
 test    | 2    | 1      | 0    | 1
```

```
        | 2    | 1        | 0    | 1
(2 rows)
```

To show as much information as possible on the same screen, partial aggregates are used. We can see active, idle, and idle-in-transaction queries. If we can see a high number of idle-in-transaction queries, it is definitely important to dig deeper, in order to figure out how long those transactions have been kept open:

```
test=# SELECT pid, xact_start, now() - xact_start AS duration
   FROM pg_stat_activity
   WHERE state LIKE '%transaction%'
   ORDER BY 3 DESC;
  pid   | xact_start                    | duration
--------+-------------------------------+-----------------
  19758 | 2017-11-26 20:27:08.168554+01 | 22:12:10.194363

(1 row)
```

The transaction in the preceding listing has been open for more than 22 hours. The main question now is: how can a transaction be open for that long? In most applications, a transaction that takes so long is highly suspicious, and potentially highly dangerous. Where does the danger come from? As we learned earlier in this book, the VACUUM command can only clean up dead rows if no transaction can see it anymore. Now, if a transaction stays open for hours or even days, the VACUUM command cannot produce useful results, which will lead to table bloat.

It is therefore highly recommended to ensure that long transactions are monitored or killed, in case they become *too* long. From version 9.6 onward, PostgreSQL has a feature called **snapshot too old**, which allows us to terminate long transactions if snapshots are around for too long.

It is also a good idea to check whether there are any long-running queries going on:

```
test=# SELECT now() - query_start AS duration, datname, query
      FROM pg_stat_activity
      WHERE state = 'active'
      ORDER BY 1 DESC;
  duration         | datname | query
-------------------+---------+---------------------------
  00:00:38.814526  | dev     | SELECT pg_sleep(10000);
  00:00:00         | test    | SELECT now() - query_start AS duration,
                                     datname, query
                               FROM  pg_stat_activity
                               WHERE state = 'active'
                               ORDER BY 1 DESC;
(2 rows)
```

In this case, all active queries are taken, and the statements calculate how long each query has already been active. Often, we see similar queries coming out on top, which can give us some valuable clues about what is happening on our system.

Treating Hibernate statements

Many **object-relational mappings (ORM)**, such as Hibernate, generate insanely long SQL statements. The trouble is this: pg_stat_activity will only store the first 1024 bytes of the query in the system view. The rest is truncated. In the case of a long query generated by an ORM such as Hibernate, the query is cut off before the interesting parts (the FROM clause, among others) actually start.

The solution to this problem is to set a config parameter in the postgresql.conf file:

```
test=# SHOW track_activity_query_size;
 track_activity_query_size
---------------------------
 1024
(1 row)
```

If we increase this parameter to a reasonably high value (maybe 32,768) and restart PostgreSQL, we will then be able to see much longer queries, and be able to detect issues more easily.

Figuring out where queries come from

When inspecting pg_stat_activity, there are some fields that will tell us where a query comes from:

```
client_addr     | inet    |
client_hostname | text    |
client_port     | integer |
```

These fields will contain IP addresses and hostnames (if configured). But what happens if every application sends their requests from the very same IP because, for example, all of the applications reside on the same application server? It will be very hard for us to see which application generated a certain query.

The solution to this problem is to ask the developers to set an `application_name` variable:

```
test=# SHOW application_name ;
 application_name
-------------------
 psql
(1 row)

test=# SET application_name TO 'some_name';
SET

test=# SHOW application_name ;
 application_name
-------------------
 some_name
(1 row)
```

If people are cooperative, the `application_name` variable will show up in the system view and make it a lot easier to see where a query comes from. The `application_name` variable can also be set as part of the connect string.

Checking for slow queries

After inspecting `pg_stat_activity`, it makes sense to take a look at slow, time-consuming queries. Basically, there are two ways to approach this problem:

- Look for individual slow queries in the log.
- Look for types of queries that take too much time.

Finding single, slow queries is the classic approach to performance tuning. By setting the `log_min_duration_statement` variable to a desired threshold, PostgreSQL will start to write a log line for each query that exceeds this threshold. By default, the slow-query log is off, as follows:

```
test=# SHOW log_min_duration_statement;
 log_min_duration_statement
----------------------------
                         -1
(1 row)
```

However, setting this variable to a reasonably good value makes perfect sense. Depending on your workload, the desired time might, of course, vary.

In many cases, the desired value might differ from database to database. Therefore, it is also possible to use the variable in a more fine-grained way:

```
test=# ALTER DATABASE test SET log_min_duration_statement TO 10000;
ALTER DATABASE
```

Setting the parameter for only a certain database makes perfect sense if your databases face different workloads.

When using the slow-query log, it is important to consider one important factor—many smaller queries might cause more load than just a handful of slow-running queries. Of course, it always makes sense to be aware of individual slow queries, but sometimes, those queries are not the problem.

Consider the following example: on your system, 1 million queries, each taking 500 milliseconds each, are executed, along with some analytical queries that are running for a couple of milliseconds each. Clearly, the real problem will never show up in the slow-query log, while every data export, every index creation, and every bulk load (which cannot be avoided in most cases anyway) will spam the log and point us in the wrong direction.

My personal recommendation, therefore, is to use a slow-query log, but use it carefully, and with caution. Most importantly, though, be aware of what we are really measuring.

The better approach, in my opinion, is to work more intensively with the `pg_stat_statements` view. It will offer aggregated information, and not just information about single queries. The `pg_stat_statements` view was discussed earlier in this book. However, the importance of the module cannot be stressed enough.

Inspecting individual queries

Sometimes, slow queries are identified, but we still don't have a clue about what is really going on. The next step is, of course, to inspect the execution plan of the query and see what happens. Identifying those key operations in the plan that are responsible for bad runtime is fairly simple. Try and use the following checklist:

- Try and see where it is in the plan that time starts to skyrocket.
- Check for missing indexes (one of the main reasons for bad performance).
- Use the EXPLAIN clause (buffers `true`, analyze `true`, and so on) to see if your query uses too many buffers.
- Turn on the `track_io_timing` parameter to figure out whether there is an I/O problem or a CPU problem (explicitly check if there is random I/O going on).
- Look for wrong estimates and try and fix them.

- Look for stored procedures that are executed too frequently.
- Try to figure out whether some of them can be marked as STABLE or IMMUTABLE, provided this is possible.

Note that pg_stat_statements does not account for parse time, so if your queries are very long (such as a query string), then pg_stat_statements might be slightly misleading.

Digging deeper with perf

In most cases, working through this tiny checklist will help you track down the majority of problems in a pretty fast and efficient way. However, even the information that's been extracted from the database engine is sometimes not enough.

The perf tool is an analysis tool for Linux that allows you to directly see which C functions are causing problems on your system. Usually, perf is not installed by default, so it is recommended that you install it. To use perf on your server, just log in to a root and run the following command:

```
perf top
```

The screen will refresh itself every couple of seconds, and you will have a chance to see what is going on live. The following listing shows you what a standard, read-only benchmark might look like:

```
Samples: 164K of event 'cycles:ppp', Event count (approx.): 109789128766
Overhead  Shared Object     Symbol
   3.10%  postgres          [.] AllocSetAlloc
   1.99%  postgres          [.] SearchCatCache
   1.51%  postgres          [.] base_yyparse
   1.42%  postgres          [.] hash_search_with_hash_value
   1.27%  libc-2.22.so      [.] vfprintf
   1.13%  libc-2.22.so      [.] _int_malloc
   0.87%  postgres          [.] palloc
   0.74%  postgres          [.] MemoryContextAllocZeroAligned
   0.66%  libc-2.22.so      [.] __strcmp_sse2_unaligned
   0.66%  [kernel]          [k] _raw_spin_lock_irqsave
   0.66%  postgres          [.] _bt_compare
   0.63%  [kernel]          [k] __fget_light
   0.62%  libc-2.22.so      [.] strlen
```

You can see that no single function takes too much CPU time in our sample, which tells us that the system is just fine.

However, this may not always be the case. There is a problem called **spinlock contention** that is quite common. Spinlocks are used by the PostgreSQL core to synchronize things such as buffer access. A spinlock is a feature provided by modern CPUs to avoid operating system interaction for small operations (such as incrementing a number). If you think you may be facing spinlock contention, the symptoms are as follows:

- Really high CPU load.
- Incredibly low throughput (queries that usually take milliseconds suddenly take seconds).
- I/O is usually low, because the CPU is busy trading locks.

In many cases, spinlock contention happens suddenly. Your system is just fine, and all of a sudden, the load goes up and the throughput drops like a stone. The `perf top` command will reveal that most of this time is spent in a `C` function called `s_lock`. If this is the case, you should try and do the following:

```
huge_pages = try                    # on, off, or try
```

Change `huge_pages` from `try` to `off`. It can be a good idea to turn off huge pages altogether at the operating system level. In general, it seems that some kernels are more prone to producing these kinds of problems than others. The Red Hat 2.6.32 series seems to be especially bad (note that I have used the word *seems* here).

The `perf` tool is also interesting if you are using PostGIS. If the top functions in the list are all GIS-related (as in, from some underlying library), you know that the problem is most likely not coming from bad PostgreSQL tuning, but is simply related to expensive operations that take time to complete.

Inspecting the log

If your system smells trouble, it makes sense to inspect the log to see what is going on. The important point is this: not all log entries are created equally. PostgreSQL has a hierarchy of log entries that range from DEBUG to PANIC.

For the administrator, the following three error levels are of great importance:

- ERROR
- FATAL
- PANIC

ERROR is used for problems such as syntax errors, permission-related problems, and more. Your log will always contain error messages. The critical factor is this—how often does a certain type of error show up? Producing millions of syntax errors is certainly not an ideal strategy for running a database server.

FATAL is scarier than ERROR; you will see messages such as could not allocate memory for shared memory name or unexpected walreceiver state. In other words, these error messages are already really scary, and will tell you that things are going wrong.

Finally, there is PANIC. If you hit this kind of message, you know that something is really, really wrong. Classic examples of PANIC are lock table being corrupted, or too many semaphores being created. These will result in a shutdown.

Checking for missing indexes

Once we are done with the first three steps, it is important to take a look at performance in general. As I have kept stating throughout this book, missing indexes are fully responsible for super bad performances. So, whenever we face a slow system, it is recommended that we check for missing indexes and deploy whatever is needed.

Usually, customers ask us to optimize the RAID level, tune the kernel, or some other fancy stuff. In reality, these complicated requests often boil down to a handful of missing indexes. By my judgement, it always makes sense to spend some extra time just checking whether all of the desired indexes are there or not. Checking for missing indexes is neither hard nor time-consuming, so it should be done all of the time, regardless of the kind of performance problem that you are facing.

Here is my favorite query to get an impression of where an index might be missing:

```
SELECT schemaname, relname, seq_scan, seq_tup_read,
        idx_scan, seq_tup_read / seq_scan AS avg
FROM   pg_stat_user_tables
WHERE  seq_scan > 0
ORDER BY seq_tup_read DESC
LIMIT 20;
```

Try and find large tables (with a high avg value) that are scanned often. These tables will typically come on top.

Checking for memory and I/O

Once we are done finding missing indexes, we can inspect the memory and I/O. To figure out what is going on, it makes sense to activate `track_io_timing`. If it is on, PostgreSQL will collect information about disk wait time and present it to you.

Often, the main question asked by a customer is: *if we add more disks, is it going to be faster?* It is possible to guess what will happen, but in general, measuring is the better and more useful strategy. Enabling `track_io_timing` will help you gather the data to really figure this out.

PostgreSQL exposes disk wait time in various ways. One way to inspect things is to take a look at `pg_stat_database`:

```
test=# \d pg_stat_database
      View "pg_catalog.pg_stat_database"
  Column         | Type             | Modifiers
-----------------+------------------+------------
  datid          | oid              |
  datname        | name             |
  . . .
  conflicts      | bigint           |
  temp_files     | bigint           |
  temp_bytes     | bigint           |
  . . .
  blk_read_time  | double precision |
  blk_write_time | double precision |
```

Note that there are two fields toward the end: `blk_read_time` and `blk_write_time`. They will tell us about the amount of time PostgreSQL has spent waiting for the operating system to respond. Note that we are not really measuring disk wait time here, but rather the time the operating system needs to return data.

If the operating system produces cache hits, this time will be fairly low. If the operating system has to do really nasty random I/O, we will see that a single block can even take a couple of milliseconds.

In many cases, high `blk_read_time` and `blk_write_time` occurs when `temp_files` and `temp_bytes` show high numbers. Also, in many cases, this points to a bad `work_mem` setting or a bad `maintenance_work_mem` setting. Remember this: if PostgreSQL cannot do things in memory, it has to spill to the disk. You can use the `temp_files` operation to detect this. Whenever there are `temp_files`, there is the chance of a nasty disk wait time.

While a global view on a per-database level makes sense, it does not yield in-depth information about the real source of trouble. Often, only a few queries are to blame for bad performance. The way to spot these is to use pg_stat_statements:

```
test=# \d pg_stat_statements
  View "public.pg_stat_statements"
  Column              | Type              | Modifiers
----------------------+-------------------+-----------
  . . .
  query               | text              |
  calls               | bigint            |
  total_time          | double precision  |
  . . .
  temp_blks_read      | bigint            |
  temp_blks_written   | bigint            |
  blk_read_time       | double precision  |
  blk_write_time      | double precision  |
```

You will be able to see, on a per-query-basis, whether there is disk wait or not. The important part is the blk_time value in combination with total_time. The ratio is what counts. In general, a query that shows more than 30% of disk wait can be seen as heavily I/O-bound.

Once we are done checking the PostgreSQL system tables, it makes sense to inspect what the vmstat command on Linux tells us. Alternatively, we can use the iostat command:

```
[hs@zenbook ~]$ vmstat 2
procs -----------memory---------- ---swap-- -----io---- -system-- ------
cpu-----
 r b swpd free buff cache si so bi bo in cs us sy id wa st
 0 0 367088 199488 96 2320388 0 2 83 96 106 156 16 6 78 0 0
 0 0 367088 198140 96 2320504 0 0 0 10 595 2624 3 1 96 0 0
 0 0 367088 191448 96 2320964 0 0 0 8 920 2957 8 2 90 0 0
```

When doing database work, we should focus our attention on three fields: bi, bo, and wa. The bi field tells us about the number of blocks read; 1,000 is the equivalent to 1 MBps. The bo field is about blocks out. It tells us about the amount of data written to the disk. In a way, bi and bo are the raw throughput. I would not consider a number to be harmful. What is a problem is high wa value. Low values for the bi and bo fields, combined with a high wa value, tells us about a potential disk bottleneck, which is most likely related to a lot of random I/O taking place on your system. The higher the wa value, the slower your queries, because you are waiting on the disk to respond.

Good raw throughput is a good thing, but sometimes, it can also point to a problem. If high throughput is needed on an **online transaction processing (OLTP)** system, it can tell you that there is not enough RAM to cache things, or that indexes are missing and PostgreSQL has to read too much data. Keep in mind that things are interconnected, and data should not be seen as isolated.

Understanding noteworthy error scenarios

After going through the basic guidelines to hunt down the most common issues that you will face in your database, the upcoming sections will discuss some of the most common error scenarios that occur in the PostgreSQL world.

Facing clog corruption

PostgreSQL has a thing called the commit log (now called `pg_xact`; it was formally known as `pg_clog`). It tracks the state of every transaction on the system, and helps PostgreSQL determine whether a row can be seen or not. In general, a transaction can be in four states:

```
#define  TRANSACTION_STATUS_IN_PROGRESS    0x00
#define  TRANSACTION_STATUS_COMMITTED       0x01
#define  TRANSACTION_STATUS_ABORTED         0x02
#define  TRANSACTION_STATUS_SUB_COMMITTED   0x03
```

The clog has a separate directory in the PostgreSQL database instance (`pg_xact`).

In the past, people have reported something called **clog corruption**, which can be caused by faulty disks or bugs in PostgreSQL that have been fixed over the years. A corrupted commit log is a pretty nasty thing to have, because all of our data is there, but PostgreSQL does not know whether things are valid or not anymore. Corruption in this area is nothing short of a total disaster.

How does the administrator figure out that the commit log is broken? Here is what we normally see:

```
ERROR: could not access status of transaction 118831
```

If PostgreSQL cannot access the status of a transaction, issues will occur. The main question is—how can this be fixed? To put it to you straight, there is no way to really fix the problem—we can only try and rescue as much data as possible.

As we've stated already, the commit log keeps two bits per transaction. This means that we have four transactions per byte, leaving us with 32,768 transactions per block. Once we have figured out which block it is, we can fake the transaction log:

```
dd if=/dev/zero of=<data directory location>/pg_clog/0001
    bs=256K count=1
```

We can use dd to fake the transaction log and set the commit status to the desired value. The core question is really—which transaction state should be used? The answer is that any state is actually wrong, because we really don't know how those transactions ended.

However, usually, it is a good idea to just set them to committed in order to lose less data. It really depends on our workload and our data, when deciding what is less disruptive.

When we have to use this technique, we should fake as little clog as is necessary. Remember, we are essentially faking the commit status, which is not a nice thing to do to a database engine.

Once we are done faking the clog, we should create a backup as fast as we can, and recreate the database instance from scratch. The system we are working with is not very trustworthy anymore, so we should try and extract data as fast as we can. Keep this in mind: the data we are about to extract could be contradictory and wrong, so we will make sure that some quality checks are imposed on whatever we are able to rescue from our database server.

Understanding checkpoint messages

Checkpoints are essential to data integrity, as well as performance. The further the checkpoints are apart, the better the performance usually is. In PostgreSQL, the default configuration is usually fairly conservative, and checkpoints are therefore comparatively fast. If a lot of data is changed in the database core at the same time, it can happen that PostgreSQL tells us that it considers checkpoints to be too frequent. The LOG file will show the following entries:

```
LOG: checkpoints are occurring too frequently (2 seconds apart)
LOG: checkpoints are occurring too frequently (3 seconds apart)
```

During heavy writing due to dump/restore or due to some other large operation, PostgreSQL might notice that the configuration parameters are too low. A message is sent to the LOG file to tell us exactly that.

If we see this kind of message, it is strongly recommended, for performance reasons, that we increase the checkpoint distances by increasing the `max_wal_size` parameter dramatically (in older versions, the setting was called `checkpoint_segments`). In recent versions of PostgreSQL, the default configuration is already a lot better than it used to be. However, writing data too frequently can still happen easily.

When we see a message about checkpoints, there is one thing that we have to keep in mind. Checkpointing too frequently is not dangerous at all—it just happens to lead to bad performance. Writing is simply a lot slower than it could be, but our data is not in danger. Increasing the distance between two checkpoints sufficiently will make the error go away, and it will speed up our database instance at the same time.

Managing corrupted data pages

PostgreSQL is a very stable database system. It protects data as much as possible, and it has proven its worth over the years. However, PostgreSQL relies on solid hardware and a filesystem that is working properly . If storage breaks, so will PostgreSQL—there isn't much that we can do about it, apart from adding replicas to make things more fail-safe.

Once in a while, it happens that the filesystem or the disk fails. But in many cases, the entire thing will not go south; just a couple of blocks become corrupted for whatever reason. Recently, we have seen this happening in virtual environments. Some virtual machines don't flush to the disk by default, which means that PostgreSQL cannot rely on things being written to the disk. This kind of behavior can lead to random problems that are hard to predict.

When a block cannot be read anymore, you might face an error message such as the following:

```
"could not read block %u in file "%s": %m"
```

The query that you are about to run will error out and stop working. Fortunately, PostgreSQL has a means of dealing with these things:

```
test=# SET zero_damaged_pages TO on;
SET
test=# SHOW zero_damaged_pages;
 zero_damaged_pages
--------------------
 on
(1 row)
```

The `zero_damaged_pages` variable is a `config` variable that allows us to deal with broken pages. Instead of throwing an error, PostgreSQL will take the block and simply fill it with zeros.

Note that this will definitely lead to data loss. But remember, the data was broken or lost before anyway, so this is simply a way to deal with the corruption that is caused by bad things happening in our storage system.

I would advise everybody to handle the `zero_damaged_pages` variable with care—be aware of what you are doing when you call it.

Careless connection management

In PostgreSQL, every database connection is a separate process. All of those processes are synchronized using shared memory (technically, in most cases, it is mapped memory, but for this example, this makes no difference). This shared memory contains the I/O cache, the list of active database connections, locks, and other vital things that make the system function properly.

When a connection is closed, it will remove all the relevant entries from the shared memory and leave the system in a sane state. However, what happens when a database connection simply crashes, for whatever reason?

The postmaster (the main process) will detect that one of the child processes is missing. Then, all of the other connections will be terminated and a roll-forward process will be initialized. Why is this necessary? When a process crashes, it might very well happen that the shared memory area is edited by the process. In other words, a crashing process might leave the shared memory in a corrupted state. Therefore, the postmaster reacts and kicks everybody out before the corruption can spread through the system. All the memory is cleaned, and everybody has to reconnect.

From an end user point of view, this feels like PostgreSQL has crashed and restarted, which is not the case. Since a process cannot react on its own crash (segmentation fault) or on some other signals, cleaning out everything is absolutely essential in order to protect your data.

The same happens if you use the `kill -9` command on a database connection. The connection cannot catch the signal (-9 cannot be caught by definition), and therefore the postmaster has to react again.

Fighting table bloat

Table bloat is one of the most important issues when dealing with PostgreSQL. When we are facing bad performance, it is always a good idea to figure out whether there are objects that need a lot more space than they are supposed to have.

How can we figure out where table bloat is happening? Check out the `pg_stat_user_tables` view:

```
test=# \d pg_stat_user_tables
   View "pg_catalog.pg_stat_user_tables"
   Column          |  Type           | Modifiers
-------------------+-----------------+-----------
   relid           | oid             |
   schemaname      | name            |
   relname         | name            |
   ...
   n_live_tup      | bigint          |
   n_dead_tup      | bigint          |
```

The `n_live_tup` and `n_dead_tup` fields give us an impression of what is going on, and we can also use `pgstattuple`.

What can we do if there is serious table bloat? The first option is to run the `VACUUM FULL` command. The trouble is that the `VACUUM FULL` clause needs a table lock. On a large table, this can be a real problem, because users cannot write to the table while it is being rewritten.

 If you are using at least PostgreSQL 9.6, you can use a tool called `pg_squeeze`. It organizes a table behind the scenes without blocking (`https://www.cybertec-postgresql.com/en/products/pg_squeeze/`). This is especially useful if you are reorganizing a very large table.

Summary

In this chapter, we have learned to how systematically approach a database system and detect the most common issues that people face with PostgreSQL. We learned about some important system tables, as well as some other important factors that can determine whether we will succeed or fail.

In the final chapter of this book, we will focus our attention on migrating to PostgreSQL. If you are using Oracle or some other database system, you might want to check out PostgreSQL. In Chapter 13, *Migrating to PostgreSQL*, we'll discuss everything that is involved with this.

Questions

1. Why do databases not administrate themselves?
2. Does PostgreSQL face corruption often?
3. Does PostgreSQL need constant care?

Migrating to PostgreSQL 13

In `Chapter 12`, *Troubleshooting PostgreSQL*, we learned how to approach the most common issues related to PostgreSQL troubleshooting. The important thing is to have a systematic approach to tracking down problems, which is exactly what is provided here.

The final chapter of this book is about moving from other databases to PostgreSQL. Many of you may still be suffering from the pain caused by commercial database license costs. I want to give all of you out there a way out and show you how data can be moved from some proprietary system to PostgreSQL. Moving to PostgreSQL makes sense not only from a financial point of view, but also makes sense if you are looking for more advanced features and more flexibility. PostgreSQL has so much to offer, and at the time of writing, new features are being added daily. The same applies to the number of tools that are available to migrate to PostgreSQL. Things are getting better and better, and developers are publishing more and better tools all the time.

The following topics will be covered in this chapter:

- Migrating SQL statements to PostgreSQL
- Moving from Oracle to PostgreSQL

By the end of this chapter, you should be able to move a basic database from some other system to PostgreSQL.

Migrating SQL statements to PostgreSQL

When moving from a database to PostgreSQL, it makes sense to take a look and figure out which database engine provides which kind of functionality. Moving the data and the structure itself is usually fairly easy. However, rewriting SQL might not be. Therefore, I decided to include a section that explicitly focuses on various advanced features of SQL and their availability in today's database engines.

Using lateral joins

In SQL, a lateral join can basically be seen as some sort of loop. This allows us to parameterize a join and execute everything inside the LATERAL clause more than once. Here is a simple example of this:

```
test=# SELECT *
   FROM generate_series(1, 4) AS x,
       LATERAL (SELECT array_agg(y)
                  FROM generate_series(1, x) AS y
              ) AS z;
 x  | array_agg
----+-----------
 1  | {1}
 2  | {1,2}
 3  | {1,2,3}
 4  | {1,2,3,4}
(4 rows)
```

The LATERAL clause will be called for each x. To the end user, it is basically some sort of loop.

Supporting lateral joins

One important SQL feature is lateral joins. The following list shows which engines support lateral joins and which don't:

- **MariaDB**: Not supported
- **MySQL**: Not supported
- **PostgreSQL**: Supported since PostgreSQL 9.3
- **SQLite**: Not supported
- **Db2 LUW**: Supported since version 9.1 (2005)
- **Oracle**: Supported since 12c
- **Microsoft SQL Server**: Supported since 2005 but using a different syntax

Using grouping sets

Grouping sets are very useful if we want to run more than one aggregate at the same time. Using grouping sets can speed up aggregation because we don't have to process the data more than once.

Here is an example of this:

```
test=# SELECT x % 2, array_agg(x)
        FROM generate_series(1, 4) AS x
        GROUP BY ROLLUP (1);
 ?column? | array_agg
----------+-----------
        0 | {2,4}
        1 | {1,3}
          | {2,4,1,3}
(3 rows)
```

PostgreSQL offers more than just the ROLLUP clause. The CUBE and GROUPING SETS clauses are also supported.

Supporting grouping sets

Grouping sets are essential for generating more than just one aggregation in a single query. The following list shows which engines support grouping sets and which don't:

- **MariaDB**: Only the ROLLUP clause has been supported since 5.1 (incomplete support).
- **MySQL**: Only the ROLLUP clause has been supported since 5.0 (incomplete support).
- **PostgreSQL**: Supported since PostgreSQL 9.5.
- **SQLite**: Not supported.
- **Db2 LUW**: Supported since at least 1999.
- **Oracle**: Supported since 9iR1 (around 2000).
- **Microsoft SQL Server**: Supported since 2008.

Using the WITH clause – common table expressions

Common table expressions are a nice way to execute things inside an SQL statement, but only once. PostgreSQL will execute all the WITH clauses and allow us to use the results throughout the query.

Here is a simplified example of this:

```
test=# WITH x AS (SELECT avg(id)
                  FROM generate_series(1, 10) AS id)
   SELECT *, y - (SELECT avg FROM x) AS diff
   FROM generate_series(1, 10) AS y
   WHERE y > (SELECT avg FROM x);
 y  | diff
----+--------------------
  6 | 0.5000000000000000
  7 | 1.5000000000000000
  8 | 2.5000000000000000
  9 | 3.5000000000000000
 10 | 4.5000000000000000
(5 rows)
```

In this example, the `WITH` clause's **common table extension** (**CTE**) calculates the average value of the time series generated by the `generate_series` function. The resulting `x` can be used just like a table—all over the query. In my example, `x` is used twice.

Supporting the WITH clause

The following list shows which engines support the `WITH` clause and which don't:

- **MariaDB**: Not supported
- **MySQL**: Not supported
- **PostgreSQL**: Supported since PostgreSQL 8.4
- **SQLite**: Supported since 3.8.3
- **Db2 LUW**: Supported since 8 (2000)
- **Oracle**: Supported since 9iR2
- **Microsoft SQL Server**: Supported since 2005

> Note that, in PostgreSQL, a CTE can even support writes (`INSERT`, `UPDATE`, and `DELETE` clauses). There is no other database I am aware of that can actually do that.

Using the WITH RECURSIVE clause

The `WITH` clause comes in two forms:

- Standard CTEs, as shown in the previous section (using the `WITH` clause)
- A method to run recursions in SQL

The simple form of a CTE was covered in the previous section. In the next section, the recursive version will be covered.

Supporting the WITH RECURSIVE clause

The following list shows which engines support the `WITH RECURSIVE` clause and which don't:

- **MariaDB**: Not supported
- **MySQL**: Not supported
- **PostgreSQL**: Supported since PostgreSQL 8.4
- **SQLite**: Supported since 3.8.3
- **Db2 LUW**: Supported since 7 (2000)
- **Oracle**: Supported since 11gR2 (in Oracle, it is usually more common to use the `CONNECT BY` clause instead of the `WITH RECURSIVE` clause)
- **Microsoft SQL Server**: Supported since 2005

Using the FILTER clause

When looking at the SQL standard itself, you will notice that the `FILTER` clause has been around since SQL (2003). However, not many systems actually support this highly useful syntax element.

Here's an example of this:

```
test=# SELECT count(*),
              count(*) FILTER (WHERE id < 5),
              count(*) FILTER (WHERE id > 2)
       FROM generate_series(1, 10) AS id;
 count | count | count
-------+-------+-------
    10 | 4 | 8
(1 row)
```

The FILTER clause is useful if a condition cannot be used inside a normal WHERE clause because some other aggregate is in need of the data.

Before the introduction of the FILTER clause, the same could be achieved using a more cumbersome form of syntax:

```
SELECT sum(CASE WHEN .. THEN 1 ELSE 0 END) AS whatever FROM some_table;
```

Supporting the FILTER clause

The following list shows which engines support the FILTER clause and which don't:

- **MariaDB**: Not supported
- **MySQL**: Not supported
- **PostgreSQL**: Supported since PostgreSQL 9.4
- **SQLite**: Not supported
- **Db2 LUW**: Not supported
- **Oracle**: Not supported
- **Microsoft SQL Server**: Not supported

Using windowing functions

Windowing and analytics have already been discussed extensively in this book. Therefore, we can jump straight into SQL compliance.

Supporting windowing and analytics

The following list shows which engines support window functions and which don't:

- **MariaDB**: Supported in latest releases
- **MySQL**: Supported in latest releases
- **PostgreSQL**: Supported since PostgreSQL 8.4
- **SQLite**: Not supported
- **Db2 LUW**: Supported since version 7
- **Oracle**: Supported since version 8i
- **Microsoft SQL Server**: Supported since 2005

Some other databases, such as Hive, Impala, Spark, and NuoDB, also support analytics.

Using ordered sets – the WITHIN GROUP clause

Ordered sets are fairly new to PostgreSQL. The difference between an ordered set and a normal aggregate is that, in the case of an ordered set, the way data is fed to the aggregate *does* make a difference. Suppose you want to find a trend in your data—the order of the data is relevant.

Here is a simple example of calculating a median value:

```
test=# SELECT id % 2,
          percentile_disc(0.5) WITHIN GROUP (ORDER BY id)
   FROM generate_series(1, 123) AS id
   GROUP BY 1;
 ?column? | percentile_disc
----------+-----------------
        0 | 62
        1 | 61
(2 rows)
```

The median can only be determined if there is sorted input.

Supporting the WITHIN GROUP clause

The following list shows which engines support windows functions and which don't:

- **MariaDB**: Not supported
- **MySQL**: Not supported
- **PostgreSQL**: Supported since PostgreSQL 9.4
- **SQLite**: Not supported
- **Db2 LUW:** Supported
- **Oracle**: Supported since version 9iR1
- **Microsoft SQL Server**: Supported, but the query has to be remodeled using the windowing function

Using the TABLESAMPLE clause

Table sampling has long been the real strength of commercial database vendors. Traditional database systems have provided sampling for many years. However, the monopoly has been broken. Since PostgreSQL 9.5, we have also had a solution to the problem of sampling.

Here's how it works:

```
test=# CREATE TABLE t_test (id int);
CREATE TABLE
test=# INSERT INTO t_test
    SELECT * FROM generate_series(1, 1000000);
INSERT 0 1000000
```

First, a table containing 1 million rows is created. Then, tests can be executed:

```
test=# SELECT count(*), avg(id)
        FROM t_test TABLESAMPLE BERNOULLI (1);
 count |        avg
-------+----------------------
 9802  |    502453.220873291165
(1 row)
test=# SELECT count(*), avg(id)
        FROM t_test TABLESAMPLE BERNOULLI (1);
 count |        avg
-------+----------------------
 10082 |    497514.321959928586
(1 row)
```

In this example, the same test is executed twice. A 1% random sample is used in each case. Both average values are pretty close to 5 million, so the result is pretty good from a statistical point of view.

Supporting the TABLESAMPLE clause

The following list shows which engines support the TABLESAMPLE clause and which don't:

- **MariaDB**: Not supported
- **MySQL**: Not supported
- **PostgreSQL**: Supported since PostgreSQL 9.5
- **SQLite**: Not supported
- **Db2 LUW**: Supported since version 8.2
- **Oracle**: Supported since version 8
- **Microsoft SQL Server**: Supported since 2005

Using limit/offset

Limiting a result in SQL is a somewhat sad story. In short, every database does things somewhat differently. Although there is actually a SQL standard on limiting results, not everybody fully supports the way things are supposed to be. The correct way to limit data is to actually use the following syntax:

```
test=# SELECT * FROM t_test FETCH FIRST 3 ROWS ONLY;
  id
  ----
   1
   2
   3
(3 rows)
```

If you have never seen this syntax before, don't worry. You are definitely not alone.

Supporting the FETCH FIRST clause

The following list shows which engines support the FETCH FIRST clause and which don't:

- **MariaDB**: Supported since 5.1 (usually, limit/offset is used)
- **MySQL**: Supported since 3.19.3 (usually, limit/offset is used)
- **PostgreSQL**: Supported since PostgreSQL 8.4 (usually, limit/offset is used)
- **SQLite**: Supported since version 2.1.0
- **Db2 LUW**: Supported since version 7
- **Oracle**: Supported since version 12c (uses subselects with the row_num function)
- **Microsoft SQL Server**: Supported since 2012 (traditionally, top-*N* is used)

As you can see, limiting result sets is quite tricky, and when you are porting a commercial database to PostgreSQL, you will most likely be confronted with some proprietary syntax.

Using the OFFSET clause

The OFFSET clause is similar to the FETCH FIRST clause. It is easy to use, but it hasn't been widely adopted. It isn't as bad as it is in the FETCH FIRST clause, but it still tends to be an issue.

Supporting the OFFSET clause

The following list shows which engines support the OFFSET clause and which don't:

- **MariaDB**: Supported since 5.1
- **MySQL**: Supported since 4.0.6
- **PostgreSQL**: Supported since PostgreSQL 6.5
- **SQLite**: Supported since version 2.1.0
- **Db2 LUW**: Supported since version 11.1
- **Oracle**: Supported since version 12c
- **Microsoft SQL Server**: Supported since 2012

As you can see, limiting result sets is quite tricky and, when you are porting a commercial database to PostgreSQL, it's likely that you will be confronted with some proprietary syntax.

Using temporal tables

Temporal tables are provided by some database engines to handle versioning. Unfortunately, there is no such thing as out-of-the-box versioning in PostgreSQL. So, if you are moving from Db2 or Oracle, there's some work ahead of you to port the desired functionality to PostgreSQL. Basically, changing the code a bit on the PostgreSQL side isn't too hard. However, it does need some manual intervention—it isn't a straight copy-and-paste job anymore.

Supporting temporal tables

The following list shows which engines support temporal tables and which don't:

- **MariaDB**: Not supported
- **MySQL**: Not supported
- **PostgreSQL**: Not supported
- **SQLite**: Not supported
- **Db2 LUW**: Supported since version 10.1
- **Oracle**: Supported since version 12cR1
- **Microsoft SQL Server**: Supported since 2016

Matching patterns in time series

At the time of writing, the most recent SQL standard (SQL 2016) provides a feature that's designed to find matches in time series. So far, only Oracle has implemented this functionality in its latest version of the product.

At this point, no other database vendor has followed them and added similar functionality. If you want to model this state-of-the art technology in PostgreSQL, you have to work with the windowing function and subselects. Matching time series patterns in Oracle is pretty powerful; there isn't just one type of query to achieve this in PostgreSQL.

Moving from Oracle to PostgreSQL

So far, we have seen how the most important advanced SQL features can be ported or used in PostgreSQL. Given this introduction, it is time to take a look at migrating Oracle database systems in particular.

These days, migrating from Oracle to PostgreSQL has become really popular due to Oracle's new license and business policy. Around the world, people are moving away from Oracle and adopting PostgreSQL.

Using the oracle_fdw extension to move data

One of my preferred methods to move people from Oracle to PostgreSQL is Laurenz Albe's `oracle_fdw` extension (`https://github.com/laurenz/oracle_fdw`). It is a **foreign data wrapper** (**FDW**) that allows you to represent a table in Oracle as a table in PostgreSQL. The `oracle_fdw` extension is one of the most sophisticated FDWs and is rock solid, well documented, free, and open source.

Installing the `oracle_fdw` extension requires you to install the Oracle client library. Fortunately, there are already RPM packages that can be used out of the box (`http://www.oracle.com/technetwork/topics/linuxx86-64soft-092277.html`). The `oracle_fdw` extension needs the OCI driver to talk to Oracle. In addition to ready-made Oracle client drivers, there is also an RPM package for the `oracle_fdw` extension itself, which is provided by the community. If you aren't using an RPM-based system, you might have to compile things on your own, which is clearly possible but a bit more labor-intensive.

Once the software has been installed, it can be enabled easily:

```
test=# CREATE EXTENSION oracle_fdw;
```

The CREATE EXTENSION clause loads the extension into your desired database. Now, a server can be created and users can be mapped to their counterparts on the Oracle side, as follows:

```
test=# CREATE SERVER oraserver FOREIGN DATA WRAPPER oracle_fdw
          OPTIONS (dbserver '//dbserver.example.com/ORADB');
test=# CREATE USER MAPPING FOR postgres SERVER oradb
          OPTIONS (user 'orauser', password 'orapass');
```

Now, it's time to fetch some data. My preferred way is to use the IMPORT FOREIGN SCHEMA clause to import the data definitions. The IMPORT FOREIGN SCHEMA clause will create a foreign table for each table in a remote schema and expose the data on the Oracle side, which can then be read easily.

The easiest way to make use of the schema import is to create separate schemas on PostgreSQL, which just hold the database schema. Then, data can be sucked into PostgreSQL easily using the FDW. The last section of this chapter, *Migrating data and schema*, regarding migrating from MySQL, shows you an example of how this can be done with MySQL/MariaDB. Keep in mind that the IMPORT FOREIGN SCHEMA clause is part of the SQL/MED standard and therefore the process is the same as it is for MySQL/MariaDB. This applies to pretty much every FDW that supports the IMPORT FOREIGN SCHEMA clause.

While the oracle_fdw extension does most of the work for us, it still makes sense to see how data types are mapped. Oracle and PostgreSQL don't provide exactly the same data types, so some mapping is done either by the oracle_fdw extension or by us manually. The following table provides an overview of how types are mapped. The left-hand column shows the Oracle types, while the right-hand column shows the potential PostgreSQL counterparts:

Oracle types	PostgreSQL types
CHAR	char, varchar, and text
NCHAR	char, varchar, and text
VARCHAR	char, varchar, and text
VARCHAR2	char, varchar, and text
NVARCHAR2	char, varchar, and text
CLOB	char, varchar, and text
LONG	char, varchar, and text
RAW	uuid and bytea

BLOB	`bytea`
BFILE	`bytea` (read-only)
LONG RAW	`bytea`
NUMBER	`numeric`, `float4`, `float8`, `char`, `varchar`, and `text`
NUMBER(n,m) with m<=0	`numeric`, `float4`, `float8`, `int2`, `int4`, `int8`, `boolean`, `char`, `varchar`, and `text`
FLOAT	`numeric`, `float4`, `float8`, `char`, `varchar`, and `text`
BINARY_FLOAT	`numeric`, `float4`, `float8`, `char`, `varchar`, and `text`
BINARY_DOUBLE	`numeric`, `float4`, `float8`, `char`, `varchar`, and `text`
DATE	`date`, `timestamp`, `timestamptz`, `char`, `varchar`, and `text`
TIMESTAMP	`date`, `timestamp`, `timestamptz`, `char`, `varchar`, and `text`
TIMESTAMP WITH TIME ZONE	`date`, `timestamp`, `timestamptz`, `char`, `varchar`, and `text`
TIMESTAMP WITH LOCAL TIME ZONE	`date`, `timestamp`, `timestamptz`, `char`, `varchar`, and `text`
INTERVAL YEAR TO MONTH	`interval`, `char`, `varchar`, and `text`
INTERVAL DAY TO SECOND	`interval`, `char`, `varchar`, and `text`
MDSYS.SDO_GEOMETRY	`geometry`

If you want to use geometries, make sure that PostGIS is installed on your database server.

The downside of the `oracle_fdw` extension is that it cannot migrate procedures out of the box. Stored procedures are a somewhat special thing and need some manual intervention.

Using ora_migrator for fast migration

While `oracle_fdw` is a good start, we can do even better. `ora_migrator` (`https://www.cybertec-postgresql.com/en/ora_migrator-moving-from-oracle-to-postgresql-even-faster/`, `https://github.com/cybertec-postgresql/ora_migrator`) has been developed on top of `oracle_fdw` and uses all its features in the most efficient way possible. How does it work? Once you have installed `ora_migrator` from our GitHub page, you can enable the extension by using the following command:

```
CREATE EXTENSION ora_migrator;
```

Once the module has been installed, it makes sense to take a look at what `ora_migrator` is doing. Let's run a sample call and inspect the output:

```
SELECT oracle_migrate(server => 'oracle', only_schemas =>
'{LAURENZ,SOCIAL}');

NOTICE: Creating staging schemas "ora_stage" and "pgsql_stage" ...
NOTICE: Creating Oracle metadata views in schema "ora_stage" ...
NOTICE: Copying definitions to PostgreSQL staging schema "pgsql_stage" ...
NOTICE: Creating schemas ...
NOTICE: Creating sequences ...
NOTICE: Creating foreign tables ...
NOTICE: Migrating table laurenz.log ...
...
NOTICE: Migrating table social.email ...
NOTICE: Migrating table laurenz.numbers ...
NOTICE: Creating UNIQUE and PRIMARY KEY constraints ...
WARNING: Error creating primary key or unique constraint on table
laurenz.badstring
DETAIL: relation "laurenz.badstring" does not exist:
WARNING: Error creating primary key or unique constraint on table
laurenz.hasnul
DETAIL: relation "laurenz.hasnul" does not exist:
NOTICE: Creating FOREIGN KEY constraints ...
NOTICE: Creating CHECK constraints ...
NOTICE: Creating indexes ...
NOTICE: Setting column default values ...
NOTICE: Dropping staging schemas ...
NOTICE: Migration completed with 4 errors.
 oracle_migrate
----------------
 4
(1 row)
```

The way `ora_migrator` works is as follows. First, it clones parts of the Oracle system catalog and puts this data into a staging schema inside a PostgreSQL database. Then, this information is transformed so that we can actually use it on the PostgreSQL side to create tables, indexes, views, and so on easily. At this stage, we perform data type conversions and so on.

Finally, data is copied over and indexes, constraints, and so on are applied.

What you have just seen is the most simplistic case. In reality, you might want to do some post-processing on your own. `oracle_migrate` is just a wrapper function and therefore you can also call the individual steps needed on your own, step by step. The documentation shows what can be done at which level and you will easily be able to migrate objects in a simple way.

In contrast to some other tools, `ora_migrator` doesn't try to do things that are actually impossible to do properly. The most important components that stay untouched by `ora_migrator` are procedures. It is basically impossible to fully and automatically convert procedures from Oracle procedures into PostgreSQL procedures. Therefore, we shouldn't attempt to transform them. In short, migrating procedures is still a partially manual process.

> If you are looking for a visual tool to migrate Oracle to PostgreSQL, consider checking out the Cybertec migrator toolkit, which can be found on my website: `https://www.cybertec-postgresql.com/en/products/cybertec-migrator/`. It offers a visual way to migrate databases and to keep track of things easily.

`ora_migrator` is being steadily improved and works for all Oracle versions, starting with version 11.2.

Using Ora2pg to migrate from Oracle

People migrated from Oracle to PostgreSQL long before FDWs existed. High license costs have plagued people for a long time, and so moving to PostgreSQL has been a natural thing to do for many years.

The alternative to the `oracle_fdw` extension is something called **Ora2pg**, which has been around for many years and can be downloaded for free from `https://github.com/darold/ora2pg`. Ora2pg has been written in Perl and has a long tradition of new releases.

The features that are provided by Ora2pg are stunning:

- Migration of the full database schema, including tables, views, sequences, and indexes (unique, primary, foreign key, and check constraints).
- Migration of privileges for users and groups.
- Migration of partitioned tables.

- Ability to export predefined functions, triggers, procedures, packages, and package bodies.
- Migration of full or partial data (using a `WHERE` clause).
- Full support of Oracle BLOB objects as PostgreSQL `bytea`.
- Ability to export Oracle views as PostgreSQL tables.
- Ability to export Oracle user-defined types.
- Basic automatic conversion of PL/SQL code to PL/pgSQL code. Note that a fully automated conversion of everything isn't possible. However, a lot of stuff can be transformed automatically.
- Ability to export Oracle tables as FDW tables.
- Ability to export materialized views.
- Ability to display detailed reports about Oracle database content.
- Assessment of the complexity of the migration process of an Oracle database.
- Migration cost assessment of PL/SQL code from a file.
- Ability to generate XML files to be used with the Pentaho data integrator (Kettle).
- Ability to export Oracle locator and spatial geometries into PostGIS.
- Ability to export database links as Oracle FDWs.
- Ability to export synonyms as views.
- Ability to export a directory as an external table or a directory for the `external_file` extension.
- Ability to dispatch a list of SQL orders over multiple PostgreSQL connections.
- Ability to perform a `diff` between Oracle and PostgreSQL databases for test purposes.

Using Ora2pg looks hard at first glance. However, it is actually a lot easier than it seems. The basic concept is as follows:

```
/usr/local/bin/ora2pg -c /some_path/new_ora2pg.conf
```

Ora2pg needs a config file to run. The config file contains all the information that's needed to handle the process. Basically, the default config file is already really nice, and it is a good starting point for most migrations. In the Ora2pg language, a migration is a project.

The configuration will drive the entire project. When you run it, Ora2pg will create a couple of directories with all the data that's been extracted from Oracle:

```
ora2pg --project_base /app/migration/ --init_project test_project
Creating project test_project.
/app/migration/test_project/
                schema/
```

```
                              dblinks/
                              directories/
                              functions/
                              grants/
                              mviews/
                              packages/
                              partitions/
                              procedures/
                              sequences/
                              synonyms/
                              tables/
                              tablespaces/
                              triggers/
                              types/
                              views/
                   sources/
                              functions/
                              mviews/
                              packages/
                              partitions/
                              procedures/
                              triggers/
                              types/
                              views/
                   data/
                   config/
                   reports/

    Generating generic configuration file
    Creating script export_schema.sh to automate all exports.
    Creating script import_all.sh to automate all imports.
```

As you can see, scripts that can just be executed are generated. The resulting data can then be imported into PostgreSQL nicely. Be prepared to change procedures here and there. Not everything can be migrated automatically, so manual intervention is necessary.

Common pitfalls

There are some very basic syntax elements that work in Oracle, but they might not work in PostgreSQL. This section lists some of the most important pitfalls to take into consideration. Of course, this list is not complete by any means, but it should point you in the right direction.

In Oracle, you may come across the following statement:

```
DELETE mytable;
```

In PostgreSQL, this statement is wrong since PostgreSQL requires that you use a FROM clause in the DELETE statement. The good news is that this kind of statement is easy to fix.

The next thing you might find is the following:

```
SELECT sysdate FROM dual;
```

PostgreSQL has neither a sysdate function nor a dual function. The dual function part is easy to fix as you can simply create a VIEW returning one line. In Oracle, the dual function works as follows:

```
SQL> desc dual
Name Null? Type
----------------------------------------- -------- -
DUMMY VARCHAR2(1)

SQL> select * from dual;

D
-
X
```

In PostgreSQL, the same can be achieved by creating the following VIEW:

```
CREATE VIEW dual AS SELECT 'X' AS dummy;
```

The sysdate function is also easy to fix. It can be replaced with the clock_timestamp() function.

Another common problem is the lack of data types, such as VARCHAR2, as well as the lack of special functions that are only supported by Oracle. A good way to get around these issues is to install the orafce extension, which provides most of the stuff that's typically needed, including the most commonly used functions. It certainly makes sense to check out https://github.com/orafce/orafce to learn more about the orafce extension. It has been around for many years and is a solid piece of software.

A recent study has shown that the orafce extension helps ensure that 73% of all Oracle SQLs can be executed on PostgreSQL without modifications if the orafce extension is around (done by NTT).

One of the most common pitfalls is the way Oracle handles outer joins. Consider the following example:

```
SELECT employee_id, manager_id
   FROM employees
   WHERE employees.manager_id(+) = employees.employee_id;
```

This kind of syntax is not provided by PostgreSQL and never will be. Therefore, the join has to be rewritten as a proper outer join. The + is highly Oracle-specific and has to be removed when moving from MySQL or MariaDB to PostgreSQL

In this chapter, you have already learned some valuable lessons about how to move from databases such as Oracle to PostgreSQL. Migrating both MySQL and MariaDB database systems to PostgreSQL is fairly easy. The reason for this is that Oracle might be expensive and a bit cumbersome from time to time. The same applies to Informix. However, both Informix and Oracle have one important thing in common: the CHECK constraints are honored properly and data types are handled properly. In general, we can safely assume that the data in those commercial systems is somewhat correct and doesn't violate the most basic rules of data integrity and common sense.

Our next candidate is different. Many things you know about commercial databases aren't true in MySQL. The term NOT NULL doesn't mean much to MySQL (unless you explicitly use strict mode). In Oracle, Informix, Db2, and all the other systems I am aware of, NOT NULL is a law that is obeyed under all circumstances. MySQL doesn't take these constraints that seriously by default. (Though, to be fair, this has been changed in recent versions. Strict mode was not **on** by default up until very recently. However, many old databases still use the old default settings.)

In the case of migrations, this causes some issues. What are you going to do with data that is technically wrong? If your NOT NULL column suddenly reveals countless NULL entries, how are you going to handle that? MySQL doesn't just insert NULL values in NOT NULL columns. It will insert an empty string or zero based on the data type, so things can get pretty nasty.

Handling data in MySQL and MariaDB

As you can probably imagine, and as you might have already noticed, I am far from unbiased when it comes to databases. However, I don't want to turn this into blind MySQL/MariaDB bashing. Our real goal is to see why MySQL and MariaDB can be such a pain in the long run. I am biased for a reason and I really want to point out why this is the case.

All of the things we are going to see are deeply scary and have serious implications on the migration process in general. I have already pointed out that MySQL is somewhat special, and this section will try to prove my point.

Again, the following examples assume that we are using a version of MySQL/MariaDB that doesn't have strict mode on, which was the case when this chapter was originally written (as of PostgreSQL 9.6). As of PostgreSQL 10.0, strict mode is already on, so most of what we are going to read here only applies to older versions of MySQL/MariaDB.

Let's get started by creating a simple table:

```
MariaDB [test]> CREATE TABLE data (
    id integer NOT NULL,
    data numeric(4, 2)
);
Query OK, 0 rows affected (0.02 sec)

MariaDB [test]> INSERT INTO data VALUES (1, 1234.5678);
Query OK, 1 row affected, 1 warning (0.01 sec)
```

So far, there's nothing special here. We have created a table consisting of two columns. The first column is explicitly marked as NOT NULL. The second column is supposed to contain a numeric value, which is limited to four digits. Finally, we have added a simple row. Can you see a potential landmine about to blow up? Most likely not. However, check the following listing:

```
MariaDB [test]> SELECT * FROM data;
+----+-------+
| id | data  |
+----+-------+
| 1  | 99.99 |
+----+-------+
1 row in set (0.00 sec)
```

If I remember correctly, we have added a four-digit number, which shouldn't have worked in the first place. However, MariaDB has simply changed my data. Sure, a warning has been issued, but this is not supposed to happen since the content of the table doesn't reflect what we have actually inserted.

Let's try to do the same thing in PostgreSQL:

```
test=# CREATE TABLE data
(
    id integer NOT NULL,
    data numeric(4, 2)
);
```

```
CREATE TABLE
test=# INSERT INTO data VALUES (1, 1234.5678);
ERROR: numeric field overflow
DETAIL: A field with precision 4, scale 2 must round to an absolute value
less than 10^2.
```

The table was created, just like it was previously, but in stark contrast to MariaDB/MySQL, PostgreSQL will error out because we are trying to insert into the table a value that is clearly not allowed. What is the point in clearly defining what we want if the database engine just doesn't care? Suppose you have won the lottery—you might have just lost a couple of million because the system has decided what is good for you.

I have been fighting commercial databases all my life, but I have never seen similar things in any of the expensive commercial systems (Oracle, Db2, Microsoft SQL Server, and so on). They might have issues of their own, but in general, the data is just fine.

Changing column definitions

Let's see what happens if you want to modify the table definition:

```
MariaDB [test]> ALTER TABLE data MODIFY data numeric(3, 2);
Query OK, 1 row affected, 1 warning (0.06 sec)
Records: 1 Duplicates: 0 Warnings: 1
```

You should see a problem here:

```
MariaDB [test]> SELECT * FROM data;
+----+------+
| id | data |
+----+------+
| 1  | 9.99 |
+----+------+
1 row in set (0.00 sec)
```

As you can see, the data has been modified again. It shouldn't have been there in the first place and has been changed all over again. Remember, you might have lost money again, or some other nice asset, because MySQL tried to be clever.

This is what happens in PostgreSQL:

```
test=# INSERT INTO data VALUES (1, 34.5678);
INSERT  0 1
test=# SELECT * FROM data;
 id  | data
-----+-------
 1   | 34.57
(1 row)
```

Now, let's change the column definition:

```
test=# ALTER TABLE data ALTER COLUMN data
    TYPE numeric(3, 2);
ERROR: numeric field overflow
DETAIL:  A field with precision 3, scale 2 must round to
an absolute value less than 10^1.
```

Again, PostgreSQL will error out and it won't allow us to do nasty things to our data. The same is expected to happen in any important database. The rule is simple: PostgreSQL and other systems won't allow us to destroy our data.

However, PostgreSQL allows you to do one thing:

```
test=# ALTER TABLE data
    ALTER COLUMN data
          TYPE numeric(3, 2)
          USING (data / 10);
ALTER TABLE
```

We can explicitly tell the system how to behave. In this case, we explicitly told PostgreSQL to divide the content of the column by 10. Developers can explicitly provide the rules that are applied to the data. PostgreSQL won't try to be smart, and for good reason:

```
test=# SELECT * FROM data;
 id  | data
-----+-------
 1   | 3.46
(1 row)
```

The data is exactly as expected.

Handling null values

We don't want to turn this into a *why MariaDB is bad* chapter, but I wanted to add a final example here, which I consider to be of high importance:

```
MariaDB [test]> UPDATE data SET id = NULL WHERE id = 1;
Query OK, 1 row affected, 1 warning (0.01 sec)
Rows matched: 1 Changed: 1 Warnings: 1
```

The id column was explicitly marked as NOT NULL:

```
MariaDB [test]> SELECT * FROM data;
+----+------+
| id | data |
+----+------+
| 0  | 9.99 |
+----+------+
1 row in set (0.00 sec)
```

Obviously, MySQL and MariaDB think that null and zero are the same thing. Let me try to explain the problem here with a simple analogy: if you know your wallet is empty, it isn't the same as not knowing how much you have. As I am writing these lines, I don't know how much money I have with me (null = unknown), but I am 100% sure that it is way more than zero (I know with certainty that there is enough to refuel my beloved car on the way home from the airport, which is hard to do if you have nothing in your pocket).

Here's more scary news:

```
MariaDB [test]> DESCRIBE data;
+-------+--------------+------+-----+---------+-------+
| Field | Type         | Null | Key | Default | Extra |
+-------+--------------+------+-----+---------+-------+
| id    | int(11)      | NO   |     | NULL    |       |
| data  | decimal(3,2) | YES  |     | NULL    |       |
+-------+--------------+------+-----+---------+-------+
2 rows in set (0.00 sec)
```

MariaDB does remember that the column is supposed to be NOT NULL; however, it simply modifies your data again.

Expecting problems

The main problem is that we might have trouble moving data to PostgreSQL. Just imagine that you want to move some data and there is a `NOT NULL` constraint on the PostgreSQL side. We know that MySQL doesn't care:

```
MariaDB [test]> SELECT
    CAST('2014-02-99 10:00:00' AS datetime) AS x,
    CAST('2014-02-09 10:00:00' AS datetime) AS y;
+------+---------------------+
| x | y |
+------+---------------------+
| NULL | 2014-02-09 10:00:00 |
+------+---------------------+
1 row in set, 1 warning (0.00 sec)
```

PostgreSQL will definitely reject February 09 (for good reason), but it might not accept the `NULL` value either if you have explicitly banned it (for good reason). What you have to do in this case is somehow fix the data to make sure that it honors the rules of your data models, which are in place for a reason. You shouldn't take this lightly, because you might have to change data that's actually wrong in the first place.

Migrating data and schema

Now that I've explained why moving to PostgreSQL is a good idea and outlined some of the most important issues, it is time for me to explain some of the possible options we have to finally get rid of MySQL/MariaDB.

Using pg_chameleon

One way to move from MySQL/MariaDB to PostgreSQL is to use Federico Campoli's tool called `pg_chameleon`, which can be downloaded for free from GitHub (`https://github.com/the4thdoctor/pg_chameleon`). It has been explicitly designed to replicate data to PostgreSQL and does a lot of work, such as converting the schema for us.

Basically, the tool performs the following four steps:

1. The `pg_chameleon` tool reads the schema and data from MySQL and creates a schema in PostgreSQL.
2. It stores MySQL's master connection information in PostgreSQL.
3. It creates primary keys and indices in PostgreSQL.
4. It replicates from MySQL/MariaDB to PostgreSQL.

The `pg_chameleon` tool provides basic support for DDLs such as CREATE, DROP, ALTER TABLE, and DROP PRIMARY KEY. However, due to the nature of MySQL/MariaDB, it doesn't support all DDLs. Instead, it covers the most important features.

However, there is more to `pg_chameleon`. I have stated extensively already that data isn't always the way it should be or is expected to be. The way `pg_chameleon` approaches this problem is to discard rubbish data and store it in a table called `sch_chameleon.t_discarded_rows`. Of course, this isn't a perfect solution but, given the fairly low-quality input, it is the only sensible solution that comes to my mind. The idea is to let developers decide what to do with all the broken rows. There is really no way for `pg_chameleon` to decide on how to handle something that has been broken by somebody else.

Recently, a lot of development has taken place and a lot of work has gone into the tool. Therefore, it is really recommended to check out the GitHub page and read through all the documentation. Features and bug fixes are being added at the time of writing this book. Given the limited scope of this chapter, full coverage isn't possible here.

 Stored procedures, triggers, and more need special treatment and can only be handled manually. The `pg_chameleon` tool cannot process these things automatically.

Using FDWs

If we want to move from MySQL/MariaDB to PostgreSQL, there is more than one way to succeed. The use of FDWs is an alternative to `pg_chameleon` and offers a way to quickly fetch the schema, as well as the data, and import it into PostgreSQL. The ability to connect MySQL and PostgreSQL has been around for quite a while, and therefore FDWs are definitely a field that can be exploited to your advantage.

Basically, the `mysql_fdw` extension works just like any other FDW out there. Compared to other, less well-known FDWs, the `mysql_fdw` extension is actually quite powerful and offers the following features:

- Writing to MySQL/MariaDB
- Connection pooling
- The WHERE clause pushdown (which means that filters that are applied on a table can actually be executed remotely for better performance)

- Column pushdown (only the columns that are needed are fetched from the remote side; older versions are used to fetch all the columns, which leads to more network traffic)
- Prepared statements on the remote side

The way to use the `mysql_fdw` extension is to make use of the IMPORT FOREIGN SCHEMA statement, which allows you to move data over to PostgreSQL. Fortunately, this is fairly easy to do on a Unix system. Let's take a look at the steps in detail:

1. The first thing we have to do is download the code from GitHub:

   ```
   git clone https://github.com/EnterpriseDB/mysql_fdw.git
   ```

2. Then, run the following commands to compile the FDW. Note that the paths might differ on your system. For this chapter, I have assumed that both MySQL and PostgreSQL are under the `/usr/local` directory, which might not be the case on your system:

   ```
   $ export PATH=/usr/local/pgsql/bin/:$PATH
   $ export PATH=/usr/local/mysql/bin/:$PATH
   $ make USE_PGXS=1
   $ make USE_PGXS=1 install
   ```

3. Once the code has been compiled, the FDW can be added to our database:

   ```
   CREATE EXTENSION mysql_fdw;
   ```

4. The next step is to create the server we want to migrate:

   ```
   CREATE SERVER migrate_me_server
       FOREIGN DATA WRAPPER mysql_fdw
       OPTIONS (host 'host.example.com', port '3306');
   ```

5. Once the server has been created, we can create the desired user mappings:

   ```
   CREATE USER MAPPING FOR postgres
       SERVER migrate_me_server
       OPTIONS (username 'joe', password 'public');
   ```

6. Finally, it's time to do the real migration. The first thing to do is import the schema. I suggest creating a special schema for the linked tables first:

   ```
   CREATE SCHEMA migration_schema;
   ```

7. When running the IMPORT FOREIGN SCHEMA statement, we can use this schema as the target schema in which all the database links will be stored. The advantage is that we can delete it conveniently after the migration.

8. Once we are done with the IMPORT FOREIGN SCHEMA statement, we can create real tables. The easiest way to do this is to use the LIKE keyword that's provided by the CREATE TABLE clause. It allows us to copy the structure of a table and create a real, local PostgreSQL table. Fortunately, this also works if the table you are cloning is just an FDW. Here's an example of this:

```
CREATE TABLE t_customer
    (LIKE migration_schema.t_customer);
```

9. Then, we can process the data:

```
INSERT INTO t_customer
    SELECT  * FROM migration_schema.t_customer
```

This is actually the point where we can correct the data, eliminate chunk rows, or do a bit of processing on the data. Given the low-quality origin of the data, it can be useful to apply constraints and so on after moving the data for the first time. It might be less painful.

Once the data has been imported, we are ready to deploy all of the constraints, indexes, and so on. At this point, you will actually start to see some nasty surprises because, as I stated previously, you can't expect the data to be rock solid. In general, migration can be pretty hard in the case of MySQL.

Summary

In this chapter, we understood how to migrate SQL statements to PostgreSQL and we learned to move a basic database from some other system to PostgreSQL. Migration is an important topic, and more and more people are adopting PostgreSQL every day.

PostgreSQL 12 has many new features, such as improved built-in partitioning, and a lot more. In the future, we will see many more developments in all the areas of PostgreSQL, especially ones that allow users to scale out more and run queries even faster. We are yet to see what the future has in store for us.

Assessments

Chapter 2

1. Transactions are at the core of any modern relational database. The idea is to be able to make operations atomic. In other words, you want everything or nothing. If you want to delete 1 million rows, for example, you want none or all of them to be gone—you don't want to be stuck with a couple of remaining rows.

2. The most important thing is that the configuration of PostgreSQL doesn't really affect the maximum length of a transaction. Therefore, you can run basically (almost) infinitely long transactions changing billions of lines with hundreds of millions of statements.

3. Not all transactions are created equally. Therefore, in many cases, you have to control the visibility of data inside your transactions. This is exactly when transaction isolation comes into play. Transaction isolation levels allow you to do exactly that.

4. Yes, definitely. Table locks lock out everybody else, which can lead to performance issues. The more table locks you can avoid, the better it is in the long run. Performance can suffer seriously.

5. Transactions and `VACUUM` are deeply related. The idea of `VACUUM` is to clean out dead rows after they have expired. If transactions are not understood by the end user, there will always be issues with table bloat.

Chapter 3

1. The answer is definitely no. If something is always good, it would be there by default. Indexes can speed up many operations, but they can also slow down things considerably. The only rule is this: think about what you are doing and what you are trying to achieve.

2. It depends on the type of index. BRIN indexes are really small and fairly cheap, while other indexes usually need a lot more space. B-trees, for example, are around 2,000 times bigger than B-trees. Trigram-based indexes are even larger in most cases.

3. The best way, in my view, is to take a look at `pg_stat_statements`, and `pg_stat_user_tables`. `seq_tup_read` in particular is a really valuable column. If you are reading a really high number of rows, there might be an index missing. In general, are -n-depth look at the query is necessary to find out what is really going on. In short: `EXPLAIN` is your friend under all circumstances.

4. Yes; since PostgreSQL 11, we have support for parallel index creation. It can speed up index creation considerably.

Chapter 5

1. There is a lot of information that's collected by the stats collector in PostgreSQL. A full overview of what there is can be found in the official PostgreSQL documentation, which is available online at `https://www.postgresql.org/docs/11/static/monitoring-stats.html`.

2. There are various ways to detect performance problems in PostgreSQL. One way is to make use of `pg_stat_statements`. Other options are to use `auto_explain` or standard PostgreSQL log files. Depending on your needs, you can decide on which method is best for you. The following blog shows you how this kind of information can be extracted from the system: `https://www.cybertec-postgresql.com/en/3-ways-to-detect-slow-queries-in-postgresql/`.

3. PostgreSQL has various options for creating logs. The most commonly used one is to simply create standard textual logs. However, you can also make use of `syslog` or the logging facilities provided by Windows (`eventlog`).

4. Actually, yes. If you are running many small queries and if you happen to write millions of lines of logs to the system, it can impact performance.

Chapter 7

1. The words function and procedure are often mixed up. However, there is actually a difference: in a procedure, you can run more than just one transaction. It can, therefore, not be part of a `SELECT` statement, and has to be executed using the `CALL` command. In contrast to that, a function has only limited transaction control, and can be part of a `SELECT`, `INSERT`, `UPDATE`, or `DELETE` statement.

2. Trusted languages limit the programmer's ability to perform system calls. They are therefore considered to be safe. Untrusted languages, however, can perform all kinds of operations, and are therefore only available to superusers in order to ensure that no security leaks are possible.

3. This question is somewhat hard to answer. Nothing is only good or only bad. The same applies to functions. They can help you to achieve your goal faster, but sometimes it can be a burden if they're used excessively. As with all things in life, functions should be used in a useful way.

4. Traditionally, PostgreSQL has been very flexible when it comes to server-side functions. The core provides support for SQL, PL/pgSQL, PL/Perl, PL/Tcl, and PL/Python. However, there are many more languages that can be installed from various sources, all of which can benefit us greatly. The more popular ones are PL/V8 (JavaScript) and PL/R.

5. A trigger is a means to automatically execute a function when rows are changed. There are various types of triggers: ROW LEVEL, which are fired for every row; STATEMENT LEVEL, which are fired for a statement; and EVENT TRIGGERS, which can be fired for a **Dynamic-Link Library (DLL)** command.

6. Basically, functions can be written in SQL, PL/pgSQL, PL/Perl, PL/Tcl, and PL/Python. Additional languages can be added on demand if needed. It depends on your use case as to which language is best, and it is highly encouraged that you experiment with them.

7. That really depends on what you are trying to do. I think there is no overall answer to this question, and most likely there will never be one. You have to check on a case-by-case basis.

Chapter 8

1. There are two levels to configure network access. In `postgresql.conf` (`listen_addresses`), you can configure the bind addresses, and open remote connections. In `pg_hba.conf`, you can tell PostgreSQL how to authenticate network connections. Depending on the IP range that a request comes from, different rules can be applied.

2. Basically, the difference between a user and a role is academic. When creating a role, the default value is NOLOGIN, which is not the case when you use CREATE USER. Otherwise, roles and users can be considered to be the same.

3. This is simple. You can use `ALTER USER` to do the job, as shown in the following example:

```
test=# ALTER USER hs PASSWORD 'abc';
ALTER ROLE
```

Keep in mind that passwords are not necessarily stored in PostgreSQL. If you are using LDAP authentication, or some other external method, the password stored in PostgreSQL won't be changed on the LDAP side.

4. RLS is a feature that allows you to limit the access of users to the content of a table. Here is an example: the `joe` user might only be allowed to see women, while the `jane` user is only allowed to see men. RLS is, therefore, a mandatory filter that's applied on a table to limit the scope of a user for a table.

Chapter 9

1. If your database is fairly small, a dump certainly makes sense. However, if your database is huge (> XXX GB), a dump might not be feasible anymore and different means can make sense such as WAL archiving. You also have to keep in mind that a dump only provides a snapshot of data—it does not provide you with point-in-time recovery. Therefore, the dump is more of an additional tool and not a replacement for WAL archiving.

2. A compressed dump is usually around 10 times faster than the PostgreSQL database that you have saved. The reason is that the database has to store the content of an index while the backup only contains definitions. This makes a huge difference in terms of space consumption. On top of that, PostgreSQL has to store additional metadata such as tuple headers and so on, which also needs space.

3. Yes, it is definitely necessary to do that.

4. Yes. If the permissions have been set properly, a `pgpass` file is perfectly safe. Keep in mind that a machine that has to back up some other database needs all of the information to connect to the target system. It makes no difference what format data is stored in.

Chapter 10

1. If you are using binary replication, the master and slave have to use the same major release of PostgreSQL. In other words, you cannot use streaming to upgrade from, say, PostgreSQL 10 to PostgreSQL 11 using a transaction log stream. Logical replication can help to bridge this gap. In addition to that, logical replication can help selectively replicate data to various systems.

2. Synchronous replication will be slower than binary replication. In general, the performance impact of short transactions will be a lot greater than for long transactions. It is hard to state a precise number as the performance decrease depends significantly on network latency. The slower your network, the slower your synchronous replication is.

3. Try to use synchronous replication only when it is absolutely necessary to reduce the impact on speed and availability. In most cases, asynchronous replication is perfectly fine and does exactly what is required by most applications. Use synchronous replication cautiously.

Chapter 12

1. You have to keep in mind that the user always knows more than the database engine itself. In addition to that, the administrator has access to a lot of external information about the operating system, hardware, user patterns, and all that. A database engine cannot decide whether a user's query is pointless or not—it does not know its purpose. Therefore, administrators and developers are always at an advantage over the database and are, therefore, necessary (and most likely always will be).

2. No. My company provides services for thousands of businesses. We rarely see cases of database corruption—and if there is corruption, it is usually caused by hardware issues.

3. Usually not, unless you are using the database in a suboptimal way. In general, PostgreSQL does a lot of stuff on its own and takes care of many things, such as VACUUM, automatically.

Other Books You May Enjoy

If you enjoyed this book, you may be interested in these other books by Packt:

PostgreSQL 11 Administration Cookbook
Simon Riggs, Gianni Ciolli, Sudheer Kumar Meesala

ISBN: 978-1-78953-758-1

- Troubleshoot open source PostgreSQL version 11 on various platforms
- Deploy best practices for planning and designing live databases
- Select and implement robust backup and recovery techniques in PostgreSQL 11
- Use pgAdmin or OmniDB to perform database administrator (DBA) tasks
- Adopt efficient replication and high availability techniques in PostgreSQL
- Improve the performance of your PostgreSQL solution

Learning PostgreSQL 11
Salahaldin Juba, Andrey Volkov

ISBN: 978-1-78953-546-4

- Understand the basics of relational databases, relational algebra, and data modeling
- Install a PostgreSQL server, create a database, and implement your data model
- Create tables and views, define indexes and stored procedures, and implement triggers
- Make use of advanced data types such as Arrays, hstore, and JSONB
- Connect your Python applications to PostgreSQL and work with data efficiently
- Identify bottlenecks to enhance reliability and performance of database applications

Leave a review - let other readers know what you think

Please share your thoughts on this book with others by leaving a review on the site that you bought it from. If you purchased the book from Amazon, please leave us an honest review on this book's Amazon page. This is vital so that other potential readers can see and use your unbiased opinion to make purchasing decisions, we can understand what our customers think about our products, and our authors can see your feedback on the title that they have worked with Packt to create. It will only take a few minutes of your time, but is valuable to other potential customers, our authors, and Packt. Thank you!

Index

Printed in Great Britain
by Amazon